PENGUIN BOOKS

PROPHET

Robin Waterfield is an authority on Gibran and his work. He has also translated a number of ancient Greek texts, chiefly for Penguin Classics and Oxford University Press, and is the consultant editor for Penguin's religious and New Age Publishing. His anthology of Kahlil Gibran's work, *The Voice of Kahlil Gibran*, is published in Arkana.

ROBIN WATERFIELD

Prophet

THE LIFE AND TIMES OF
KAHLIL GIBRAN

PENGUIN BOOKS

PENGUIN BOOKS

Published by the Penguin Group
Penguin Books Ltd, 27 Wrights Lane, London W8 5TZ, England
Penguin Putnam Inc., 375 Hudson Street, New York, New York 10014, USA
Penguin Books Australia Ltd, Ringwood, Victoria, Australia
Penguin Books Canada Ltd, 10 Alcorn Avenue, Toronto, Ontario, Canada M4V 3B2
Penguin Books (NZ) Ltd, Private Bag 102902, NSMC, Auckland, New Zealand

Penguin Books Ltd, Registered Offices: Harmondsworth, Middlesex, England

First published by Allen Lane The Penguin Press 1998
Published in Penguin Books 1999
1 3 5 7 9 10 8 6 4 2

Printed in England by Clays Ltd, St Ives plc

To the wild and the only ones

Contents

List of Illustrations

Preface and Acknowledgements

Thanks largely to his book *The Prophet* (whose seventy-fifth anniversary coincides with the first publication of this biography), Kahlil Gibran is one of the most famous and popular writers in the modern world, with book sales numbering in eight figures in the English language alone and making him probably the best-selling individual poet of all time after Shakespeare and Lao-tzu – but this describes only one aspect of his talent. He was also a gifted artist, and indeed specialized in painting and drawing for some years before he really turned to writing. But so far we have said only what he did, and no one wants to be known by their work alone. He loved and was loved by a number of women, and much of the history of his life is the history of their lives, because what remains of him, apart from his writings and paintings, is often little more than a portrait refracted through the medium of his main female friends. He hobnobbed with the rich and famous of Boston and New York – and claimed an affinity with the poor of the world. He suffered devastating personal tragedies, and yet is known for the peace and optimism of his most popular work. He seems, we will find, to have created a number of personalities for himself, and even to have been something of a chameleon, and yet, as his continuing book sales testify, his appeal is not that of a superficial thinker.

There are a number of reasons why a biography of Gibran is timely now. It seems to me that we are better placed, at the end of the 1990s, to understand him than ever before. This is a result partly of the quality of some of the earlier research into his life, particularly the Gibrans' book on their namesake (see the bibliography), but more of factors which are rather harder to explain. Because of our own recent past, we can instinctively gain a number of insights into a character such as Gibran's. We now have considerable experience of gurus: we understand their attraction, and know some of the pitfalls of their attempts to perpetuate themselves; we understand more about narcissism and creativity; we are familiar with the cult of personality; we acknowledge the desperate insecurity of the immigrant and the lengths to which he or she may be driven in the quest for apparent security; we recognize without shuddering the ambivalent sexuality of many aesthetes such as Gibran. A couple of times in the book I speak of resonances between Gibran's era and our own present or recent past; it seems to me that there is also a resonance between his character and the profile of certain icons of the late twentieth century. There has been no one else to my knowledge quite like him (and that is another good reason for a biography), so there is no point in drawing direct comparisons because they would quickly prove hollow. All the same, there are echoes. If Gibran had been born into our own time, he would, I think, have been either a guru or a media pundit.

Despite the admirable thoroughness of the book by Jean and Kahlil Gibran, a great deal of work remained to be done. Their book is the starting-point for all future research in the sense that they made available, for the first time, far more material about Gibran than had previously been known. However, a reader of the Gibrans' book may still find it hard, within the welter of factual information, to gain a rounded impression of the man himself. It is my purpose, on the other hand, to put flesh on to the bones of the events of Gibran's life, and not eschew comment where comment is needed to lead the reader towards understanding his character – which should be the purpose of all biography. At much the same time as the publication of the Gibrans' book, in the early 1970s, there were also published two editions (one legal, one illegal) of the main sources of information about Gibran – the letters between him and Mary Haskell, and her diaries and journals. However, none of these three books is entirely reliable when it quotes from letters and journals, and the wealth of material available in Mary Haskell's journals is such that only a tiny proportion of the whole has been published. A fresh reading of them was clearly essential, and it proved astonishing how many important clues to Gibran's character had been omitted from these earlier books. This is one reason why I have chosen to refer fairly fully in the notes to Mary Haskell's journals, as an aid to future writers on Gibran.

Gibran's life also presents peculiar problems of interpretation, which turn the biographer, beyond being a writer, into a detective. On the one hand, since he has generally been considered a literary lightweight, his life and work have failed to attract the kind of scholarly attention which might have resulted in a greater body of original interview material, or in the preservation of more of his correspondence. And so, despite the fact that he died only sixty or so years ago, there are gaps in our knowledge of his life, not just in the sense of stretches of time about which we have little or no information, but also in the sense that there are major stretches of time when we have to rely more or less on a single reporter, with little objective means of assessing the record. It is now too late: there is no one alive who remembers him. On the other hand, because of the kind of man he was, he has attracted much adulatory, imaginative and uncritical reporting, with dismally low standards of accuracy. For both these reasons, then, a serious biographer often has to weigh up conflicting evidence, assess the reliability of sources, and in general behave as much like an academic as a conventional writer.

Apart from books and collections of letters, there are also two oral sources of information in Lebanon. Surprisingly, the one which promised riches turned out to be more or less worthless, and the other, which seemed risky, turned out to be important. The worthless source consists of the stories told about Gibran in Lebanon, particularly in his home village, Bsharri. Some of these stories have unfortunately become enshrined in the literature. The reason these tales are worthless is this: Gibran left Bsharri in 1895, when he was twelve. No one knew he was going to become so famous, and his departure was one among many from the region at the time. He was forgotten. But later, from the 1930s onwards, when it became clear, even to the largely illiterate villagers, that this long-forgotten son of theirs had achieved world-wide fame, suddenly every greybeard had a story about Gibran!

The second oral source is a single individual – my friend Nadeem Naimy. His importance is that he is the nephew of Mikhail Naimy, Gibran's closest friend and confidant in New York. Not long after

Gibran's death, Mikhail returned to Lebanon, and Nadeem was brought up in the same house as his uncle, imbibing stories about Gibran. This is not just a case of relying on Nadeem's childhood memories, since Mikhail died in 1988, at the venerable age of 99, by which time Nadeem was a respected academic in his fifties. The value of Nadeem as a source lay not so much in his supplying me with original material, but in his confirming the essential accuracy and honesty of his uncle's own book on Gibran. This is important because Mikhail Naimy's book – while admittedly being a pen-portrait rather than a proper biography – has been much vilified, despite the fact that, where cross-checking was possible, he invariably turned out to have been close to the truth, at least where his broad brush-strokes were concerned. Mikhail's book is known to be fairly accurate for the period after 1916, when he met and became friendly with Gibran, but was regarded as inaccurate and spiteful for the earlier period. However, it now appears that at least some of the material for the earlier part of the book was supplied to Mikhail by Mary Haskell herself. Immediately after Gibran's death, the two of them met several times in New York and had long conversations late into the night – the kind of conversation in which truths are revealed and souls are bared. Some of the substance of these conversations made its way into Mikhail's book, while some also found a place in Nadeem's memory. It is highly significant, though ignored by other biographers and critics, that Mary (who lived until 1964) reviewed the English edition of Naimy's book in the Savannah *Morning News* for 19 November 1950. Here was her opportunity to criticize the book as inaccurate – but there is not a word of such reproach throughout the whole review.

The reason I have gone on at some length about my approach to this book and the sources is because the portrait I have given of Gibran is considerably different from that to be found elsewhere, and from the impression readers might have gained from reading *The Prophet* or any of his other works. It is not so much that it is different in substance from earlier portraits, but it varies in a large number of details, and cumulatively these details do make quite a difference. Therefore, in all honesty, I should not disguise my attitudes and sources. This is another reason for my somewhat full end-notes.

Apart from trying to give an accurate impression of the major events of Gibran's life, and to understand the man, I also try to set all the important aspects of Gibran's life briefly in context. We are all conditioned by our contexts. This is a truism, but one that it is easy to forget. Numerous biographies apply the standards of the 1990s (or whenever they were written) to assess their subjects; historians of philosophy read Plato and Parmenides as if these ancient Greeks were familiar with the works of Wittgenstein and Frege; archaeologists interpret fragments according to the *Zeitgeist* of their own era. I have done my best to avoid this trap. So by placing Gibran's life and work in context, this book is not only a literary biography, but draws on social history as well. The overall aim, then, is to gain a balanced view of Gibran as both a person and a writer – to show that he is not a fringe, flaky figure of fun, nor yet (perhaps) a divinely inspired prophet, but a man of his times, who has managed to reach out beyond his times. Just as in his private life he was a chameleon, so in his public life he was somewhat of a 'cultural ventriloquist' (David Reynolds's nice phrase for Walt Whitman), popularizing and making timeless some trends of the times.

This book is not meant to be an exposé of certain more or less titillating aspects of Gibran's life. There is a deplorable side to many modern biographies: they revel in their subject's feet of clay. There may be skeletons in his cupboard – but whose cupboard is bare? Human beings are always complex creatures. So let me say from the start that I believe the value of his work outshines his peccadilloes. Would that we could all turn our complexes and the psychological knots formed by our upbringing and surroundings into sources of creative energy and strength! Nor, again, is this book a work of philosophical analysis or of literary criticism, although I hope that academic students of Gibran may profit from my work. Of course, since it is a literary biography, I summarize the content of many of Gibran's works in their biographical context, but I invariably assume, as a biographer must, the reader's familiarity with the detailed content of his books. It would take another book, and one of a different kind, to analyse 'Gibranism', or even to decide whether or not there is such a thing. In fact, in Gibran's case, for reasons that will become clear as the book progresses, I believe the attempt to be somewhat misguided:

he was a poet rather than a philosopher, which is to say that he had little or no desire to construct a coherent body of thought.

In preparing this book, I have incurred a great many debts. Before going any further, however, I must mention my UK editor Peter Carson. One way or another, we go back quite a long way now, and he has always been generous with his time, encouragement and support. Next, during my research travels, I met with an astonishing, heart-warming degree of generosity and kindness. A number of new friendships have been forged; people sacrificed their floor-space and their time, gave me books and advice. In this context the name of Nadeem Naimy must come first, but I would also like to thank particularly Michael F. Brown and Sylvia Kennick Brown, Eric Dugdale, Consuelo Dutschke, Akram and Jodi Khater, Robert and Roberta Matthews, Anita Mukand, Raja and Zorine Roy-Singh, David and Therese Stanford, and of course my long-suffering family – Briji, Julian and Kathy. As for the others, each of you knows what part you have played in this book. So thanks to: Tim Bates, Martin Buckley, Suheil Bushrui, John Bussanich, Jonathan Clark, Lindsay Clarke, Juan Cole, Father Denis Como SJ, Richard Copeland, Charles F. Cummings, Sarah Deco, Carl and Judy Ernst, Doucet Devin Fischer, Brian Gallagher, Marc Gascoigne, Pamela Goldstein, Alessandra Guiffrida, Patrick Harpur, Brad Inwood, Wahib Kayrouz, Émile and Marlene Khater, Bill Koshland, James Kraft, Christina Kraus, Penny Lawrence, Richard Leigh, Toinette Lippe, Paul Maiteny, William Merryman, Charles and Promilla Powell, Howard Powell, Mohamed Ragab, Connie Reuveni, Jeff Rice, Lily Richards, Erika Rockett, Mohammed Rouda, Pradeep and Jane Roy-Singh, Tania Sammons, Niko Scharer, John Schlapobersky, Sarah Shields, Graham Simon, Henryk and Juanita Skolimowski, Sarah Smith, Richard Smoley, Anna South, Philip Stadter, Janet Tyrrell, John Walbridge, Nick Waterfield, Bob Weil and Simon Winder.

Numerous bookshops have assisted, more or less knowingly, in providing me with resources. The work of research would be vastly longer and more trying if it were not for the patience and kindness of librarians. My thanks go to staff at the following libraries, museums and archive centres: the British Library; Northwestern University

Library; the National Archives (Northeast Region), New York; the New York Public Library; the Columbia University Libraries; the New York University Tamiment Institute Library, in the Elmer Holmes Bobst Library; Williams College Library; Yale University Library; the Hilles, Houghton, Lamont, Pusey and Widener Libraries of Harvard University; Radcliffe College Schlesinger Library; Boston Public Library; the Davis and Wilson Libraries of the University of North Carolina at Chapel Hill; the Harry Ransom Humanities Research Center at the University of Texas at Austin; the Library of Congress in Washington; the Perkins Library, Duke University; the Telfair Museum of Art; the Smithsonian National Museum of American Art; and the Centre historique des Archives nationales, Paris.

A number of these libraries have holdings of Gibran's letters. Mary Haskell's journals and papers are deposited among the Minis Family Papers, Southern Historical Collection, in the Wilson Library of the University of North Carolina at Chapel Hill; Josephine Preston Peabody's journals and papers are deposited in the Houghton Library of Harvard University. For the sake of art historians I will add that the major public repositories of Gibran's paintings and drawings are: the Gibran Museum, Bsharri, Lebanon; the Telfair Museum of Art, Savannah, Georgia; the Metropolitan Museum of Art, New York; The Fogg Art Museum, Cambridge, Massachusetts; the Brooklyn Museum, New York; and the Newark Museum, Newark, New Jersey.

The untitled poem by Witter Bynner is reprinted with permission of the Witter Bynner Foundation for Poetry; for permission to quote from Suheil Bushrui, *An Introduction to Kahlil Gibran* and *Blue Flame*, I thank Suheil Bushrui. Excerpts from Mary Haskell's diaries and journals are reprinted by kind permission of Charles Haskell, and from Gibran's unpublished letters by generous permission of his cousin, Kahlil Gibran.

The photograph of Fred Holland Day by Reginald Craigie is reproduced with the permission of the Norwood Historical Society, F. Holland Day Collection, Norwood, Massachusetts. The photographs of Mary Haskell, Charlotte Teller and Emilie Michel, and the Gibran drawing of Albert Pinkham Ryder, are reproduced from the Minis Family Papers, the Manuscripts Department, Wilson Library, the University of North Carolina at Chapel Hill, North Carolina. The photograph of various members of the Pen Club is reproduced with the kind permission of Nadeem Naimy. The Rose O'Neill portrait of Gibran is reproduced with the permission of the National Museum of American Art, Smithsonian Institution (Gift of the Smithsonian Women's Committee in memory of Adelyn Dohme Breeskin). The Jean Delville painting 'L'Amour des âmes' ('Love of Souls') is reproduced with the permission of the Musée d'Ixelles, Brussels. The self-portrait of Gibran, the photograph of his New York studio, 'The Head of Orpheus Floating Down the River Hebrus to the Sea', the untitled portrait of a woman with death's head, 'The Great Longing' and 'The Heavenly Mother' are all reproduced with the permission of the Telfair Museum of Art, Savannah, Georgia (gift of Mary Haskell Minis). All reasonable attempts have been made to contact copyright holders of text and illustrative material.

Prophet

εἰ δὲ Σύρος, τί τὸ θαῦμα; μίαν, ξένε, πατρίδα κόσμον
ναίομεν, ἓν θνατοὺς πάντας ἔτικτε Χάος.

So what if I am Syrian?
The world we live in, my friend, is a single country,
And we are all children of a single Abyss.

Meleager of Gadara

Wer immer strebend sich bemüht, den können wir erlösen.

We can save those who constantly strive upward.

Goethe

Overture

In the summer of 1921, when walking in the Catskills near Cahoonzie with his best friend Mikhail Naimy, about 100 miles from their homes in New York, Kahlil Gibran suddenly stopped and broke the companionable silence between them. He called out to Naimy by his familiar name: 'Mischa!' Naimy stopped and saw distress on his companion's face. 'Mischa!' Gibran said. 'I am a false alarm.'

This is a crucial episode in Gibran's life. He was a very reserved and private person, even to the extent of glorifying what he called his 'aloneness' and condemning curiosity about others. It is difficult to know the inmost thoughts of anyone, but especially of those who deliberately hide themselves from others. So although there are occasions in Gibran's life when it is possible to guess at what is going on under the surface, we are hardly ever afforded the kind of glimpse that this story of Naimy gives us.

'I am a false alarm.' At the very least, then, he felt that he was not practising what he preached. This was a time when he was working on *The Prophet*, and as a result of public readings of extracts from the book was becoming identified with that role. To his American friends he had long been the 'master' or the 'prophet', but now he was gaining a wider appreciative audience. He was telling his confidante, Mary Haskell, that it was crucial for him to live this philosophy, not just to write it, and that he wanted to be a teacher, to awaken people to consciousness. An alarm wakes people up; if Gibran felt he was a false alarm, he felt that he really had no right to play the part of awakener himself.

Why might he feel this? Curiously, it is possible to speculate with some plausibility as to at least some of the thoughts that might have been passing through Gibran's mind before he burst out with this confession. Naimy used to try to persuade Gibran that they should both return to Lebanon from the States so as to put their precepts into practice. They were both writing Romantic poetry and stories in praise of a life of simplicity, lived in rural surroundings, away from the distractions and machinations of the city. Only in the countryside could a man develop his soul and learn to know God. In letters at this time Gibran often expressed a longing for Lebanon in just these terms. And so, I guess, Naimy's presence triggered this train of thought in Gibran. He could have returned at any time, but something kept him back. In letters he spoke of 'golden chains' keeping him in New York: the image is very precise, because he stayed there largely for financial and materialistic reasons. He was trapped by his own desire for fame and recognition – the almost inevitable yearning of an immigrant – which he felt could be fulfilled only in New York. He was never fully a Westerner, and yet he could not re-commit himself to the East. And so he could not return. He could advise others of the necessity of the unadorned life, but he could not make the break and experience it for himself.

Two important and interesting questions Kahlil Gibran's life raises are the extent to which we, as readers, have a right to demand that a writer live up to his precepts, and the extent to which personal experience is necessary to validate spiritual teaching. At an early age Gibran created or accepted a persona for himself. Like all such masks, it was to a degree untrue to the reality, yet as time went by he became more and more committed to living within its parameters. The gap between the man and the myth grew increasingly wide. The man was insecure, worldly, sexual; the myth projected a knowledgeable, ascetic prophet. It is to his credit that he was aware of the gap, since many of us live our masks as if they were our true selves. But with that awareness, and being a person of considerable sensitivity, Gibran must have felt the gap sometimes as an unbearable tension – precisely the tension that he was expressing by admitting, in a private moment, that he was a false alarm.

And so a further importance of this isolated incident is that it shows Gibran to have been human after all. We usually look in vain in the extant records for such signs. Rather, his life appears to have been composed, plotted. It evolved organically out of the persona he chose to adopt – that of wounded Romantic, shading into that of poet and prophet – but even an organic development of a persona remains two-dimensional. Whether Gibran was talking to friends or to a public audience, the impression he projected was the same. He constantly played the role. As an insecure young immigrant he soon learnt that this role could win him ready acceptance, and even adulation; such positive feedback entrenched the role-playing until it became second nature. But once in a while his first nature prodded him into awareness: anyone who ignores his true nature is bound to remain, to some extent, a false alarm.

I

From East to West

There was luggage everywhere: sacks tied up with string, leather suitcases bulging open and suffering from an inadequate number of locks or hinges, shapeless bundles, wickerwork, crates. Piled on trolleys, heaped on one another, these tottering tokens of poverty, hope and desperation towered above the head of the small 12-year-old boy as he gazed in wonder around him, while remaining careful not to lose sight of the rest of his family. It was hard to remember, in these crowded, modern surroundings, that the whole trip had started on a few hired mules, which had carried him and his family from his home village of Bsharri down to the town of Beirut, 5,000 miles to the east.

The babel of excited voices swelled around him as more and more people disembarked from the ship. This was not the huge and exciting Dutch steamship *Spaarndam* which had brought him across the Atlantic from Boulogne. The *Spaarndam* had docked in New York itself, to let off the wealthy first-class passengers, and their slight social inferiors from the cabin class. But Gibran Khalil Gibran was not so privileged. He had travelled steerage, and along with all steerage passengers his entry into the United States of America had to be processed through Ellis Island. Their feet had hardly touched American soil – they had scarcely absorbed the wooded shoreline, the factories, cranes, the squalid piers, and the houses beyond – before they were herded on to another, smaller boat, which took them the half mile to Ellis Island.

By now he was used to shuffling along in queues, clutching some treasured possession and the hand of one of his younger sisters. By now he was used to the cacophony of voices around him. The

Spaarndam had carried mainly Russians, Austrians and Hungarians, who had embarked at Rotterdam. Khalil, along with a few other Syrians and some Greeks, had joined the ship in Boulogne, just before it set out for the voyage across the Atlantic Ocean. They were a small minority on the ship, as they would also be in North America, and by the time they climbed on board the best places on the steerage deck had already been taken by the sombre Europeans with their strange dark hats, shawls and clothing.[1] Although the *Spaarndam* was nowhere near as crowded as many of the immigrant ships that plied the Atlantic in the frenzied years of immigration into the United States, Khalil had also grown accustomed to the proximity of numerous unwashed and even seasick human bodies. Steerage was an experience best forgotten, and in later years he would rarely mention the trip to any of his friends, as far as we know.

Back home he had heard so much talk about 'al-Nayurk' (New York) and 'Amrika' that the idea of being refused entry never occurred to him; and his elder half-brother Peter had always spoken encouragingly about their future in America, as if there were never any doubt. But once they reached northern Europe, helped by the network of Syrians scattered around the Mediterranean to travel from Beirut to Marseilles, via Egypt and probably Italy, and then around the Iberian peninsula to Boulogne, they found that the officers of the Dutch Steamship Company would require them to submit to a medical examination before they allowed them on board the ship. The point was that there would be another medical examination on Ellis Island. Although this was very cursory, and rarely lasted longer than a few seconds (they were looking for obvious ailments, especially the eye disease trachoma), a certain percentage of potential immigrants were turned away at this eleventh hour. For about 2 per cent of the hopefuls, the closest they got to the freedom of America was the sight of the Statue of Liberty in New York bay; half of them were turned back for legal reasons, half because of poor health. In either case they were undesirables: they would not contribute to the moral and physical development of the great new country. Two per cent is a small proportion, but considering how many millions of people passed through Ellis Island in its years, between 1892 and 1954, as the processing facility for the most stupendous immigration movement the world has ever seen, it represents a not insignificant number of broken dreams. So every shipping company required its steerage passengers to submit to fumigation and a medical examination, because if the officers on Ellis Island refused someone entry, it was the shipping company itself which had to take the unfortunate person back across the Atlantic, at its own expense.

Ellis Island was named by generations of immigrants 'Island of Hopes, Island of Dreams'. Dreams can be broken; dreams can turn to nightmares. The Ellis Island experience was at least uncomfortable, at worst terrifying and alien. The Statue of Liberty promised to accept the 'weary and forsaken', but some had already reached their limit by the time they arrived. Several thousand suicides are reported as having taken place on Ellis Island. Today tourists visit a gleaming museum, the present incarnation of the immigration building (though not the one which Gibran would have seen, since the new one was not completed until 1900). Just off to one side of the museum, however, there are rows of dilapidated and dismal old dormitory and administrative buildings. In a sense they give a more accurate impression of what Ellis Island must have been like than does the spotless museum, for all its authentic exhibits. And there must have been a dreamlike quality to the whole process, as one queued endlessly, exhausted after the uncomfortable Atlantic voyage, and with one's senses bombarded by unfamiliar data and people firing questions in an incomprehensible language. Immigrants were presented with forms to fill in; they were 'marshalled, herded, divided, subdivided, sorted, sifted, searched, fumigated'.[2] And that day it was hot. It was 17 June 1895, and in later years Gibran would try and fail to become used to the stifling heat of a succession of New York summers.

In her excellent thesis on Gibran, Suhail Hanna states, 'The date of his first arrival in the United States is disputed.'[3] It is true that there used to be some doubt whether the family emigrated in 1894 or 1895, but the only precise date that has been confidently given is 25 June 1895, and that has never been disputed.[4] But it is wrong. We know that it was in fact 17 June 1895 because Ellis Island, like all good bureaucratic departments, was required to keep meticulous records. The legibility of the handwriting varies from entry to entry, but there, lodged in the New York office of the National Archives, Northeastern

Section,[5] the following passengers are listed as arrivals in New York on 17 June, each carrying two items of luggage, having joined the *Spaarndam* in Boulogne and found accommodation on the main decks:

Poutros Rhamé, aged 20, merchant
Camil Rhamé, aged 40
Jubran Rhamé, aged 11
Marianna Rhamé, aged 9
Sultané Rhamé, aged 7

There are some slight anomalies here, which might explain why previous biographers have missed the entry, if they bothered to look. In the first place, the family came in under the name of Rhamé. Kamila – this is the usual spelling of Gibran's mother's name – had previously been married to a cousin of hers, Hanna Abd-al-Salaam Rhamé, who had died in Brazil, while reconnoitring the country with a view to emigration; he left her with one son, Butrus or Peter. Since Kamila's second husband, the father of young Khalil, Marianna and Sultana, had stayed behind in Lebanon, Peter was the head of the party of immigrants; this must be the reason why they used his name. A second anomaly is that their destination is listed as New York, when in fact they headed straight off to Boston, which appears always to have been their intended destination. It seems likely that this is just a clerical error, due perhaps to some combination of the heat, laziness, the mechanical nature of the questioning process, and language difficulties.

A final oddity is that young Khalil's age is given as eleven. There is no difficulty about knowing the date of Gibran's birth. 'To-day is my birthday,' he wrote to Josephine Peabody on 6 January 1906. 'Now I am twenty-three years of age.'[6] Other similar remarks to friends and correspondents over the years corroborate this evidence: he was born on 6 January 1883. We can only speculate as to why the register should give his age as eleven.

The full and proper Arabic name of the boy who would later become known to the world as Kahlil Gibran may be transliterated Gibran Khalil Gibran, with the extra forename and the aspirated 'K'. So he would have entered America as Gibran (or Jubran, or Jibran) Khalil Rhamé. In Boston, as soon as there are records of him, he is

Kahlil Gibran. The family must have reverted to their proper surname once they were past the immigration facility, and Gibran more or less accepted the Westernization of his name by dropping the initial forename, and changing 'Khalil' to 'Kahlil'.

So the Rhamés were successfully processed. They stepped forward as a family unit to submit to examination and interrogation, clutching papers from the old country and the money needed by US law to prove that they were not just freeloaders. At last, under the prominent flag, with its stripes and forty-four stars, their names were written on labels and pinned to their lapels, and they were allowed to set foot in fabled al-Nayurk. They had probably been able to change their money on Ellis Island and buy tickets for the boat trip to Boston, and get a meal. Years later Marianna remembered that they also spent a night there,[7] which was not uncommon. On busy days the immigration facility was expected to process up to 5,000 people a day, and backlogs were frequent.

In a sense, the Gibrans' emigration to America was conditioned by four events that had taken place in Lebanon some sixty years earlier, in 1834. First, the men's college at 'Aintura, which had been closed in 1775 with the suppression of the Jesuits in the region, was reopened by the Lazarist Fathers. Second, the American missions decided to move their Mediterranean printing press from Malta to Beirut. Third, Eli Smith, an American Presbyterian missionary, opened a girls' school in Beirut. And fourth, Ibrahim Pasha, the Syrian ruler, initiated a wide programme of primary education for boys, modelled on the system inaugurated by his father, the great Muhammad 'Ali, in Egypt. But in order to understand the importance of these events, we need to step even further back in time.

Nowadays the images conjured up in the mind by the mention of the country Lebanon are most likely to be of war-torn Beirut, though older people will remember the attractions of this city, the 'Paris of the East', before the troubles started in 1975. The contrast between beauty and strife is not inappropriate. One way or another, Lebanon, one of the most beautiful countries in the world, has always suffered. About ten miles north of Beirut, where the Nahr al-Kalb (the Dog River, the ancient Lycus) empties into the Mediterranean, the face of the limestone rock has nineteen inscriptions carved into it, in almost as many languages. A spur of the mountains there used to come right down to the sea, and these inscriptions have been left by the military leaders of various nations as they led their armies over the outcrop and into or out of the country, perhaps having subdued it, perhaps simply on their way elsewhere. They begin with Rameses II of Egypt, commemorating a victory over the Hittites in 1300 BC, and end in 1946 with the departure of the French occupying forces.[8] Canaanites and Amorites came from the south; Hittites and Kurds from Anatolia; Persians from the east; Egyptians from the Nile valley; Greeks, Romans and Crusaders from Europe; Mongols and Turks from Central Asia. More recently the French and British, driven by greed to deceive the Arab nationalists, tried to carve up the area between themselves; and now, in the late 1990s, Lebanon is partially occupied by Syrian troops and there is the notorious Israeli 'buffer zone' in the south of the country.

Until 1946 Lebanon was not even a country in its own right, although it had been a part of many empires. In 1920 the state of 'Greater Lebanon' was proudly announced, incorporating the coastal towns as well as the mountain ranges and the Biqa' valley, and in 1926 it was formally declared a separate country, a parliamentary republic with a new constitution; but it was still occupied by French troops. Only after they left was final independence gained, for Syria on 17 April 1946, and for Lebanon on 31 December 1946. For most of recent history Lebanon was part of 'Syria', which referred to the countries known now as Syria, Lebanon, Jordan and Israel; and this Syria was in turn part of various Muslim empires, culminating of course in the Ottoman Empire. But the narrow strip of land between the Mediterranean coast and the borders of modern Syria always clung on to its own traditions, especially in the strongholds of the mountains, which conquerors tended to bypass.

Modern Lebanon occupies a little less than 4,000 square miles (about half the size of Wales or New Jersey). A fertile narrow coastal strip, often no more than a few hundred yards wide, rises into magnificent mountain ranges whose peaks climb like a wall to over 9,000 feet in some places. Rivers run down sheer gorges dividing long spurs which lead up to the ridge of the Mount Lebanon range. In some places the transition from coast to mountain is shocking in its suddenness; in others there are terraced foothills, dotted with citrus orchards and olive groves. Terraces corrugate even the most unlikely and sheer hillsides, though all too often nowadays they are abandoned and unworked. In Gibran's time, however, they would have been the sites of intensive farming. The coastline, perfect for trading, was where cities developed early in history – Tripoli, Byblos, Beirut, Tyre and Sidon, the homes of the Phoenician traders, who invented the alphabet and, just possibly, explored across the Atlantic Ocean as far as North America, forging a route retraced 2,000 years later by Kahlil Gibran and his family.

On the mountains, the fabled cedar forests of history have by now mostly disappeared; only a very few truly ancient trees remain, and, despite some attempts at replanting, only a few isolated groves survive. But these highlands are still breathtakingly beautiful, provided one can get away from ski lodges and other ferro-concrete monstrosities: as life in Beirut becomes increasingly stressful and polluted, more and more people are building second homes in the mountains. The snow-capped peaks give their name to the country as a whole, for the Semitic word for 'white' is *lubnan*. Bsharri, where the Gibran family came from, is high in the mountains, overlooking the Wadi Qadisha or Sacred Valley, nestling under the huge bulk of Mount Lebanon within an area of devastating natural beauty, with streams, crags, mountains, cedars, the cultivated Koura plateau, an abundance of flowers, wild animals and ancient ruins. In the summer, browns and greens predominate in the foreground, with purple, veiled blues and rosy mists in the distance, as one looks, for instance, across the Biqa' valley from the Lebanon range to the Anti-Lebanon mountains, only slightly less prominent and awesome than Mount Lebanon itself. Closer up, the cliffs of the highest parts of the mountains change colour in the evening from grey to honey to rosy pink. In the winter deep snow covers the ground for up to six months, cutting off mountain communities from one another and leaving them to their own resources.

Typically, for centuries the inhabitants of Mount Lebanon lived in small and often quite isolated villages. They were peasant farmers, independent and hardy, with terraced smallholdings clinging to the sides of mountains, farming sheep and cultivating vines, olives and other fruit trees, and cereal crops. The area as a whole was never self-sufficient, and imports increased in the nineteenth century, when growing contact with the outside world encouraged these mountain-dwellers to develop their ancient skills in growing mulberry trees for the cultivation of silkworms, to feed European hunger for silk thread. Land prices rose and eventually a few large landowners parcelled out most of the land among themselves.

Mount Lebanon is such a natural stronghold that one can find there survivals, bypassed by history, seemingly from an earlier age. Most noticeable – and most important for Lebanon's subsequent history – are a number of unique religious sects, two of which we will turn to shortly. But until recently the social structure of Lebanon was also an atavism. As with many traditional cultures, the family was all-important, with the father very much the *paterfamilias*, dominating the family with his income and autocracy. And this reliance on a single authority figure extended outwards. Until the middle of the last century, Lebanon had one of the last surviving feudal systems in the world. The topography of the place encourages such a system, since until the construction of modern roads travel across the ravines even to nearby villages would have been arduous, so that each village had to govern itself. Given the relatively recent disappearance of feudalism there, traces still remain; when the Western press gives prominence to individual 'warlords' with their followers, it is not being inaccurate. And when we come to consider the chaos generated by Gibran's will, we will meet again the phenomenon of warring clans.

Two authority figures are particularly important in Lebanese history, since they both extended Lebanon's influence beyond the mountains and down to the coast. They both created short-lived independent countries, whose boundaries more or less coincide with those of modern Lebanon. Both are, of course, still national heroes nowadays, as Lebanon still struggles for full independence. The first was the Druze Fakhr-al-Din II (1572–1635), a colourful figure who resisted the Turks and, after his exile, was misled by the Medicis of Florence into expecting their support; whereupon he returned to his kingdom and was beheaded, or possibly strangled, by the Turks. The second was Bashir II (1790–1840), from the powerful Shihab clan, which had taken over as the controlling family of Lebanon once Fakhr-al-Din's Ma'nid line had become extinct in 1697. Bashir's defiance acted as a red rag to the Turks, whose empire was by now beginning to disintegrate, much to the interest of the European superpowers, who hoped to pick up the pieces. Anyway, by this stage the Turks needed an excuse to exert greater direct authority over Lebanon. The means were not far to seek.

In the early centuries of Christianity, various sects flourished around crucial matters of dogma. One such sect were the Monotheletes, who tried to reconcile the debate over whether Christ had one or two natures by claiming that he had two natures, divine and human, but only one will – that he was, as far as his will was concerned, completely unified with God. Saint Maron (350–433) brought Monothelitism to the area now known as Lebanon, where it thrived. Even when the doctrine was condemned at the Council of Chalcedon in 451, the sect remained, more or less overlooked and forgotten, within its mountain home. It was only when the heresy was officially outlawed at the Third Council of Constantinople in 680 that more positive steps towards independence were taken, and the first patriarch, John Maro (Yuhanna Marun), was appointed. Five hundred years later, however, after contact with the Crusaders, the sect rejoined the rest of the world. Officially renouncing its heresy, the Maronite Church sought unification with the Catholic Church of Rome. This was granted, and the Maronite Church came to rise high in Rome's favour. In 1510, overlooking its earlier status as a heretic sect, Pope Leo X famously described it as a 'rose among thorns', an offshoot of the true Church surrounded by infidels and heretics. Nowadays there are scarcely any noticeable differences between the Maronite Church and Roman Catholicism in general. It was, and continues to be, the most populous of the ten or so Christian sects represented in Lebanon.

In the early eleventh century, al-Hakim, the Fatimid caliph reigning in Egypt, who some writers believe to have been insane, proclaimed himself divine. One of his main disciples was his vizier, a Persian Isma'ili theologian called Hamzah ibn 'Ali ibn Ahmad al-Zuzani, who had come to Cairo in 1016. There was a strong streak of Messianic fervour within the Isma'ili sect, and Hamzah saw al-Hakim as a true incarnation of God. He declared a new religion, and he sent as a missionary Muhammad al-Darazi, 'the tailor', to preach the gospel in Mount Lebanon. Al-Darazi was so successful that he set himself up as a spiritual leader in his own right, as a result of which Hamzah had him assassinated and replaced by al-Muqtana Baha'-al-Din. Persecuted by orthodox Muslims, the new sect (known as the Druze after al-Darazi, though they call themselves al-Muwahhidun, 'the unitarians') became incredibly secretive. Their former missionary activities ceased, and ever since then one has to be born into a Druze family to be a member, beginning as *juhhal* ('ignorant') and, if God wills it, becoming *'uqqal* ('intelligent') and thereby gaining access to the sect's sacred books and rituals. Over the centuries various aspects of their beliefs and practices have become known, but they remain shrouded in myth and speculation by outsiders. As for al-Hakim, he disappeared in mysterious circumstances in 1021; though probably assassinated by his sister, the Druze believe he was taken into heaven, and they look forward to a second coming.

Between them, these two sects, Christian and quasi-Muslim (the Druze do not adhere, or adhere strictly, to all the five pillars of Islam), constituted the majority of the population of Lebanon. The Christians greatly outnumbered the Druze,[9] but, distinguished by little more than their religious observances and their clothing, Druze, Muslims and Maronites lived together in relative peace for centuries in the mountains. Often villages would be inhabited more or less exclusively by members of one sect or the other, but they coexisted in many villages, and of course traded and dealt with one another. But there was always an awareness of differences between religions and sects; it was not at all uncommon to introduce oneself as, say, 'Aziz Shihab, a Maronite'.[10] By and large the Druze were the majority in southern Lebanon, while the Maronites were dominant in the north. Gibran was brought up a Maronite Christian; his native village, Bsharri, had long been an important centre for the sect. His grandfather on his mother's side was a priest.

In 1756, the status quo received a rude shake-up when the ruling Shihab emirs converted from the Druze religion to Maronite Christianity. In a sense the district of Lebanon came to have two rulers – the emir and the Maronite patriarch. The stage was set for simmering hostility between the two sects, and the breakdown in amicable relations was hastened by the high-handed attitude of the Maronite emirs towards the Druze barons, who lost many of their ancestral privileges and lands. The same arrogance was reflected at all levels of society. '[The Maronites'] leading men amassed riches. They kept studs, their wives and daughters were apparelled in silks and satins and blazed with jewelry. The few Druzes who still inhabited the town were reduced to insignificance as hewers of wood and drawers of water.'[11] The Druze looked to the Turks, but in fact help came from an unexpected quarter. When Ibrahim Pasha became the ruler of Syria, he supported the Druze against the Christians.

By 1811, as a result of diplomacy and assassination, Ibrahim's father, Muhammad 'Ali, had established himself as absolute ruler in Egypt, Sudan and Arabia. In effect, he controlled a lesser empire within the Ottoman Empire. Relations with the Ottoman emperor, Mahmud II, in Constantinople were naturally uneasy, although Muhammad 'Ali did everything he could at first to avoid giving offence and to appear to be no more than a loyal vassal. Nevertheless, he coveted Syria, and in 1831 he sent in his son Ibrahim with an army to depose the Ottoman pasha and establish himself instead. Bashir II, the Christian ruler of Lebanon, helped Ibrahim achieve his aims, but Ibrahim rewarded him by inclining towards the Druze underdogs of Syrian society. Meanwhile, the European powers sided with the Turks to make sure that Ibrahim did not extend his kingdom too far northwards. His rule soon proved unpopular and his Christian subjects waited for the tide to turn against Muhammad 'Ali.

And, of course, the tide did turn. Britain was concerned about her trade routes to India, France wanted to expand from Algeria into Egypt; both nations wanted to lay claim to Palestine and Syria too. In short, they wanted Muhammad 'Ali out of Egypt. On 5 July 1840 the Quadruple Alliance was formed between Britain, Russia, Germany and Austria, with the express intention of defending the integrity of Turkey – in other words, of seeing that Muhammad 'Ali did not become too powerful. A European fleet assembled off the Syrian coast to attack Ibrahim. The Maronites seized the opportunity to rise up in rebellion. Before long Ibrahim had fled to Egypt, and in the chaos Bashir II was deposed and killed for having supported him.

The Christians installed Bashir III as emir, but he was weak and could not afford them the protection to which they had become accustomed. The Ottoman government soon deposed him and, both recognizing and exacerbating the status quo, divided the mountains into two cantons, one Druze and Muslim, and the other Maronite – an action which served only to encourage the growth of communal and local loyalties. In the early 1840s, egged on by the Turks, the Druze rose up against the Christians, remembering decades of arrogant overlordship. The violence left several hundred villagers dead. The cantonization of Lebanon was no real solution: many Christians lived in the south, and many Muslims (especially Shi'a) and Druze lived in the north. Life became one of occasional skirmishes, leading ultimately in the 1850s to an uneasy stand-off. Re-enter, stage left from Europe, the two superpowers France and England. Catholic France put its weight behind the Maronites and fanned their dreams of dominance, while England – paradoxically for a Christian nation – backed the Druze. The upshot was a brief period of savage civil war in 1859 and 1860. The Druze successfully captured towns and villages and massacred any Christians they found. News of the atrocities shocked the Western world. Estimates of the casualties vary between 5,000 and 11,000, with several thousand further refugee deaths.

Peace was restored only when the superpowers again sent a fleet to the eastern Mediterranean, threatening intervention. The Christians demanded reparation, but the Druze ringleaders received only a mock trial in the Turkish courts, and there were no executions, although there had been a number of condemnations for war crimes.[12] Kahlil Gibran's mother Kamila would have been about five years old at the time of the 1860 massacres. The date of his father's birth is unknown, but he was presumably alive. In fact, however, they were relatively untouched by these terrible events, since the Druze raids did not penetrate as far north as Bsharri.

As a ploy to regain strict control over the area, all this proved singularly unsuccessful for the Turks. The crumbling, decadent empire had been forced to rely more than once on European intervention, and the European powers assisted in the establishment of a less authoritarian form of Turkish control, known as the Règlement Organique. This was an era of reform throughout the Ottoman Empire. Syria was divided into three vilayets or provinces, and three smaller administrative units called sanjaks, one of which was Lebanon. For the first time the name 'Lebanon' became the official designation of a state, or at least a quasi-state. Originally the name had been restricted to Jabal Lubnan, Mount Lebanon itself, in the north, but as the Maronites moved south in the late eighteenth century they brought the name with them to stand for the whole area in which they lived. And now the term received international recognition. Peace and prosperity came to Lebanon (albeit more to the Christians than to the other sects and religions) after the horrid period of anarchy; roads were built, agriculture improved. The truth of the old saying at last became apparent – 'Fortunate is he who owns even a goat's pen in the Mountain.' And along with all these advances came the leisure for education.

The Turks had always been suspicious of Western influence on the various parts of their empire. In Syria, Western missionaries would creep in, only to be expelled as part of some sultan's or pasha's fundamentalist crackdown.[13] But Muhammad 'Ali of Egypt had favoured European education as a means of bringing his people out of the Middle Ages – and also perhaps as a form of subtle defiance against the sultan in Constantinople. His son Ibrahim carried these educational reforms into Syria and Lebanon, and in 1834 allowed Protestant missions back into the country, which had previously been dominated by Catholics. Under the more tolerant post-1860 regime, Ibrahim's reforms proved to be only the thin end of the wedge. 'By the end of the nineteenth century,' Kamal Salibi says, 'Lebanon was easily the most advanced part of the Ottoman Empire in the field of popular education.'[14] And this, it should be noted, despite the fact that the Sultan 'Abd-al-Hamid II (1876–1909), who was eventually deposed by the Young Turks, employed secret police and informers in some parts of his empire against intellectuals.

The Turks were right to be suspicious of the influence of Western education. The importance of intellectuals in the growth of the Arab nationalist movement cannot be overestimated. The dramatic story of Arab nationalism would take us too far afield, although it is one in which Gibran played a minor role; it is told with clarity and great authority by George Antonius, whose book on the subject begins: 'The story of the Arab national movement opens in Syria in 1847, with the foundation in Bairut of a modest literary society under

American patronage.'[15] As it happens, I am placing the start of the story a little further back, in 1834, but he is right to recognize the importance of Arab intellectuals. As a result of the changes of 1834, the general level of education in the region rose dramatically. Books, previously more or less unknown, became widely disseminated; the education of women was a particularly impressive break with tradition, and came to be copied elsewhere in the Arab world. The eventual upshot was that, considering its size, Lebanon provided a disproportionate number of important intellectuals who fostered nationalism throughout the Arab world.

Ibrahim's tolerant rule opened the door to Western missionary enterprise; the opportunity was seized by, especially, the French and Americans. Not to be outdone by foreign missionaries and local ecclesiastics, the government also sponsored the establishment of schools. Newspapers began to be published, books were being written. The Syrian Protestant College, forerunner to the famous American University of Beirut, was founded in 1866. Knowledge became recognized as the essential prerequisite for political and spiritual freedom. The liberal American magazine *The Independent* ran in its issue for 30 April 1907 an interview with an anonymous 'very well known' Syrian expatriate, 'who is under sentence of death for his utterances against Turkish misrule'. The interview is fascinating for its glimpses of rural life on Mount Lebanon, and at one point the young Syrian has this to say:

> Great changes have come in the minds of our people since I was a boy. They were like cattle in the old days and took the blows of their rulers as a matter of course, not knowing that such a thing as freedom for the common people existed. But at the time when I was going to mission school new knowledge began to get about and there were whisperings of discontent that became louder and louder.[16]

All this forms the context, the broad background, to the wave of Lebanese emigration in the late nineteenth century, of which the entry of most of the Gibran family into America was a tiny fragment – but one that, through Kahlil Gibran, would prove to have enormous consequences for the Arab literary world and for the lives of his millions of readers since. For, as we shall see, Gibran could never have become precisely the kind of writer he was were it not for the influence on him of particular people he met in Boston.

The largest concentration of Syrian immigrants could be found in New York; by 1900 half the Syrians in America lived there. They lived (and still live) in Brooklyn around Atlantic Avenue, but more especially in those days around Washington Street in Manhattan. The district has now largely given way to the development of roads, but at the time it was a bustling 'Little Syria', full of the sights and sounds and scents of the old country. But there were also groups of Syrian immigrants in all the major cities, especially on the east coast, and the odd Syrian family or individual might be found anywhere in the United States. They spread out and assimilated somewhat more readily than many other races. One of the main reasons for their diffusion was that the job many Lebanese men, and some women, undertook was peddling. Familiar in their fezzes, open jackets and baggy *shirwal* trousers, they were often the first to bring fresh fish or fruit, silk or lace or dry goods of all descriptions, door to door in their baskets to the houses of the outlying communities of the United States.

Born traders, the Syrians on reaching this country naturally turn to some form of buying and selling as the readiest means of gaining a livelihood. The peddler's basket represents, in numberless instances, their first venture here in business. After this comes the small basement store, then the larger store on the level of the street, then an additional store, or the factory, or the office of the importer. The basement store, before it gives way to its successor, often becomes a center where peddlers are supplied, or from which they are sent out by the proprietor on some basis of profit-sharing. There may also be a short cut from it directly to the factory. Every branch of commerce and many branches of manufacture have been entered by this immigrant people.

But all Syrians here are not traders or manufacturers. Large numbers of them are factory operatives, mine workers, brass polishers, merchants, carpenters, masons, and even farmers. There are also Syrian priests, lawyers, doctors, ministers, writers, editors, teachers, and musicians.[17]

On the whole, they were very successful. Whereas in 1910 the average income per year in America was $382, the Syrian average was closer to $1,000. By then there were over 100,000 Syrians in America.

They were quick to exploit the vast pool of cheap labour in New York, which was the China or Taiwan of its day in terms of the manufacture of inexpensive goods; with the help of a network of Syrian immigrants to other countries, they moved into the export business. They also sent more money back to relatives in Syria and Lebanon than did any other ethnic group in the States.

Contrary to popular beliefs,[18] the search for political freedom was a rare reason for emigration from the Middle East, and the desire for intellectual freedom applies only to the few intellectuals. The search for the good life, for greater wealth and comfort, was invariably the primary motivation, at least in the case of the earliest wave of emigrants – a trickle in the 1870s, a stream by the 1880s and 1890s. Land prices were rising; under the influence of Western medicines, the population of Syria doubled between 1830 and 1890; the opening of the Suez Canal in 1869 diverted some trade away from the coastal ports.[19] It is noticeable, however, that the majority of the emigrants from Lebanon were Maronite Christians, rather than Muslims or Druze. Perhaps the memory of the 1860 massacres lingered. Perhaps the Christians were, on the whole, better educated, and therefore had a higher level of expectations, which they were not finding fulfilled in their native land. Or perhaps it was simply that America was a Christian country, and therefore more congenial to Christian immigrants. Lacking any evidence to the contrary, it seems reasonable to attribute economic motives to the Gibran family's departure. And all we know about Kahlil's mother Kamila suggests that she was ambitious for her children, and might well have felt that their growth would be stunted in Bsharri. But then there is the question of Gibran's father. Why did he remain behind? Was the rest of the family in some sense trying to escape from him? The issue is complicated by contradictions in the evidence; here we meet for the first time Gibran's facility at myth-making, at creating a smokescreen behind which he could hide – or, less charitably put, at telling lies and half-truths.

Given the role of the father in a traditional Lebanese family, it is curious, in the first place, that Khalil Sa'd Gibran should have allowed the family to divide in this way. Even though the mother was invariably the power within the home, a decision as important as family emigration would hardly have been taken without the connivance, or at least concession, of Gibran's father. But then, strange things did happen to families who emigrated. Parents might go on ahead of their children, waiting perhaps as many as fifteen years until they felt they had carved out a way of life in the new country and could send for their offspring. Gregory Orfalea cites one case where, as with the Gibrans, the father, a 'wastrel', was the only one to remain behind.[20] As a matter of fact, however, it was far from unknown for the head of the family to stay in Lebanon and yet remain, as much as possible, the patriarch: he would be consulted by letter on all major family decisions.[21] Unfortunately there is no way now of knowing whether this was the system employed by the Gibrans.

According to the most authoritative account to date of Gibran's life, his father was an irascible and boastful bully, a heavy drinker and a gambler. He owned a walnut grove thirty-five miles from Bsharri, but preferred not to work if he could help it. The family lived in a crumbling stone house with a mud roof, until that more or less collapsed and they moved, to Kamila's shame, into one floor of a four-storey house on public land in the village – the village equivalent of council housing, except that they paid in political allegiance to the village headman rather than in rent. Family life was uncomfortable, with tension between Khalil and strong-willed Kamila. The last straw came in 1891 when, as a result of his involvement in some financial irregularity (he had collected taxes for the village headman), Khalil was arrested and found guilty. As punishment, he was stripped in 1894 of all his remaining property. Although to salvage her pride Kamila had tried desperately to prove her husband's innocence, she was now irredeemably estranged from him, and she took her family to try to build a new life for them and for herself in America.

Since the sources for this account are largely unacknowledged, and since it comes from a book written by relatives of Gibran (albeit not very close relatives),[22] we are left to assume that the main source is family tradition, which, though it may exaggerate, is rarely untrue. Gibran's own portrait of his early life, however, as told piecemeal to American friends, especially Mary Haskell, over the years, is quite different. He admitted, of course, that his father had been in trouble with the law, but protested his innocence, and the corruption of the local judiciary; his father was ruined, he said, because he refused to bribe his way out of the false charge. He even denied that his mother left his father, and said that they were expecting him to catch up with them (perhaps this was the tale Kamila told her younger children to console them). Rather than being irascible, his father was 'imperious', and came from a long line of noble warriors and horsemen. He never punished his son or gave him an order. In one famous story the elder Khalil, irritated at religious intolerance in the village, generously buys oil from a muleteer of another Christian denomination, and even invites him into his house for supper.

Not only did the father become transformed, but their poverty – the sign of the father's failure – also vanished. 'His was what is called in the East a "fortunate" birth,' said his friend, the artist and writer Claude Bragdon, who must have got his information from Gibran himself, 'for he was brought up in an atmosphere of love, beauty and abundance. Not only were his people affluent and cultured, but his mother's family, from far back, was the most musical in all the countryside.'[23] In Bsharri they lived, according to Gibran, in a big house surrounded by family antiques and heirlooms, with a whole room just for weaponry. He was descended, on his father's side, from owners of a 'palace' in Bsharri, and on his mother's side from a grandfather who was 'the richest man in Lebanon'. He compared their life of poverty in Boston with his father's life back home in Lebanon with his horses and servants. His childhood memories, he claimed, included being dressed up, aged two-and-a-half, like a French officer in honour of a visit to his father by a French admiral – a ritual frequently repeated afterwards, sometimes three or four times a week, in honour of various guests. Even more grandiosely, he claimed to have met the Kaiser when he was a child, because his father 'was one of the body appointed to do him honor'. His uncle, he claimed, knew Henry Irving and 'everybody in Europe best worth knowing in his day'. He told how whenever he went out riding his father made sure he was accompanied by two attendants, and mentions in passing that his father had a hunting-suit made in Vienna. At another point he claimed that he had a good deal of money to spend on his childish artistic and engineering projects. This is certainly not a picture of family poverty brought on by a lazy slob of a father. 'Have you ever lived near enough to simple people to eat at their tables and share their work?' his friend, editor, confidante and quasi-lover Mary Haskell once asked him. 'No,' replied Kahlil, 'but I'd love to.'[24]

Well, perhaps both pictures are true – the first objectively true, and the second true in the eyes of a boy deprived of his father at an early age, when he was too young to understand the tensions and rifts between his parents. There does seem to be an element of compensation, as if Gibran was even faintly aware of his father's nature, and therefore in later life glossed over his defects. This is borne out by consideration of the fact that the first chapter of the life of Gibran by his close friend and associate Mikhail Naimy also contains stories of the elder Khalil's drunkenness, crudity and cruelty – and, because Naimy never refers to any sources, we are led to believe that Gibran himself was the origin of these stories. If so, he was giving one set of impressions to Mary Haskell and another set to Naimy. We shall find that this is far from unlikely; there is plenty of evidence that Gibran liked to please people and liked to be liked and that in pursuit of this aim he spoke and acted as he believed his audience would want him to speak and act. 'I don't want anyone to find me out,' he once told Mary,[25] and he seems to have been successful at wearing his various disguises. He even tried to pretend in some contexts that the year of his birth was unknown. The question for a biographer then becomes: did this man have a centre at all? Where is the core around which all these masks cohered?

Many of the other memories of his childhood days he mentioned to his friends are almost unbelievably whimsical and romantic. He told Mary Haskell of 'Fakry' (as she spells the name in her journal), the local wise man of the village who could tell a person's character and future from a single glimpse of his features, and of a time when his father took him out riding at sunrise to see a tribe 'in which the men for generations had always of intent married only beautiful women'. She recorded how he once asked the local doctor, Selim Dahir, whether doctors could graft a human being on to a horse and create a centaur, and how impressed Gibran was with the courage and nobility of the band of sixty-eight horsemen – an old sheikh and his descendants down to his great-grandsons – riding out to greet the sun. He told her of a mysterious meeting with a woman in the mountains of Lebanon and how she got him to light her fire because he was 'the first-born of his father'; the woman gave him a sacred silver ring in exchange.[26] He told Barbara

Young, the confidante of his later years, 'of a day when a great rain was falling, and it called to him, called his name, and he slipped off his little garments and ran out naked to answer the call of the rain, ran until his mother and his nurse, breathless, caught up with him and bore him struggling and protesting into the house', or again of a time when he planted scraps of paper in the ground, so that they would grow into sheets for him to draw and write on.[27]

And, of course, his stories about his childhood often stressed his precocious, delicate and artistic nature. At the age of six he was given a book of Leonardo reproductions by his mother; after looking through it for a few minutes, he was moved to passionate tears and ran from the room to be alone. He liked to make out that he was somehow different from the rest – lonely, sad, thoughtful and serious – and he told of early but often astonishingly mature attempts at writing, painting, engineering and sculpture, of dreams of Jesus Christ and a mystical communion with the beautiful surrounding countryside, of being beaten up at school as a sissy.[28] His childhood schooling, in fact, was probably irregular at best. We should certainly take with a considerable pinch of salt his later claim to have had tutors for German, French and English.[29] The Maronites in northern Lebanon were notoriously uneducated, since Protestant schooling had not penetrated to all the Catholic villages. Apart from some rudimentary teaching at the hands of the priests, the most important educational influence was Selim Dahir, about whom very little is known. He was the local doctor, and, not untypically, the most learned man in the village. He seems to have taken Gibran under his wing at an early age, introduced him to the world of books and encouraged him in his boyish artistic aspirations, if this is not too pretentious a way to express it, given that the boy was probably under ten years old. Certainly, it seems that as a young boy he liked to spend time alone, and was constantly sketching.[30] However, we should surely disbelieve him when he tells Mary that some romantic ballads he wrote before emigrating became popular in Syria and Egypt.[31]

Kamila may have been an important source of learning. Kahlil once told Mary that she was a learned woman, fluent in French, Italian, Spanish and English as well as Arabic, that she had read and travelled widely, and had a cosmopolitan selection of friends and acquaintances from all over the world.[32] Even allowing for wild exaggeration, it is clear from all accounts that she was bright, flirtatious and gifted. She was the daughter of the village priest, but according to interviews with members of her family was not educated.[33] She probably felt herself stifled in Bsharri, and like many mothers tried to live her ambitions vicariously through her children – and particularly her talented son Kahlil. She even told him that she thought he might one day be a great man, and her attitude towards him, he said, was that he was her teacher rather than she his.[34] She was undoubtedly the dominant educational and emotional influence on the young boy, sheltering him from his more practically minded father, allowing him his moods and fancies,[35] pandering to his delicacy.[36] She encouraged his artistic and literary side,[37] not only with words but, for example, by giving him the Leonardo book. She had a good singing voice, and would sing to him for hours, instilling in him the tales of Lebanon and a sense of rhythm and poetry. Photographs exist of her, showing a small-framed woman with a strong, lined, slightly pinched face, and heavy-lidded eyes that distract one from the sense of humour evident elsewhere in the features. 'I am indebted for all that I call "I" to women,' Gibran wrote later in life,[38] and the first of these women was undoubtedly his mother. For all that, she remains a somewhat shadowy figure. She died in 1903, and we are left with an impression of Gibran's sentimental attachment to her memory, but little else.

The lives of the rest of his family – his sisters and half-brother – will play only a peripheral part, though their deaths will briefly occupy centre stage. On arriving in the United States of America, the five-strong family caught a boat straight for Boston, where cousins and more distant relatives were already living, in the Syrian quarter of the South End, the second biggest Syrian community in the country. It would not take Gibran long to break out of this ghetto and begin to fulfil Kamila's dreams of his great future. As a natural chameleon, it would prove easier for him than for many other immigrants to assimilate into American society – even Boston society – and win acceptance. The only question was how it would happen. And here chance had a crucial part to play.

2

Beautiful Dreamer

The Boston in which the Gibrans settled was a vibrant city, with a population of some half a million, and growing fast.[1] Growth had been helped by enormous land-engineering projects undertaken earlier in the century. The South End – the area where the Gibrans settled – was until 1850 the South Bay; Beach Street, later one of the South End's main thoroughfares, was aptly named. Then the whole of the South Bay was filled in. The fantastic scale of the work reflected the city's civic pride and ambitions for the future. And the sense of energetic modernity had not been hindered by the Great Fire of 1872, which served – leaving aside the tragic aspects – to clear the ground for massive rebuilding, and for an enlightened programme creating the 'Emerald Necklace' of Boston's parks.[2] The architecture of many of the buildings constructed in the last quarter of the nineteenth century in Boston displays the same sense of pride. Above all, perhaps, stands the incomparable Public Library, opened in 1895 in all its Renaissance splendour; its interior is adorned with specially commissioned murals and statues, a vast collection of books, and fountains playing in the inner sanctum of a cloistered courtyard. Henry James found it all 'pomp and circumstance', but then Henry James was a conservative grouch.[3] Numerous other public buildings and institutions, many still surviving, arose at this time and attest to the city's sense of self: the Boston Society of Natural History, the Harvard Medical School, the several universities in Cambridge and Boston itself, the Boston Symphony Orchestra, and so on. This Boston, the 'Athens of America', was the creation of the wealthy elite, the Boston Brahmins.

The South End, it was originally thought, would house the genteel middle classes and parvenus of Boston, while the aristocracy continued to cluster around Charles Street, Beacon Hill and the Back Bay. And so the typical architecture of the South End was a spacious, red, bow-fronted house with an outlook on to a square or, more commonly, a narrow cobbled street. But property speculators who eagerly bought up land and houses there were to be disappointed, overtaken by the tide of events – or, to be exact, the tide of immigration. By 1900 an astonishing 74 per cent of Boston's population was foreign-born. The South End became one of the main areas in Boston for immigrants, and privately owned bow-fronted houses gave way to tenement and lodging houses. Union Park, for instance, was originally a pleasant square of private houses; by 1874, two of the houses had become lodging houses, and by 1902 only seven out of the fifty-three houses remained as private residences.[4]

As one wanders around the South End today, it is easy to catch the odd glimpse back through time to the 1890s. It is not just that some of the old buildings are still standing, but that the district has kept its ghetto atmosphere, though it is less polyglot now than it was then. Almost all of Boston's Chinese live there, in a few blocks constituting a typical modern American Chinatown. There were some 500 Chinese there in the 1890s too, but at the time a certain part of it (around Tyler Street and the now demolished Oliver Place) was home to several hundred Syrians. A few Lebanese families remain there nowadays, but by and large, in typical Syrian immigrant fashion, they have assimilated into American society and moved elsewhere. If they retain a link with the district, it is likely to be as landlords to the Chinese.

Many of the tenements currently occupied by the Chinese were rapidly thrown up in the 1880s to accommodate the growing immigrant population. As soon as they were built, they were evidently slums in the making, and were decried as such by some of the more far-sighted and liberal members of Boston society. The powers that be, however, turned a deaf ear to their pleas, and the immigrants themselves had no voice with which to complain. Besides, it is better to live in cramped conditions with all one's family in a single room, or perhaps two, than to live on the streets. But they did live in considerable squalor. In 1912 one observer wrote about one of the South End streets:

Its multifarious business bursts through the narrow shop doors, and overruns the basements, the sidewalk, the street itself, in pushcarts and open-air stands. Its multitudinous population bursts through the greasy tenement doors, and floods the corridors, the doorsteps, the gutters, the side-streets, pushing in and out among the pushcarts, all day long and half the night beside. Rarely as Harrison Avenue is caught asleep, even more rarely is it found clean. Nothing less than a fire or flood would cleanse this street.[5]

Even this picture of the slums is somewhat genteel. They could be places of high infant mortality, where rats and paupers scrabbled for refuse and every epidemic left a devastating trail of death. Often apartments in the tenement buildings had no running water, and so no sanitation. In the heat of a Boston summer the stench of rotting food and human waste was appalling.

Boston was a city of contrasts and a city of traditions. Of particular relevance to this book is not just the contrast, typical of America then as now, between rich and poor, but that between a rigid conservatism, inherited from their Puritan forebears, and a tolerance for progressiveness in the arts. The paradox of Boston is that it is innately conventional, and yet has fostered a number of radical movements. The Boston tradition which was to play the largest part in young Gibran's life was the one which had manifested most famously earlier in the century in a city at the forefront of the anti-slavery movement. Led particularly by the ladies – and society as a whole was led by them at the time – Boston was filled with charities.

Even here there are contrasting attitudes. On the one hand, it is perfectly clear that the Proper Bostonians felt threatened by the vast numbers of immigrants and were often reluctant to lend a helping hand. On the other hand, the charities were founded, fuelled and run by determined society ladies such as Annie Adams Fields, who organized the Friendly Visitors to visit poor homes, become as intimate as possible with an immigrant family, and help them to help themselves – to find jobs, to get children into school, to improve sanitation. Various witnesses attest to either side of this divide. While many praised Boston's charities, William Dean Howells, most famous as the author of *The Rise of Silas Lapham*, wrote *A Traveller from Alturia* in 1894, in which the protagonist, the transparently named

Mr Homos, is shocked on visiting Boston at the gulf between the rich and the poor, at the exploitation by the rich of the poor, and at the complacency of the rich. In the same year, Edward Everett Hale covered much the same ground in *If Jesus Came to Boston*. They and others like them exposed the hollowness of self-satisfied syllogisms such as: our society fosters individual initiative; that is how we made it to the top; therefore if we succumb to sentiment and help the poor, we will in fact be ruining their chances of following in our footsteps.[6]

However, it may be that this was a minority view – the view of the highly privileged minority constituting the Boston Brahmins and those who imitated their mores. Something of the arrogance of the Brahmins is wittily captured in the verse Dr John Collins Bossidy made up about them in 1910:

> And this is good old Boston
> The home of the bean and the cod,
> Where the Lowells talk to the Cabots,
> And the Cabots talk only to God.

On the face of things, though, the Bostonians were proud of their charitable achievements. One local writer said in 1903:

> To cope with these new conditions [the influx of immigrants] the same efforts are being made in Boston as elsewhere in America. The attempt to amalgamate the diverse elements into a common citizenship goes forward through hundreds of agencies – the public schools, the social settlements, the organization of charities, secular and religious, designed to meet every conceivable need of the unfortunate, but in such a way as to create citizens instead of paupers.[7]

When assessing the charitable movements of North America and Europe in Victorian times, it is important to remember above all that there were fewer guaranteed public rights than nowadays, so that there was a genuine vacuum which could be filled only by private charities, short of social welfare legislation. There was a need, then, and they undoubtedly did good work. Nevertheless, they were blinkered in a number of respects. What underlay the charities was invariably the Protestant work ethic and the Protestant virtues of sobriety and thrift. They concentrated on educating and 'improving' the poor, and there was a gulf between the charitable ladies of high society and the more radical socialist and communist thinkers who were beginning to advocate the redistribution of wealth. In the long run, the charities of the nineteenth century were often protective of class and property interests. In Boston, the charitable ladies exercised a degree of discrimination: they distinguished between the deserving and the undeserving poor. Quite often, the Syrian way of life was incomprehensible to them, and therefore shocking. They could not understand why the men seemed to loaf in idleness while the women went out to work; since they equated regular working hours with the virtue of industriousness, they could not understand more relaxed Eastern habits. And somehow the Syrians acquired a name as liars and deceivers.

Nevertheless, the way out of the slums, for at least one young Syrian immigrant, was a chance result of charity. The consequences for Kahlil Gibran were immeasurable. On arriving in Boston, the Gibran family settled in the heart of the Syrian district, lodging in a house at 9 Oliver Place, a tenement square off Beach Street. There was a Maronite church near by at 78 Tyler Street. Later Gibran would talk of 'tenements crowded with the ghosts of despair and the gasps of the dying'.[8] Even allowing for some poetic exaggeration, they clearly made an impression on him as horrific places. I do not think we should imagine him scampering among the refuse and the pushcarts on the street. Kahlil comes across as a serious child, little given to scampering anywhere, devoted more to his books and his drawing.

Kamila set to work immediately in the usual Syrian fashion, as a peddler. She hawked lace and linen around the wealthy houses of Boston, and within a year had saved enough money to set Peter up with a small dry goods store at 61 Beach Street, where a Chinese poultry shop now stands. Pinning their hopes for financial security on Peter and his shop, Marianna and Sultana helped him out there, while Kahlil, the privileged male child, went to school. The records of the Quincy School, which was situated at 88 Tyler Street, state that 'Kahlil Gibran jr. alias Assad' entered the school on 30 September 1895 and left on 22 September 1898.[9] Family tradition has it that Kahlil thrived at the school and showed many signs of his later genius, but he himself was curiously silent in later life about his school years, apart from remembering that he was bright enough to advance rapidly through the classes, and was a favourite of the teachers.[10] We can assume, however, that Gibran would have taken well to his first formal schooling, and that he was probably still too shy to put himself forward much. He certainly profited from his introduction to English literature, and presumably studied 'the three Rs' in some form or other, but we know little of what other kinds of schoolwork he did in these years, and nothing of anyone else at the school. No friendships appear to have been formed, and it may well be accurate to think of him as aloof from his peers.

The charitable institution that was to play such a momentous part in Gibran's life was situated on the other side of Tyler Street, at number 93. Denison House, which has since been demolished, was one of a number of 'Settlement Houses' in poor parts of Boston. The object of these Settlement Houses was to provide a base from which to help the local community, and to that end they were permanently staffed by a few resident social workers, with more brought in for particular activities. The guiding spirit of Denison House, and for many years its most active staff member, was a woman called Helena Stuart Dudley. Under her aegis, Denison House offered a five-pronged service: an open door, clubs and classes, education, job-oriented training, and emergency relief work. She also opened baths and a clinic in the house, and arranged for a gymnasium to be set up in a disused chapel near by.

Helena Stuart Dudley was simply the most famous person on the staff of Denison House, however. Far more significant a role in Kahlil's life was to be played by the art teacher there, one Florence Peirce,[11] who recognized the boy's talent and brought it to the attention of an eminent Boston social worker called Jessie Fremont Beale. And Ms Beale was interested enough to write to another friend of hers, in a letter dated 25 November 1896:

My dear Mr Day:
I am wondering if you may happen to have an artist friend who would care to become interested in a little Assyrian boy Kahlil G. He is not connected with any society, so any one befriending the little chap would be entirely

free to do with him what would seem in their judgment wise. He strolled into a drawing class at the College Settlement on Tyler Street last winter and showed a sufficient ability to make Miss Peirce feel that he was capable of some day earning his living in a better way than by selling matches or newspapers on the street, if some one would only help him to get an artistic education.

His future will certainly be that of a street fakir if something is not done for him at once. The family are horribly poor, living on Oliver Place, and will insist upon having some financial assistance from this little boy just as soon as the law will allow unless he is on the road to something better . . . I fear you will feel this request in regard to Kahlil almost an intrusion, but I am so interested in the little fellow myself, and yet so utterly helpless, that I feel as if I must try to find some one else who can be of real use to him.

Born in 1864 to a millionaire father, Fred Holland Day was a leader of the Boston avant-garde and the centre of a group of young Decadent poets and artists, such as Ralph Adams Cram, Louise Guiney and Herbert Copeland, who called themselves the Visionists. The walls of the rooms where they met, at 3 Province Court, were decorated with oriental and esoteric symbols. Rich, eccentric, a bibliomaniac and devotee of Keats and Balzac, and with a strong attraction towards young men in an era that did not tolerate homosexuality, he and his friends were a cross between the English Decadents and the Pre-Raphaelite Brotherhood. Day himself visited England several times, first in 1889–90, when he came across 'the chic homosexuality, publicly flaunted, of so many of the English aesthetes'.[12] Greatly impressed, Day reinvented himself and came back to Boston a dandy in the Whistler style, sporting 'an opera cloak, a broad black hat, a long cigarette holder with a flat Russian cigarette in it, and a convincingly aesthetic bearing'.[13] Even in the office Day could be found wearing 'pajamas, a turban and yellow dressing gown . . . with red slippers that turn up at the toes. He writes only by the light of forty-one candles and burns incense to a squat Number Ten Joss.'[14] He remained friends with the doomed consumptive Aubrey Beardsley, and with other English luminaries such as Edmund Gosse, and was instrumental in the erection of the first Keats memorial, Anne Whitney's bust, in Hampstead Parish Church, London, in 1894.

Day and his circle certainly took on the Decadent motto 'Art for art's sake', but they hero-worshipped William Morris as much as Oscar Wilde, the Rossettis and Ruskin alongside Ernest Dowson or Beardsley, combining ultra-modern Decadence with Pre-Raphaelite medievalism. Their fascination with the occult, which Day began to study after meeting Yeats, their dabbling in drugs and their languid aestheticism did not stop them originating some important publishing projects. Two short-lived arts magazines – *The Mahogany Tree* and *The Knight Errant*[15] – were the first of their kind in the country and, for all their commercial failure (hastened by their noble refusal to tolerate advertising), may be said to have established the medium of the 'little magazine' in North America; of equal importance was the publishing house of Copeland and Day, set up to rival and emulate Morris's Kelmscott Press, with its 'missal-like editions'.[16] For a few years this small publishing house brought out books whose design and hand-made paper quality were and remain second to none in North America. As well as introducing the American public to the British avant-garde, they also published the new generation of American poets and writers – people such as Louise Guiney, Bliss Carman and Stephen Crane.

As characters, there was something slightly second-rate about the Visionists. They did not quite have the stature of their Decadent counterparts in Britain; they did not quite 'burn always with this hard, gem-like flame', as the Decadents' prophet, Walter Pater, had urged them. 'They were smugly cliquish, enamored of the exotic and the bizarre, contemptuous of the normal or average, in costume, in behavior, in art. They tried, of course, to be bohemian, but they were frequently self-conscious and played their roles with mixed success.'[17] They tried hard to *épater le bourgeois*, and to appear fashionably wicked, but never achieved the notoriety of Oscar Wilde and the others in London. In part, probably, this was due to differences between Boston and London: while Boston certainly had its rigidities and scruples, it was also a more accommodating environment for aestheticism, and thus in a sense the Visionists were tilting against windmills.

However, they were not entirely imitative. They had some home-grown idiosyncrasies and some undeniable original talents. Chief among the former was their practice of founding monarchist quasi-esoteric orders, such as the Order of the White Rose, which used to meet in Day's mansion.[18] Chief among the latter were the architectural expertise of Ralph Adams Cram, who initiated a Gothic revival in Boston to counteract the established classicism, and Day's own talent as a photographer. Until the rise of Alfred Stieglitz, Day was considered the finest pictorial photographer in the United States; in fact, if Day had not fallen out with Stieglitz and Edward Steichen, he might well have become the leader of the Photo-Secession Group, which revolutionized American photography at the beginning of the century, insisting and demonstrating that photography could be fine art, and could penetrate beneath the surface of the world. As much as anything, it was probably his being snubbed by the Photo-Secessionists that caused him gradually to withdraw from the world. He spent the last sixteen years of his life, until his death in 1933, wrapped up in bed.[19]

This was the unashamedly *fin-de-siècle* world into the margins of which Jessie Fremont Beale's letter pitched the 13-year-old Gibran. What was her purpose in writing the letter? Did she want someone to give him extra tuition in art, or, as has been suggested, to take him on as a model? Probably she had no perfectly clear idea herself, but Day took the bait by asking to see some of Gibran's work, and they met on 9 December 1896. Once Day had met him, his 'intoxication with male beauty'[20] guaranteed that he would take the good-looking young boy under his wing. In any case, he had occasionally trawled the slums of the South End in the search for models, using his charitable work as a home librarian to visit places otherwise alien to him. As a photographer, Day specialized in portraits. In 1898 he scandalized Boston by putting on display a full-frontal male nude photographic portrait – as a 'Study for the Crucifixion'! Very commonly, however, his model was a young man, sometimes nude, but more often dressed up and in a pastoral or exotic setting. For instance, he frequently had his muscular young black servant, Alfred Tanneyhill, pose as a Nubian king, draped loosely in a lion skin and seated on a throne. In the late 1890s, Gibran sat as his model for a number of fine portraits, while Day acted as his mentor as well, encouraging his talents as an artist, and introducing him to the world of Romantic literature.

Some of these portraits are charged with a certain sultry sexual energy. Although in the earliest photographs Gibran appears a young innocent, in some of the later ones he looks at the camera with cunning in his eyes and a sneer on his lips, as if he knew what was going through Day's mind and was daring him to take things just that little bit further. Nevertheless, it is safest to assume that their relationship was not overtly sexual. It is not clear that Day ever took his passion for young men further than the stage of tortured longing. For all his flamboyance in dress and appearance, he was an awkward man, often shy in the company of others. At first, in fact, he nearly lost sight of Gibran. Although the two met a few times in the spring of 1897, the Gibran family moved house in the summer and neither Jessie Fremont Beale nor Day could find them. Jessie Beale wanted to invite the three children to summer camp, while Day no doubt wanted to continue working with his promising young model. However, contact was re-established in the autumn, and from then on, for a number of years, Gibran clearly considered Day his patron and his friend.

Day had two crucial and lifelong influences on Gibran: in the first place, he gave him his voice; in the second place, he gave him his pretensions. The first of these is relatively easy to discuss, the second more speculative. Gibran was a frequent visitor at Day's studio. Sometimes he sat for him; more often he simply hung around, absorbing the atmosphere of artistic Boston. Later he was allowed to help out in the studio. When we come to Gibran's relationship with Josephine Peabody, we will find clear evidence of an immature tendency to hero-worship her, to put her on a high pedestal. It is extremely likely that Gibran began by worshipping Day in the same way. He was still only 13 years old when they met, and here was an exotic, colourful character who was prepared to introduce him to the wonderful world of literature and art, which he had already begun to glimpse through his reading and his drawing. Here was an established artist who was prepared to comment seriously on his youthful sketches and teach him to improve. If Day adored Gibran in his way, Gibran undoubtedly reciprocated the feeling. To Day, Gibran was not only an attractive young man, but also an unspoiled genius – a type of the noble savage with which Romantic America was obsessed. He had no desire to spoil his young protégé with formal art training. To Gibran, Day was a role-model.

Day gave Gibran his voice by introducing him to literary classics such as Shakespeare and Tolstoy, but above all by getting him to read the Romantics. At first, Day would read aloud to the boy, but as Gibran became more fluent in English he lent him books to take home, and encouraged him to visit the Public Library in Copley Square. The Romantics, for all the revolutionary impact they had on Western consciousness, are hard to categorize and define: they are a rag-bag of artists and writers, and there are specific differences between, say, the English Romantics and those on the Continent. In *The Mirror of Art* Baudelaire famously declared that 'Romanticism is precisely situated neither in choice of subject nor in exact truth, but in a mode of feeling.' This is to say that Romanticism is indefinable, since feelings are subjective. Nevertheless, there are certain common features to those artists and writers who are classifiable as Romantics. Their common features may be summarized as: the conviction that individual sensibility was the only criterion of aesthetic judgement (and hence an emphasis on relativism, subjectivity, autobiography and self-portraiture); a search for freedom from the established rules of their chosen medium (and also often a quasi-political liberalism too); a strong emphasis on the imagination, amounting at times almost to deification; a revolt against the mechanism of eighteenth-century philosophy and a preference for the mystical and Platonic; an attraction to the natural world as a potential conveyor of the mystery of things, of a more perfect world, accessible to the imagination rather than to the senses. Anyone reading Gibran's works will find all of these features: he was a Romantic to the core, and it was Fred Holland Day who made him so. Gibran was a young teenager, his mind a *tabula rasa* on which Day imprinted his own predilections.

Day introduced Gibran to the Pre-Raphaelites as well. The Pre-Raphaelites may perhaps be defined as Romantics with a tinge of sometimes brooding nostalgia; they shared many of the traits of the Romantics, but added a greater concern with detail and pictorial accuracy, a deep love-affair with fantasy, and a tendency, perhaps inherited from Goethe, to idealize Woman. Consider Swinburne, who was for a long time Gibran's favourite poet, with his many Arthurian poems, or shorter gems such as 'Atalanta in Calydon', 'Laus Veneris', 'The Leper' and 'The Leave-taking': all of them are filled with a sense of nostalgia, not just for past times, but for lost love, an ideal that cannot be attained. In his novel *The Last Puritan*, George Santayana describes the whole movement as infused with a 'sickly aestheticism',[21] but it was a view of life which was to have a lasting effect on Gibran.

Moreover, it was Day who helped to turn Gibran into something of a revolutionary. Here is the excellent summary by Richard Le Gallienne, himself a prominent Decadent, of the Romanticism of late Victorian England:

> Though, of course, it had its foolish, and even its dangerous sides, there was real, and indeed inevitable, change behind it. Many and various currents of thought had converged to bring it about, and particularly the teachings of such popularizers of evolutionary science as Huxley and Tyndall. The theological conceptions of our fathers had suffered serious disintegration, and the social sanctions and restrictions founded upon them were rapidly losing their authority. A larger and deeper spirituality, a more human morality, in which the influence of Walt Whitman counted for much, was breaking the old moulds and making for a freer exercise of vital emotions and functions than had been considered proper, or had been even possible before . . . The significance of the '90s is that they began to apply all the new ideas that had been for some time accumulating from the disintegrating action of scientific and philosophic thought on every kind of spiritual, moral, social and artistic convention, and all forms of authority demanding obedience merely as authority.[22]

All these Romantic currents were in the air – a new social order, increased access to the divine. Under Day's influence, Gibran drank it all in with innocent eclecticism.

It is worth pausing, at this formative stage in Gibran's life, to generalize. If he was imbibing the Romantics, what philosophy was he, consciously or unconsciously, taking in? 'Romanticism was a revolt of the individual.'[23] The individual's particular moods and feelings become the focus, as opposed to Realism's attempt to be objective. Oscar Wilde, ever the pithy exaggerator, still captured something of the times when he said: 'For what is Truth? In matters of art, it is one's last mood.' This radical subjectivism was extolled not only by

Symbolist poets and painters,[24] but by academic philosophers too, in the face of the growing scientism of the age. F. H. Bradley said: 'Nothing in the end is real but what is felt, and for me, nothing in the end is real but what I feel.'[25] In artistic and poetic terms, this relativism has the following consequence:

> Every feeling or sensation we have, every moment of consciousness, is different from every other: and it is, in consequence, impossible to render our sensations as we actually experience them through the conventional and universal language of ordinary literature. Each poet has his unique personality: each of his moments has its special tone, its special combination of elements. And it is the poet's task to find, to invent, the special language which will alone be capable of expressing his personality and feelings. Such a language must make use of symbols: what is so special, so fleeting and so vague cannot be conveyed by direct statement or description, but only by a succession of words, of images, which will serve to suggest it to the reader.[26]

There is a sense in which children and teenagers are natural Romantics: they are preoccupied with their own universes and with attempts to express them, before becoming engaged, in their late teens and early twenties, with wider, more abstract issues. Gibran had a quick intellect, and was the more inclined to absorb Day's teachings because of the flattering effect acceptance by an eminent artist had on him. So it is hardly surprising that Gibran should have become a fully fledged Romantic, and remained so all his life. Out of the cadences of the Bible and the free verse of Walt Whitman, he eventually forged his own 'special language', to convey his message to future generations.

We can recreate the scene. It is the winter of 1897. Gibran is 14 years old, suffering the turmoils of puberty.[27] Outside it is as cold as only a Boston winter can be, with ice frozen hard into the ground and the wind blowing off the Atlantic. He has walked through 'straight, gloomy streets, piled with six feet of snow in the middle' and 'frosts that made the snow sing under wheels or runners'.[28] But here in Day's studio it is warm, with a crackling fire burning in the hearth. Perhaps Day has shown him his latest photographs and excited the boy's admiration; perhaps he has talked to him of schemes for the future and invited his participation. At any rate, Kahlil basks in more than the warmth of the fire. He feels that Day is a great man, and yet he feels strangely at home. A companionable silence falls on the room until Day languorously picks up a slim volume of verse from the floor and reads some lines of love poetry that seem to come from another age. Then he picks up another book and, with an ambiguous look in his eye, reads from Walt Whitman. Kahlil is too young and innocent to pick up the homoerotic references, but he is entranced by the daring freedom of the verse and the passion of the poet's voice. The evening has to come to an end some time, and with regret Kahlil takes his leave, but they make an appointment for the near future, and Day presses into his hand a volume of Keats, perhaps, or Emerson, or Maeterlinck, which Kahlil will labour through deep into the night at home, feeling that the struggle is worthwhile because the book was recommended to him by Fred Holland Day.

This book is not the appropriate medium for undertaking an academic study of the formative influences on Gibran's mind. It has already been attempted, not entirely satisfactorily.[29] However, a few points may be made. First, the influence of Nietzsche on the young Gibran has probably been exaggerated. It is not clear that Gibran knew any of Nietzsche's works in any detail before 1908 or so. However, he may well have come across Nietzschean ideas, either as paraphrased by Fred Holland Day, or as filtered through one or more of a number of sources: perhaps the novelist Gabriele D'Annunzio, whom Gibran rated highly, or the essayist Maurice Maeterlinck, whom Gibran adored, or Ibsen's *Brand*, or popular paraphrases in the Arabic press. So here Gibran found someone who had the courage to assert with trenchant and bitter humour that art was one of the highest manifestations of man's highest faculty, the will to power. The noble man has perfect self-possession, and fears neither the opinions of others nor the approach of death. There is nothing negative about his life or the way he expresses his will: in all he does – in his art, if he is an artist – he affirms life. Under Nietzsche's influence, Gibran came to question the value of the religion of his birth and particularly the stifling power of the priesthood. A religion of love had been warped by the hatred and prejudices of its practitioners; priests had turned a religion for the common people into a means of oppression. Gibran was no out-and-out Nietzschean, however: he never lost his belief in some kind of god. It was the general trend in America at this time to think of Nietzsche as a kind of robust Emersonian, railing against soullessness. Moreover, under Day's guidance his extracurricular education was eclectic and random, and so, ironically alongside Nietzsche, who was a staunch opponent of all two-world theories, Gibran came to value the platonizing Romantics and Maurice Maeterlinck.

The case of Maeterlinck is familiar. Considered a genius of the highest rank in his day, he is now hardly known at all. A Belgian, born in 1862, he began his literary career as a playwright. In 1890 his play *Princess Maleine* was hailed by no less a critic than Octave Mirbeau as a masterpiece, 'as good as Shakespeare'. His first prose work, a collection of essays entitled *The Treasure of the Humble*, was published in 1896, and soon translated into English. It made a deep impression on the aesthetic world on both sides of the Atlantic. Even Louise Guiney, who was no fan of his Symbolist plays, said that the book had made her respect him.[30] When Day read it to Gibran, its effect was overwhelming:

> Mr Day read to him out of the newly translated *Trésor des Humbles* of Maeterlinck one day, and the boy would not let him go till he had read the whole volume at a sitting. Then he borrowed it. Then he had to own it himself.[31]

Maeterlinck had the great gift in his many volumes of essays of making accessible and reasonable some profound and abstruse ideas. Anyone of a Romantic or even thoughtful turn of mind will be astonished to find many of his or her insights already expressed, and then illuminated, in Maeterlinck's pages. His tone is always frank, lucid and honest; he enquires without dogmatism, and an extraordinary wealth of interesting and unusual ideas populates his pages. Gibran's later comment on him is astute. He described Maeterlinck as 'of the first rank', but immediately went on to say that 'there are grades in that rank. He is great as an essayist, not as a creative artist.'[32] If there is a common theme to the essays in *The Treasure of the Humble* it is how Maeterlinck uses his studies of thinkers of the past to suggest that if we want to understand the secrets of the universe we must first make for ourselves a home in the metaphysical realm, which we do not just by the use of intellect, but by intuition and sensibility too.

So, for instance, in 'Silence', the first essay in the book, Maeterlinck counselled his readers not to be afraid of silence but to profit from it. In 'The Awakening of the Soul' he argued that an aesthetic revolution was taking place – that the new movement in art and poetry heralded the dawning of a more spiritual age, with less emphasis on materialism and science. This idea was by no means new: many poets throughout the nineteenth century had been saying the same, but Maeterlinck puts a characteristic spin on it by claiming that no writer or thinker, however great, works in isolation: his soul is 'the flower of the multitude'. That is, no revolution can happen until the human race as a whole, or some significant portion of it, has subliminally, in the 'Oversoul' (or 'collective unconscious'), prepared the ground.

Other essays in the collection speak of the ennobling power of sorrow and of how love is often born out of sorrow, of how women are nearer God than men, of how we access the deeper currents of life only at special moments, which constitute a kind of rebirth. He stresses throughout these and other essays that human beings do have access to the divine world: 'Can it be that man is nothing but a frightened god?' Love, he argues, is the power that enables us to 'issue forth' from ourselves and into this other world – and since love is often born out of grief, then the suffering of experience can help too. However, poets too can open the door; beauty is the food of the soul, and poets and artists can nudge us in that direction.

Now, these are undeniably attractive ideas, powerfully phrased. Gibran's mind, I have suggested, was a *tabula rasa*, though perhaps already with an innate delicate leaning in the direction of Romanticism. Every single one of these themes of Maeterlinck's will be expressed with absolute fidelity in Gibran's written work.

This chapter is fundamentally concerned with Gibran's formation, his education. Prompted initially by Day's tutelage, Gibran read widely, and continued to do so, and to visit the theatre, for the next dozen or so years. In later years he even provided Mary Haskell and others with lists of his favourite authors, while adding that he had grown out of some of them. No doubt these lists are incomplete, but they include, among poets, Blake, Swinburne, Dowson, Whitman and Rossetti; among fiction-writers, Tolstoy, Anatole France and Gabriele D'Annunzio; among playwrights, O'Neill, Ibsen and Strindberg; among thinkers, Nietzsche, Ernest Renan, Edward Carpenter and H. G. Wells.[33] In art his tastes were catholic, ranging from Greek art, through masters such as Michelangelo, Leonardo and Titian, to contemporary practitioners such as Redon, Rodin and Ryder; he generally found something good to say about most artists and schools of art except Cubism. In music he liked Beethoven in particular, and Wagner with some qualification.[34] In all fields of artistic endeavour he reserved a high place for Eastern practitioners.

One of the writers in this list, like Maeterlinck, is another unjustly forgotten figure – highly thought of in his day, but hardly a household name today. This is Edward Carpenter, whose influence on Gibran can be assessed by the fact that Gibran would later describe him as 'the greatest', while adding (in 1913), 'though I can't read him any longer'.[35] Although it was certainly Day or someone from his circle who introduced Gibran to Carpenter, it is unclear how much of his work Gibran was familiar with in the 1890s; quite a bit of it was not published until the 1900s, or even later. Here, then, I shall summarize only Carpenter's earliest works. He was born in 1844 and died in 1929; for a while he was an Anglican priest, but he left the church in 1874 and lived most of his life in the Yorkshire countryside as a sandal-maker and smallholder.

It is quite likely that Gibran first thought of him as a Whitmanesque poet. Though English, Carpenter had made two pilgrimages to America to meet Whitman, and he imitated not just his style of verse, but also his use of poetry to express social themes. In *Towards Democracy* (a copy of which Gibran was to give to Josephine Peabody) and *Who Shall Command the Heart?*, for instance, he called for sexual freedom, celebrated nature and the physical in true Whitmanesque style, spoke of a higher 'Mysterious Being', portrayed a possible future – here the influence of William Morris is clear – where there is no disease, people do only the work they enjoy, and there is no greed or private property, and suggested that only lovers truly know what death is.

More important than his poetry, however, are his essays; like Maeterlinck, he was a prolific essayist. He is astonishingly modern. His themes are vegetarianism, sex-reform, anti-vivisection, pantheism, economic reform, socialism, anarchism, Marxism, biological theories, pacifism, music, poetry, pollution, penal reform, female emancipation and liberation. He focused on practical questions: the environment and the negligent appropriation of nature by capitalism; the brutalizing effects of industrial work; social alienation; the philistinism of bourgeois cultural life; society's sexual codes. He fell squarely into the idealist tradition, but was less bossy than Whitman, less tortured than the Decadents, less elitist than many. He had a genuine empathy with the common sense and integrity of the working class, which he hoped would lead to the transformation of society.

Perhaps most unusually for the time he was openly homosexual, comfortable with it, and a passionate advocate for the recognition of homosexuality as a valid, natural manifestation of human sexuality. Like Whitman, he celebrated 'comradeship' and found cultural justification for homosexuality in his studies particularly of ancient Greek society and 'primitive folk'. He popularized the work of early sexologists such as Richard von Krafft-Ebing who argued that homosexuality (Carpenter preferred the phrase 'homogenic love') was perfectly natural. Carpenter claimed that men with a 'Uranian' temperament – sensitive and emotional – form a large class in society and do essential work; they are the artists, educationalists, philanthropists. Love in all its forms and manifestations is acceptable; homosexual love is not morbid or degenerate, and hostility towards homosexuals is caused merely by ignorance and misunderstanding. Although a lot of this is based on work others had done, Carpenter always wrote clearly and accessibly; he wrote to educate people at large. It seems likely that his work on homosexuality would have reached a wider audience if it had not been for the crackdown following the sensational trial of Oscar Wilde in 1895.[36]

He is equally modern in feel when it comes to his views on women and marriage. From an idealistic position he argues that only the meeting of soul-mates is true marriage, whereas everything else is a 'squalid perversity' because the man is half-grown and the woman is a serf. How, then, is marriage to become not a life-sentence, but 'the indwelling place of Love'? By the liberation of women, by education for both sexes, and by marriage not necessarily having to be for life. The liberation of women, he argues, is not just a case of changing laws, but changing attitudes. Quoting Havelock Ellis, he says that at present woman is regarded as 'a cross between an angel and an idiot', which is a travesty of womanhood. As for the social liberation of women, his proposals are dramatic and sweeping. He argues that women will never truly be free until the capitalist system which leads to the idea of ownership has been eliminated; he wants to see women in politics, and he wants to see a greater emphasis on educating women, so that they, as mothers, can educate the next generation of men and women.[37]

This, then, is a précis of some of the views of the writer Gibran found one of the greatest. But here there is a puzzle: for Gibran was opposed to the liberation of women, unsympathetic to much socialist politics, and apparently averse to homosexuality.[38] Why, then, did he tell Mary that in his view Carpenter was the greatest? Was it to please Mary, who was a modern woman and would have approved of Carpenter's views? This is unlikely, because it is also Mary who is the recipient of his admissions about women's liberation, socialism and so on. It seems that Gibran had conveniently forgotten all those aspects of Carpenter of which he did not approve, and remembered only those aspects with which he was sympathetic – his Whitmanesque passion, his fondness for nature and denigration of civilization as a disease afflicting societies, his celebration of the power of love and discussions of reincarnation and the higher self.

Nietzsche, Maeterlinck, Carpenter, the Romantics in general – who else were major influences? In a promissory way, because some of this will become clear only later in the book, Rousseau enters the list here for his idealization of nature. An honourable mention must go to Emerson, not just as a source of Romantic and mystical ideas, but probably also of Gibran's tendency, under Day's tutelage, towards pagan pantheism. He may also have shown Gibran the possibilities inherent in an oracular and pithy style of writing, rather than coherent argument. From Whitman Gibran inherited a certain breadth of vision and ideas on freedom, and, from a stylistic point of view, the Biblical cadences of his prose-poetry and the autobiographical tone of his work. Both Emerson and Whitman in their respective ways taught that each of us has a greater self that we can grow into – an idea that young Gibran, rootless in Boston, took to with ease, since it seems to provide a way out of exile and into a promised homeland. Finally, just as William Blake was a decisive influence on Gibran's painting, especially in his younger days, so he gave the young Gibran a network of powerful ideas: the definition of virtue and vice in terms of innocence and experience; the idea that the life-force in all living creatures is sacred; the belief in the unity of all religions; the preference of personal religion over a perceived tyranny of the priesthood, and relatedly a celebration of the poor and downtrodden; trust in the imagination and a mistrust of reason; the image (which could also have been gleaned from Emerson or Whitman, in fact) that the poet is a prophet, with a sacred mission on this earth.[39]

We do not know how many of these authors Gibran met through Fred Holland Day, or how deeply Gibran had read any one of them. We will find good reasons to think his acquaintance with Rousseau, for example, came about through certain of his predecessors in Arabic literature. However, they are all authors with whom Gibran evinces a degree of familiarity at an early or relatively early age, and it is a safe bet that most of them were introduced to him by Day, or at any rate that Day started him off in these directions. Even when Gibran was on his own, Day was the invisible mentor against whose approval or disapproval Gibran would measure his reading.

So, in one way or another, Day moulded Gibran's mind.[40] In order to understand the rest of his influence on Gibran, we need to try to put ourselves into Gibran's shoes. Here was a young boy whose life had so far consisted of an impoverished and tense childhood in Lebanon, from which he had been uprooted to live in slum conditions in a strange country. He knew he had some talent at drawing, and probably, like many teenagers, entertained dreams of a grand future. The fictions he created later about his noble background could well have stemmed from such childhood fantasies.

Then from time to time he is transported out of the slums and into another world altogether. The agent of this transformation is an exotic individual who dresses in Eastern clothing and smokes a hookah. He lavishes attention on Kahlil and is clearly not short of money. No wonder Kahlil becomes so attached to him. But here is the point: this man, this magical man, changes the scruffy slum kid into a Middle Eastern princeling. He has him dress up in exotic Eastern clothing and pose with a haughty look on his face; he has him wear a burnous and look down at the camera with the hint of a disdainful sneer. He gives Kahlil glimpses into another world, a rich world full of art and interesting figures, and seems to suggest that he could belong there. And the slum boy is hooked – so hooked that there is no turning back for him, ever. At some point he decides: whatever it is that Day sees in him, he will live up to it. There must be things of great value in him; he must really be of noble blood, physically or metaphorically. It never occurred to him that this other side of him was merely a figment of Day's imagination – the same imagination that could transform Alfred Tanneyhill into a Nubian king, or some other slum child into an Arcadian shepherd boy, or himself into Christ crucified.

In short, the enduring legacy of Fred Holland Day to Kahlil Gibran was not just that he educated him and thereby gave him his voice, but also convinced him that there was more to him than meets the undiscerning eye. Gibran was perfectly prepared to re-invent himself to please this ambiguous father-figure. Day once lent him a book on classical Greek mythology, and Gibran returned it, saying, 'I am no longer a Catholic; I am a pagan.'[41] And what did Day do with his willing and malleable acolyte? By making him out to seem to be more than he was, he gave him an inflated sense of his own importance. Now, of course, this is not necessarily in itself a bad thing to have: such people are often motivated to get things done, and often those things are worth doing. After all, for a writer to put pen to paper in the first place he must believe that he has something to say that it is important for other people to hear. Since a precise sense of one's own importance is rare, this is more likely to arise out of an exaggerated sense of importance. Louise Guiney once wrote to Day, with reference to Gibran: 'America has a subtle effect on its foreign-born children, on Orientals in particular: they come out of a grave ripened civilization into an air where no values are fixed, and it goes very badly to their heads.'[42] This is exactly right: Day exposed Gibran to a world where he felt that anything was possible, and that he was the person to achieve it. But deep in his heart he always knew that he was not this exotic figure, looking down on the world from on high, and a tension was set up which will underlie a great deal of Gibran's life. In moments of weakness or honesty he will confess to his intimates that he feels himself to be somewhat of a fraud, but from now on, as a result of Day's influence, he is committed to creating a mythology about himself – of never showing his true self to people, but only what they want or expect to see. As this book progresses, aspects of this myth, and the tensions it created in Gibran's life, will constantly recur.

Meanwhile, as an artist too he was making rapid strides. Immature sketches are still extant, and it is possible to trace his progress from copying the style of others to struggling to achieve a style of his own among the Pre-Raphaelite and Decadent influences surrounding him. Day even allowed Gibran to submit illustrations for a book of poems he was publishing through the firm of Copeland and Day, but in the event they were not used. However, strange though it may seem, the teenager did manage to find an outlet for at least one of his drawings. In a secondhand bookshop in Boston, an 1898 copy of *Omar Khayyam* by Nathan Haskell Dole, published by L. C. Page and Company, recently turned up with a portrait of the Persian poet on the outside cover, signed 'K. Gibran'.[43] Dole was at the time such a popular writer that this would have been an important commission for anyone, let alone a 15-year-old.

Gibran used to claim that he had had several drawings published by 1898, but so far nothing else has come to light. He was perhaps embroidering the truth – a hypothesis that becomes more plausible given that he later told Mary Haskell that when he was 13 or 14 people were writing newspaper articles and even pamphlets about his drawings and designs.[44] There is some basis for this claim, but not as much as he made out. It does seem to be true that he had a couple of designs for book covers accepted. He sold cipher covers, which publishers could use as they wished.[45] Day himself used one for a volume of poetry by Lilla Cabot Perry which Copeland and Day were publishing, and another design adorned the cover of a collection of Maeterlinck's essays, *Wisdom and Destiny*, published by Macmillan.[46] As for 'articles and even pamphlets', at best this is a reference to an article in the New York arts periodical *The Critic*, for 2 April 1898, which tells of a 'Syrian youth' who walked unannounced into the office of the publishers Scribner's with a portfolio of 'oriental' designs for covers, which were immediately snapped up. Assuming that this 'Syrian youth' was Gibran – and it may well have been, although there is no other record of a trip to New York at this time – the article did at least give a basis for Gibran's fancy to develop.

It seems likely that it was Day who provided him with the introductions that gained him at least some of these early commissions. And Day was also instrumental in gaining him a toehold in wider Boston society. We know of at least one occasion when he recommended the young boy as a model to another artist – in this case Lilla Cabot Perry. Despite her artistic inclinations and her friendship with the notorious Mr Day, Lilla and her husband Thomas Sergeant Perry were immensely well connected Proper Bostonians; this was Kahlil's first glimpse into the rarefied atmosphere of high society, where later in life he would travel with ease.[47]

There was one other occasion in 1898 when he would mix with the great and the good – an occasion that was to prove very important in his life. On 8 March an exhibition of Day's photography opened at the Boston Camera Club. The reviewers surpassed one another in lavishing praise on the work. Kahlil had been the model for a number of these photographs by Day, so naturally he was invited to the exhibition. One of his portraits was bought by Sarah Choate Sears, a wealthy Bostonian society hostess, who was later to become something of a patroness of Gibran. But of more significance was a casual meeting with a young aspiring poetess and playwright called Josephine Preston Peabody, who was then 23 years old, to Gibran's 15. She was small, but attractive, with a striking wide-eyed beauty, and Gibran later claimed that it was love at first sight – or at least that she made a great impression on him straight away.[48] At the time, however, they exchanged no more than a sentence or two.

Kahlil's mother and half-brother Peter were conspiring, however, to remove him from this exciting new world, in which he met beautiful women, mingled with high-society Bostonians, had designs accepted by publishers, and dipped into the aesthetic world of Day and his companions. At the level of rumour, some sources claim that Gibran's family wanted to remove him from the reach of Day, who they thought was at least a bad influence on Gibran, and possibly had sexual designs on him. It is more plausible to suggest, as Naimy does in his biography, that they wanted to get him away from some wicked woman, since Gibran later told Mary Haskell that he had been initiated into sex when he was fifteen – that is, round about this time in Boston – by a married woman twice his age.[49] They decided that Kahlil should return to Syria to complete his education – and he does not seem to have kicked up a fuss about the decision. It was far from uncommon for the children of first-generation immigrants to be sent back to Syria for their schooling. Family tradition has it that he himself was somewhat homesick, and missed his father, but this sits awkwardly with the picture of a young man trying to gain a foothold in Western society, desperately improving his English, and fast acquiring influential friends. Later, Gibran would come to regard Western society as no better than what he had left behind in Syria,[50] but at this stage he seems to have been enchanted by the West. Perhaps there were family rows, but he was after all still only 15 – still a schoolboy, whose artistic pursuits were strictly extra-curricular – and he bowed to family authority. His teacher Florence Peirce, however, was not pleased: she felt that North America was the place for Gibran to pursue a career in art, and that little good would come of an interruption to that objective.[51]

No doubt the Gibrans could afford to send him on the trip, because otherwise they would not have decided to do so. Nevertheless, his new-found friends rallied round and got together a fund, organized by Day, to contribute to his expenses. After a brief summer holiday at Louise Guiney's new home at Five Islands on the coast of Maine, a charitable occasion on which he was accompanied by some other slum boys, Gibran set sail for Lebanon late in August 1898. Years later, in 1919, he told Mary:

> When I was a boy . . . and was going to Syria, on my own decision – when I had chosen my boat and bought my ticket, I suddenly, two or three days before the sailing, changed my mind – for no apparent reason – changed it absolutely – and took back my ticket and exchanged it for one on the next steamer. The steamer on which I had first bought passage was lost, and 700 or 800 people on her, just a few hours out of New York.[52]

What Gibran is referring to is presumably the sinking of the ship *La Bourgogne*, as reported, for instance, in the *New York Times* for 7 July 1898. After colliding with the British ship *Cromartyshire*, the passenger steamer went down on 6 July off Sable Island with the loss of 562 lives, including all but eight of its complement of seventy-five 'Assyrian' passengers. The way he told the story to Mary looks as if it was influenced by the rash of similar stories following the sinking of the *Titanic* in 1912, and it seems unlikely that such a young boy would have been free to make and break his own travel arrangements like this. But perhaps he persuaded Peter to change the date of his departure so that he could go to Five Islands.

Be that as it may, it must have been quite a voyage for a 15-year-old all alone, and the sinking of *La Bourgogne* would only have added to his excitement. But before he left he had one final pleasant task to perform. He had drawn Josephine Peabody from memory, and he entrusted the drawing to Day to forward on to her. Here is some of the entry from Josephine Peabody's journal for 15 September 1898:

> Cheered by the mail which brings me . . . a note from F. H. Day with a delicate little drawing which he says was left for me by a little Syrian boy (a protégé of his whom I saw for a few moments last winter at the photograph view) – Kahlil Gibran. Says FHD, 'He is now on his way to . . . study Arabic literature and philosophy. He always kept a bright memory of you and wished that you would not forget him.' What a sweet little happening is such a thing as this. I had not forgotten the boy: but there were crowds of people there and I only had a word or two with him because I saw that he was shy, and we smiled at each other once or twice across the rooms.

It was to be the first of many entries about Kahlil Gibran.

3

A Smile and a Tear

The Syria to which Gibran returned was little changed from the one he had left. Despite its recent growth, the town of Beirut still resembled an overgrown seaside village. It was a far cry from the sprawling city of today; the villages up in the hills or further north and south along the coast were still separate villages, not indistinguishable parts of a bustling conurbation. When we picture Gibran at college there, we should not imagine the international scene of a modern university, but a small parochial town. He was there solely to recover his Arabic roots.

There are few hard facts about Gibran's years at college in Syria. Like his childhood in Boston, it was another period of his life about which he chose to say little (at least, to his Western friends, whose records survive), and then usually only about external matters, rather than those experiences which shaped him. It is as if to his Western friends he wanted to downplay his Eastern side – to present himself as a blank sheet upon which the West could imprint its alien injunctions. Or rather, it may be that he had already been shaped, chiefly by Fred Holland Day, and saw what he had been given in Boston as infinitely more important and precious than anything he could gain in Syria. Perhaps, then, on his arrival in Beirut, he felt sophisticated and cosmopolitan. There are traces of just such youthful arrogance.

Nor is the record of his years in college in Beirut helped by his constant embellishment of his childhood and family background, which we have already noted. So, for instance, in the midst of a long and largely fanciful reminiscence of his Lebanon days to Mary Haskell on 25 August 1915, he says: 'I threw away a fortune, so to speak, in college. I was among the richest youths, not only of Syria but of Egypt and Northern Africa and India – and I spent like them, or sometimes better.'

Gibran arrived in Beirut towards the end of 1898 to begin a three-year course of study at the Maronite Catholic college Madrasat-al-Hikmah.[1] Legend has it that he was enrolled in a junior class for the study of Arabic, because his knowledge of Arabic literature and grammar was found to be patchy and it was felt that he first needed a thorough grounding in the basics, but that he found this slight to his dignity intolerable. He protested long and loud to Father Yusuf Haddad, a teacher at the college, flaunting his knowledge of English literature and threatening to change over to the rival Protestant American University at Beirut. Somehow, the 15-year-old boy managed to win Father Haddad over to his side, and the teacher then persuaded the headmaster that Gibran was a pupil of promise, and should be allowed a more flexible routine. Perhaps because of his limited knowledge of Arabic, he was granted long periods when he could study the set texts without being tested on his knowledge of them. The curriculum would have been based largely on Arabic and French literature, though there were some lectures on current affairs and history.

There is no doubt that Gibran was happy to immerse himself in the Arabic language and literature. In this respect he flourished at the college, and read widely in the books set him by his Arabic teacher, Father Haddad. He read classical Arabic literature from all periods, and discovered the myths and poetry of his country; he studied the more recent Arabic Christian writings, especially the Arabic translation of the Bible. It is also likely, given the pervasive French influence in the college, that he became proficient enough at French to begin to read French literature too.

So this was a side of college life that he did not find irksome, but at the same time it must have tried the teachers' patience that, even after having been granted these concessions, the boy was still an unruly and mischievous student, who resented what he later described as the 'rigid hand' of the college authorities. He cut classes and avoided some of his religious duties, such as making his confession before taking communion; he filled his notebooks with sketches, often cartoons of the teachers, rather than lecture notes. Most extraordinarily he claimed once to have thrown a dictionary at a teacher who was insulting his class; the teacher tried to attack Gibran, but the rest of the class restrained him, and he was fired the next day.[2] Gibran maintained later that the college tolerated his rebellious attitude towards authority because they were aware how serious he was about his reading and how hard he studied in his own time.[3]

There is a somewhat simpler explanation available, even if it is more prosaic than this legendary version. The fact of the matter is that Gibran was regarded in some ways rather like a foreign student in a university today. He was attending courses and classes of his own free will, and paying for the privilege, but he was not a full-time student, nor was he working for a degree.[4] To an extent, then, he was there of his own free choice. This makes his behaviour at the college, and the concessions the authorities granted him, more comprehensible, though less romantic. And it seems that Gibran cultivated an aura of foreign aloofness: he wore his hair longer than was the fashion in Syria, and preferred to be seen in his own company, with a book or a sketch pad, rather than with his fellow students.

There were two events in his final year at al-Hikmah which Gibran did like to recall in later years. The first was his collaboration with a couple of other students to produce a student magazine called *Al-Manarah* (*The Beacon*).[5] His chief partner in this short-lived enterprise was Yusuf Huwayyik, the nephew of the Maronite Patriarch, who was to remain a lifelong friend of Gibran.[6] Gibran was the editor, designer, artist and chief contributor to the magazine, while Huwayyik was, so to speak, its business manager, which presumably involved drumming up sales to fellow students. Despite Huwayyik's important connections in Syrian society, compared with Gibran's humble origins, Gibran later told Mary Haskell that he took Huwayyik under his wing and taught him to draw.[7] The adult Huwayyik would become a sculptor of some talent.

The second incident which Gibran was fond of recalling was that in his final year he was made the 'college poet'.[8] The very existence of such an institution and title at the school reflects the high honour in which poetry was and still is held in Arabic societies. All the students were given a topic – the same topic – on which to write a poem, and the composer of the piece judged by the teachers to be the best was the college poet for that year. Mary Haskell's account of Gibran's recollections of this episode is unusually confused, and includes a vision of Jesus comforting Gibran and perhaps assuring him of his success in the competition;[9] but at any rate what is clear is that Gibran's confidence was hugely boosted by his winning of the prize. It seems likely that he already saw himself as someone who would try to make a living and achieve recognition as a creative artist, and so it is no wonder that it meant so much to him to carry off this school prize. No wonder, also, that his father's reaction to his son's literary pretensions was at the very least a deep disappointment to him.

The village of Bsharri lies only some forty miles, as the crow flies, north-north-east of Beirut, though it is considerably further by road. Gibran's contacts with his father seem to have been few and far between. At first he intended to spend the whole of every summer vacation staying with his father, but now, with the extra maturity caused not just by a few years of growth, but also by the exciting experiences of aesthetic Boston, Gibran was able to see his father for the coarse man he appears to have been. On one occasion, in particular, Gibran was badly hurt by his father, and his poetry was the cause of it. He had just had a poem published (he doesn't say whether this was in a student magazine or some more prestigious medium) and was feeling rather full of himself. At his father's house that evening was, among others, Selim Dahir, Gibran's childhood tutor, whom the teenaged Gibran was naturally anxious to impress. One of the women present praised his poem and he was asked to read something else he had written. His father pulled a contemptuous face and said that he doubted the guests would be interested in such things. But the guests insisted, and Gibran read a poem. It was his first 'public' poetry reading, and the poem went down well with everyone except his father, who said, 'I hope we shall never have any more of this stuff – this sick-mindedness.'[10] From a father, this kind of comment is always bound to sting. Add the fact of Selim Dahir being there, and the painful sensitivity of a teenager, and you have a recipe for mutual antagonism and unhappiness. Gibran once told Mary Haskell that during his college years he used to woo death, which may be a Keatsian exaggeration, but points towards a degree of sadness stemming from somewhere – perhaps from the breakdown of the relationship with his father.[11]

Whether as a direct result of this incident, or just because of a general rift between Kahlil and his father, he began to stay with cousins rather than with his father when he visited Bsharri. In fact, he stayed in the Gibran family's first home in Bsharri – the one they had been forced to leave because of its worsening state of dilapidation. Even if the structure of the place had been improved, in other respects things were just as bad: Gibran's cousin N'oula Gibran always remembered the rats and bugs infesting the place.[12] However, in the West we should remember that in the East, especially in the villages, people have a more stoical attitude towards such frequent visitors to their homes.

Meanwhile, back in Boston, Josephine Peabody was becoming intrigued by the young Syrian. When she visited Fred Holland Day in December 1898, Day showed her some of Gibran's sketches and the two of them agreed 'that the boy was made to be one of the prophets', basing this judgement on the 'spiritual' quality of his drawings. She also wrote: 'There is no avoiding that young personality. You are filled with recognition and radiant delight.'[13] She is, then, our first witness to the quality we will meet time and again in this book: Gibran had charisma. She decided to write to thank him for the drawing of her he had given her just before he left for Syria. She also told Gibran she had met with Day, who had shown her more of the drawings Gibran had left with him for safe keeping. Josephine's comment was: 'You have eyes to see and ears to hear. After you have pointed out the beautiful inwardness of things, other people less fortunate may be able to see too, and to be cheered by that vision.' This undoubtedly represented her sincere belief, but it can only have fed Gibran's ego. She goes on in this letter, dated 12 December 1898, to ask whether he can find enough peace, quiet and solitude to grow in. 'You know what Maeterlinck says of silence in *The Treasure of the Humble*. Well, I think you listen to silences: and I hope that you will come back some day and tell us what you have heard.' She ends by inviting him to write back to her.

Throughout their relationship, Josephine is incredibly naïve. She surely can have had no idea that the teenager she was writing to was already half-infatuated with her; otherwise it would have been cruel teasing to tell him how she kept his picture of her close by her side and expected great things of him. What is more, she was a published poet, and she treated Gibran as a fellow artist. Gibran's studied aloofness at college was certainly part of an artistic pose, and he liked to drop into his conversations in Beirut the names of poets and artists he had met in Boston. What a boost to his ego, and to his ambitions, this letter must have been!

Of course, he took up her offer to reply. In fact, he was later to claim that he wrote three letters to her.[14] Only one got through, however. Written on a page torn out of a school notebook, it is full of charming mistakes in English grammar and spelling.[15] He tells how overjoyed he was to receive her letter: 'And as I says that the hope of getting a letter from you was almost dead, tell your letter arived which did tell me a gread more than what was in it of words.' He tells her: 'I will keepe your friendship in midesst of my heart, and over that many many milles of land and sea I will allways have a sertane love for you and will keep the thought of you near my heart and will be no sepperation between you and my mind.' Calling her 'Miss Beabody', he describes how he was struck by her when they first met at Fred Holland Day's exhibition and agrees with her that he loves silent and quiet places, and can hear beautiful music there. He signs off 'From your far far friend, Kahlil Gibran', and accompanied the letter with a pen sketch of Josephine inscribed on the back: 'Remember the far far little Syrian.'

Josephine was delighted by his letter, and told Fred Holland Day about it. She also began trying to interest some of her artistic Boston friends in his drawings. The ground was being prepared for his entry into wider circles of Boston society upon his eventual return. She drafted a letter of reply and thanks to him, but apparently did not send it: the draft is extant, but there is no record of its receipt by Gibran. In this letter, dated 3 July 1899, she adopts a far more judicious tone than in her first enthusiastic epistle. Perhaps she was alarmed by the youthful fervour with which Kahlil had replied. She takes on an auntly persona, telling him to work hard and thanking him for the drawing. In the fashion of a newspaper advice column, she tells him:

'It is as wrong for an Artist to be idle and forgetful as for a Prince to neglect his people. It is really the rulers of men who were born to work.'

It seems likely that Day and Gibran were in communication during this period too, but there are no extant letters. However, we do know that Day once sent his young protégé a cheque for $50, nominally to pay for some drawings Gibran had sent him. This too hugely increased Gibran's reputation in Bsharri: $50 was an exceptional sum in those days in the village, before it became spoiled by the influx of royalties from Gibran's estate. People began to think that there might be some truth to this strange teenager's stories about his wealthy and influential friends in America.

Gibran was at college in Beirut from 1898 until 1901 – from the ages of 15 to 18. These are generally critical years in the development of a young person's view of the world. We are very short of information about his time at school, but some of the earliest writings he published later, after his return to the States, are set in Lebanon. They should be able to tell us something of his experiences there during his college years. Here we immediately face something of a crux in Gibran scholarship.

The Broken Wings (*Al-Ajnihah al-Mutakassirah*) was first published in Arabic in New York by Mir'at al-Gharb in 1912, although it was originally written several years earlier, and then substantially revised prior to publication.[16] The book is unique among Gibran's writings in consisting of the longest sustained narrative he ever wrote. All his other works are either anthologies of short poems and prose-poems, or at most short stories or one-act plays; even *The Prophet* and *The Garden of the Prophet* are actually collections of short homilies on various topics held together by the single character of Almustafa the Prophet, just as his longest book, *Jesus, The Son of Man*, is a collection of short pieces about Jesus.

The story-line of *The Broken Wings* is very simple and can be swiftly told: a young man in Beirut around the turn of the century meets a young woman, Salma Karama; they fall in love, but her father has betrothed her to the nephew of a powerful churchman. After the marriage the two young lovers meet occasionally in secret, and chastely, but the archbishop finds out about their meetings and confines Salma to the house. A few years later Salma dies in childbirth. Thus the 'broken wings' of the title are the wings of love on which the young couple first explore the exalted domain of love, only to find themselves brought abruptly down to earth by harsh realities.[17]

What makes the novella so special is the insight with which Gibran treats the youthful emotions of the protagonists and the subtlety of his descriptions of feeling and place. What makes the book distinctive of the young Gibran are some typical themes: sympathy for the plight of Eastern women;[18] championing womanhood in general; the idea that wealth is a positive impediment to happiness; criticism of the greed and worldly power of high-ranking clerics; eulogy of the mother; and above all the Romantic theme of the power of love to elevate us into a world of transcendent reality. Love is truth, beauty, God, everything. Nor is this love only the love of God for man (or vice versa): it lives fully in the love a human lover has for his or her soul-mate. Time and again in his writings, Gibran returned to the topic of the power of love, a power to transform our lives for ever. But he also remained aware of the rarity of true love, and believed that this was due as much as anything to the fact that true love is dangerous and revolutionary: it shatters the wall of social conventions. *The Broken Wings* was criticized in certain Arab quarters for portraying a married woman secretly meeting a man who was not her husband, but for Gibran this was only a fragment of the power of love. Other stories show love's contempt for social divisions, for the supposed bond of a loveless marriage – and even for time itself, as reincarnated lovers meet after centuries apart.[19]

The protagonist of *The Broken Wings* speaks in the first person; the superficial details of time and setting correspond to features of Gibran's own life; readers are inevitably impressed by the insight Gibran displays into young love and pain. It is hard for them to resist thinking that the novella is autobiographical. Biographers and commentators have been more or less unanimous in claiming that the book is pure autobiography.

But what biographers were unaware of until the early 1970s is that we have Gibran's own words on the matter. On 20 December 1911 he met his friend Mary Haskell, to whom *The Broken Wings* is dedicated, and outlined the plot to her. As recorded in Mary's journal, Gibran stated categorically that the book was *not* autobiographical: 'Not one of the experiences in the book has been mine. Not one of the characters has been studied from a model, nor one of the events taken from real life . . . Nothing personal to me is in this book.'

That should be the end of the matter. It would, after all, only increase our admiration for Gibran as a writer that he could so fully enter into the soul of a broken-hearted young lover without having had any such experiences himself. However, as we have already seen, Gibran was something of a chameleon. He was perfectly capable of not telling Mary the complete truth, of saying what he thought would please her. At the end of 1911, their relationship was delicately poised: while still professing undying love for each other, Gibran had recently moved to New York, while Mary had stayed in Boston, where her school was. They now met more rarely, and whenever they did, each was anxious not to say anything that might hurt the other. Under these circumstances, it is plausible to think that Gibran might have been disingenuous, to say the least, about the earlier affair: everyone knows the lingering power of a first, teenage love.

So there is still room for speculation based on the autobiographical impression the novella gives us. And then we find that Professor Hawi interviewed people close to the Gibran family in Lebanon in the 1950s, and discovered that while Gibran was over there at the turn of the century he *had* fallen in love with a young girl. This happened not in Beirut, it is true, but in Bsharri, and her name was not Salma Karama, but Hala al-Dahir. Nor was their relationship broken off because she was betrothed to someone else, but simply because Kahlil Gibran was too low-born for the likes of Hala's brother. After all, he was the son of that ruffian Khalil: possibly here we glimpse another reason for Gibran's estrangement from his father. And following Kahlil's and Hala's enforced separation, they did take to clandestine meetings, as in the book. As recently as 1987 a descendant of Hala al-Dahir confirmed the story to the travel writer Charles Glass.[20]

At this point the biographer of Gibran is caught between the devil and the deep blue sea, since, in fact, both sources of information are unreliable. Gibran, as we will find time and again, was more concerned to present to Mary his mythical persona than any solid reality, so that it is often hard to believe the things he told her; and the interviews conducted by Hawi and Glass fall squarely into the category mentioned in the Preface of retrospective memories. I needed a trustworthy source to tip the scales one way or the other. It was interesting to note that Mikhail Naimy omits the story from his biography, when it would have meshed perfectly with his dramatic reconstructions of Gibran's youth. An interview with his nephew, Nadeem Naimy, confirmed that Gibran had made it clear to his uncle too that there was no basis of fact in *The Broken Wings*. It seems, then, that in this instance Gibran was not lying to Mary: the book is not autobiographical.

Chronologically, in terms of publication, *The Broken Wings* came after two collections of short stories, both of which were published in New York by the newspaper *Al-Mohajer* (*The Immigrant*). *Ara'is al-Muruj*, which is perhaps most accurately translated as *Brides of the Meadows*, but which has been translated into English as *Nymphs of the Valley* (the title under which Gibran referred to the book in English conversation) and as *Spirit Brides*, was published in 1906, and *Spirits Rebellious* (*Al-Arwah al-Mutamarridah*) followed two years later. Although occasional poems, especially early poems, take Lebanon as their background, the majority of them have no specific setting. As Gibran grew more confident in his 'prophetic' role, he moved further away from the concrete and particular. Where once Lebanon had been the homeland whose wrongs he set out to right, he expanded his horizons until the injustices of the whole world were his to correct. *Nymphs of the Valley*, *Spirits Rebellious* and *The Broken Wings* are the only whole books of Gibran which are set entirely in Lebanon.

Nymphs of the Valley contains three short stories. In the first, 'The Ash of Centuries and the Immortal Flame', a young man, Nathan, prays to Astarte to spare the life of his beloved who is ill, but she dies. Crushed by grief, he wanders disconsolate and out of his mind. Two thousand years later, however, in the same location in Lebanon, a certain Ali al-Husaini explores the ruins of Astarte's temple – and almost remembers. Overwhelmed by love, he has a vague intimation of his beloved. The next morning he meets a young woman for the first time, and they recognize each other instantly: they are Nathan and his beloved reincarnated. Their love has survived the ages to be born again in them.

In 'Marta al-Baniyah' a poor and innocent village girl, an orphan, is seduced and then cast aside by a rich man from Beirut. By then she has already had his child, and she is condemned to work as a prostitute in order to make enough money to feed herself and her child. The narrator hears her story and is taken to meet Marta, who is now on her death-bed; he comforts her with a Christian humanitarian sermon, and she dies in peace.

'Yuhanna the Madman' has nourished himself on the beauty of his native countryside and the pure words of Jesus in the Bible, which he finds scarcely reflected at all in the services he attends at church and in the attitudes and lifestyles of the monks and priests. Matters come to a head when he is roughly treated by some monks from a rich monastery when his cattle stray on to their land. They end by imprisoning him, provoked by his accusations of hypocrisy. His mother has to pay for his release with her last precious possession. Yuhanna now embarks on a crusade; he tries to urge the people to challenge the authority of the priests, in the name of true Christianity, but although they appreciate what he is saying they cannot follow him. Yuhanna is arrested, but remains silent in court, as Jesus had done before him. He has something of the 'magnificent sorrow' of which Maeterlinck spoke in *Wisdom and Destiny*.[21] As a result of his treatment by the authorities, people become suspicious of him, and he becomes increasingly alienated from the world. He is a lone voice, crying in the wilderness, defined as mad by the world.

Many overlapping themes and ideas occur in the four short stories that make up *Spirits Rebellious*. 'Rose al-Hani' is a powerful evocation of the idea that love scorns convention. When true love calls, nothing can stand in its way. A young woman – no more than a girl, really – is married off to a rich old man. Her husband is kind enough, and looks after her, but she cannot be a true wife to him, especially after she discovers her soul-mate. For a while she lives a hypocritical life – married to one man but in love with another – before she gains the courage of her love and, ignoring the social repercussions, goes to live with her beloved. She relishes the insults cast at her, because she sees society as corrupt and its laws as impediments to people's birthright, which is happiness and a life in the Spirit. Just as in *The Broken Wings*, Gibran sets out his stall as one who is firmly opposed to arranged marriages, and prefers the heavenly inspiration of Romantic love.

A second story in the collection, 'The Bridal Bed', touches on similar topics. On the very day of her wedding to an arranged husband, Layla sees her beloved, Salim, and realizes the mistake she has made. She has been duped by society's lies and laws, and her father's social ambitions.[22] She and Salim meet in the garden, but he refuses to run away with her. Rather than lose him, she stabs him to death, and then kills herself over his body, having called the wedding guests out to the garden to see what she has done and to hear her sermon on life and love.

In 'The Cry of the Graves', Gibran's theme is the oppression of individuals by man-made laws. Shocked by the inhumanity of what passes for justice among men, Gibran protests against blind adherence to the laws – blind in the sense that it turns a blind eye to worse injustices being perpetrated by those in authority. In fact, these sanctioned injustices may even justify the so-called 'crimes' for which criminals are being punished. How else are the oppressed poor to fight back against institutionalized injustice, except by breaking the so-called laws?

Finally, in 'Khalil the Heretic', two women rescue a young man, Khalil, from a blizzard. They find that he has been expelled from the nearby monastery for, in effect, living too Christ-like a life, as opposed to the material and worldly aims of the rest of the monks, who are in league with the local sheikh to oppress the already impoverished peasants. As he recovers from his ordeal, he explains his predicament to the women and wins not just two converts, but the love of the younger one, Miriam. Her mother, Rachel, reveals how her husband was unjustly killed by the authorities. The local sheikh arrests Khalil as a potential troublemaker, and at his trial before the shiekh, with all the local villagers present, Khalil delivers a long, impassioned speech addressed directly to the poor people, outlining the causes of their hardships. When the sheikh orders his men to kill Khalil, the villagers intervene and prevent it. They free Khalil and he lives among them as a hero and a preacher: he frees them from their dependence on local landlords, and frees their souls with his words of religious wisdom.

This bare outline of the stories of *Spirits Rebellious* and *Nymphs of the Valley* cannot do justice to the actual stories themselves. Certainly one of the things Gibran gained from his childhood and student years in Lebanon was an abiding love for the countryside, and a strong sense of place informs all these seven short stories, as well as *The Broken Wings*, and communicates Gibran's love for his native land to his readers. This love stayed with Gibran all his life, and we will misunderstand him if we see him as the type of immigrant who longed for all things Western and despised his native land. It is true that he often criticized the Syrians themselves,[23] but he never lost his love for the countryside, and eventually his yearning for home fused with his metaphysical nostalgia for a transcendent homeland.[24]

There are powerful ideas in these early writings, and they are powerfully expressed. In many ways it is a shame that the fame of Gibran's later work (especially *The Prophet*, of course) has eclipsed the fame of these earlier works. But it is these for which he became known in the Arab world, and which helped to initiate a revolution in Arabic literature. Gibran's early works had an enormous effect on the Arab world: he attracted both censure and adulation, and was caricatured as having started a school of 'Gibranism'. To us these early works are bound to seem immature, but in their own context and time, they were clearly extremely powerful. Consider the following extract from one of Khalil the Heretic's speeches, which is an impassioned plea to personified Liberty:[25]

From the depths of these depths
We call you, O Liberty – hear us!
From the corners of this darkness
We raise our hands in supplication – turn your gaze towards us!
On the expanse of these snows
We lay ourselves prostrate before you – have compassion upon us!

We stand before your terrible throne
Wearing the blood-smeared garments of our fathers;
Covering our heads with the dust of the tombs mingled with their remains;
Drawing the swords which have been sheathed in their entrails;

Raising the spears that have pierced their breasts;
Dragging the chains that have withered their feet;
Crying aloud cries that have wounded their throats,
And lamentations that have filled the darkness of their prisons;
Praying prayers that have sprung out of the pain of their hearts –
Listen, O Liberty, and hear us!

In schools and offices
Despairing youth calls upon you;
In the churches and mosques
The forsaken book invites you;
In the councils and courts
The neglected law implores you –
Have pity, O Liberty, and save us.

And so on: this is only a small part of the speech. It seems clear that Gibran spent a good deal of his time during his student days in Beirut with his eyes open. It is easy to imagine the kind of student conversations, late into the night, that he may have had with Huwayyik and other close friends. Judging by the preaching tone of many of Gibran's early stories, it is also easy to imagine that he liked to lead these conversations, and was already beginning to perceive himself as someone with a special mission in life, to educate others in some field or other. This is an early sign of his arrogant and domineering mannerisms. But change was in the air in Lebanon, and Gibran absorbed the charged atmosphere.[26] He had left Syria before as a child, and in Boston had formed no close friendships in the Syrian community, preferring the company of white Americans; but now, as a young man, his Arabism was awoken. All the same, it is clear that, even with his eyes open to the almost feudal oppression of the poor in Lebanon, he was seeing things through spectacles which had already acquired a tint.

We have seen how, under the influence of Fred Holland Day, the young Gibran became steeped in the ideas of the Romantics and, probably, of Nietzsche. Many Romantics had been calling for a new social order. Moreover, either or both of these influences, especially if added to a dash of native temperament, could have led to the dark pessimism which runs throughout these early works. In the case of Romanticism, the contrast between high Romantic ideals and the cruel realities of life could have tipped the scales in that direction; and in *Thus Spake Zarathustra*, Nietzsche has his prophet deliver a radical denunciation of the present state of humanity. So in these early works of Gibran the oppression of peasants in Lebanon is generalized until *all* man-made laws are seen as tyrannical. Perhaps thanks indirectly to Rousseau, whose writings had influenced an earlier generation of Arabic writers,[27] Gibran believed passionately in the essential goodness of people – a goodness which shines out in natural surroundings such as the countryside, but which is constrained, distorted and imprisoned by wealth, cities and all forms of organizations, including the Church.

As well as the influence of Maeterlinck, there is much of Edward Carpenter in these early works. Carpenter too – and in a far more directly political fashion – had inveighed against tyranny and taken the part of the downtrodden, had celebrated Nature in a Rousseauistic fashion and urged the centrality of love as a unifying and universal power, and had discarded, both in his life and on paper, society's conventions. He declared, 'I am as a child before thee – all conventions, luxuries, all refinements of civilization, acquisitions, formulated rules, rights, prescriptions, and whatever constitutes a barrier – I discard.'[28]

I am not suggesting for a minute that Gibran did not sincerely and genuinely feel sorrow at the oppression of Lebanese women or of the poor, but I am suggesting that had Gibran come under the influence in Boston of, say, James Russell Lowell rather than Fred Holland Day, he might have sincerely and genuinely felt an entirely different range of emotions. This fusion of life and literature in Gibran is an aspect of the dichotomy already noted in the last chapter, between man and myth. If Gibran found it difficult to separate his true self from the image created for him by Day and others, and later from the image he created for himself, he also found it difficult to separate life and literature. So do we all, of course: we are all conditioned by various sources. The difficulties begin only if our conditioned selves become the sum total of our being, and if the imitation of reality that is found in books and ideas replaces the reality of events in the outside world.

My point is not that Gibran was directly borrowing themes and topics. It is rather that, having had Romantic sensibility benignly ingrained in him by Day, a great deal else follows at the particular level. He was bound to focus on examples of innocent, persecuted women, rather than on any other type; he was bound to notice cases of social abuse rather than of justice, and the tyranny of the Church rather than all the good it does. He had determined to live the kind of life dictated by Day's photographs of him and the ideas he had picked up from his mentor, and this decision conditioned the rest of his life.[29]

In most of Gibran's stories from this period, a philosophy of resignation rather than action appears to be dominant, and some will find this not at all to their taste. It may be that at the time of publication Gibran saw himself, living in remote America as he did, as attempting to provide an ideological impetus which could be followed up by his countrymen back home. He seems to feel that following the dictates of Love is the answer. If so, he had at least one august predecessor. Honoré de Balzac's hero Louis Lambert, in the book of that title, is a character on whom Gibran might have modelled himself, were there any evidence that he had read the book (which was published in 1834). At one point Balzac puts the following words into Lambert's mouth:

> 'The law,' said he, 'never puts a check on the enterprises of the rich and the great, but crushes the poor, who, on the contrary, need protection.'
>
> His kind heart did not therefore allow him to sympathise in political ideas: his system led rather to the passive obedience of which Jesus had set the example.[30]

So it is a pure form of Jesus' teaching that Gibran has Khalil the Heretic follow to achieve his revolution; but all the same, Gibran can scarcely be said to have gained from his years as a student in Syria any sense of a practical, political solution to the country's problems. Robin Ostle's summary of Gibran's early work is sound:

> One is grateful for the frequent attractiveness and originality of his prose style, and also for the interest of some of the social comment in the earlier works. Yet the conclusion has to be that much of Jibran's work descends to

the level of an unsubtle primitivism with a vaguely defined role of primacy for the heart and the emotions. It is the escapism of a rootless and somewhat unbalanced individual which is not always made more palatable by a significant literary talent.[31]

In Gibran's early thought love is more commonly a means of self-realization, rather than a catalyst of any broader changes. In a poem first published in 1914, 'The Storm', the protagonist Yusuf al-Fakhri explicitly turns his back on political solutions and restricts himself to living as good a life as he can on his own in the countryside. It is to Gibran's credit that he is aware of the bleakness of his message: he does not portray his protagonists in these early works as heroes, but as heretics, madmen, hermits.[32] It is only in a later work, *The Prophet*, that the same criticism of civilization is given a more positive twist, and therefore the protagonist becomes a hero. Like his contemporaries Krishnamurti and Gurdjieff, Gibran seems to believe that individual self-realization is the best way forward. Perhaps such a person sets an example which others may follow; perhaps 'wakefulness of the soul', as Yusuf al-Fakhri is made to put it, prompts wakefulness in others. At any rate, as far as Gibran's individuals are concerned, and in true Romantic fashion, Love is not a still, small voice, but a raging, all-consuming fire. It is not an epiphenomenon of chemicals in our brain, but an eternal, external, pre-existent force which can be accessed by meeting one's beloved or soul-mate. Even if these ideas are somewhat hackneyed in the West today, consider their impact on the Arabic world for which they were written round about the turn of the century, when women had no freedom to choose with whom they spent their lives. And throughout his life, Gibran retained the conviction that Christ had come for the poor and the oppressed, not to institute a vast, worldly organization like the Church. Considering that Gibran has Khalil the Heretic say, 'The clergyman erects his temple upon the graves and bones of the devoted worshippers',[33] it is no wonder that some of his early work was condemned from the pulpits of Lebanon. Gibran even went so far as to tell Mary Haskell that he was excommunicated for *Nymphs of the Valley*, but this is probably an exaggeration; on another occasion she reports him as saying that the Maronite Church considered excommunicating him, rather than that they actually did so. Perhaps some priests condemned him as a heretic, but it seems unlikely that he was excommunicated from the Church as a whole.[34]

This analysis of three of Gibran's early works has taken us somewhat ahead of a strictly chronological account of his life, since they were all published after his return from Syria to the United States. However, understanding the content of these works set in Lebanon does round out our otherwise sketchy impressions of his life there from 1898 to 1902. In short, by the end of his student days in Beirut, it may not be going too far to say that what began as youthful arrogance, leading to irritation with school authorities, had become a maturer social sense of righteous indignation. Gibran had become one of the angry young men of his generation in the Arab world. All he wanted to see, he wrote in 1908, was some simple kindness; it was the lack of this that made him angry.[35]

It was time, however, for him to leave Lebanon and return to Boston. He cannot have known that he would never return to his native land. Many times throughout his life he would express to various correspondents the desire, the physical ache, to return home to Lebanon, but it never happened. The actual sequence of events and the route of his journey back to the States is somewhat confused. It is not clear exactly when he left the college: it may have been late in 1901 or early in 1902. And what did he do with himself in the months prior to his departure from Lebanon? There is a unique letter from Gibran to his father, dating from April 1902. In it Gibran first discussed his sisters' health. His father had received a letter from Boston telling him that one or both of his daughters were ill. Gibran suggests that this is a practical joke, since the letter was written on 1 April, and assures him that Mr Day has kept him informed with news of his family, and that both his sisters are well. He then goes on to say:

I am still in Beirut, although I might be away from home for a whole month touring Syria and Palestine or Egypt and Sudan with an American family for whom I have great respect. For this reason I do not know how long my stay will last in Beirut. However, I am here for personal benefit which makes it necessary for me to remain in this country a while in order to please those who care for my future. Do not ever doubt my judgement regarding what is good for me and for the fortification and betterment of my future.[36]

Apart from the clear tone of filial independence in the last sentence, the rest of the quoted part of the letter is unclear. Who were the American family? Perhaps some people he had met in Beirut in the gap after leaving college. However, nothing seems to have come of this prospective trip. Who does he mean by 'the people who care for my future'? Apart from the fact that he seems to be excluding his father from that category, we do not know to whom he is referring: perhaps his mother and the rest of his family in Boston; perhaps Day and his circle, who might have been encouraging him to stay as long as possible in Beirut to absorb as much of his native culture as he could.

In May 1908, when the friendship between Gibran and Mary Haskell was in its early stages, he told her a curious story about his time in Beirut. He said that there was a beautiful young widow, aged only 22, with whom he was much taken. Her name was Sultana Tabet. He wrote to her, but her notes back to him were formal and cool. They used to exchange books and talk poetry and literature, but never anything personal. Suddenly she died, and after her death Gibran was given by a friend of hers a few personal items and a packet of seventeen letters to him, written but never sent. They were tender and passionate love letters. She had taken to the grave the secret of her love for the young student.[37] There is absolutely no way to check the authenticity of this story. To me, I have to say, it sounds like a teenage fantasy; he even endows the glamorous lady with the habit of wearing a white rose behind her ear. But truth, as they say, is often stranger than fiction. In this case, the fiction (if such it was) was at least based on a real character: Sultana Tabet was the sister of a college friend of Gibran called Ayub Tabet, who later became a prominent Syrian and then Lebanese nationalist, and in 1915 fled into exile to New York, where he and Gibran renewed their acquaintance.[38]

Another puzzle: who was funding Gibran's stay in Beirut? Presumably it was basically his family in Boston. Gibran was clearly the favoured child, on whom his family's hopes for improvement rested, and they will have sent him all the money they could spare to pay for his education. But it also seems possible to me that Gibran was being financially supported by Day as well. We know of that single $50 cheque: there may have been more. Interestingly, Day came as far east as Algeria round about this time, but there is no record of his having met up with Gibran, though they were clearly in touch by letter throughout Gibran's stay in the East. Day had also taken an interest in Gibran's family while he was away: some of his photographs of Sultana and other members of the family date from this period.

At any rate, that Gibran was in adequate funds from somewhere is strongly suggested by the fact that the next time we hear of him he is in Paris, having stopped over in Athens on the way from Beirut, and moreover is using this city as a basis for travel to London (where he claimed to have met Annie Besant, among others) and Munich.[39] Was this simply a staging-post on his journey back to Boston, or was he lingering on the way back? He told Mary that while he was there he sold some diamonds – but this may be part of his fantasy of childhood wealth.[40] It is possible that Gibran attended a few public lessons on art there: at any rate, that is what Mikhail Naimy seems to suggest.[41] But if he was intending to enrol as a student at some art college, his plans were tragically curtailed. According to his sister Marianna's later recollections, it was while Gibran was in Paris that he learnt of his sister Sultana's death, reading about it 'in a paper', rather than receiving the letter from home which had been sent to Beirut.[42]

Sultana died aged 14 on 4 April 1902. For two years she had suffered from glandular swellings on both sides of her neck; later chronic diarrhoea and nephritis set in. By two months before her death, her feet and lower legs were also grossly swollen. This was probably due to protein deficiency brought on by her bowel disease, but the basic illness bears all the hallmarks of tuberculosis. On hearing about the death, Gibran no longer lingered in Europe, but caught the first available boat back to America. He arrived two weeks after Sultana's death, to find the family still numb from the shock of the tragedy. They were now living at 7 Tyler Street, just around the corner from their former Oliver Place apartment, and no less dingy. Family and friends did not know whether to make the occasion one of celebration for the homecoming, or to renew their mourning for Sultana.

Now, what would anyone do, on returning home to a family in shock at a young daughter's cruel death? Conversation on other topics might be awkward, but necessary for a while so as not to touch too abruptly on sensitive areas; but at some point mention would have to be made of the death, and tears would have to be shed. Astonishingly, as Marianna clearly recalled, Gibran avoided mentioning Sultana even once. Not surprisingly, this hurt his mother a great deal. Perhaps he was frightened of opening the floodgates of tears in himself and others by talking about her; perhaps he was too full of himself and his years away. At any rate, the 19-year-old boy had already learned to hide behind a wall erected between himself and even those closest to him.

4

She

For some reason, Gibran waited six months before getting in touch with Josephine Peabody. These six months are more or less a complete blank in his life, so it is useless to speculate about the reason for this delay, though it is true that Josephine was in England for the summer months, at least, that year. He did ask Fred Holland Day about her, but he avoided direct contact. It is probably safest to imagine him picking up the threads of his former life in Boston, and working hard at his English, because by the time we once more have extant letters, starting in November of this year, 1902, his English is considerably improved. Since, when he and Josephine first meet again, he has read all her published books, perhaps he was also preparing for the meeting.

Josephine Preston Peabody – who called herself by her family name, 'Posy', in her diaries – had been brought up in a privileged environment in New York by artistic parents until her father's death in 1884, when she was seven. This event heralded the family's slow decline into poverty and their return to Boston, from where both parents originally came. A gifted writer, she had already had several poems published while she was still at school. Her diaries reveal a girl, and then a young woman, who was deeply in love with life, literature and romance, but whose circumstances afforded little hope of fulfilment in any of these areas, despite her ambitions. She spent a year or so at Radcliffe College, but was too enamoured of life to take to the dusty atmosphere of the Cambridge lecture halls. Her poetry continued to be published and, to her delight, to be admired by the right kind of Cambridge intellectual; she counted among her friends the poets Edward Arlington Robinson and Louise Guiney, and was published by Copeland and Day, among others. For all her private sorrows, she emitted an air of beauty and joy, and these were undoubtedly the qualities that initially attracted young Kahlil to her.

There has been a great deal of misunderstanding about the relationship between Gibran and Josephine. It was an important relationship for him, however, so it is important to be clear about it. Gibran wrote to her on 5 November 1902, renewing the acquaintance. She replied, and he invited himself to her house on 16 November, when, as it turned out, she was having other friends around as well. They talked politely, recalling their meeting and the letters that passed between them, discussing her books. Then there are entries in her diaries or journals recording visits from or meetings with Kahlil on 21 November (when he brought round a whole lot of drawings for her to see, which convinced her that he was a boy genius). By 6 January 1903, they had already met a further six times.

As frequent as their meetings were, they were preceded, accompanied and followed by letters, or more usually notes, from him to her. In the first two notes she is 'My dear Miss Peabody'; in the next two 'My dear friend'; in the next two 'Dear friend'. On 23 December she is 'Sweet friend', and on 8 January 1903, two days after his twentieth birthday, he addresses her as 'Sweet Consolation'. After that his notes to her rarely begin with a form of address: they are on such good terms that he just plunges into the message of the letter, perhaps addressing her as 'Sweet Love' (17 February 1903) or the like in the course of the letter. Also, from January 1903 onwards, he signs his letters with one or another of various stylized versions of his initials, G.K.G., in Arabic. She too adopted this short form in order to refer to him in her diaries and journals: it was their secret code.

This torrent of letters and meetings continued until August 1903; in March, for instance, Gibran wrote to her thirteen times, and they met several times that month as well. Their relationship, whatever its nature, was obviously intense. At the time Josephine was living at 36 Linnaean Street, Cambridge, so we should imagine Kahlil trudging out to Cambridge across the Charles River in the freezing cold and snow of a winter that was exceptionally cold even by usual Boston standards. There is a gap in letter-writing (or extant letters), though not in visits, from August to October, by which time things seem to have cooled between them, although she is still 'beloved' in his letters, and remains so in the twenty or so letters he wrote her between then and 1906. Finally, in 1906, she metamorphoses into 'Godmother', 'My beloved Godmother', or the like, a less personal appellation which before then Gibran had used only rarely of her.

The tone of the letters also changes. At first, tentatively, he sends her gifts (a piece of Syrian embroidery, a flute, commonly a drawing or a poem); she sometimes reciprocates in kind. By January 1903, he is writing to her in the vein which he maintains for the rest of their relationship. In response to a poem she sent him, for instance, he says: 'To be sure of possessing your sweet words, and that I can read them and reread them when ever I wish, is to realise that I owe you all. And I know not how to reward you since I believe that all what I can do is allready yours.' He claims that she already knows him, and has only to close her eyes and look deep into his soul to understand him; he suggests that they share each other's grief and sorrow; she is so present to him when he works that he can describe a drawing he has done as 'more of your work than mine'.[1]

The trigger for this deepening of their relationship was perhaps a joint visit to see Wagner's *Parsifal* in Boston on the evening of Gibran's twentieth birthday, 6 January 1903. The music certainly had a profound effect on him; he says that it seemed to want to take him Home, and yet Home was so far away, and this made him need her. And so she became his Consolation and in his letters he portrays himself as a deeply wounded poet and artist, in need of the consolation she offers and embodies.[2] There is a pleading or self-pitying aspect to this: the emphasis in the letters on his melancholy, sadness, tears, illnesses, weakness, pain and so on gets rather monotonous. He even wonders at one point if he is going blind: 'So early? But blindness can not prevent my seeing you and your beauty in me . . .'[3] He talks of this world as a prison and himself as an exile in it; his homeland is another world to be reached only on death, a world of infinite love and beauty. The only redeeming feature in it is her, and his pure love for her. She is the 'mother of his heart' or of his 'soul', or simply 'beloved Mother'. She is the inspiration for his work. When she is away, he sees nothing but darkness; when she is ill, he suffers too.

It should immediately be said that Gibran did have good reasons for suffering. Josephine was his lifeline throughout a very difficult and painful period at home. He had returned home to find not only Sultana dead, but both his mother and his elder half-brother Peter very ill. His mother had some form of cancer, and Peter, like Sultana, had tuberculosis. By the end of February or early March 1903, Peter had become too ill to carry on his business, and Kahlil was forced, much against his will and predilections, to take it over, especially since Peter was in debt to several people, and funds were urgently needed.[4] At the same time, the Gibrans had no stable home, but were moving from one tenement to another within the Syrian ghetto, presumably at the whim of their landlords rather than as a result of choice, since no apartment seems to have been preferable to the one before it.

Peter died on 12 March. Kahlil wrote to Josephine:

The wound is so deep, the beloved brother is gone; Ah it is so bitter, bitter.

Poor mother has buryed her heart twice in the same year.

I am blinde now, can see nothing but this paper, how much I need strenght to console the poor sick mother, I can say no more, write to me, and send Her, that is all I need of you, yes, sorrow is so deep, deep, deep.

And his mother died on 28 June of the same year. Gibran wrote more or less identical black-bordered notes to his two Boston friends, Day and Josephine, telling them of her death and expressing his grief. Gibran was out on the evening that his mother died, and when he returned to find her dead, he fainted, 'and the blood came out of his nose and mouth'.[5] And even apart from these family tragedies, Gibran was writing to Josephine in early March about the death of another child, perhaps the child of some friends or relatives, who had also died, impressing him with sorrow and the knowledge of the frailty of life.

Josephine too was going through a critical time. A life of genteel poverty had become one of real hardship. She was forced to scrabble for work and move to increasingly smaller and meaner houses. Without a doubt, they both felt that life was treating them cruelly, and sympathy for each other's situations became a strong bond between them throughout 1903. However, one cannot escape the feeling that Gibran received more sympathy than he gave. Josephine had a strong streak of stoicism and humour, which allowed her to rise above her circumstances and take pleasure in small things even when larger events were bleak. Gibran shows no such characteristics. Even his attempts to express sympathy tend to devolve into expressions of the corresponding pain *he* feels about her pain. It is difficult for him to enter into another person's world and ignore himself, which is of course what it takes to sympathize with someone else. Similarly, even during the period of his mother's last illness, Gibran was spending quite a few evenings out at Josephine's or round at Fred Holland Day's house. In a letter to Josephine, Kahlil poetically contrasted the duty of having to watch over the dying woman who was the mother of his body with the pleasure of loving Josephine, the mother of his soul.[6] It should be stressed that, in Lebanese terms, this is quite extraordinary, and highly culpable behaviour: one does not leave the bedside of one's dying mother; it is no mere duty to look after her. Since by then he was working all day at the shop, he left almost the entire burden of nursing to his surviving sister, Marianna. Again, there is more than a trace here of an inability to see beyond his own pain to that of others – but this is a symptom of the kind of monomaniacal and exploitative selfishness which Gibran shares with many other creative people.

In Gibran's letter of 12 March, quoted above, he refers to a female spirit he calls simply 'Her'. This figure, 'She', first appears in a note of 26 February, and from then on recurs time and again. She is Womanhood, Goethe's *das Ewigweibliche*, especially in her guise as Mother, and quite often, throughout Gibran's letters to Josephine, one gets the impression that Josephine is not so much a flesh-and-blood living person to Gibran as a vehicle for Her. He implores her more than once to 'send Her', and tells her in detail dreams of his in which She appears in pure white robes. It is true that Gibran often expresses his love for Josephine, and his notes and letters contain all the usual lover's complaints about the slowness of time between their meetings, and the conviction that their spirits have some natural affinity, and assurances that he thinks of her every waking moment of the day, and so on. Nevertheless, it is hard to resist the sense that, to put it this way, the capitalizations with which he addresses her – 'Beloved', 'Godmother', and so on – are significant. There is no doubt that he was deeply and genuinely in love with her, but it also seems clear that he put her on too high a pedestal to see her as a real person. Mysterious and pure, she is the one who can heal his soul, who understands him with perfect insight, who inspires his work. This presumably also helps to explain why he found it hard to sympathize with her problems: goddesses (she is 'divine' for him a couple of times, and once a nymph) do not have worldly crises.

If Gibran adored Josephine, how did Josephine feel about Gibran? Only one of her letters to him is extant, and that dates from later in their relationship.[7] It is sometimes possible to guess at some of the content of earlier letters from Gibran's responses in his own letters, but we do have her jottings in her diaries and, more extensively, her journal, which refers some dozen times to Gibran. These documents shed a very interesting light on the relationship. Josephine, remember, was about eight years older than Kahlil. So in her diaries and journal she talks of him as 'the Syrian boy' or 'the boy', and she appears always aware not only of the age difference between them, but of her extra maturity. 'One was a child, and the other a young woman grown up', she writes of them at one point, though they could both be 'childish' together.[8]

Or again, in her journal for 9 May 1903, for instance, when she was ill, Gibran comes to visit and appears 'disproportionately anxious'. She goes on: 'We reversed our usual ministry. He was very old and wise; and I was very young and docile and pleased to be revived with news of how great and glorious I am. We were almost funnier than ever.'

'We were almost funnier than ever.' Josephine is keenly aware of the anomaly of their relationship. Sometimes there is an almost cynical tone to her account of their meetings:

Also he holding out his hands for mine with a benign air, I gave him my hands which he stroked and surveyed with care and compassion. 'What do you see?' I asked him. And he said, 'They are a little pale, yet; yes, a little pale.' Then he must needs draw a picture; and I say, 'Now, shall we look at the Picture-Book?' Which we do with nods of satisfaction over each . . . And then after much more talk we look at the vase of white roses that had been sent to me – critically. And I give him one, and he goes home.

It is almost as if she is laughing at him, or at them – at their solemnity. It does not seem to be a relationship that she takes seriously as a love affair.[9]

As early as 13 December 1902, apparently, Gibran had revealed the height of the pedestal upon which he was prepared to place Josephine. She wrote in her journal, somewhat confusingly: 'I was (not) amazed and appalled and not appalled at the boy's way of assuming that I know all things, and that it isn't necessary to tell me things in English or even to talk at all. If I see much of him, I shall become a Buddha.' She finds his attention flattering, but not to be taken altogether seriously.

A little detective work supplements the impression journal entries like these afford us. For instance, in her diary for 23 October 1903 she notes that she wrote to Gibran, and in her parallel journal for the same day we read: 'Today I wrote eight letters; – three to answer superfluous questions; two 'cause I *had* to write 'em; one to Miss Marbury ... one to Applebro's ... one to my pupil.' Now, since Gibran was not her pupil (she took in pupils for tuition), nor plainly was he Miss Marbury or Applebro's, then she wrote to him on 23 October either in response to a superfluous question or because she felt she had to – most likely the latter.

In other words, as a relationship, it is clear that it was more or less one-sided. She naïvely encouraged him by not rejecting his declarations of love, but only he was actually in love. Love rarely enters her journal for these months at all, and then not in a context attached to Gibran or anyone, only as an abstract force. In fact, her journals commonly reveal the uncertainty she felt that she had not pledged her heart and mind to anyone. In comparison with Gibran's youthful certainty of his love for her, she is uncommitted to him or anyone else. Her journals are filled with other people, places, activities, her work, hopes and fears: Kahlil is only one person in this parade. By contrast, later journal entries from the latter half of 1905, charting her developing relationship with Lionel Marks, the man she was to marry in 1906, are truly delightful in the way they show her blossoming in response to Lionel's loving attentions, and devoting more and more of her journal space to him alone.

What, then, did she get out of the relationship? Why did she reply to his impassioned letters, comfort him, let him come to her house so often? The answer is found in a pencilled, scribbled message in an abandoned diary. She used an old 1902 diary as a 1903 diary for about a month – scribbling down appointments, mail received and sent, that kind of thing – before turning the book over to hasty ideas and messages to herself, and a partial dream diary, dating from 1903 to 1905. On the page for 24 March there is an unmistakable reference to her young Syrian suitor:

And to this child of God chiefly my gratitude is due because to him my Soul is no poor foreigner without the franchise. The gifts it holds out [*illegible*] fully expecting not to be heard, he takes with joy, and to him they are substance, richness, gifts indeed. Out of its [*illegible*] hands he takes strength, joy and fullness: and it stands regarding him, hearing his thanks – once and for all set free – a glorious and liberated life. God bless him, that he takes of me my gifts that I would give.

As I have already remarked, Josephine was going through a tough time. Her financial situation was wretched, and she felt she was not achieving the recognition she deserved as a writer (the recognition she was later to receive). In addition, she believed powerfully in *giving* – of herself, if she had nothing material to give.[10] Her inner life, lived out on the pages of her journals, is intense: she debates moral issues, affirms her Christianity, struggles with poverty and hardship, feels ecstasy at bathing naked in a cold, secluded stream, feels that sometimes she gives too much and has to withdraw to preserve her integrity. It would be too simple just to say that Gibran flattered her by idolizing her work along with herself: he was also someone to whom she could give the poetic gifts with which she felt she had been blessed. This was how he let her experience the freedom of soul to which she refers. He responded to her poetry, and freed her from doubting 'that it was given me to be remembered as something beautiful'.[11] Her self-confidence had been undermined, and Kahlil helped to restore it.

In addition, she genuinely wanted to look after Gibran. She felt that he was a 'genius', an 'angel' and a 'prophet' in the making, with 'natural insight'.[12] Perhaps most tellingly, in December 1902 she wrote a poem in which she imagined Gibran's childhood in the Lebanese hills; although at first the poem was entitled 'His Boyhood', she later changed the title to 'The Prophet'. Apart from her natural and Christian compassion for his suffering, there was a desire to nurture a young talent. In a letter to her friend Mary Mason, dated 25 January 1903, she wrote: 'I have a marvelous and beautiful tale to relate of a genius of a creature I'm trying to godmother now. He is a Syrian boy. He writes Arabic poetry all night; and he draws (much better than William Blake) all day.' Apart from encouragement, and telling her friends about him, she was also able to supply concrete assistance: in May 1903 she arranged for some of his drawings to be included in an exhibition at Wellesley College, where she was teaching. In another letter to Mary Mason, written on 6 September, she describes him as her 'charge', someone in her care or responsibility. This is not how one refers to a loved one.[13]

At any rate, it should be perfectly clear that their relationship was not sexual, even though this has apparently been suggested by those taken to be Gibran's most authoritative biographers.[14] This shows a total lack of understanding of the nature of their relationship, which was that between an infatuated young man, little more than a boy, and a maturer young woman. In fact, in one note to Josephine, Gibran expressly eschews any physical side to their relationship: 'And my love give birth to no desire, bring no selfishness into existence . . . It is the weak spirit that yield to the flesh. Weak spirits can not love.'[15]

Nevertheless, I think it possible to charge Josephine with naïveté, even within the context of the relatively innocent times in which they were living. Here is an immature young man, pouring out expressions of the profoundest love for her. At some stage, surely, and sooner rather than later, she should have let him know, firmly and clearly, that she was not a candidate for a love affair with him. She should have been a little cooler in inviting him to visit, in allowing him to sketch her and her friends, in letting him share her life to the extent that he did in the early months of 1903. But she did none of these things. She accepted his presence and his presents; on every visit he would show her more drawings he had done and poems he had written, some for the first time in English, and gratefully receive her compliments and her encouragement.

Naturally, when the end came it was stormy. We do not know what Gibran said or did, but something made her furious enough to tear up all his letters to her from the end of August to the end of October 1903. During the summer he had been writing to her and visiting her quite often, as usual, even though she was living further out of Boston in the suburb of Arlington (before moving back to Cambridge in September). But on 10 October she received a letter from him which contained what she described, without going into any details, as an 'infuriating suggestion'. When he visited her two days later, they did not get on: 'Everyone depressed' was her only comment. And the next day she recorded in her diary: 'Look over old letters and tear up.'

Of course, there is no way of knowing what it was that Gibran had suggested. The possibilities range from something sexual to a sure-fire way of improving her financial position. Whatever it was, it annoyed her enough to make her feel she had to destroy all record of it. Since she destroyed only letters from the end of August, presumably this 'suggestion' was something that had been building up for a while. In other words, she must have destroyed only those letters which in some way heralded the 'infuriating suggestion'.

In any case, the overall result of the row was a distinct cooling of his ardour. Never again does he pour out his love for her in his still-broken English; never again does he speak so directly of her as the vehicle of 'Her'. Further references to 'Her' in his letters to Josephine are more wistful, as if telling her of something she might be interested to hear. Whatever the actual cause of their row, it looks as though it forced Josephine to face up to the fact that things had gone far enough, and to tell him to withdraw. Significantly, he becomes 'the boy' again in her journals, rather than the more intimate coded Arabic initials. He responded to this slap-down well: he still wrote to her with affection, and still saw her sometimes, but he accepted with sorrow that she was not to be his.

If there is something slightly mannered about Gibran's attitude to Josephine Peabody – something that doesn't ring quite true – this is, I think, a result of that feature of Gibran's life noted in the last chapter, his conditioning by Romanticism. Gibran's relationship towards her seems almost to have been plotted from the pages of a Romantic novel; literature and life fuse once again. In a valuable book, Ridge defined the characteristics of the Romantic hero:

> The romantic hero plays several roles. He is a poet-prophet, man of sensibility, psychopath, solitary, wanderer, criminal, rebel, seeker, prototype of the

Messiah. He is the fatal man, the pale genius, the ostracized magus, the victim of fate . . . He is convinced that there has never been another like him and he feels superior because he is in fact exceptional. He is always a titan because his happiness and sorrow always exceed the emotional capacity of an ordinary man.[16]

Now, Ridge is here defining the characteristics of a Romantic hero *from a novel*; but Gibran conforms to all or most of these features *in his actual life*. He appears to have plotted his life from the pages of the books Day and Josephine gave him to read.

So, for instance, Gibran was a great admirer of Swinburne and D'Annunzio, two of the chief purveyors of the image of the *femme fatale*. Gibran was therefore 'in thrall' to Josephine as one should be, after Keats, to a *belle dame sans merci*, and his attitude towards her generally conforms, though in a somewhat insipid fashion, to that of a Romantic hero towards a *femme fatale*: he is passive, he adores her, his love causes him pain, and he complains more than he sympathizes. But if it is right to suggest that Gibran was looking for a *femme fatale*, Josephine in fact made a poor candidate for such a role. She had the requisite aristocracy, but no further hint of exoticism; she represented eternal womanhood for Gibran, and she was aesthetic and beautiful, but not in a pale and cruel way; she had many admirers, to whom she did not commit herself for quite a while – unattainability is an important feature of a *femme fatale* – but there is no sign that she treated her suitors with anger, boredom and scorn, or that they saw her as a potential sexual cannibal. In 'Atalanta in Calydon' Swinburne describes the Fatal Woman as 'adorable, detestable': Josephine was the former, but not the latter. She was closer to the Ideal Beloved of the Pre-Raphaelites than to the *femme fatale* of the Decadents.

Josephine was Gibran's first love, and their relationship has ended in aridity. Three members of his immediate family, including his beloved mother, have died prematurely. The importance of his affair with Josephine is that it has reinforced a lesson Gibran is well on the way to learning anyway. The angry young man, convinced of the evil of social conditions in his homeland in Syria and of the general tyranny of man-made laws, now bears some personal scars as well. He picks at these scars for a long time in his writing, adding a certain resigned acceptance of sadness to the elements of a personal philosophy that we have noted in the previous chapter. And I do mean to imply a degree of artificiality in the suggestion that he picks at the scars of his grief to help him create a literary persona: there is no evidence that he mourned the deaths in his family for very long, and in the story 'Rose al-Hani', published just a few years later in *Spirits Rebellious*, he says: 'When death stretches out its hand and slaps you violently, no more than a day and a night will pass before you feel the touch of the fingers of life, and you will smile and rejoice.'[17]

Within a year of the break-up of his relationship with Josephine, Gibran had begun to write for an influential Arabic-language newspaper, *Al-Mohajer*, published in New York by Amin Goryeb. Gibran had approached Goryeb, when he was on a visit to Boston, with a view to publishing some of his drawings, but the far-sighted newspaperman was more interested in the prose-poems Gibran also showed him from his notebooks. In due course, from 1906, Gibran had a regular column in the newspaper, entitled 'Tears and Laughter'. The title is perfect: the bitter-sweet taste of Gibran's personal philosophy is evident throughout his published works.

The very first piece in *Al-Mohajer* was called 'A Vision', and it sets the tone.[18] Gibran uses a simple allegory between a caged bird and the heart behind its cage of ribs to make the point that the human heart can be wounded by man-made rules and regulations which deny it life and love. It is probably relevant to remember that in Arabic the word *asfourieh*, which means 'bird cage', also means 'lunatic asylum'. We see Gibran's familiar emphasis on the emptiness of human law, in combination with a statement of the life-giving potential of love and, this time, with a darker degree of gloom than in the later works surveyed in the previous chapter. Whereas in those later works Gibran claims that love will always fulfil itself one way or another, that love is boundless, that lovers are bound to find each other in spite of social conventions or even death, in this early piece he claims that love can be denied.

However, I say only that on this occasion there is a greater degree of pessimism, because it is hard to pin down a poet like Gibran. Works published at more or less the same time of his life reveal either despair or hope.[19] It is certainly impossible to assert with conviction that his experiences with the deaths of members of his family and with Josephine embittered him in any long-lasting way. It is more the case that they taught him something about the importance of sorrow in human life. Tears and laughter become the two poles of human existence. Both afford genuine and valid insights, and both are a source of artistic creativity.[20] In fact, without sorrow many things in life remain hidden. Even as late as 1920 he was still arguing that sorrow is a kind of summons, calling one to find the solution to it, which will convey insights into oneself and the world.[21] He asks for 'a tear to purify my heart and give me understanding of life's secrets and hidden things'.[22] He feels that the water of tears washes away a number of delusions, and that 'love makes suffering a delight and grief a joy'.[23] The more simple thought is that a person can know joy only by contrast, if he or she has known sadness.[24]

So along with occasional assertions born of deep despair, particularly at the social injustices of the world, we also find radiant optimism. At one moment he can conclude a story by saying, 'So is man's burden: a tragedy played on the stage of time. Many are the spectators that applaud; few are they that comprehend and know.'[25] At another he can state: 'All things were and are ever marching toward truth.'[26] Along with the relative gloom about interpersonal love just noted in 'A Vision', we find tales such as 'The Beloved' or 'The Tale of a Friend' in which interpersonal love has the ability to transform a person's life miraculously for the better, and all unhappiness is a result of failing to find one's allotted soul-mate.

As in *The Broken Wings*, *Nymphs of the Valley* and *Spirits Rebellious*, so in these shorter poems, stories and prose-poems, the contrast between natural and man-made laws is prominent. Human laws not only oppress the poor, they impede the natural flow of love. Nature is the domain of love. Gibran's primitivism is very marked in a number of these early pieces. He calls for a return to nature, and equates this with a return to morality and the possibility of true interpersonal love. In an unpublished piece, *Falsafat al-Din wa al-Tadayyun* (*The Philosophy of Religion and Religiosity*), which is stored at the Gibran Museum in Bsharri, he suggests the foundation of an ideal community in Lebanon (or in theory anywhere else which is unspoiled territory), away from the corrupting reach of civilization, law and institutional religion, where the inhabitants can live in harmony with nature and God, and can rediscover their inherent divinity.[27]

While remaining convinced that the rich, by their very wealth, somehow exclude themselves from happiness and humanity (a view which will, of course, begin to be toned down in the 1920s as Gibran himself starts to acquire some money), he is also equally convinced of the 'brotherhood of man'. There is no real contradiction or tension here. For Gibran the brotherhood of man is man's natural state, which has become overlaid and corrupted by so-called civilization and its baubles. In a similar vein, there are occasional hints that Gibran believed in the unity of all religions. This is an ideal for him: while he recognizes that, as things are, there are different forms of worship, he believes that everyone and everything arises out of the same universal spirit, and that this *single* Universal Soul, which is God, should or could be the object of a *single* religion, beyond the differences of dogma which currently pollute the various religions.[28]

Two final themes in these early pieces are worth mentioning: self-reflective thoughts about the work of the poet, and a recurrent emphasis on death.[29] The two themes are interrelated in that the poet is above all one whose connection with this world is tenuous; he lives as much in some transcendent world as in this world of harsh realities and so is, in a sense, seeking or preparing for death, as the philosopher does in Plato's *Phaedo*. For Gibran death is at once the end of suffering and a transmigration to a realm of eternal love, a place where lost lovers can be reunited. The personal sorrows of his life had convinced him that life is a vale of tears to be lived through with resignation until the moment of death. The only possible redeeming feature of life is love, but that is extremely rare, constrained as we are by the trappings of civilization.

As before, there is plenty here that recalls familiar Romantic themes – the role of the poet, the sweet attraction of death, the connection between sorrow and beauty. It does seem to me, as I have already said, that in his writings, as in his life, Gibran tried out the role of tormented Romantic to see if it would fit, and to see what effect it would have on Josephine and his wider audience. But this does not necessarily impugn the depth of his feelings. The image we have of ourselves invariably conditions what we feel; in Gibran's case that image centred on Romanticism and its themes. And he was well placed to play the role. His Syrian background gave him a head start: it made him slightly mysterious and exotic,[30] and enabled him to get away with expressing himself, even in his relationship with Josephine, in an emotional way normally found only in the pages of novels or poetry. Josephine's treatment of him just gave him the excuse to acquire the melancholy habits and wounded eyes of the Romantic hero.

Gibran continued to see Josephine, and they even fell by inertia into the same modes of thought and conversation, but there is something tired about it all now. They were becoming companions rather than friends. Late in December 1903 Gibran shed the burden of Peter's shop, but it is quite unclear how, after this, he and his surviving sister Marianna intended to make a living. Marianna worked for much of her life in the sweatshop of the fashionable Newbury Street dressmaker Miss Teahan, but they cannot have expected to do more than scrape by on her income. One suspects that Gibran was expecting to rely on Marianna while hoping to make a living as a writer and artist – and, as we have already seen, he did soon begin to win some newspaper commissions. But first it was his drawing that seemed to offer some hope. For Fred Holland Day, who was still a constant friend and guiding light in Gibran's life, offered to let Gibran use his studio to put on an exhibition of his drawings, along with some paintings by Langrel Harris, an acquaintance of Day who had died in 1903. As a photographer, Day had achieved quite a bit of fame, and even more notoriety,[31] so an exhibition at his studio was bound to attract serious interest. Gibran leapt at the chance.

The exhibition was scheduled to open at the end of April 1904, and throughout the early months of the year, when he was not laid up in bed with a bout of the flu that was to plague him almost every winter of his life, Gibran was working to produce enough drawings of sufficient quality to please both himself and his mentors. Meanwhile, Fred Holland Day had a simple but elegant invitation card printed, with the following unpunctuated message:

Your company with friends is requested at an exhibition of drawings studies and designs by Mr Gibran Kahlil Gibran together with a small collection of minatures [*sic*] and sketches by the late Mr Langrel Harris to be held at the studio of Mr F. Holland Day 29 Harcourt Building 23 Irvington Street Boston on the afternoons of April 30th to May 10th inclusive from one until five o'clock.

A catalogue was prepared, with the name of Boston socialite Sarah Choate Sears prominently mentioned, since she had already bought one of Gibran's sketches in 1903; she also owned one of Day's photographic portraits of Gibran, bought in 1898. Josephine lent five of the drawings Gibran had given her to enhance the exhibition, and helped to mount and hang pictures. But the most significant part she had to play was to invite a number of her friends.

On 2 May, the Boston *Evening Transcript* ran a review of the exhibition. It was everything the 21-year-old artist might have hoped for. The first critical attention he received was extremely favourable:

Mr Gibran is a young Syrian, who, in his drawings, manifests the poetical and imaginative temperament of his race, and a remarkable vein of individual invention. The ponderous beauty and nobility of certain of his pictorial fancies are wonderful, and the tragic import of other conceptions is dreadful. All told, his drawings make a profound impression and, considering his age, the qualities shown in them are extraordinary for originality and depth of symbolic significance . . . The earnest desire to give expression to metaphysical ideas has triumphantly prevailed over technical limitations to the extent that the imagination is greatly stirred by the abstract or moral beauty of the thought. There are faces here which haunt the memory with something of the spell cast upon the fancy by the visions of dreamland . . .

Not surprisingly, the review drew larger numbers to the exhibition and a few pieces were sold, sometimes to prominent members of Boston society. Charles Peabody, a critic and professor at Harvard University, bought one; Mrs Sears bought another.

The *Evening Transcript* review is so remarkable that one wonders whether it might not have been written by Day himself or one of his associates; there were a number of influential critics and artists in his circle. What was it about Gibran's early drawings that led Josephine Peabody to call him a genius (though she had stopped doing so by now) and to such an outstanding review? It seems to me that he was perfectly in tune with the times. It is difficult to say precisely what influences Gibran had absorbed in his artistic development, though even to the untrained eye there are clear touches of Pre-Raphaelitism about some of his female figures, and the aura of Symbolist painters such as Eugène Carrière, Maurice Denis, Odilon Redon and Gustave Moreau is unmistakable, especially in his composition.[32] At this stage many of his drawings show firmer lines than he was given to later in his career, when he generally preferred vaguer outlines and forms. What the reviewer called the 'metaphysical' aspect of his drawings shows in his choice of figures – Christ-like heads, winged angels, and so on – but also in a certain wistful quality, as if expressing nostalgia for that transcendent realm to which his writings alluded. And he had already adopted the technique, which is prominent throughout his artistic career, of placing in the background of his drawings vague ectoplasmic figures, often female, to hint at the further dimensions of supernatural life.[33] The picture which most completely prefigures Gibran's work is Jean Delville's 'Love of Souls' (1900), which is, of course, itself reminiscent of certain works of William Blake, such as 'The Reunion of the Soul and the Body'. In Delville's painting, the combination of Rodinesque sculptural anatomical precision with metaphysical symbolism is typical of Gibran at this stage, as is the swirling Carrière-like background. In Gibran's middle period, however, in the early 1910s, Carrière's misty outlines would come to be the dominant influence. It seems to have been a convention of the times to use a veil of mist as a symbol for the dim access the normal human mind has to higher worlds,[34] and Gibran was constantly striving to communicate a sense of these transcendental realms.

Gibran's pictures are meant to evoke or inspire rather than define. In a similar vein, Redon claimed to place 'the logic of the visible at the service of the invisible'.[35] Puvis de Chavannes, whose murals Gibran would have seen in the Boston Public Library, was another master of strange stillnesses and lonely landscapes, suggestive of mystery. The Pre-Raphaelites had developed the technique of creating an aura of mystery by the posed arrangements of figures, but it was the Symbolists who often added the disturbing or even macabre touch – the hint of other realms which Gibran was undoubtedly trying to capture. There is an undeniable quality to those of Gibran's early drawings which survive, but not enough to deserve the label of 'genius' which Josephine applied to him. He seems to me to have more skill as a drawer than a painter.

A number of the French painters whose work, I have suggested, may have been influential on the young Gibran were brought to the public's attention above all by Joris-Karl Huysmans' 1884 novel *À Rebours* (*Against Nature*). This extraordinary book – as much treatise as novel, as much sly mocker of Decadence as champion of its causes – portrays a morbidly sensitive protagonist who follows the aloofness practised by the French Symbolist poets to its logical conclusion and locks himself away in his house, devoting himself to stimulating his senses in bizarre and decadent ways. In aesthetic terms 'Decadence' refers not to a state of corruption and decay as to the pursuit of art for art's sake and a devotion to the theories of Symbolism, perhaps with a tinge of self-indulgence and amorality, or at least a disillusionment with the morality promoted by human civilizations and an emphasis on the individual rather than the mass of humanity. There is a sentence in one of D'Annunzio's novels which for me perfectly summarizes the Decadent hero: 'Will, in abdicating, had yielded the sceptre to instinct, and the aesthetic sense was substituted for the moral.'[36] However, there is also a late Symbolist or quasi-Decadent phase of art, when the aloofness and absolute relativism of the artist becomes diluted.[37] In this phase poetry and painting are taken to have important salvational messages for the common run of humanity. This is an accurate brief for either Gibran's writing or his drawing and painting. If he needs labelling, he is a late Symbolist or Romantic, following as usual in the footsteps of his mentor Fred Holland Day.

Six years previously, Gibran had met Josephine Peabody at an exhibition of Day's photographs. Now, at an exhibition of his own work in Day's studio, he met the woman who would make an even more lasting impression on his life – and, ironically, it was due to Josephine that he met her. Josephine had been pressing Lionel Marks, the man who would soon become her successful suitor, to bring his friend

Mary Haskell to the show. In 1904, at the time of the exhibition, Mary Haskell was thirty years old. She was a wealthy woman, originally from South Carolina, who had come north as a university student and stayed to help her sister Louise (there were, in all, five sisters and four brothers) run a private school in Boston. When Louise married in 1903, Mary stayed on as the school's headmistress. She was in many ways a modern woman – involved in the women's labour movement, a supporter of the radical union the International Workers of the World, fluent in German, interested in art and literature, concerned about educational reform (for instance, she initiated the practice of educational visits to museums, and was a fan of Montessori), dabbling lightly in the occult.[38] She used Emerson and Wordsworth as well as the Bible for the morning assemblies at her school. She counted among her friends English Walling, the founder of the NAACP ('a spirit like the North Star'),[39] and the composer Arthur Farwell. She was in some respects the opposite of Josephine. She was more worldly and practical, with the ability to run her school through good times and bad. Her attitude towards the countryside was different from Josephine's Romanticism: Mary regularly spent her summers with the Sierra Club in California on tough hiking and climbing expeditions, covering thirty to forty miles a day. She was given to occasional outbursts of 'unseemly' behaviour, such as speeding in her automobile or stripping naked on an isolated camping trip. She was distant from most of her siblings and felt she had had an unhappy childhood; she was often, secretly, miserable and used to contemplate suicide.[40]

As she was browsing around the exhibition, 'a little dark young man' approached her and offered to explain the pictures to her, heavily laden as they were with symbols.[41] She found him interesting, and he was certainly attracted to her – perhaps not immediately attracted physically, because she was not enormously good-looking, but he liked her mind.[42] Many years later he told Mary that he was fed up with being Boston high society's performing monkey, something exotic and unusual, and liked her immediately because she treated him simply as an individual, and was interested enough in what he had to say to ask pertinent questions.[43] Another sign of her interest was that she also solicited Day's help in explaining Harris's paintings to her.

Was Gibran a performing monkey? To a certain extent, yes. He was Day's protégé and had been noised abroad by Josephine as a genius. Very commonly, when his visits to Josephine coincided with the presence of other guests, he would charm them by sketching them. This in turn led to his being invited to other houses, expressly to sketch people. It is not impossible that he was paid for some of these portraits. He was a male version of Edith Wharton's Lily Bart in *The House of Mirth* – cultivating his talent to win and then maintain a place in society, to break past Bostonian reluctance to accept strangers, particularly when they had come from another country. Santayana has left us with a scornful portrait of a Boston parlour of the period, and this is the setting in which we should picture Gibran, head bowed over paper, silent while idle chatter takes place around him, but absorbing everything.

> The room was littered with little sofas, little arm-chairs, little tables, with plants flowering in porcelain jars, and flowers flaunting in cut-glass bowls, photographs in silver frames, work-baskets, cushions, foot-stools, books, and magazines, while the walls were a mosaic of trivial decorations . . . étagères with nick-nacks and bric-à-brac, feeble water-colours, sentimental engravings, and slanting mirrors in showy frames.[44]

However, if Gibran described himself in 1922 as a performing monkey, it was with the help of a liberal dose of hindsight. At the time there is no sign that he felt embarrassed or mistreated or underestimated. On the contrary, he was probably flattered, and saw what was happening to him as a way out of the slums, and one which offered the possibility of fulfilling his artistic potential, so that he would not have to work as a drudge. He seems to have seized the opportunity offered by Day and Josephine with both hands. He probably even thought that his talents were at last being appreciated. Years later he admitted to Mary that he was rather proud of himself in those days.[45]

Josephine Peabody brought, or was, 'Her'. She introduced him to powerful and interesting friends and acquaintances. Her frank admiration of his work gave him the confidence to continue and develop. She was the recipient of his love. And finally she was indirectly responsible for his meeting Mary Haskell. On 30 May 1906, three weeks before her wedding to Lionel Marks, as a farewell acknowledgement Gibran wrote a short note to Josephine in which he quoted the book of Genesis and compared her effect on his life to that of God creating the universe. For all its effusive exaggeration, it is not an inappropriate image. Gibran himself called her the mother of his soul. She created his emotional life more fully than anyone, and so enabled him to live and feel as an artist for the rest of his life. If it had not been her, it would have been someone else: Gibran was an artist waiting to happen. But it was her, and Gibran's acknowledgement of her influence is a touching and unusual piece of modesty, very different in tone from the prophetic arrogance that would characterize a great deal of his relationship with Mary Haskell.

5

City of Light

For all Gibran's later statements, it is not clear that Mary Haskell immediately made that much of an impression on him. Their first meetings were purely practical, since she invited him to exhibit the same pictures he had shown in Day's studio in her school, at 314 Marlborough Street, more or less as soon as the first exhibition was over. And so the first entry in her diary about Gibran, on 14 May 1904, reads simply: 'Mr. Gibran to see ab. pictures.' The exhibition opened on 17 May and ran for a week. It was not a success: not a single drawing was sold. Nevertheless, it did bring Gibran and Mary into closer contact. The formality of 'Mr. Gibran' was dissolved by 21 May when she refers to him in her diary as 'K.' and then on 4 June as 'Kahlil'. By 29 June they appear to be on quite good terms: 'Kahlil and I made screen for kitchen, out of clothes-horse and bin-lap.'

Kahlil divided his time between working at Day's studio and visiting either Josephine or Mary. Josephine was still in the emotional doldrums: she had started the year brimming with ideas for poems and plays, but was too caught up in daily living to find the time to pursue them. As a result of her depression and Gibran's temperamental melancholia, their relationship at this time was uneasy, and occasionally quarrelsome. As usual, Kahlil's way in to Mary's circle was through his talent as a drawer: he would impress her and her friends by sketching them, or rapidly outlining some symbolic figure. He spent a few summer weeks up at Day's beach house in Five Islands, Maine. Presumably, he also spent some time at home, but as usual we know little or nothing of his life there. He was living at 35 Edinboro Street by now – another tenement in another tenement block in the polyglot South End. Marianna was still working at the sweatshop, but there is no sign that he was bringing in any income at all. It is not at all impossible that Day was supporting him financially. Gibran was not idle, however: he was filling his notebooks with sketches and with the first of the poems and the prose-poems which were to have such a profound effect on Arabic literature. From now on, although he continued to draw, references to poetry become as frequent as references to sketches: he is beginning to find his feet in another medium.

We have already seen, in the previous chapter, how in 1904 Gibran began to write for the New-York-based Arabic newspaper *Al-Mohajer*. His pieces – at first incidental, later more regular – gained him a high degree of popularity. The Gibrans have pinpointed one aspect of his appeal:

> Four years of college in Beirut had not fully equipped him to perfect his writing in Arabic . . . He was forced to resort to his essentially peasant's ear when putting down his thoughts. Ignoring much of the traditional vocabulary and form of classical Arabic, he began to develop a style which reflected the ordinary language he had heard as a child in Besharri and to which he was still exposed in the South End. This use of the colloquial was more a product of his isolation than of a specific intent, but it appealed to thousands of Arab immigrants.[1]

Other aspects of his style, however, were not so naïve. He was undoubtedly well read in Arabic as well as Western literature, and it is possible to trace a number of influences, as we have done in previous chapters.

The Gibrans are right, however, to suggest that what was unique about Gibran was his popular appeal. This was due in part to the simplicity of his language and the straightforwardness of his ideas, but also in part to his being the right person at the right place at the right time. There was a budding Romantic tradition in Arabic literature, being developed by writers such as Francis Marrash, but Gibran was one of the first to popularize it. In order for anyone to achieve popular recognition, he must be able to gain the ears or eyes of a wide audience. Another way in which Gibran was the right person at the right time is that there was a thriving Arabic newspaper scene in the United States; many of the papers circulated widely and were highly influential in shaping the immigrants' views about their new environment and the life they had left behind in the Middle East. In their new environment, the Syrian immigrants were open to new ideas and forms of expression. Gibran provided them with both.

Some of these newspapers were set up for sectarian religious or political purposes; these tended not to last for long, since their audiences were too limited. Others lasted for half a dozen years or more, despite being fairly highbrow in content. As well as *Al-Mohajer*, to which Gibran contributed regularly, his writings also found a home in *Mir'at al-Gharb* (*The Mirror of the West*), and later in *Al-Funun* (*The Arts*, 1913–19) and *As-Sa'ih* (*The Traveller*, 1912–31). Later the increasing assimilation of the immigrant population to America, and the fact that a new generation of Arabic children spoke English, generated a need for papers such as *The Syrian World*, published in English between 1926 and 1932. But more on this later, since Gibran was essentially involved in its establishment.

These newspapers represent only the tip of the iceberg – albeit the influential tip. Between 1890 and 1940 the Syrians in New York published no fewer than fifty-one Arabic-language periodicals. Editors of a successful paper such as *Al-Hoda*, which was begun in 1898 by Naoum and Salloum Mokarzel, gained a great deal of prestige and authority within the Arabic immigrant community. The papers typically included news from the homeland and from America, immigrant success stories, feature items, a wealth of advertisements, and a literary column. Editorials might offer advice on assimilation and champion the cause of Arab independence abroad. They made the careers of writers such as Gibran, Amin Rihani, Nasib 'Arida, Mikhail Naimy and 'Abd al-Masih Haddad – though none of these writers except Gibran found a way to break out into truly international fame.

Josephine was still far more prominent in Gibran's life than Mary. It was Josephine on whom he tried out his early poetry, attempting to explain what he was up to in his Arabic poems, and taking his first tottering steps in English composition. One of these immature prose-poems remains, dating probably from 1904, among Josephine's papers in Harvard University Library. It begins:

It was there that I heard unseen great wings moving about me.
And as I turned my eyes, I saw thee standing before me as the cedars of God in Lebanon.
I knew thee because the light was in thine eyes and the motherly smile on thine lips.
You blessed me with a touch and whispered to my soul these words
'Follow me, child, I am thy guide;
I shall reveal what sorrow doth hide.'

On 13 September Gibran wrote to Josephine in some distress, saying that he was lost in a sea of worldly troubles. Whatever these were, he had recovered from them sufficiently by the middle of November to face a far worse tragedy with, apparently, considerable equanimity. On the evening of Friday, 11 November, Harcourt Studios, the building containing Day's studio and that of forty other artists, burnt to the ground. It was a major fire, causing an estimated $200,000 worth of damage at contemporary prices, and obliterating the work of a number of artists. Day lost a great deal, including not just his own work but some Beardsley pictures he owned; the disaster probably hastened his decline and withdrawal from the world. Naturally enough, Gibran stored his portfolio in Day's studio where he worked rather than in the unsavoury tenement where he lived. Apart from the few sketches he had given to friends or sold, all his work was destroyed.

The following Monday, in response to a note from Josephine (who had been out of town at the time of the fire), Gibran wrote:

Yes, beloved, the years of Love's labor are lost. And you know: She came Saturday night – and O – how much of untold sad things she tolde. Do not be sad, beloved, for there must be an – unknown beautiful reason behinde it all.

He was obviously pleased with this phraseology and sentiment, because he wrote in very similar terms to Mary the next day – without, of course, mentioning 'Her', whose vehicle Josephine was.[2] His note to Josephine has a sketch to the left of the message of smoke rising from coals and a hand, palm down, appearing out of a cloud to receive the smoke. The 'fortitude' of his note reassured her, and she found hope for him in the situation. In her journal she wrote, 'And after all, the most glorious thing one can have . . . is surely this knowledge that one Lives Again and rises, singing, from the death and ashes of an earlier self.'[3] In fact, this is similar to how Gibran himself viewed the disaster in later years: people's expressions of sorrow, he said, led him to believe that he might have some talent, and that gave him the impetus to undertake further and better work.[4]

In his note to Mary, Gibran said that he was thinking about paying her a visit. In fact, he did not visit her again until October 1905, by which time he was at a loose end, emotionally speaking, since Josephine had more or less entirely withdrawn her affection for him and was devoting herself to Lionel Marks. Gibran plays hardly any part in Josephine's diaries and journals for this period, except when she has occasion to record a visit from him. Perhaps in acknowledgement of the ending of their relationship, Gibran had given her a beautiful present for her birthday on 30 May that year – a short story in elaborate Arabic calligraphy, with richly decorated colourful borders.

By the time he saw Mary again in October, Gibran had some achievements to talk about. Not only had he become quite a regular contributor to *Al-Mohajer*, but the newspaper had also published a short monograph of his, no more than a dozen pages in length, on music. Following a preface which likens the conversation of a loved one to music, Gibran whisks at a rapid and unscholarly pace through the importance of music in ancient cultures, lingering longer over four particular Persian modes. The essay concludes by calling on his readers to worship composers ancient and modern, from Orpheus to Mozart. The general tone of the piece is nostalgic and melancholic. Nadeem Naimy, commenting that 'The Gibran it [the booklet] reveals is a flowery sentimentalist', translates a short typical extract from it in which Gibran addresses music directly:

> Oh you, wine of the heart that uplifts its drinker to the heights of the world of imagination: you ethereal waves, bearing the soul's phantoms; you sea of sensibility and tenderness; to your waves we lend our souls and to your uttermost depths we trust our hearts. Carry those hearts away beyond the world of matter and show us what is hidden deep in the world of the unknown.[5]

As Hawi comments: 'His descriptions of music are so vague that we could as well apply them to poetry, love or any other subject which can excite emotion in the heart.'[6] Amin Goryeb must have been truly committed to fostering the Romantic revolution to have published this juvenile booklet by Gibran, but it shows as clearly as any of Gibran's writings at this period his commitment to the cause into which he was initiated by Day.

During the winter of 1905 to 1906 Gibran visited both Josephine and Mary occasionally. Neither was being particularly welcoming, and in any case he was working hard to recoup his losses in the Harcourt Studios fire. In February news of Josephine's and Lionel's engagement began to circulate, and Josephine's life took a turn for the better with the critical and popular acceptance of her play *Wings*, which called for female emancipation. Lionel and Josephine were married on 21 June. There is some evidence that Gibran felt betrayed enough by the transference of her time and energy to Lionel to suffer from pique. It is not true to say that he did not reply to her wedding invitation, since he wrote on 20 June sending his regrets for being unable to attend the ceremony and assuring his 'godmother', in his usual florid way, that he would be thinking of them both.[7] But there is no record of his acknowledging their marriage with a gift, and it is certainly true that when Josephine wrote to him, as she did to all her Boston friends, during her honeymoon in Europe, he failed to reply to her letters. She was puzzled enough to write to Fred Holland Day and ask what was up. For all the bravery of his writings, Gibran can still appear emotionally insecure and immature.

So Josephine had clearly left Gibran's life: there are only two notes from him to her dating from after her wedding.[8] At the same time, Mary was not yet a part of his life: they seem to have met only twice in 1905, and not at all in 1906. Day was presumably there for him as much as he was for anyone, and he had other friends,[9] but what was he to do for female company? Where was 'She'?

The appendix to later editions of the Gibrans' biography of their cousin makes fascinating reading. It tells, among other things, how, after the original publication of their book in 1974, they received a phone call out of the blue from a woman who asked whether they were aware that her aunt had had an affair with Gibran. This led eventually to their acquisition of sixty-six letters from Gibran to Gertrude Barrie, 'pianist, feminist, lover', who seems to have had an enlightened attitude towards the bestowing of her sexual favours: she had a number of lovers. The Gibrans afford us no more than a glimpse of the relationship with Kahlil: they have reproduced only a tiny proportion of the letters, and they did not allow me to see either these letters or any of the Gibran material in their possession.[10]

Gibran met Gertrude Barrie, a concert pianist *manquée* who now made a living as a piano teacher, some time in 1906 through the offices of a mutual friend, Salim Sarkis, a translator and newspaper editor associated for a time with the paper *Mir'at al-Gharb* in New York. Later, in 1908, Sarkis wrote rather coarsely to Barrie, saying: 'When I wanted to give you a sample of the Syrian I gave you Gibran. And I do not regret it. Do you?' The affair – for such it certainly was, with all the sexual connotations of the word – continued for at least two years, and Gibran was still writing to her from Paris. Gibran's tone in his letters to her is decidedly erotic and utterly familiar. He calls his body a slave to his passion, and calls her 'wicked' and 'devilish'. Her studio was only a few minutes' walk from the Syrian ghetto, and it is clear from the letters that Gibran spent quite a few evenings, late into the night, alone there with her. She used to leave a light in the window to indicate that she was in and available.

Gibran returned to Boston after his two years in Paris to find the affair finished, but he and Gertrude Barrie remained in touch as friends at least until her marriage in 1922. Some of the extant letters in the Gibrans' possession date from way past the ending of their affair, and there is a letter to Gibran from a certain D. Weston Eliot, written in March 1919, in which he hopes that 'Miss Barrie' will have acted as a go-between so that Eliot can renew the acquaintance with Gibran he used to have fifteen years earlier. So they remained in affectionate, but not intimate, contact for many years.

Like Josephine and Mary, Gertrude was a few years older than Gibran. However, the part she played in Gibran's life was clearly more earthy and less ethereal than that of the other older women. She was less a vehicle for Romantic notions than a real, available person. There was no talk between the two of them of marriage or anything like that: this was just fun. The affair was not without its cost, however: while writing high-flown pieces on the value of spiritual love, he was engaged in an earthy affair. It increased the tension between the myth and the man. The persona Gibran was beginning to present to the world at large was that of a delicate, otherworldly figure, not the type to conduct such an affair. And indeed the public was taken in: his secret affair with Gertrude was not disclosed for some seventy years.

So we picture Gibran in the latter half of 1906 in high spirits. He has a beautiful lover and, relishing his budding role as the people's prophet, his work is going well. With only a slight pang he brushes Josephine out of his life and buries himself in his work and in the soft flesh of a receptive woman. In addition to his newspaper pieces, *Nymphs of the Valley* has just been published. He is still reliant on his sister Marianna for a regular income, but he is increasingly committed to making a living by pen and pencil. Years later Marianna humbly recalled her role in his life at this time: she cooked and kept house so that he could be free to work and explore the outside world of which she was somewhat terrified – not least because she had not yet learnt to read and speak English.

His name was now well enough known among the Syrian immigrant population that, at a time of feuding between the Maronite and Orthodox communities, one of the devices *Al-Mohajer* used to try to restore calm was to print on their front page a drawing by Gibran of an angel extending its two hands to the two rival factions. At the same time they published an article by Amin Rihani, another well-known young immigrant writer, in which he condemned the conflict and typically located the problems in the people's dependence on the clergy of their churches. Within a few years Gibran's and Rihani's lives were to become more closely intertwined.

Meanwhile, Mary was undergoing some kind of spiritual crisis – one that would make her utterly receptive to Gibran's adopted persona. First, in the summer of 1906 she rediscovered God, not in the sense that she was inclined to return to church, but as a presence in her life; second, her beloved mentor Sarah Armstrong died in October. Mary mourned her deeply, and frequently reread her letters. References to her are underlined in her diaries and journals, so she must have reread those too, so as to relive past times. She even tried to get in touch with her by spiritualist means, apparently to no avail.

Mary had a wide circle of friends and acquaintances, but two in particular were to play an important part in the somewhat tangled and incestuous web of relationships involving Gibran. Charlotte Teller came from an eminent Colorado family. Her father, James B. Teller, later rose to become the Attorney-General of the state, while her uncle, Henry Teller, was a famous and respected Senator. Charlotte was the very type of a modern woman. Living in New York, she wanted to become a famous writer, especially of plays, and as well as writing incidental pieces for newspapers and magazines she also had novels published both under her own name and under the pseudonym of John Brangwyn. She broke up with her husband in 1904, reverted to her maiden name, and was committed to the cause of women's emancipation. She was sexy, vivacious and outgoing, several years younger than Mary, and had a strong interest in Theosophy. We can imagine her and Mary deep in conversation, or exchanging breathless, gossipy letters. Their relationship sometimes seems to resemble that of best friends at a girls' school; occasionally, for instance, Charlotte slept over in Mary's room when she was in Boston and they had talked too late into the night.[11] But in actual fact Mary was supporting Charlotte financially while she attempted to reinvent herself as a playwright.

The other woman in this triangle of three formidable women who were soon to play such a major part in Gibran's life was the bewitching, dark-haired French teacher at Mary's school, Émilie Michel, or Micheline, as she was familiarly known. Frustratingly little is known about this woman, who aspired to be an actress and to whom Gibran probably dedicated *Spirits Rebellious*,[12] but Gibran's portraits show her to have been a beautiful young woman. She came from a poor background, and was plagued by a serious illness which would eventually paralyse her and kill her young in 1931. Mary says at one point that she 'inevitably holds the hearts of men', which helps to bring the portrait alive.[13] She joined the Haskell-Dean School at the beginning of the academic year in 1906,[14] and was soon a firm favourite not only with the pupils but also with Mary herself.

Suddenly, out of the blue, Gibran re-entered Mary's life.[15] He went round for tea on 6 January 1907, and stayed, as she noted in her diary, until 10.15. It cannot have been coincidence that this was his birthday, so they must have been in touch with each other beforehand to set things up. He brought her a copy of *Nymphs of the Valley* (which was illegible to her, of course), and, recognizing her greater age,[16] wrote on the flyleaf, 'With the love of a strong child to Mary Elizabeth Haskell, from Kahlil.' Typically, he drew two pictures for her while he was there: this was still his way into Boston society.

Still there was nothing particular between them. The next time Gibran came round to her house was eleven months later, for dinner on 7 December, when he drew his self-portrait, using the mirror on her desk. They have now known each other on and off – mostly off – for three and a half years, and there is absolutely no sign of any intimacy between them, or of anything more than her polite interest in a talented young man, several years her junior. Things started to change in January the next year, 1908 – a momentous year for Gibran. The catalyst for the change was the relationship between Gibran and Mary's other two friends, especially Micheline. They began to get on so well together that Mary was inevitably drawn in by the magnetic power of their friendship and love – so much so that, even though she was the older woman of the foursome, love was in the air and she basked in the warmth of it.

On 19 January she had Kahlil round to dinner by himself, although she saw Charlotte later and no doubt told her about him. Charlotte was apparently on an extended visit to Boston, however, because Mary was able to introduce the two of them to each other on the 27th. Kahlil drew Charlotte, of course, and the portrait went well. More importantly, Charlotte and Gibran hit it off together. They discovered a shared interest in Symbolism and matters occult. Three days later Mary had Gibran round for dinner again, this time because she had also invited Josephine and Lionel Marks. The evening was not a success: one gets the distinct impression from Josephine's diary that Kahlil sulked. Mary did not try to repeat the experiment, and in fact began to drift away from the literary and high-society crowd of which the Markses were a part. Likewise, Gibran was drifting away from Fred Holland Day. This separation may not have been entirely his doing, since Day, as I have already mentioned, was becoming increasingly reclusive. But perhaps Gibran saw his future as lying with his present protectress, and felt that he had gained all Day had to offer him.

If Gibran did somehow guess that his future lay with Mary, February was to prove him right beyond his wildest dreams. It started on a good note, too. On Sunday the 2nd, Mary wrote to Gibran with a proposition – that he should come round to the school and draw from life at least once a week. Ever open to educational possibilities, she had already displayed several of his pictures, including the portrait of Charlotte, in the school for the girls' edification. Now she wanted him to come and draw in front of the girls, so that they could see an artist at work. And the person she chose as his first model was Micheline. The first portrait did not come out well, however. Gibran returned to the school four more times that month, and each time Micheline sat for him. Mary found the whole arrangement deeply satisfying. She loved the tableau created, on 11 February, as Micheline read French poetry aloud while Gibran sketched her. She described it as 'exquisite', but later events suggest that there was probably also a sexual charge passing between the artist and his model. At the same time Charlotte sat again for Gibran on another visit to Boston. They got on well, and perhaps continued the discussion they had started in January on reincarnation, a belief of Gibran with which the mystically inclined Charlotte was in full sympathy. She wrote to Mary, 'He seems to be an early-age brother of mine – as though if I were often with him I might recall actual scenes in those Egyptian times in which I *know* I lived.'[17] In return he told Mary that he felt he had known Charlotte in one of his previous lives, and that she troubled his thoughts.[18]

Like Josephine, Mary recognized Kahlil's talents and wanted to do something to foster them: Gibran had the ability to arouse this emotion in his older women friends. Unlike Josephine, Mary was well placed to carry out her intentions. No doubt she paid him for these visits to the school, and she also wrote to him on 22 February offering $100 for two symbolic drawings he had done. More importantly – far more importantly – she offered to pay for him to attend art school in Paris for a year. He was over the moon. He hugged the secret to himself, telling only Marianna and Amin Goryeb in New York. In his letter to Goryeb, he looks forward to his time there as the beginning of a whole new chapter in the story of his life, and acknowledges Mary as a 'she-angel' who is paving his way to intellectual and financial success. Goryeb had clearly been telling Gibran that his future lay in New York, because Gibran says that it is the presence of this she-angel that is keeping him in Boston.[19] He assures Goryeb that he will continue to write for *Al-Mohajer* even while he is in Paris – and will write even better, given the inspiration the 'City of Light' will afford him.

So Mary steps into Josephine's shoes as Gibran's protectress. It is hardly surprising, then, to find that epithets he used to apply to Josephine, he now applies to her: she is, for instance, the 'mother of his heart'.[20] But again it needs to be stressed that all the time up until his departure for Paris in July, there is no sign that he was in love with her, or she with him. He writes to her with affection, recognizes the enormous debt he owes her, and treats her as a mother, or at least someone he can rely on and confide in. In a letter of 25 March 1908, for instance, he tells her that he dreamt the night before of Christ – which is perhaps not the kind of dream you tell all and sundry. He trusts her not to mock or disbelieve him. Anything which he takes seriously is taken with the utmost seriousness by her. She also offers to be his agent while he is in Paris: he will send her pictures, and she will try to get a good price for them in the States. And for her part, she talks of feeling a 'sense of companionship' with Gibran, and is happy that he no longer feels he has to talk only of 'winged things' with her, and can relax and be a normal human being.

Had Mary been in love with Gibran at this stage, her behaviour would have been perverse in the extreme. For there is no doubt that she was gently pushing Gibran and Micheline together. Despite the secret presence of Gertrude Barrie in the background, Gibran seems not to have been slow to respond. Throughout March, he was not only drawing her in public in the school, but going round to her apartment alone, and several times the three of them dined together at one or other of the two women's places. It is noticeable that Micheline stops being 'Mademoiselle' in Mary's diary, and begins to be Micheline: their relationship is no longer that of headmistress to staff member. They are a circle of friends; they sit up together late into the night, talking philosophy and Theosophy, righting the wrongs of the world, watching Gibran draw and listening to his tales of exotic Syria.

Much the same pattern continued throughout March and April. Gibran created his familiar symbolic drawings for Mary and drew her friends – and her for the first time on 24 April. Marianna came with Gibran to dinner, presumably to meet his benefactress. Again, just as Josephine did, Mary introduced Gibran to her friends. He had become her protégé and she showed him off, with something of the pride of a mother hen. In return he sent her his typically effusive letters and gave her copies of his books, including *Spirits Rebellious*, which was published in March of that year.

The mother hen was nurturing not just her Syrian charge, but also the blossoming affair between him and Micheline. When Gibran was shy, she made him kiss Micheline, and she watched over the agonies and ecstasies of young love. On 19 May they were having a 'hard time, both sobbing broken-heartedly', but two days later all was well with them again. She recorded that Micheline was gloriously happy, and when Gibran came round to dine with her alone, the conversation frequently turned to Micheline.

By the same token, when Micheline and Mary were alone together, the conversation turned to Gibran. On 5 May they had a long, frank discussion about Gibran over dinner. They spoke in French, 'because the servants are always about and we always talk of Kahlil, and they will think us both mad on the subject if they hear us say "He" any more.' Micheline told her about a talk she had had with Kahlil in which she had said that Paris would change him – so much so that he might forget her. 'You may forget everything else,' she told him, 'but remember that I give you my affection because you deserve it. Guard those qualities that were worthy of Micheline's heart, so that in the future you may deserve the hearts of other women.'

There can be little doubt, then, that Micheline and Gibran were in love.[21] They also consummated their relationship sexually. There are no extant letters or anything to provide concrete evidence of this, but with the certainty of the affair with Gertrude Barrie to guide us, most doubts are swept away. They were both young, free, modern people, in an era which was just beginning to emerge from under the repression of the Victorian period and admit its sexuality. The extraordinary promiscuity of the 1920s was not far off. Baudelaire's book, *Les Fleurs du mal*, containing some of the most highly charged erotic poems ever written, was readily available; Mirbeau's *The Diary of a Chambermaid* spoke easily and freely of sex; Decadent writers such as Gabriele D'Annunzio (a favourite of Gibran), Rachilde and Rémy de Gourmont were even going so far as to flaunt a fairly perverse kind of sexuality.

But Micheline, at any rate, paid heavily and painfully for her relationship with Gibran. She became pregnant, but the pregnancy was ectopic, and she had to have an abortion, probably in France. The first, Arabic edition of Mikhail Naimy's book revealed some of the facts of Micheline's pregnancy, but they were omitted from later Arabic editions, and also from the English edition. This led to charges of falsehood: it was said that he left out the story of her pregnancy because he knew it was a lie. In fact, however, he left it out because he had qualms of a different sort: he did not know whether or not Micheline was still alive, and he wanted to avoid giving offence. Moreover, it was Mary Haskell herself who told Naimy that Micheline had an ectopic pregnancy, in one of their late-night talks in Gibran's studio after his death. In later years, when Kahlil and Mary talked about the possibility of their having sex, he showed himself to be well aware of the dangers of unwanted pregnancy: this episode with Micheline certainly scarred him for life.

In other respects too it was not an easy time for a tortured Romantic. Having put Woman on so high a pedestal, what was one to do with one's natural sexual urges? Sleeping with the object of one's dreams would bring her down to earth. Gibran idealized Josephine Peabody, and never slept with her. He never consummated his affair with Mary Haskell either. These were the two women who were most important to him – who inspired him in his work. It is noticeable that throughout his career as an artist, the majority of his portrayals of womanhood – and She is a predominant theme – are sexless, with the genital area obscured. Gertrude Barrie and Micheline, however, were available – and not least in the sense that they were not carriers of Ideal Womanhood for Gibran. They were his equals, or so he felt, and with them he could fall innocently in love and have a passionate physical affair without engaging his soul.

There may have been others as well. In a 1908 letter of Gibran to his friend Jamil Malouf, he recounted an episode with an unnamed poetess which may have been sexual in nature. And a woman called Mary Qahwaji came forward after Gibran's death with the claim that Gibran had been in love with her at this time, despite the fact that she was married.[22] In Mary Qahwaji's case, there is no hint necessarily of impropriety, but there is a gap in the record that we do need to fill, since Gibran once confessed to Mary Haskell that before he met her, or knew her well, he had had a number of affairs, starting with his initiation into sex at the age of fifteen by an older married woman. He was concerned with Mary to downplay the number of sexual liaisons he had had in the past, and there is no way we can know how many women there had been in his life, beyond recording that he was certainly not a virgin when he met Gertrude Barrie and Micheline.

In May and June of 1908, the talk must all have been of Paris. Not only was Gibran going there, but so was Micheline, ostensibly to see her parents, and Mary and her father were planning a European tour in the summer as well. After a farewell dinner for Kahlil on 9 June, Mary and he travelled on the 10th to New York where they dined with Charlotte, before Mary left for the South, to pick up her father and attend her sister Marion's wedding, while Gibran returned to Boston. Some time in June Kahlil wrote a sweet farewell note to Fred Holland Day. Recognizing that Day was now hard to get to, and that they were unlikely to meet before he sailed, he says that he still hopes they might see each other some time so that Day can offer him advice and guidance for the future, and then 'you, dear Brother, who first opened the eyes of my childhood to light, will give wings to my manhood'. After this, they met and corresponded sporadically, but were never again as close as they had been during Kahlil's teens. When he came back from Paris he felt he had changed, moved on, and yet he found Day stuck in the same old Decadent mode. But when he set sail for Europe on 1 July, on the T.S. *Rotterdam* of the Holland-American line, he had in his bag a copy of Bulfinch's *Mythology*, a typical gift from his old mentor Day.

In Paris, Gibran coincided with his old school friend, Yusuf Huwayyik, and Huwayyik later wrote an account of his time there with Gibran. The book has the virtue of readability, but he chose to write it largely as a series of dramatized conversations. Since the book was written a great many years after he and Gibran were in Paris, we are bound to doubt the reliability of these conversations. Nevertheless, there is a ring of veracity about Huwayyik's book, largely because he is not concerned to present a tabloid version of Gibran's life. There are discrepancies between his account and Mary Haskell's journals in minor details, but these are mostly unimportant, and attributable to faulty memory rather than falsification.[23]

More awkward is the fact that there is virtually no overlap between any of the stories Huwayyik tells about Gibran in Paris, and any of the stories Gibran told Mary, either in his letters to her at the time, or in later conversations. However, only in two cases is this mismatch glaring. Gibran told Mary in 1920 that he had once accepted an invitation to dine with three Lebanese bishops who were visiting Paris. They were all over him, he claimed, because he was the darling of Lebanon, but they did not know that Huwayyik, who was also at the dinner party, had told him that they had been responsible for his excommunication. He denounced them to their faces as hypocrites. There are very good reasons to doubt the truth of this story, not only because it would surely have been too good for Huwayyik to omit, and because it is unlikely that Gibran was ever excommunicated in any meaningful sense of the word,[24] but also because he had already told her, some years before, a less dramatic version of the same story. In the original version, rather than raging at their hypocrisy, he only made it clear that he did not intend to change the tone of what he was writing to satisfy them.[25] As usual, Gibran is trying to impress Mary with his high moral stand; this is one of the reasons for his strange habit of lying.

The other undoubtedly fictitious tale is as follows. As we will see from time to time throughout this book, Gibran liked to exaggerate his importance to Syria as a political figure. Presumably he couldn't get away with this in the company of his Eastern friends, but he certainly laid it on thick for Mary, who was the recipient of his tales of the political importance of his family in the Middle East and of how he was offered high-ranking posts in the government. Just after Christmas 1917 he also told her that agents of the Ottoman Empire had tried to assassinate him while he was in Paris, and he showed her a scar on his arm which he claimed came from a bullet. Surely this is a lie – not just because Huwayyik doesn't include the story in his book, but because Gibran was in constant touch with Mary throughout his stay in Paris, and would hardly have omitted to mention it.

The trouble with this habitual lying is that it makes one doubt almost every colourful story recorded in Mary Haskell's journals. Another melodramatic one from his time in Paris is that there was a talented Polish artist living above him who went mad, destroyed almost all his own work, and eventually killed himself. Gibran and the others living in the house bought his remaining pieces – a little head of a girl, in Gibran's case – to raise money to give to the Polish man's poor mother.[26] In this case, there is no objective reason to doubt the story: Huwayyik may not have known about this incident, since it may have taken place before he arrived in Paris. The description of the location certainly fits the time Gibran was living at 14 Avenue du Maine, on the ground floor, rather than his later studio at number 54 on the same street. But still one wonders how much Gibran has embroidered the facts. Perhaps he bought the piece in a shop and the shopkeeper told him the story; perhaps the Polish artist did live above him, but simply left town. The trouble is that we will never know: Gibran constantly reminds his biographer of the boy who cried 'Wolf!'

But Gibran loved Paris. And here he was, living in the Latin Quarter – the heart of the city of artists and freethinkers! It was the art capital of the world; literally thousands of artists from all over the globe were living there. But certain elements of his old life followed him to Paris. Micheline was already there, and she helped him to find a studio and get settled; Mary and her father arrived by the end of July, after a brief tour of Ireland and England. However, they stayed only a few days, and Mary was too busy sight-seeing and visiting old friends to spend very much time with her protégé. Besides, she was there with her father, which was not the context in which he was accustomed to see her. He spent the evening of 31 July at her hotel, and on 4 August she visited his studio at 14 Avenue du Maine. Then she was gone, and by then Micheline had left too, for an extended visit with her family in Nevers. In a letter to Mary written on 13 July, Gibran seems to express – although in very broken English – his understanding that he has to let Micheline go, if she is to fulfil her aspirations to become a stage actress.

This was already his third letter to Mary. He wrote to her once from the boat, and on the 11th, in a burst of high spirits, he, Micheline and a friend of hers called Marguerite had co-authored a letter in three hands. For instance, Marguerite wrote: 'Je sais que Micheline est folle ce soir,' and then Kahlil broke in with, 'And yet in Syria they say that fools are the friends of God,' to which Micheline added, 'This explains why I am K's friend!!!' And Gibran continued to write to Mary, though not with the same frequency, throughout his stay in Paris, which lasted until 22 October 1910: thirty of his letters from this period exist, though unfortunately only the first three pages of one of hers. This is a pity, because we would like to see her side of their developing epistolary relationship, and to know, for instance, how she reacted to the death of her father in the spring of 1910.

Even after the departure of his Boston friends, Kahlil was not truly alone in Paris. As he told Mary much later, his published work had already made him famous in the Arabic-speaking world by the time he arrived in Paris.[27] There was, and still is, a thriving Lebanese population there, and Gibran was not short of invitations to dine and visit, though he chose to refuse most of them. He had started work at the Académie Julian on 28 July, and although Huwayyik's book covers little but their social life, which centred on certain cafés and their two studios, the overriding impression we receive from his letters to Mary, in so far as they deal with the externals of his Paris life, is of an earnest young man determined to make the most of his sponsored time in the 'City of Light'. His life was not all work and no play, but play was a visit to the Louvre rather than the Moulin Rouge, or an earnest discussion about life and art around a café table rather than a flirtation with any of the available women there. Huwayyik expressly says that Gibran was bashful with Parisian women, and was no Don Juan.[28] He presents himself as the frivolous one, and Gibran as the serious one, inclined to melancholy, wearing his hair long, unable to dance. It is true that Gibran later told Mary that he met many available women in Paris, and refused at least one offer of sex, but given Huwayyik's testimony we should probably assume that nothing came of any of these meetings. My impression is that he avoided as many as he attended of the wild café parties he told Mary about.[29]

A major part of the reason for this earnestness – this inability to let go, one might say – was that Gibran came to Paris already with a sense of his own importance. He had had three books published (two books and a monograph, anyway) and a large number of incidental poems and pieces. He had been lionized by certain elements of Boston society. His ambition runs like a thread through Huwayyik's account. He sees himself as a man with a mission – to awaken the Arab world to the wrongs being perpetrated in the name of authority. He feels he may be a genius of some kind. If he is to fulfil himself, he must not waste his time in Paris. It is only in keeping with this high self-estimation that to acquaintances in Paris he continued the fiction he had already begun in America that he came from a wealthy and noble family in Lebanon.[30]

However, his sense of importance may in this instance have led him to stray from the best route to fulfilling his mission, in so far as that involved learning the ropes as an artist. For he quickly became impatient with the Académie Julian. The Académie was founded by Rodolphe Julian in 1868, and had rapidly grown to become the largest private academy in Paris, with a number of *ateliers* all over the city. There was no entrance requirement, so that students could start immediately and prepare under expert supervision for entrance, most usually, to the École des Beaux-Arts. This was one of the reasons the Académie Julian was popular among foreign students.[31] Would-be artists of both sexes were welcomed, and the regime was flexible. There were courses in drawing (especially of the human figure), painting and sculpture, to which students could be admitted for as little as a few days, or for as much as a whole year: it was up to them, and they paid in advance. In its time, the Académie Julian had admitted quite a few famous artists: Gibran was following in the footsteps of such as Henri Matisse, John Singer Sargent, Fernand Khnopff, Edmund Dulac, Édouard Vuillard, Maurice Denis, Marcel Duchamp and Pierre Bonnard. As the eclecticism of this list demonstrates, the Académie Julian was famous for allowing its students to develop their own individual talents, rather than imposing the methods and philosophy of one particular school on them.

Gibran started work there with a great deal of enthusiasm, and joined the *atelier* of Jean-Paul Laurens.[32] He wrote to Mary about learning how to paint, learning to use his eyes more, as an artist, and about wrestling with colour. But already by early November a sour note has crept in: he complains that his teachers tell him off for making the model more beautiful than she really is, whereas he thinks he has never captured her essential beauty. Then in the New Year he informs her that he has been working for a few weeks in the studio of Pierre Marcel-Béronneau. Although it was perfectly legitimate, given the flexible routine of the Académie Julian, for students to attend more than one Académie or more than one teacher, Gibran used his sympathy towards Béronneau as an excuse to leave the Académie Julian altogether by early February 1909. And he might well have been more at home at the Béronneau studio. Béronneau was a Symbolist, a pupil of Gustave Moreau, and Gibran readily acknowledged himself as a 'small Berinau [*sic*]'. Gibran was confirmed in his aspiration to be a Symbolist painter, but it may well be argued that he always lacked some of the basic appreciation of line and structure that the more realistic Laurens might have imparted to him. As Huwayyik perceptively says, Gibran was an ideas man, more a writer than an artist. He knew *what* he wanted to say, but lacked some of the basic skills to communicate his ideas through the medium of painting.[33]

Béronneau closed his studio for the summer of 1909, but when it reopened in October Gibran did not return to him. He told Mary that he felt, and his friends agreed, that he had gained all he could from the man. This is hardly the attitude of a humble student. For the rest of his time in Paris, Gibran does not appear to have apprenticed himself seriously to any teacher (though he mentions that he was receiving criticism from a certain Richard Miller, an art teacher in Paris);[34] he hired models, sharing the cost with Huwayyik, and practised assiduously on his own. He spent hours studying the work of other artists he admired in the museums and galleries, imbibing their styles and techniques. In one letter to Mary he lists a number of them, but marks Eugène Carrière as his favourite.

Gibran did undoubtedly profit from Paris. With the help of his teachers, his friends and hard work, he transformed himself from a skilful drawer to someone who was at least not afraid of using colours and had some familiarity with oils, water colours and pastels. The crowning success of his time in Paris came when in 1910 the Société Nationale des Beaux-Arts accepted one of his canvases – a moody study of a female model that Gibran entitled 'Autumn' – for its spring Salon. They asked for a further six pictures for the autumn Salon that October, but by then Gibran had already decided to leave Paris, for reasons that are not entirely clear. He hated the winters there. The cheap accommodation he could afford was damp and hard to heat, and he was ill on and off for much of the winter of 1908 to 1909. He was always on the lookout for better studios – but they did not come cheap. So one of his reasons for leaving Paris may have been merely the difficulty of finding a studio which combined comfort with cheapness. He may also have been worried about how long he could go on staying in Paris at Mary's expense. The details of their financial arrangement are unclear. At first he was due to spend only a year in Paris, though at a later stage of the planning this expanded to a year in Paris and a year in Italy.[35] Perhaps he had even agreed with her from the start that he would stay only for as long as it took to use up a certain amount of her money. At any rate, he seems to have been invariably short of money in Paris, despite the fact that he supplemented his allowance from Mary by teaching drawing from the winter of 1909 to 1910, while complaining about how tiring it was.[36]

A major artistic project which Gibran conceived in Paris and initiated there was what he later came to refer to as the 'Temple of Art'. The idea was to do a series of pencil portraits – always Gibran's best medium – of famous men and women artists of the day, with a few of Gibran's heroes from past times thrown in for good measure. He started in December 1909 with Paul Bartlett, the American sculptor whose statue of Lafayette stood in front of the steps of the Louvre, and continued with Debussy, Edmond Rostand and Henri Rochefort. He wanted to include Rodin, but found it hard to pin the man down to an appointment. He hoped also to draw Sarah Bernhardt, Pierre Loti and others. Despite Huwayyik's insistence that Gibran's acquaintance with Rodin was fleeting and minimal, there seems no good reason to doubt the veracity of Gibran's letters to Mary in which he claims to have met him twice during his time in Paris. On neither occasion was any degree of intimacy attained, however – which becomes important in the light, or shadow, of one of the most notorious lies Gibran perpetuated about himself in later years.[37] In the meantime, it seems likely that the beautiful head of Rodin which Gibran drew for his series was done from memory, or from a photograph. He must have seemed to the impressionable Gibran the very personification of art, with his flowing white beard and Bohemian lifestyle.

Back in Boston, Mary was looking after Gibran's interests. Not only did she take care of his sister Marianna, who was desperately lonely without Kahlil and had gone through a period of illness herself, but she also arranged for another exhibition of Gibran's work at Wellesley College, which at Josephine Peabody's urging had included some of his work in an earlier exhibition in 1903. The review in the college newspaper was somewhat non-committal, preferring to describe the paintings rather than assess their merits.[38]

Naturally, Gibran did not get as much writing done in Paris as he did before and after his time there. Nevertheless, he was still regularly contributing pieces for Amin Goryeb's *Al-Mohajer*, one of which – 'The Day of My Birth' (also translated as 'My Birthday' in some collections) – was dedicated to Mary Haskell. He sent her a copy of the newspaper, which she received with great pleasure, even though she couldn't read the poem. He also achieved a notable literary success when one of the stories from *Nymphs of the Valley*, 'Marta al-Baniyah', was translated into French and anthologized in a prestigious collection of the best new writers from around the world. It must have been pleasant for Mary at last to be able to read one of his stories. Moreover, his intellectual life was developing. He discovered Renan's unorthodox and humanist interpretation of Christ ('He saw [Jesus] in light and not in twilight'),[39] read Balzac, became familiar with Voltaire, for the first time read the complete works of Nietzsche, continued his acquaintance with Tolstoy and Rousseau. Although his spoken French was apparently far from fluent, there is no reason to think that he could not read the language competently.

As well as marking a significant departure in his development as an artist, Paris was also a watershed for Gibran in a number of other ways. In the first place, it marked the end of his affair with Micheline. We cannot track her movements exactly, but by late October 1908 she had left France and was back in America, living in New York and trying to make her way as an actress (while being supported financially by Mary). She was not successful. When she wrote to Gibran in late October 1908, perhaps deliberately she did not give him her address in New York. When her name cropped up in a letter to Mary in December 1909 he said that he had nothing to say to Micheline any more, and although he paid her a visit when she was in Paris in July 1910, there was no hint of intimacy. We cannot know exactly what caused the end of their affair; Kahlil once implied to Mary that it was he who pulled back – that Micheline wanted him more than he wanted her – but this is too vague to allow us to guess at any details.[40] However, the emotional stresses surrounding unwanted pregnancies and abortions have been sufficient to tear many couples apart.

It is not clear that any other woman filled the gap left by Micheline. Charlotte visited Paris in the summer of 1909, and although she and Gibran spent quite a bit of time together, seeing the sights in and around Paris, their relationship does not seem to have built up the intensity it was to gain a couple of years later in New York. She sat for him and they both wrote to Mary independently saying how well they had got on with each other, but Gibran also contrived to give Charlotte the impression that he was a bit of a man-about-town, and had already had a number of affairs in Paris. Perhaps he was merely trying to impress her. As already noted, Huwayyik gives us the opposite impression, that although there were women in Paris who were attracted towards Gibran, his friend was too moral to take advantage of his good looks. But Huwayyik also adds that he and Gibran were not constantly in each other's pockets. In three of his letters to Mary in late 1909 and early 1910 Gibran mentions a young, beautiful American actress he had met, called Marie Doro, with whom he was getting on well. She also posed for him.[41] Maybe he had an affair with her, although he expressly told Mary that 'Miss Doro' did not 'feed his heart'. In any case, this was *after* Charlotte's visit to Paris.

The most curious aspect of Gibran's romantic life is the increasing intimacy with which he addressed Mary in his letters to her. At first his letters were what one might expect from a younger man writing, at least partly out of duty, to his benefactress. He gave her news of his work, accommodation, mutual friends; he complained of his health when he was ill, and told her when he got better; he described his visits to Syrian acquaintances in Paris, worried about his sister in Boston, and thanked her when he received money from her. But, as Josephine had been before her, she also took on the role of his 'Consolation'. He went through periods of loneliness in Paris, but – or so he told her – found solace in thinking of her. In this context, he mentioned in passing the unhappiness of past years, and quoted from Keats's *Ode to a Nightingale*: 'I have been half in love with easeful Death.' Along with attributing this role to her went a greater presumption of her love for him, fuller declarations of the warmth of his feelings for her, and a distinctly increased intensity of tone when he was addressing personal thoughts and sentiments to her. His rapidly improving English enabled him to convey this intensity with greater subtlety than he ever did in any of his letters to Josephine, so that there was nothing in the letters that she might not, if she so chose, take as more than the innocent effusion of a close, emotionally expressive friend. But the minimal conclusion to be drawn from this is that Gibran was one of those people who find it easier to be intimate by letter than face to face. We will see the same phenomenon when we come to consider his epistolary love affair with May Ziadeh.

Another important turning-point for Gibran in Paris concerns his politicization. Paris was a hotbed of Syrian dissidents, and Gibran certainly came into contact with some of them. One, a poet called Sukrui Ghanim, was explicitly described as a friend in a letter to Mary.[42] Although Gibran was always too self-absorbed to be in any complete sense a political animal, his friendship with Ghanim and others must have helped turn his earlier Romantic anger about injustice into a more sharply focused desire to influence Lebanon's future. Personally, I find implausible the story he told Mary later that while he was in Paris a delegation arrived from the Young Turks offering him a high position in the newly established government in Constantinople, which he refused.[43] He was hardly famous as a political figure, only as an angry young writer. Nevertheless, on his return to the United States he did make an attempt to be more involved in Syrian groups there, and this can be attributed to his contact with Syrian political thinkers in Paris. But the Syrian who was to have the greatest influence on him, and engagement in his life, was Amin Rihani, whose acquaintance he had already made through the pages of *Al-Mohajer*, but whom he met for the first time in Paris. The two became fast friends, and spent a month together in London in the summer of 1910. Rihani was an older man (he was born in 1876), with a more established reputation in the Arab world as a writer, and Gibran admired him immensely, describing him as a 'great poet'.[44] It is not going too far to say that for some time he aspired to follow in his footsteps. In return, Gibran introduced him to the world of art.

The final rite of passage that Kahlil underwent during his years in Paris was the death of his father in June 1909. In recent months they had become somewhat reconciled, which Gibran more than once attributed to his growing fame. As soon as he began to make his mark as a writer, his father revised his earlier negative view of his prospects in that field, and was proud of his son and his rebellion against society.[45] Yet Gibran does not seem to have mourned very deeply. After a platitudinous paragraph in his letter to Mary about how his father is now resting in the bosom of God and has been reunited with the other dead members of the family, he went straight on with a normal, newsy letter. There is no sign even of any attempt to win her sympathy for his loss, as we might have expected given his behaviour at the time of the deaths of his mother, sister and half-brother.

Gibran changed in Paris. It was, as he later acknowledged, a time of self-discovery.[46] He arrived back in the States on the last day of October 1910 still just as dependent on Mary, but otherwise more self-assured, more confident that the future held great things in store for him. He now felt he had outgrown Boston.

6

The Beacon of Fame

At the very least, Paris gave Gibran some idea of what he had been missing. As soon as he was back in Boston, he began looking for a better studio. It had to be in a better location, away from the South End, yet it had to be cheap enough for Mary to afford to pay the rent, and small enough for Marianna to feel comfortable. Within a few days he had found somewhere suitable, at 18 West Cedar Street, in the Beacon Hill district of Boston.

It is a short walk from the Tyler Street–Oliver Place district of the South End to Beacon Hill. You can stroll across the Boston Common, with the golden dome of the State House beckoning you on towards grander things. The walk takes only twenty minutes, but Gibran's move there was more than just a change from tenement to studio. Beacon Hill was, and is, one of the eminently desirable areas of Boston. There could be no clearer symbol of Gibran's desire to get on. Even today, as you ascend the hill across the Common, you enter a different universe; throughout the summer the South End is discreetly veiled from sight by the trees of the Common. The narrow streets of Beacon Hill still give a distinct impression of age, gentility and privilege, somewhat reminiscent of Kensington in London. It is easy to imagine the streets cobbled. Cars seem an intrusive modernism; at the most horse-drawn carriages should wait under the flowering pears of Pinckney Street, where Thoreau once lived, and where in Gibran's time Fred Holland Day had his *pied à terre*.[1]

Nothing sums up the immensity of the distance Gibran travelled in that twenty minutes better than a story Henry Adams tells in *The Education of Henry Adams*:

> One of the commonest boy-games of winter, inherited directly from the eighteenth century, was a game of war on Boston Common. In old days the two hostile forces were called North Enders and South Enders. In 1850 the North Enders still survived as a legend, but in practice it was a battle of the Latin School against all comers . . . Whenever on a half-holiday the weather was soft enough to soften the snow, the Common was apt to be the scene of a fight, which began in daylight with the Latin School in force, rushing their opponents down to Tremont Street, and which generally ended at dark by the Latin School dwindling in numbers and disappearing. As the Latin School grew weak, the roughs and young blackguards grew strong. As long as snowballs were the only weapon, no one was much hurt, but a stone may be put in a snowball, and in the dark a stick or a slungshot in the hands of a boy is as effective as a knife.[2]

Of course, this predates Gibran's move by a fair number of years, and the culture of the South End, at any rate, had changed with immigration, but these rivalries between different parts of a city linger, and, as anyone who has made that twenty-minute walk across the Common will attest, Adams's story remains a perfect symbol of the difference between the two locations – or indeed of that between any two neighbouring urban districts whose youth differ in terms of gentility and street-wisdom.

The incline of the Beacon Hill area affords good light for artists' studios, and 18 West Cedar Street is a tall building on a corner, taller than the trees and unshaded by other houses. When Mary first visited the studio she recorded her impressions. On the wall opposite the door, a yellow tapestry gleamed and shone; on the east wall, against a dark blue tapestry, Gibran had hung the death mask of a beautiful young woman found dead in the Seine; another wall sported a piece of red silk with a Japanese print, and Beethoven's death mask on a piece of oriental linen with embroidered ends. There were also two or three old bits of gilded wood-carving and a small case of books, with a series called 'Masters in Art' the most conspicuous things among them.

So Gibran had set himself up in a perfect Romantic environment, complete with tributes to death and beauty. In other respects, however, the move was a failure. Gibran may have become used to moving in international circles – for instance, he listed six nationalities among his Paris friends[3] – but Marianna was like a fish out of water. Her English was still poor, and so she was trapped within an isolated world, removed from her familiar haunts. With only her brother to talk to, her devotion to him quickly became a nuisance, as she followed him around, and left him little time or space in which to work. With the death of their father, Kahlil was all her family now. For his part, however, he seemed to feel, in a most un-Lebanese fashion, that he had outgrown his family along with much else of his past; at any rate, when he moved to New York a few months later, there is little sign that he found Marianna too difficult to discard.

The intensity of his epistolary feelings for Mary climaxed in the note he wrote her from New York on landing from Europe – 'I must see you before seeing other faces. O, you are so near now.' He was lonely in Boston; she was the only familiar face, and they fell into the habit of meeting two or three times a week. Perhaps they would visit a museum or go to the theatre together; more typically, he came round for dinner, or after dinner, either alone or to meet other friends of hers. His Paris pictures arrived early in November and she had several of them hanging in her rooms; he would explain them to her guests. Several times he read Swinburne aloud to her – no doubt as a way of improving his English pronunciation, as well as of sharing his favourite poet. She commonly lapsed into a teacherly mode where his English was concerned.

Less than six weeks pass in this fashion, with Mary's diary recording little more than the bare externals of their life together, with one long entry in which he told her about his family. Her entry for 10 December therefore comes as a bombshell. They spent most of the day together, partly at the museum, and then in the evening: 'K. . . . told me he loved me and would marry me if he could.' It is hard to gauge her response as written down in her diary: 'I said my age made it out of the question.' She certainly valued his friendship, because she explained to him, with uncommon good sense, that she did not want to 'spoil a good friendship for a poor love-affair'.[4]

She made it clear, then, that she did not love him, but wanted him as her friend. What thoughts must have passed through her mind that night? Perhaps she reckoned that friendship was as good a basis for a lasting relationship as any; perhaps her age – 10 December was the eve of her thirty-seventh birthday – was a factor in making her change her mind. At any rate, the next day, as she recorded in a single sentence appended to the previous diary entry, Kahlil came to visit in the afternoon, before her party, and she told him that she would marry him. It would prove to be an ambiguous birthday present to herself, in the sense that it would initiate years of agonizing over what she refers to in her journals as the 'sex-question', and then, later, an extended period of self-chastisement over the pain she feels, with Gibran's encouragement, that she has caused him.

They do not appear to have shown any immediate reaction. Mary did not talk in her diaries and journals about her feelings as a fiancée, and there was no sign of the kind of conversations one might expect about their future together. Nor was there any indication that they told their friends. It is as if they felt unsure of themselves, or perhaps things had been left completely open-ended: 'We'll get married *some day*.' The only sign of an increase of intimacy was that they now saw each other pretty much every day. Mary continued to record his visits – or, in one instance, his deliberate absence: on 14 December she was expecting Micheline from New York, so Kahlil stayed away – and the trivia of their lives together. We read about which plays they visited, whom he drew, where he went for models, and so on. He suffered from his usual winter flu, and she worried about his unhealthy habits of smoking and heavy coffee-drinking. She arranged for him to meet and draw people like Charles Eliot, the famous ex-president of Harvard University who had instituted the elective system whereby students could choose from a wide range of courses. She helped him compose letters to Sarah Bernhardt, for instance, whom he wanted to draw for his Temple of Art. She continued to behave more like his patron than his fiancée.

This is what seems to have been happening. During his time in Paris, Gibran built up an intense longing for the absent Mary – so much so that, he told her later, he decided two months before leaving Paris that he would ask her to marry him.[5] But this intensity of feeling was one-sided: Mary cared for him, but not at all in that kind of way. Since this is the 1900s, and since Gibran was always reserved about emotional display, he had failed to communicate his feelings to her, and their relationship had entered a comfortable routine. In the first place, then, Mary had little warning of his declaration of 10 December; in the second place, they found it hard to break out of the habitual pattern of their relationship and begin the work of reconstructing it as something else, something more.

However, in January 1911 a slightly more emotional note occasionally creeps in. Mary remarked, for instance, that she was beginning to care for him more. However, it is far from clear to what extent they showed their feelings for each other. In an entry in the Memoranda section at the end of her diary for this period, Mary chided herself for being undemonstrative, and even though on 7 January in the main diary she recorded that she cared for Gibran, in this Memoranda section she added a note for this day that she restrained herself. There is still a distinct feeling of distance between them. They behaved more like good friends than a potential married couple. They shared their enthusiasm for Francis Thompson's poetry, discussed politics and the Arabic language – that kind of thing. The reason for this hesitancy is at last revealed at the end of January. They had been talking about the possibility of her sending him to Paris again, and on 28 January she elaborated the idea. She wanted him to go to Paris for a couple of years as a kind of test of his feelings for her. Though he told her that he was absolutely certain, and needed no such test, it is clear that she was not sure of the wisdom of their engagement. And on the same evening he told her that if she said to him that they should not marry, he would accept it. These hardly sound like the words of a passionate lover. What kind of lover seeds an escape-route in his partner's mind?

Moreover, a couple of weeks earlier, on 12 January, they had talked, apparently in the abstract, about marriage – but of course no conversation about marriage could be entirely abstract under these circumstances. So when Kahlil asserted, in the context of a discussion about happy marriages, that he believed happiness to be a rare experience, it must have set up some weird vibrations in the room. He almost seems to accept that she does not love him: if there is understanding between a couple, he says, everything else will fall into place. Later he even went so far as to say that understanding, rather than love, ought to be the basis of a marriage – though he admits, when pressed, that he would want to see love present in his own marriage.[6] All this is oddly dispassionate. Mary too seems to have done her best to put up barriers against marriage. Apart from her age, she made sure that he knew of her other financial commitments – that as well as supporting him, she was also giving money to Charlotte, Micheline and several others. She told him that these commitments would prevent their marrying for at least two years.[7]

The apparent coolness of their relationship was offset by a cosy evening on 3 February when they told each other about their past love affairs. For his part, he told her of three previous affairs.[8] Despite the strange nature of their relationship, in the middle of February she told Charlotte that she and Kahlil planned to get married when they could. Charlotte, apparently, was pleased: 'She said she had hoped since she saw him in Paris that it might be.'[9] So perhaps Gibran had revealed something of his feelings to Charlotte in Paris – the feelings he left Mary only to guess at in his letters. Charlotte, however, seems to have been the only other person to know about their engagement. Mary's sister Louise guessed that something was going on, and Mary wanted to tell her, but Gibran talked her out of it.[10]

And so the laborious game continued. Early in March they talk about sex, and Gibran reveals himself to be a freethinker: 'I believe the day will come when we shall not have laws about the use of the body in matters of sex.' He doesn't mind about Mary's previous affairs, as long as personal growth came out of it. But at the end of March Mary confides to her diary that she has doubts about their relationship. She doesn't want to give Kahlil up, but at the same time she doesn't want to give up work either. She doesn't want a plain, ordinary life, but one filled with adventure. For instance, she loves going on hiking and camping trips, but he had told her that he felt himself too frail to join her on them; perhaps he was embarrassed that, as they discovered, she could run faster than him. She had always wanted someone physically strong as a husband. Moreover, she still worries about her age: there isn't enough time for them to have several children, or possibly any. Besides, Kahlil had told her on 1 March that he didn't think he was strong enough to tolerate children. Maybe she should just devote herself to work. She wonders whether he goes through such agonies of doubt and self-analysis, or whether it is her age that makes her worry. 'Sometimes,' she says, 'he seems a stranger, sometimes even an actual foe, and I'm so hostile!'[11]

The conclusion is plain to anyone reading Mary Haskell's journals and diaries. She did not love Gibran enough to marry him. And so she decided, on 14 April, to tell him that she would not be his wife – that it would be a 'blunder' for them to get married. She told him the next day. At first he was shocked and turned pale, but she talked for a long time, explaining that she felt there were greater things in store for him than marriage to her. She told him that she did now feel genuine passion and desire for him, but that her age was for her an insurmountable barrier. They wept together in silence for a long time, and eventually he left, saying, 'You've given me a new heart tonight.' Over the next few days she became reconciled to the idea of not living with him: 'It hurts! But it's right.' In fact, she felt that her rejection of him as a husband had brought them even closer together, and would enable him to grow as an artist and as a man. She even told him only two days later that she hoped he would marry some day.[12] Kahlil, however, refused to discuss her rejection. This worried her a bit, but she interpreted it as signifying that he knew she was right, and that in fact he never really wanted to marry her. She was consoled by the thought that they loved each other, although not in a marrying way – not in a sexual way. Theirs was a deep, loving friendship, and that was more than enough. Gibran agreed with her, spoke of the last veil between them having been dropped, and said that all along he had been afraid of marriage.[13] However, this is far from the end of the story: as it turned out, they talked of the possibility of marriage and sex on and off for another few years.

She was wrong, though, about his silence, and he was being hypocritical, or perhaps reassuring, in agreeing with her that their union was now more complete than if they had had sex or been married. His silence hid suffering and a seething sense of having been wronged, which developed into a long-held grudge against Mary for her behaviour during these early months of 1911. Some years later, something triggered a six-month period of recrimination, when Kahlil told her how much she had hurt him – tortured him, he says – at the time, and she chastised herself in front of him and in the pages of her journals for her 'brutality'. All this makes unpleasant reading in the journals, because he rubbed salt in her wounds whenever she gave him the opportunity, which was virtually every time they met in the second half of 1915. The dialogue continued by letter too. He went on and on about it. He told her that she would say hurtful things to his face, then apologize by letter . . . and then do it all over again the next time they met. Like a spoiled child, he felt that she singled him out for cruel treatment, while being gracious to all the rest of her friends. But with forced magnanimity, he pretended to place all the pain she caused him in the context of the fact that he was born to suffer, and had grown great through suffering.[14]

Meanwhile, to return to 1911, what of Gibran's work? His regime, Mary reported, was that he worked for six hours a day, and then read and wrote letters or visited the library.[15] In this period – inevitably, since it is straight after Paris – most of his work was painting. He produced works with titles like 'Contemplation' and 'Weariness', and a number of portraits. He took models where he could find them – especially his sister and cousins, Mary's friends and relations – and added the actor David Bispham to the Temple of Art series. Mary clearly relished and felt comfortable with the role of his business manager: she introduced him to useful people, and helped him compose letters to Isabella Stewart Gardner, for example, whose patronage or interest could open many doors for him. It seems as though Mary was more comfortable in this role than as Gibran's lover or future wife. She rejoiced to see him growing in confidence in his work with colour and oils, and crowed with delight when doors into society opened for him. In fact, it was precisely such an evening – when she introduced him to some people called Greene, and they promised to arrange further introductions for him – that made her predict a great future for Gibran, and feel that she would impede him if they were married. That was the evening when she finally came to the decision not to marry him.

One painting Gibran was working on at the time started life as an imaginative portrait of Orpheus, but for lack of a male model ended as a Sappho. Mary and he, however, familiarly called the figure 'Rose Sleeves', after the colour of her flowing gown. This picture came to be one of Mary's favourites, and always occupied a prominent position in her collection of Gibran's works. Objectively, it is not a great painting – it is an immature study in oils – but Mary was fond of it perhaps because she had been involved throughout the period of its gestation and birth, and because it reminded her of this delicate and emotional phase of their lives. Since it is no more than a portrait of a woman in a robe, with no symbolical title, she may also have taken it to herald a trend she welcomed, that of an increasing streak of realism in Gibran's work, which she saw as a sign of maturity.[16] He was particularly pleased with a portrait of Charlotte, which he described as 'my first picture as far as technique is concerned'. Generally, though, he confessed to a weakness in portraiture: 'I am too much in love with my own self – my inner conception. I must learn to look only upon what I see.'[17]

He was also writing a little. On 12 January 1911 he presented Mary with another Arabic poem dedicated to her, called 'We and You', in which 'We' are the poets, enlightened by sorrow, and 'You' are the masses, trapped by attachment to an unthinking materialism, the killers of Jesus and Socrates. This poem had been published late the previous year in *Mir'at al-Gharb* rather than *Al-Mohajer*, since Gibran's main contact at *Al-Mohajer*, Amin Goryeb, had returned to Lebanon in 1909. But Najib Diab, the editor of *Mir'at al-Gharb*, was eager to pick up where Goryeb had left off.

His sojourn in Paris had not harmed his reputation in the Arabic world. He had continued to produce occasional pieces, and his fame had spread as a result of his published books. On 27 January, when Mary teasingly asked him if he thought he could write poetry as well as Francis Thompson, he denied it, but added, with a blush, that even when he was 19 years old his writing had been compared to that of D'Annunzio. Now that he has read D'Annunzio, he says, he realizes that the comparison is exaggerated, but he still feels that he has already done some work that will survive – though he also feels that the best is yet to come. He is never satisfied with anything he has written, and is always trying to do better.

His fame within the American Syrian community was starting to gain him invitations as a speaker. On 19 November 1910 he lectured to the Syrian Student Club, and on 25 February 1911 he spoke at the Boston branch of the Golden Links Society (*Al-Halaqat al-*

Dhahabiyah), recommending that Syria try to solve her own problems, without relying on Turkey or any other greater power. Just as a man must first learn to stand on his own two feet before he can make a mark in his community, so Syria must look to her own resources in order to become established in the community of nations. Next he harangued his audience with the argument that they should not expect American citizenship automatically to alleviate their problems, and should be wary of the promises of the American state, since all states were corrupt. They should put aside the petty squabbles of Druze versus Maronite, Christian versus Muslim, and the allegiances they inherited from their homeland, and each man should look to his own resources to make good in America.

At the end of April 1911 he lectured to a Syrian gathering in New York in a far quieter mood, taking as his theme the idea that art enlarges and ennobles our lives. This position of authority within the Syrian community in America would continue and grow all his life, until he became their spokesman and idol. For Syrians in America, as for those in the home country, Gibran was a symbol of what was possible: an immigrant who made good not at trade or some kind of business (there were a number of Syrian immigrants who were extremely successful in the commercial field), but on his own, in literature, and eventually in English literature, winning international stardom.

The irrepressible Charlotte, bubbling with news of New York and Theosophy, came to Boston for a prolonged visit in February. Her stay this time cemented her relationship with Kahlil. She sat for him at length, and he enthused to Mary – perhaps not with great tact – about the current that flowed between them.[18] She and Kahlil also confirmed each other in their belief in reincarnation, and he told them, with extraordinary confidence, about his past lives: 'Twice in Syria – short lives only; once in Italy till I was 25; in Greece till 22; in Egypt till an old, old age; several times, maybe six or seven in Chaldea; once in India; and in Persia once – all as a human being. I don't know anything about my lives before then.' In response Charlotte and Mary speculated that Gibran was Rossetti and Blake reborn. Working on a naïve theory of reincarnation, they found significance in the fact that Blake died in 1827, while Rossetti was born in 1828, and that Rossetti in turn died in 1882, while Gibran was born in 1883.[19]

Gibran also entertained them by inducing a trance state. He claimed to have discovered recently that he could separate his astral body from his physical body and enter a realm in which 'truths about the biggest things were given me in simpler, clearer forms than I had ever known them', though he didn't remember anything when he came back. The women were fascinated, of course, and they persuaded him to induce this trance state then and there, so that they could question him and see what great truths he was able to transmit to them. The results were so vague and disappointing, however, that Charlotte seemed to doubt the authenticity of the state, but, when pushed, fell back and said that he shouldn't misuse this gift. All that Mary recorded about the results was: 'Questioning got little – except that we saw a round light and heard music. Felt soothed after it and then like dancing.' On leaving the trance state, Gibran dramatically gave a sort of shudder and looked around as if everything in the room were strange. He continued experimenting with this trance state for some time, to see if he could bring back any great truths, but nothing happened and he discontinued the practice some time in the summer of 1911. Mary seems to have felt uneasy about the trances, however, and in April she persuaded Kahlil to let her talk to Dr Morton Prince about them. Prince was a very eminent Boston 'alienist', the author of works such as *The Dissociation of a Personality: A Biographical Study in Abnormal Psychology* (1908), whose pioneer work on dissociation, including the phenomenon of mediumship (or channelling, as it is now known) is receiving some attention once more, in the 1990s, in the context of the new outbreak of Multiple Personality Disorder. However, it is not clear that she ever did consult Dr Prince, or if so what came of it. Probably she did not, because by April they had other things on their minds.[20]

Charlotte's visit also stirred up Gibran's restless feeling that he had outgrown Boston. He found it unexciting and restrictive, and he was often somewhat depressed in the first months of 1911.[21] New York was stimulating, New York was the place to be. He wrote to Huwayyik that he felt himself to be in exile in Boston.[22] As early as November 1910 Charlotte was writing to Mary about the then purely hypothetical possibility of Gibran coming to live in New York. At some stage this vague possibility became a probability: Mary clearly offered to pay the rent on a studio in New York if Gibran could find a suitable one. This was an important moment: without New York, Gibran would never have come to the attention of the wider world, and his move to New York would have been impossible without Mary. Therefore, Gibran – and any of his readers who appreciate his work – are utterly indebted to Mary Haskell.

Gibran was ecstatic, especially when Mary also offered to persuade Charlotte to sit for him again, in his own studio in New York. The idea brought him close to tears.[23] Charlotte told them that he could stay in her flat while he looked for a studio (she was due to be away touring with a repertory group, as one of their lesser actresses), and the whole trip also coincided with the talk he was due to give to some Syrians in New York on 29 April.

Now, there are some peculiarities here. In the first place, Gibran seems prepared to sacrifice his sister Marianna, who clearly doted on her elder brother, to his ambition, which required him to be in New York. He resolved this difficulty when on 17 April Mary promised to look after Marianna – which in effect meant having her round for dinner once in a while, and probably supporting her financially. The second oddity is how Gibran squared his planned departure to New York with his profession of love for Mary and desire to marry her. The two things were going on together. Mary's journal for 6 April, for instance, is filled with the prospect of Kahlil going to live in New York – but this is nine days before she told him that she didn't want to marry him. Perhaps Gibran was expecting her to give up her school and come to New York with him. In conversation with Marianna Gibran on 17 April she seems to imply that she had considered it.

Taking all with all – the curious lack of passion in their relationship, and now his plans to leave her in Boston – it seems to me that the most likely scenario is this. Their 'engagement' was never formalized. The understanding was – until she broke it off – that they would get married one day. Mary was waiting for her admiration for her talented protégé to develop into passion and love, and Kahlil was waiting for her to free herself from her other obligations and commit herself wholeheartedly to him. Once Mary began to think that she would hold him back – that he needed to be in New York to make a name for himself – she withdrew her commitment to marriage, and immediately helped firm up his plans for going to New York.

And so, at the end of April, Kahlil Gibran left Boston for New York. He was to return often – especially to see his sister and Mary – but the city which had fostered his youthful artistic strivings was no longer his home. Condemned to an immigrant slum ghetto on his arrival in Boston in 1895, and considered exotic throughout his efforts to break out of this mould and into wider society, Gibran was finally acknowledged as one of Boston's favoured sons in 1977.

Copley Square is the very heart of Boston. Surrounded by the Boston Public Library and other architectural delights, old and new, the pavements, patches of lawn, and fountains into which tourists superstitiously throw small change have so far received the addition of only two monuments. As a runner, I was fascinated by the memorial of the Boston marathon, set into the pavement, recording every winner since its inception in 1897. The only other monument is a raised pink-marble plinth on the pavement directly opposite the entrance to the imposing library. On the plinth is a bronze plaque engraved: 'Kahlil Gibran 1883–1931, poet, painter.' A young Gibran, with hair swept back off his high forehead in the style he favoured in Paris, and hand resting on forehead in thoughtful artistic pose, rests his other hand on a volume entitled *The Prophet*. Beside him are the boughs of a Lebanese cedar tree. This bronze plaque is the work of Kahlil Gibran the younger, a sculptor and a resident of Boston. Inscribed in the marble next to the plaque are the proud civic words: 'Kahlil Gibran, a native of Besharri, Lebanon, found literary and artistic sustenance in the Denison Settlement House, the Boston Public Schools and the Boston Public Library. A grateful city acknowledges the greater harmony among men and strengthened universality of spirit given by Kahlil Gibran to the people of the world in return.' On the front of the plinth is a quote from Gibran: 'It was in my heart to help a little because I was helped much.'

It is not difficult to see why Gibran was prepared to give up the daily presence of the woman he found such a source of strength, apparently, and to abandon his sister. On 4 June, while Mary was visiting him for the first time in New York, he told her: 'I'm hungry to establish myself in America. Eventually I must be in New York. This is the city where pictures are made and sold.' Gibran always was highly ambitious: he once wrote to his friend and editor Amin Goryeb of his feeling that 'I came to this world to write my name upon the face of life with big letters.'[24] Besides, as a result of occasional visits, he already knew people from the Syrian community there, which was larger and more important than in Boston, and they knew him through his writings for their newspapers, whose offices were in New York, and through his books. Influential friends like Amin Goryeb had been encouraging him to come to New York for years, telling him that his future lay there. Whereas in 1908 he had told Goryeb that the presence of a 'she-angel' – Mary – kept him in Boston, there was now nothing to detain him: he had offered her lifelong partnership, and she had refused.

New York was undoubtedly the place for an ambitious young man to be. The closest we can get to understanding the expansive spirit of the times is to think of the late 1960s. Revolution was in the air. The suffragette movement was gathering pace, while Emma Goldman and Margaret Sanger were preaching free love and birth control respectively. Socialists such as Bill Haywood were convinced that they were going to change the face of American society for ever, just as critics such as Gertrude Stein were sure that Cubism was going to sweep away all forms of realism in art for good. In a fascinating book, historian and literary critic Martin Green perceptively focused his account of the times on two events in 1913 – the Armory Show which introduced the American public to the latest trends in European art,[25] and the Paterson Strike Pageant, which displayed the claims of the working man from the palace of Madison Square Gardens. Those at the cutting edge of New York society, such as Mabel Dodge, were involved in both projects.

And this was the beginning of the heyday of Greenwich Village. Its charm and quaintness attracted those with taste but little money. Here art and politics became fused or confused: both bohemians and radicals were convinced that America was on the eve of a renaissance – the one group favouring a revolution in individual consciousness, the other social change. As Richwine puts it: 'Socialism, free love, anarchism, free verse, poetry and politics were all the same cause to most of the Villagers.'[26] It would take the war to blunt the edge of their ardour and to separate the two strands of politics and art.

The Village was alive and buzzing. There was the Liberal Club at 137 MacDougal Street, proclaiming itself, with deliberately broad vagueness, 'a meeting-place for those interested in new ideas'. In its brief history it attracted many of the movers and shakers of Village life. The values of the time included self-expression and psychological adjustment (Freudian ideas were popular), paganism and living for the moment, liberty and female equality. Art was considered to have socially redemptive power, in the sense that it could give people new values, and then those people would create a new social order.[27] James Oppenheim's magazine *The Seven Arts* was subtitled 'An Expression of Artists for the Community'; the first issue, published in November 1916, contained the following editorial:

It is our faith and the faith of many, that we are living in the first days of a renascent period, a time which means for America the coming of that national self-consciousness which is the beginning of greatness. In all such epochs the arts cease to be private matters: they become not only the expression of the national life but a means to its enhancement. Our arts show signs of this change. It is the aim of *The Seven Arts* to become a channel for the flow of these tendencies: an expression of our American arts which shall be fundamentally an expression of our American life. We have no tradition to continue: we have no school of style to build up. What we ask of the writer is simply self-expression without regard to current magazine standards. We should prefer that portion of his work which is done through a joyous necessity of the writer himself.

Of course, not everyone was swept away in the excitement of the times. Don Marquis, best remembered nowadays for his comic *archy and mehitabel* poems, wrote a savage satire which was first serialized and then published in book form in 1916. *Hermione and Her Little Group of Serious Thinkers*, in a mixture of poetry and prose, introduces us to Hermione and her group of 'Advanced Women' who hear lectures from the Swami Brandranath (an obvious caricature of Rabindranath Tagore, who had received the Nobel Prize for Literature in 1913 and made a triumphant tour of America in 1916). His subjects include the cosmos, transmigration of souls, and meditation ('seeking the Silences'). Hermione and her group use a lot of muddled Freudian terminology; they are opposed to materialism, and non-artistic people are called 'Earth People'. They are pacifists, and in favour of Russia because it is so soulful; they read Nietzsche, the *Bhagavad Gita* and some appalling free verse written by Fothergil Finch. Hermione herself frequently gets confused between the Exotic, the Erotic and the Esoteric, though she somehow feels they are all important. The Best People, she is sure, have astral bodies, and she attempts to read auras and discern the sensitivity of plants. They cover each of these and numerous other topics – sex education, Bergson, evolution and so on – in an evening, and yet decry superficiality.

The Village felt itself to be different from the rest of the country – in the forefront of thinking. As a symbol of its difference, 'On the evening of 23 January 1917, six people climbed the Washington Square Arch and proclaimed the Village an independent republic. They held a picnic and a bonfire there, and hung Chinese lanterns and red balloons; and, accompanied by the firing of toy pistols, Gertrude Smith . . . read aloud a declaration of independence.'[28]

This, then, in brief, was the Village in which Kahlil Gibran found himself at the end of April 1911, ensconced in Charlotte's flat at 164 Waverley Place. Gibran settled in, made himself known to his Syrian friends – especially Amin Rihani, who was now living in New York – and began both to look for a suitable studio and to sample the energy of New York. Within days he was making useful contacts. Mary's old friend, the composer Arthur Farwell, introduced him to the galleries of the art dealers, while Rihani arranged for him to illustrate his *The Book of Khalid*, which was due out later in the year.[29] He and Rihani became almost inseparable, with Gibran nurturing the admiration for the older man he had developed in Paris.

Everything about New York delighted Gibran and, caught up in the excitement of the spirit of the times, he was filled with a sense that he belonged there, and would flourish and prosper. His letters to Mary in Boston were ecstatic. 'I gaze with thousand eyes and listen with thousand ears all through the day.'[30] He loved the Metropolitan Museum, thanked her for sending him more money, dreaded a dinner-party organized by Salloum Mokarzel, an important Syrian editor, at which he was to meet the Turkish ambassador; the party turned out to be 'wonderful', of course, though he expressed sorrow that Syria was a Turkish province. He drew Farwell for his Temple of Art series, read *Thus Spake Zarathustra* in English, and established himself in the Syrian community. Mary's letters to him are mostly lost, but they appear to have been bright, breezy and filled with news, though she must have felt strange after their almost daily contact in Boston.

Saturday 6 May could serve as a typical day. He drew Rihani and considered it the best work he had done since returning from Paris. Micheline came for a visit and they renewed their acquaintance. Then some Syrian friends arrived and talked incessantly until Gibran had to ask them to leave, so that he could prepare for going out to give a talk at some Syrian club on 'The Destiny of Nations'. The talk went so well that they wanted him to give another one the next week. Gibran concluded: 'I wish I was more than one Kahlil!'[31]

Charlotte returned on 15 May, having left the repertory tour early, so Gibran moved into a small room at 28 West 9th Street, where Rihani was staying. Although the room was not as suitable for work, Gibran continued as busy as ever. He began another painting of Charlotte, met and drew both Richard Le Gallienne and the poet Edwin Markham – and each meeting led to further contacts, such as Charles Edward Russell, the eminent socialist who stood, unsuccessfully, for both the governorship of New York and the US Senate. Gibran's world was truly expanding fast. After the restrictions he had felt in Boston, he felt free and expansive. In a 1920 letter to Mikhail Naimy he said of Boston: 'The souls of its inhabitants are petrified.'[32] He undoubtedly felt no such thing about New Yorkers.

Mary came to New York on 1 June for an extended visit. The three friends – Kahlil, Mary and Charlotte – opened their circle to admit Rihani too, whom Kahlil had introduced to Charlotte a few days earlier. However, the evening the four of them first met was not a success. In a fit of childlike enthusiasm, they decided to dress up. The women wore finery and make-up, while the men dressed in Syrian clothing. This created an artificial atmosphere, and although in units of two or three they remained firm friends, and even lovers, the foursome was never attempted again.[33]

Charlotte left on 5 June to visit her family in Denver, and for the next five days Mary and Kahlil explored New York together. They visited museums and saw the sights, discovered Gonfarone's, which was to remain their favourite restaurant together for many years, read together and, as usual, he sketched for her. She recorded how well he looked, and how obviously he was thriving on New York life. He found a studio to rent during the summer, so that he could move out of the room where he was staying, which was so small and dark that for painting and drawing he had to impose on Rihani and make use of his room.

They also, of course, talked endlessly. Most of their conversations have the flavour of two people still getting to know each other – for instance, Mary explained to him at length her views on friendship and why Charlotte was so important to her. Occasionally, they talked more impersonally, and in the spirit of the Village, about 'the Absolute' and how beautiful a man was when he truly expressed himself. One of their conversations concerned money and wills. Mary told him that she had left him $5,000 in her will, but now wanted to give him the whole amount immediately. He protested, but eventually accepted the money, because he didn't want to sell his pictures now, before he had made enough of a name for them to fetch their proper value. In return he offered to leave her all his pictures in his will, and on 16 June he drafted just such a will, a copy of which Mary kept in her journal. He left her all his pictures and money, while leaving his literary work to either Marianna or Amin Goryeb. Most of his personal effects went to his sister also, while his body was to be buried in his home town, Bsharri. It might seem strange (or far-sighted) for a 28-year-old to be making a will, but Gibran told Mary – with unerring prophecy – that he felt he would live for only fifteen or twenty more years, while she would live to be more than seventy.[34]

When Mary returned to Boston, Gibran followed her shortly, to spend time with his sister, and to holiday with Fred Holland Day in Maine. But Mary left for her usual vigorous summer trip to the California wilderness on 18 June, while Kahlil divided his time between Boston and New York, revising his book *The Broken Wings* (despite feeling that he had outgrown it), illustrating Rihani's *The Book of Khalid*, completing Charlotte's portrait, which was now called 'Isis', and working on other pictures too. He worked hard all summer, interrupted by brief holidays with Marianna and Day, and by a bout of flu. He and Mary met again briefly in Boston in mid-September when Mary returned from the West, but then Gibran returned to New York to put more serious effort into finding a viable studio.

It is very hard to assess the precise nature of their relationship at this time. There are copious expressions of closeness – for instance, when he is alone in New York, Gibran claimed to summon Mary's presence before beginning any piece of work – but at the same time one gets the distinct impression that the distance between Boston and New York was matched by a certain emotional distance between the two of them. I don't mean that they were not getting on, but that they were still uncertain of each other. They no longer had the formality of future marriage between them – though Charlotte was urging Mary to work on Kahlil to renew his offer, which she was then to accept – and they were not lovers in a sexual sense. Their conversations and letters, and Mary's record in her journals, veer between warm friendship and the relationship of a patron and a protégé. She gave him money, bought him clothes, recorded in an almost maternal fashion how well he looked and his achievements, and at the same time they were each the other's 'dearly beloved' in their letters.

It didn't take Gibran long on his return to New York in the last couple of weeks of September to find himself a studio. The one he had taken for the summer was at 51 West 10th Street, a purpose-built block of artists' studios, and another one – number 30, which had a balcony – soon became vacant. He snapped it up, and wrote triumphantly to Mary that he had found a 'little, humble studio' for $20 a week. She wanted him to find somewhere better and grander, but he said that the light was adequate, and that it would be good enough for the time being.

The red-brick block of artists' studios at 51 West 10th Street, between the Avenue of the Americas and 5th Avenue, was known simply as 'the Studio Building'. Said to be the first building in New York built especially for artists, it was demolished in the early 1950s, despite considerable protest from Village historians and residents, to make way for an upmarket apartment block. This is the north end of

Greenwich Village: the shops are slightly seedy, but plenty of older buildings remain on the opposite side of the street and the area as a whole has a somewhat genteel, old-fashioned feel to it, like certain parts of Bloomsbury in London.

Gibran returned to Boston to pack up his belongings and arrange for them to be shipped to New York. Boston had one last treat to offer him. On 28 September he and Mary went to the Drama League to hear W. B. Yeats talk on Synge, and they were invited backstage afterwards by a friend of Mary. Gibran wangled an appointment with Yeats to draw him for his Temple of Art series, and this meeting took place on 1 October. It is a good drawing and it was much admired by Yeats's friend Lady Gregory, who also sat for Gibran a couple of weeks later, since she was in Boston too with the Irish Players, the group formed by herself and Yeats. She also gave him two tickets for the Irish Players, which he and Mary made use of on their last evening together. Then Gibran was off to New York.

He had successfully disentangled himself from Boston. The beacon of fame summoned him to New York. Wanting to escape from his role as 'Romantic Eastern prodigy', he made the mistake many others have before and since of thinking that geographical distance can create psychological influence. It was not so easy to shake off the conditioning he had received from Fred Holland Day. But he reassured Mary that, despite the move, he did want their relationship to continue, and repeated that however many miles there were between them she was always present when he worked, as his inspiration and guiding light and invisible critic.[35] He described the nature of their relationship as 'friendship mixed with passion'.[36] They wept together a bit at the prospect of his departure, but they got on so well together in the course of Gibran's final two weeks in Boston that something must have seemed permanent between them. One of the most important things that happened between them concerned a new oil painting of his which he gave her. A solitary figure, naked but of indeterminate sex, stands alone in a bleak, turbulent landscape, with its hands on the back of its head in a gesture of pain. Mary christened the painting 'The Beholder' and wrote him a four-page interpretation of it, with which he was delighted. Mary recorded his reaction as follows: 'I want to say that this will enable me to paint pictures. It sets one free to work and gives one confidence, when one knows that what he does will be so understood. And it is very wonderful to be understood in one's innermost.'[37]

Even a miserable dinner-party she gave only brought them closer together, since, as she put it, she realized how different he was from other people, and how he had gradually won her away from their world and closer to his. Gibran, trying out a new role, pontificated – 'I'm afraid most people live in the little things' – and told her how much it hurt him to see people do so. Before long this pontificating will become second nature to him, as his confidence increases in New York and adulation comes his way. Previously Mary has been his single close fan, but in New York many more were waiting. Gibran, ambitious and longing to be loved, would revel in it, and discard those who did not pay him what he felt was his due.

7

Mother Mary

By the end of 1911, the pattern of the relationship between Kahlil and Mary was fixed into the groove it was to occupy for much of the next twelve years. They would meet several times a year, for longer or shorter periods, either when she travelled to New York or when he came to Boston. These visits often happened around other events: in late November or early December each year, for instance, Mary came to New York for the Head Mistresses' Association Meeting, and she also stopped off on her way west for her annual summer holiday. During these visits she stayed with Charlotte, or occasionally Micheline, or, if neither of them was free, at a boarding-house. She and Kahlil would meet, exchange news and views, visit a museum, take a ride on a bus, and walk in Central Park with its litter, muddy lake and bullfrogs. They used to eat out at Child's, or one of the cheaper restaurants (Gonfarone's was a favourite), rather than at Delmonico's or Martin's or Moretti's. They might frame some pictures or go over some of his latest compositions. Gibran tended to go to Boston in the summer on his way to a friend's house on the coast – wherever he had been invited that year – and he usually went around Christmas and the New Year as well. On these Boston visits, he would spend alternate days with Mary and Marianna.

Nor was it just the external pattern that became fixed: the emotional and psychological dynamics of their relationship also rapidly came to occupy a small, and in certain respects stifling, spectrum. Given the centrality of Mary to Gibran's life, it is worth spending some time over certain features of their relationship. Despite the physical distance between them, Mary's devotion to Gibran only increased over the next few years. Her journals constantly apply to him adulatory epithets; she marvels (and worries) at the amount of work he does, seeing him as a higher being who is being used by the gods to bring forth a body of work for the benefit of future generations, even though the present generation may not appreciate him. She reflects on how much greater than her he is and how much she has to grow to understand him. These are constant threads in her journals, particularly up to about 1915; after then, they become somewhat rarer.[1] Here are some examples: 'O Glorious Kahlil!! Transcendent, timeless spirit!' 'To him . . . who gives the Absolute a voice.' 'He is truth itself and able to discern reality; therefore he speaks truth and reveals Reality.' 'Americans don't yet know that K. is *very great*.' 'He is *seeing* and *creating the future – and destroying the dead things in the present*.' 'The strongest being I [have] ever known . . . All that power, that passion, that sensitiveness, that beauty, crowded through one small living being into form! I wonder whether K. as the gods' creation may not need to resist the gods' zeal in using him.' 'I kissed his Hand – the world will be handless when that hand goes.' 'Great, suffering, godlike Kahlil!' 'I felt as if Christ had been sitting [where Kahlil had been] as well as K. – the two friends . . . Kahlil is one of the group that include [*sic*] Christ and Buddha and Michael Angelo and Shakespere [*sic*] and others as great.'[2]

For his part – and there really is no other way to put it – his ego and vanity grow the more she presents herself as his devoted disciple, and over the years as increased success comes his way. There are certain people whose sense of self is so slight that they model themselves not just on others, but on what others believe them to be. Mary Haskell believed Kahlil Gibran to be a Christ-like figure, and as the years went by he grew into that role, and for her part she adapted herself to it. At times she seems to let herself be a doormat on which he can wipe his anger at her past behaviour, and so far from sticking up for herself, she merely chastises herself mercilessly, agreeing with everything he says.[3] By 1914 she had put herself in a totally passive state in relation to him. She herself admitted this at one point: 'We spoke of my tendency of old to be dependent on K. – something we'd never spoken of before.'[4] She trusted him absolutely to do what was right for them both. If she pushed him at all, even to choose pictures for a possible exhibition, he got irritated and she later found fault with herself for not trusting him.[5] Once, in June 1913, she watched Kahlil treat a visitor – no less a person than the eminent painter and critic Walter Pach – with arrogant rudeness, and she dared to tell him off, which led to an argument – and then to pages and pages of self-recrimination in her journal.[6] She was a clever, active woman – but she was evidently emotionally insecure. 'I felt like a baby being tended by a giant,' she said, after one of their meetings.[7] She recorded more than once his admission that he was domineering – not with her, but in groups: he loved to take them over and be the centre of attention.[8]

Very commonly the pattern of their conversations was that she asked questions and he delivered sententious opinions on everything under the sun, from national characteristics (a recurring topic) to art and poetry and politics. There are too many examples of this to quote: they occur on almost every page of the journals. It should be remembered that Gibran was largely an autodidact, and that such people often come across as pompous and opinionated. She often used to prepare questions for him, based on their latest meeting. He told her things in a preaching fashion, she went away and digested what he had said, and then returned later with further questions, or to tell him how wise and wonderful he was. 'We both knew I had come to tell him what I had been learning that week,' she said, revealingly, at one point.[9] With her permission, he was generally her lord and master, and he took full advantage of the situation.

Particularly upsetting for Mary was the fact that he tried to keep their friendship secret. They used to go out together to museums and restaurants, but he never introduced her to his friends when she came to New York, and he went to great lengths to make sure that they would not be identified in anyone's mind as lovers. So, for instance, he refused to stay with her when he visited Boston, and he would not let her come up to his studio late at night, despite the fact that in her opinion it was a nice 'clean' building where 'no slanders arise' if one stayed late in someone's studio. Of course, he could always argue, with perfect plausibility, that he was doing this for her own sake, so that she should not acquire a reputation as a loose woman, but it still upset her. She was kept in the background. He dedicated poems and books to her, by initial, and inscribed these same initials on some of his paintings, but she was never allowed in person into his circle of friends in New York. Was she then no more to him than a source of income, she asked herself? Didn't she deserve public recognition as his friend and patron? His stifling of her used to make her cry, but she lacked the strength to forge the relationship afresh into something involving a higher degree of empowerment for herself.[10]

An especially irritating (to me) aspect of this syndrome of control is that he does not allow her to have full experiences of her own: if she tells him of something she has felt, or some insight she has gained, he is likely to say: 'Exactly! That's what I meant when I said . . .', and so divert the conversation away from her experience and towards his own. He has always had her insights and experiences first, and better. Here are a few instances. In September 1922 she had an important experience: travelling on the Boston subway she felt she had perceived sheer Existence – the Platonic form, so to speak, not attached to any particular individuals. She was clearly bursting to tell him about it, but he just said, more or less, 'Yes, isn't it wonderful when that happens?' as if it were an everyday occurrence, and then moved the conversation on to other topics. On another occasion she remarked how she found it difficult to attend to all the petty details of life and at the same time 'live in the larger consciousness'. Instead of talking about this important problem in the abstract, or as it related to her, he said, 'That's it! There's the curse of my life!' Once she tried to talk about the not unimportant matter that she was negotiating to buy another school, but he soon diverted the conversation back to himself and his work. She intended to teach herself Arabic so that she could read his work in the original, but he put her off. A particularly clear case occurred on 23 July 1916. She told him how she saw a 'little darkey child'[11] seize her mother's hand with exquisite ecstasy of faith and delight, and it made her wonder why all of us can't trust in God like that every moment. Kahlil immediately seized the opportunity for self-aggrandizement: 'Yes,' he said, 'it is those of us who have done that who have given most to the race.'[12]

Still, no one knows what makes any relationship work. And theirs certainly did seem to work, in its fashion. Their letters to each other are full of expressions of love; they kiss and caress and hold hands and so on when they are together. Although she regretted that he was not more forthcoming with fond expressions,[13] terms of endearment litter the pages of their letters, and tales of tenderness crop up now and again in her journals.[14] And although, as we shall see, Gibran may have taken other lovers, it is certain that Mary didn't. She at any rate found her relationship with Gibran perfectly satisfying for many years. From the outside, and judged by modern standards, the power dynamics seem lopsided, overbalanced in his favour, but since this did not concern her at the time, perhaps we should not dwell on it. It is worth recording, though, that later, after Gibran's death, by which time she had been emotionally separated from him for a number of years, she could look back and tell Mikhail Naimy that by the end of her relationship with Gibran she knew she was being used, but tolerated it in order to support Gibran's career.

But there are more obvious flaws to Gibran's character. For one thing, there is his lying. True, Mary could not be expected to spot some of the worst cases (such as his complete fabrications about his childhood and family), but there are a number of other instances, both glaring and minor, which she might well have been aware of. When he told her, in the winter of 1917, that he had been shot by a Turkish agent in Paris, surely she must at least have wondered why he hadn't told her about this in his letters at the time.[15] Likewise, when in 1918 the publicity for his first English-language book, *The Madman*, boasted that Rodin had described Gibran as the Blake of the twentieth century, she must have known that this was a fabrication, passed on by Gibran to the publisher, because he had written to her from Paris about his meetings with Rodin, and would surely have mentioned such a great compliment. If her memory was good, she might have remembered the different versions of the story of his meeting in Paris with the Maronite bishops.[16] On 25 August 1920, he told her that he was impervious to psychological pain, and so did not remember when people had been unkind to him. She must have remembered how he tortured her, or got her to torture herself, for at least six months by reminding her of how horrible, as he saw it, she had been to him in 1911 – not that she saw it as torture, rather as clearing the air between them; but he was clearly remembering psychological pain. He was always writing to her and others about his bouts of ill health, but then asserted on 20 April 1920 that he didn't think about sickness and health: 'I experience neither to such a degree that it gets a grip on my mind.' Or again, on 10 September 1917 he refused one of a batch of neckties she had bought him, because it had a sheen and he claimed that he didn't like to wear anything that would draw people's attention to him. This is in keeping with his musing aloud on 30 June 1915, that he wished he could wear white, 'but it is so conspicuous . . . I want above all things not to be looked at.' And yet there is a photograph in existence from the late 1910s showing Gibran wearing a gleaming white suit.[17]

There are other trivial cases, such as the question of whether he does or does not read lowbrow fiction – 'trash', as he called it – and whether he can or cannot eat lobster.[18] More curious is the fact that he once admitted to Mary that he did tell lies. 'I've told many lies,' he said, 'and I've felt fears, but I've never been unclean' – by which he meant that he'd never acted out of underhand motives or for 'secret profit'. Yet little over a year later he modestly asserted, 'I'm not wonderful and I'm not good. There's just one thing I am – I'm honest.'[19] On another occasion he told her, 'One may lie to other people, but not to one's self – not all alone, in bed at night, before going to sleep.'[20] But it may be straining to find more than the usual impersonal homily in this case.

A final unappetizing aspect of Gibran's character which sheds light on the nature of his relationship with Mary is the incredibly high assessment he has of himself. It is not just that he regards himself as a great artist and a profound writer: this estimation – which may not even be an over-estimation – is perhaps excusable, since every creative artist has to feel that she has something to offer the world, otherwise she would not put pen to paper, or brush to canvas, in the first place. It is rather the enormity of his self-estimation which is staggering.[21]

Throughout the pages of Mary's journals we read his proud comments on his achievements, and what other people think of him. He loves it, for instance, that some of his friends have gone off the work of the eminent painter Arthur B. Davies, on the grounds that 'When the gods arrive the half-gods go.'[22] We also read that he feels he is capable of mighty things, that he has a 'message' to deliver: however high Mary ascends in estimating his talents, he matches her step for step; however much she feels he has suffered, he prompts her to realize it more and more.[23] He feels he could go alone to a remote spot in Mount Lebanon, and within a month have fifty disciples camping out there just to be near him. The comparison with Christ is irrepressible: Gibran clearly considered himself a prophet as well as a poet.[24] The high points of his full-blown estimation of himself come when he claims to be able to do everything Michelangelo ever did, and to have intuited Einstein's theories of relativity several years before Einstein himself published them.[25] By the 1920s his self-apotheosis occasionally attains bizarre proportions, as when he says, 'Thousands of times I've been drawn up from the earth by the sun as dew, and risen into cloud, then fallen as rain, and gone down into the earth, and sought the sea. And I've blown with the wind, everywhere. I've been rock too, but I'm more of an air person.' Less bizarrely, but no less grandiosely, a few months later he claims: 'Whatever any man or woman does or says, I can understand the motive of it – and more, I can bless it. And I do.' He claimed to have greater insight into the meaning of life and death than the Buddha had, and to have united his consciousness with that of the planet and the universe.[26]

Often, of course, he is not so direct, but when he is criticizing people for their small-mindedness (which, after Edward Carpenter, he likes to call 'local' thinking),[27] we are inevitably supposed to feel that he has risen above such things. Or when he and Mary talk in the abstract about the features of genius, we cannot help thinking that they both feel that his insight into the matter has been gained merely by introspection. It is certainly explicit that when he developed his theory that some individuals express the collective soul of a race, and that they are the race's fathers, while all the others are children, Mary immediately identified him as such a 'race father'; and elsewhere he asserted, with pointed self-reference, that people always resent it when a person can see a little more or a little further than they can.[28] Where the relationship between Mary and Kahlil is concerned, there can surely be only one conclusion: her loving adoration blinded her to these flaws in his character. She hero-worshipped him; he could do no wrong.

These characteristics of Gibran raise some interesting issues. In the first place, the whole syndrome raises questions about Gibran's credibility. We don't expect most categories of writer to live the philosophy or implicit philosophy they promulgate in their books: a thriller writer with a string of macho heroes may be a wimp, for all we care. Things start to get more difficult, however, with philosophers: it is disappointing to find Immanuel Kant arguing for the sanctity and dignity of human life, and yet in his private life supporting the death penalty. The border has definitely been crossed in the case of moralizing preachers such as Gibran. Here we expect, and we have a right to expect, that the teacher will practise what he preaches and speak from his own personal experience. Gibran was well aware of this. As early as 1912 he told Mary: 'I have to live the absolute life, must be what I believe in, practise what I preach, or what I practise and what I preach are nothing.' In *Sand and Foam* he was to write: 'Everything I have imprisoned in expression, I must free by my deeds.' Again, on *The Prophet* in particular, he said: 'In *The Prophet* I have imprisoned certain ideals, and it is my desire to live those ideals . . . Just writing them would seem to me false.'[29] Gibran wrote as if he knew more than others, and certainly presented himself to others as just such a gifted person, even a messiah of some kind. There is indeed, in my opinion, considerable value in his work – and yet it cannot be said that he had risen above the very flaws he counsels others to avoid. 'Truth is the will and purpose of God in man,' he tells us – and yet he lies in his private life.[30] His writings are riddled with glorification of Woman and womanhood – and yet he treats Mary Haskell badly. He even undervalues the importance of personal experience: 'I don't depend on experience for understanding, as you know . . . I can get the life of an experience without actually going through it.'[31] This, to me, explains the hit-and-miss nature of his insights: sometimes he is spot on, sometimes he is too vague. Actual experience is essential in spiritual work of all kinds, because without it speculation is just guesswork. He was, as he and Mary often say, in love with the Absolute, but he did not really know how to go about translating that aspiration into reality.

In the second place, we can delve beneath these and other aspects of Gibran's character, and discover some underlying complex or explanation for them. The following are features, some or all of which indicate the presence of a strong, though not necessarily pathological streak of narcissism in a person. Such a person wants to please people, not to hurt them, and to be appreciated by them. Anyone who shows signs of not appreciating a narcissistic person is rejected, often harshly. Narcissistic people feel vulnerable, and are easily slighted. In consequence, then, they are invariably charming, since they do their best to please people. They are hungry for the acknowledgement from others which feeds their sense of being special.

Creative people are often narcissistic, for obvious reasons: they want their work to be appreciated and fame gives them positive feedback; they have a restless, even hyperactive drive towards external recognition and prestige; they have an awareness of their talents which may give them an inflated sense of self-esteem, particularly in a society which overvalues artistic creativity; and a narcissistic person's desire for recognition gives him the ability to work the hard and long hours required by creative work. Likewise, narcissism is commonly associated with role-playing. 'A feeling of high personal value may result from an identification with the prestige inherent in a collective role.'[32]

Narcissistic people find it hard to empathize with others, because they are too wrapped up in themselves; by the same token, they find it difficult to enter into a full relationship with another person as a living, breathing person, not only because they are self-centred, but because they have a tendency to idealize their partners. The typical childhood environment for a narcissistic personality (and, interestingly, for alcoholics) involves insecurity and a lack of guiding values; the loss of the father or a quick-tempered father; and a devoted mother, who idealizes the child and pins all her hopes for the future on him or her. Men with strong narcissistic tendencies will often look for a mother substitute in female relationships; because they tend to idealize their partners, they may abjure sex altogether.

I am not suggesting that Gibran suffered from pathological narcissism in the strict, clinical sense, but I am suggesting that he had more prominent narcissistic traits than most people. As a matter of fact, it hardly needs much elaboration to demonstrate that the match between Gibran's profile and that of a narcissistic person as listed above is remarkably precise.

We have met Gibran the chameleon, who adapts himself to the

demands of East and West, of Boston literati and Syrian traders. His charm was legendary in New York circles: people described him as 'irresistible', and Claude Bragdon said, 'In any company of his intimates he was the center of a charmed attention.'[33] We have seen that he is capable of taking offence and holding a grudge when he feels slighted. We know that he loved to be loved; once he even makes an archetypally narcissistic comment when he says, 'Other people's interest in our work is the most creative influence we can have'[34] – a statement with which plenty of creative people would disagree. It goes without saying that he was highly creative. His hyperactivity is frequently remarked upon by Mary in her journals, and she takes steps to get him to do something about it.[35] Relatedly, he occasionally expressed dissatisfaction, almost disgust at times, with his earlier work, and felt driven to do more and better.[36] We have found plenty of evidence of what the psychologist Kohut calls the 'grandiose self'. Where role-playing is concerned, we have already seen how the teenaged Gibran was a virtual *tabula rasa* on which Fred Holland Day imprinted the role of melancholic Romantic; in New York, it is clear, he took on the role of prophet or guru. We have seen that he found it hard to empathize with Mary, and easier to divert conversations back to himself. We have noted his tendency to idealize Josephine Peabody. He suffered from precisely the kind of childhood environment which tends to produce a narcissistic personality. His predilection for older women fits in with the narcissist's desire for a mother substitute, and in this context it is perhaps worth mentioning that, of course, Mary Haskell shared a name with the Mother of Christ, who received particularly high regard in the Maronite Church of Gibran's childhood. He once told her he felt like her son.[37]

It might be argued that the tenderness of their relationship shows that Gibran was not narcissistic, at least in the sense that he had the ability to form such a close friendship. However, the only real evidence for this closeness is the number of terms of endearment that occur in his letters to her, and it is legitimate to question the value of these as evidence, since they continue long after their relationship has cooled to a companionable friendship. There are certain watersheds in their relationship. Those relating to their sex life will be considered shortly, but for now it is worth mentioning that in September 1915 they talked about how they had tried to make their relationship personal, but failed. In May 1917 Mary wondered aloud whether she would ever again talk as much with Kahlil as she used to, or he with her, and he said, 'Probably not,' but consoled her with the thought that 'One can be saying a great deal more in silence.' These are important landmarks in a cooling relationship – and yet she was still, constantly, 'Beloved Mary' in his letters, and even as late as April 1922, he could say to her, 'You are a thousand times nearer to me now than you ever were before.'[38]

Mary played a number of roles in Gibran's life – editor, friend, patron, sounding-board for ideas – but one of them was confidante, and several times he comes close to admitting his narcissistic nature. We have already seen that he liked to be the centre of attention. More tellingly, he confessed to her on several occasions, in different ways, how strong the urge was in him to be 'loved and admired and looked up to'.[39] He said that he felt an urge to fulfil the high opinions people had of him,[40] and found odd ways of making himself attractive to others: 'I tell people just what I think now, and they love it. If it makes them suffer they come back again and want to suffer more.'[41]

A considerable number of pages in Mary's diaries and journals are devoted to the question of sex – not just in an impersonal way, but mostly recording conversations she had with Kahlil on the subject, and her own thoughts about their relationship in this respect. Naturally, these entries occur most frequently in the earlier years of their relationship; after all, that was when they came close to marrying. It was unfortunate for Mary that although she was slow to feel physical desire for Gibran – preferring, she admits, a more rugged type of man – she did eventually come to want sex with him, but by then his ardour had cooled.

The topic of sex began to enter their conversations, between themselves or with friends present, in March and April 1911, but they were careful to keep the discussions impersonal. They talked about, and denounced, the social stigma attached to premarital sex; they discussed the nature of lust and chastity. But it should be remembered that at this time they were still engaged to be married, so the subject cannot have been entirely abstract to them. It must have left a charge in the atmosphere.

In December that year they were still talking about sex and marriage as if they were topics unrelated to their own lives, as they would continue to do now and then throughout the years of their friendship.[42] Oddly, however, the topic had definitely become personal by February 1912, several months *after* the ending of their engagement and Gibran's move to New York.[43] On a visit to New York, she passed the night of 18 February in a restless sleep. All her subdued and subliminal pondering on whether she and Kahlil should get married, or should have sex, erupted in a dream in which a voice told her that Kahlil must have all or nothing. The next day, on a visit to his studio as usual, the atmosphere was soft and peaceful, and she offered herself to him. However, this was no wholehearted offer: at the same time she told him that she thought a man a coward if he let a woman be his mistress. Under the circumstances, Gibran hardly had any choice: he made what Mary calls 'the great refusal'. She offered to be his mistress, and he said words to the effect of 'Thanks – but no thanks.'[44]

This was far from being the end of the matter, however. She visited him again over Easter that year and summarized the most important topic of their conversations in an enormous entry in her diary, which begins on the page for 1 March and ends on the page for 20 April. The whole entry is devoted to the issue of their sex life. She is still contemplating being his mistress for his sake. She leaves us in no doubt that this is what *he* wanted: he had told her that he couldn't take another year like 1911 with, as she puts it, 'the extreme pain of complete intimacy of feeling and thought with unceasing inhibitions on expression'. But she protested, on the grounds that this kind of love is 'debasing for him to give and humiliating for me to receive'. She feels the danger of losing everything – that the sexual side of their relationship would inevitably end, and would take with it their friendship and companionship, which she values highly. On the other hand, she argues with herself, his love for her is so much 'more beautiful, more delicate, more understanding and satisfying than that of any other man', that even if becoming his 'paramour' is 'second best', it is still better than anyone else's best, so why not do so? She very nearly wrote a note to Gibran saying that she would be his mistress, but then changed her mind. The letter that she did eventually write, on her return to Boston, made him a different kind of offer: if it was too painful for him to be with her, while she consistently refused sex, then perhaps they should just make a clean break and stop seeing each other altogether. Gibran hastened to reply, somewhat ambiguously, saying at first that of course it did not cause him more pain than pleasure to see her, and then going on to say that pain and pleasure were inseparable anyway. Whatever she was to make of this, he did end with an unambiguous declaration of love for her.[45]

In April Gibran came to Boston, and they had a long heart-to-heart conversation in the Public Gardens, mostly about his past affairs and attitude towards sex. She was, as we will see in the next chapter, worried and not a little jealous about what was going on behind her back in New York. She told her diary that he had always been reserved with her, where physical contact was concerned, and had never explicitly asked her for 'intercourse', though she knew that he desired her. But that evening, when he visited her at home, 'for the first time I knew the peace and sweetness of his touch and his kisses on my body. He caressed me; that was all. But there was an infinite feeling of expansion and freedom of heart now that not even the fastening of my garments said "Thou shalt not".' Afterwards, she felt deeply contented, and mused that perhaps it hadn't been marriage with Gibran she had been wanting all along, but this 'nearness'. She reckons they love each other perfectly as things are, and so she promises to herself to renounce any further thoughts of marriage.

The next night they didn't get the opportunity to pursue the subject further, either by word or deed, because shortly after Gibran had arrived at her house, Mary had an unexpected visit from her brother Adam and his wife. She felt very awkward and hesitated about letting them in, which created an odd atmosphere in the house when she did finally allow them to enter. Gibran told her many years later that this was very painful for him. He felt as if Mary was embarrassed that he was foreign and didn't want him to meet her family for that reason. For him, he said, this was a turning-point, when he decided that he could not marry or be intimate with her, but would have to confine their love to the spiritual plane.[46]

The next day they continued their interrupted discussion, whispering together in the corner of a room in the Boston Public Library. Mary stressed that she would not marry him because of the difference in their ages,[47] but held out the possibility that they might one day have sex. The day after that was Gibran's final day on this highly charged visit to Boston. He came round to her house in Cambridge as usual. What were his thoughts? Had he already made up his mind to keep their affair purely platonic? They are lying together on the sofa, and she tells him that she no longer has any 'injunction' against intercourse, and will accept whatever he chooses. Contrary to their talk the day before about waiting until the time was right, this seems to be a blatant offer. But again he turns her down, saying that he loves her not only for today, but for tomorrow and the next day too. Mary writes her diary now for some unknown future reader: 'So it is that we have never had intercourse. I write all this out because it is so clear to me. And if another eye even than K's sees it I don't care. For it is all to his honor – and I am living refutation of any idea held by anybody of lightness on his part in sex matters or love relations with women.' She is trying to convince herself that there is no foundation to the rumours reaching her from New York that he is having affairs there. She finds it unthinkable that Gibran could so gently and politely refuse her offers of sex and yet be a rake in New York. Unfortunately, of course, this is not good evidence, especially in view of the fact that he may already have decided to confine their love to the spiritual realm.

It was not so easy to calm her restless mind and instincts. In June 1912, when Kahlil was in Boston, she again offered herself to him, saying that she was willing to try a contraceptive method so that they could have sex – but again he refused, on the grounds that the risks of pregnancy were too great.[48] On a visit to New York in September she asked him whether it might be a relief for him to see her married to someone else. He responded to her question with another question: would it in any way disturb the completeness of their mutual understanding? She said that she supposed not, but went on to say that she had sometimes thought of marrying just for companionship, so that she would not end her days solely in the company of women, but now rejected this as a ground for marriage. She told Kahlil that in any case she would not get married until he was successful.[49] For his part he added, on the subject of marriage, that daily life with the same person now seemed unthinkable to him, which must have seemed like a slap in the face to Mary.[50] Nevertheless, throughout the autumn of that year Mary found her desire to marry Kahlil resurfacing in her mind, and debated with herself the possibility and wisdom of becoming his mistress.[51]

The subject continued to surface in a living way for the next couple of years. There were times when they came close to having sex together, but it never quite happened. In early September 1913, the topic arose again between them. Mary expressed the wish that she was a cheap actress, experienced in matters of sex and contraception, so that they could have sex together. The next day she wished she hadn't said it, and apologized, because it made it sound as though Gibran was pressuring her to go to bed with him, which he wasn't. She told him that whether the 'sex-element' in their lives increased, decreased, or stayed the same, she would accept it. He said nothing, but she felt his approval.[52]

The topic of sex was in the air that day, because Mary agreed to be sketched, in the nude, by Gibran's friend, the eminent painter Arthur B. Davies, who had achieved prominence that year because as president of the prestigious American Association of Painters and Sculptors he had been instrumental in preparing the hugely successful Armory Show.[53] When she told Gibran, he was horrified, and told her that Davies wouldn't know what to make of it, and might imagine that she was looking for sex with him. Together they composed a letter to Davies, explaining that she did not want to continue with the sitting. Though they followed the letter up with a visit to Davies's studio at the time Mary was due to go and continue the session, the topic did not arise in face-to-face conversation. Curiously, Gibran's intuition about Davies having a 'divided personality',[54] and not always having the purest motives where sex was concerned, was correct: after Davies's death in 1928 he was discovered to have been living a double life, with a second wife, by whom he had a child, and with whom he lived half the time under an assumed name.

At the beginning of 1914, they again decided against having sex together on the grounds that they had perfect union already, and that it would be highly inexpedient, given that contraception was uncertain and abortion illegal, and that society still ostracized the woman in an unmarried sexual relationship.[55] This episode epitomizes the confused nature of their thinking on the subject: are they refusing to have sex because they already have perfect union and a kind of spiritual sex, or because it is not practical? It is hard not to see an element of special pleading – that is, to think that they have already decided not to have sex, not to become that intimate, and are scrabbling for reasons to reinforce and justify their abstinence. In any case, during her visit to New York in April, and again in June, they kissed and caressed each other freely – but resisted the temptation, on the grounds that they wanted their relationship to last, and sex would make it short-lived.[56]

Gibran reinforced the message of abstinence in a letter to her describing a convenient dream he'd had in which the two of them had, with obvious symbolism and regret, thrown a statue of Aphrodite back into the sea.[57] But on her visit to New York in December they came closer than ever before to consummating their relationship sexually. It started over dinner with Mary asking him if he liked her figure now that she had put on some weight: he had told her earlier in the year that her build was too 'athletic'.[58] Back in his studio 'I showed him my calf and pressed my skirt against the upper leg so he'd see it . . . "I'm just as well covered all over," said I. I asked if he'd look at me and see for himself . . . We warmed the room and I undressed.' Kahlil was full of admiration for her figure[59] – but he was also, in Mary's euphemism, 'moved', and explained that he couldn't help it: 'Women of your type move men.' So she got dressed again, to avoid 'the sex complication'. But Kahlil put his arms around her neck and kissed her on the breast as they stood there in his studio. 'I felt that touch all night and for three days after.' She expressed surprise that Kahlil was 'moved': after all, wasn't he used to seeing the naked women who acted as his models? He explained that he kept his relationship with his models totally impersonal, but it was different with her because they loved each other.

Now it is Mary's turn to express regret that they don't have sex. She longs for the touch of his body, she tells her journal, and thinks it would bring them closer, but she can see now that it is not going to happen, and consoles herself with the idea that their mutual abstention also brings them together. His logic is that 'the physical thing' can exist without love, therefore love can be unimpaired even in its complete absence. However, he agrees that she would be harder to resist if she were younger.[60]

When he came to Boston for the New Year a few days later, she expressed sadness that she now felt she had to restrain herself and not touch him and kiss him so much, for fear of 'moving' him and making things difficult for him. He admitted that he did want sex with her, but they agreed that the risks were too great. She seemed to be about to suggest that they go to bed together, but this conversation put the chill on it. Kahlil went on to ask her help: he feels he must devote his energy to trying to get established in the world, and that he doesn't have energy left over to resist her sexually. So he asks her to try not to do anything that might arouse him, and so divert him from the task at hand – his mission in the world. At this she, of course, immediately chastises herself for making life hard for him, and resolves not to bring the matter up again, in word or deed. Two days later, however, it is he who kisses and caresses her with passion, until she has to distract him by suggesting that they look through some pictures together in a magazine (one of their favourite pastimes).[61]

Not surprisingly, all this agonizing and rationalizing over whether or not they should have sex took its toll. That day, New Year's Eve 1914, a few days before Kahlil's thirty-first birthday and not long after her forty-first, was the last time they came close. In the following June Mary sorrowfully recorded his lack of dependence on her: from now on the relationship is one of companionable friendship, with no passion to discompose them. 'Less and less,' she reported in her journal, 'he needs to see me . . . Bodily he makes me more and more remote and all his physical goes into his inner creative life or at least turns not to me.' Watching him at work, she was deeply impressed: 'I would no more touch or move him than a man would approach sexually his wife in childbirth.'[62]

And so from now on there are fewer and fewer references in her journals to them kissing or caressing. If they did kiss, it was likely to be on the hand or cheek, not the lips. On 28 June 1915, Kahlil announced that his sex drive was dead. He said that he struggled to make it so, and succeeded, leaving 'other centres uppermost'.[63] Later in the year, perhaps in some kind of consolation, he argued – had he been reading Plato's *Symposium*? – that physical children were not the only kind of children, nor was physical intercourse the only kind of intercourse. 'You and I, for instance,' he said, 'have many kinds of intercourse all the time.' Whereas cows have intercourse for the purpose of producing more cows, souls have intercourse for the purpose of producing more soul. 'Small sex' (the sex of the lesser, physical self) is temporary, while 'large sex' (ethereal, spiritual sex) endures.[64] At times they remind themselves that they are as close as two human beings can get, and never needed sex to complete their union: it would have endangered, not enhanced, their relationship. By this stage, Mary feels she too is on the way to conquering her sexuality, by putting her attention on 'the larger life' when sexual energy reared its ugly head.[65]

Poor Mary! At first she didn't want sex, while he did, and by the time she really wanted it with him, he claimed to have risen above such things, and made her feel foolish for distracting him with such a base matter. She was condemned to a childless, dry existence. On 14 November 1914, he tried to put all the blame on to her: 'If I ever stop being intimate with you,' he said, 'I tell you truly it will be because you won't let me still be.' In fact, though, his self-imposed celibacy had a great deal to do with it, and then after that the truth was more humdrum: they simply drifted apart.

Gibran admitted that he was selfish.[66] Was he in this relationship with Mary for what he could get out of it? Was he even playing with her, using her adoration of him as a means of stringing her along? As early as April 1912 he had gone off the idea of marrying her or having any kind of daily, intimate relationship with her. But he didn't tell her so at the time. Of course, there were occasions when he was tempted to make love to her: in certain circumstances the instincts do have a habit of overriding the heart or head. But as far as we can tell, from April 1912 he did not want a serious relationship with her. What did he want, then?

In the first place, it goes almost without saying, he was getting narcissistic feedback: she was his chief and most devoted disciple. There is also no point in ignoring the financial side. I don't want to go as far as to suggest that Gibran kept Mary dangling on his hook just so that she would continue to support him financially, but of course it must have occurred to him that he didn't want to jeopardize his main source of income. To repeat: I don't necessarily mean to imply that he was sly or underhand in this respect – 'unclean', as he would have put it[67] – but he was an intelligent man, and he would surely have considered every aspect of the situation. Even if the price was entertaining her when he would rather have been working, it was a price well worth paying.[68] Mary herself later told Mikhail Naimy that Gibran was peculiarly interested in money.

The precise details of their financial arrangement are unknown. We know that she paid his rent, and often bought him clothes. In the spring of 1913 they worked out that all told, up to that date – that is, in the previous five years – she had given him $7,440. She sent him regular small sums of money, and occasionally gave him substantial lump sums as well – $5,000 in June 1911, $1,000 in February 1913, $1,200 in December 1913 (which was apparently *all* the profits from her school for that year), an unspecified sum in March 1915, $1,000 in November 1915, an unspecified sum again in February 1916. Given that in 1910 the average annual income in America was $382, and that in 1920 in New York the average was $1,144 a year, healthy amounts of money are involved in her gifts. Early in 1913 she also transferred a whole lot of her securities into his name, which were worth perhaps several thousand dollars; he sold some of these later in the year to raise cash, but invested the rest through Mary's stockbroker, Mr Moors. At the start of their friendship she used to buy pictures from him; later he would give them to her (as it were in repayment of his debt), although once, as late as November 1919, she said that she 'engaged' him to do a painting for her. He was aware how indebted he was to her – your money and your love have kept me alive for the last year, he told her in April 1914 – and he often tried to tell her, especially after she had accused him of allowing money to be the only bond between them, that this was not so, and that their love was primary.[69]

Moreover, in the early years of their relationship she was a constant presence in his mind, advising him, helping him, inspiring his work, even when she was not actually there in person. Gibran claimed that they were in constant telepathic communication.[70] When they were together, they drew thoughts and ideas out of each other's minds. She also performed the incredibly useful service of improving his English, and in later years this role developed until she was effectively his

English-language editor. He would not submit books until they had been checked by her, and when they met he would often dictate to her, or they would copy pieces out together. She used to carry his work back home with her to check, and send him her comments by post if she was not due to make a visit in person. Even after her marriage to Florance Minis, she continued to edit his work – but behind Florance's back, because he disapproved of her relationship with Gibran.[71]

One way or another, then, there was plenty for Gibran in his relationship with Mary Haskell. In keeping with the fact that the power dynamics were imbalanced in his favour, there was rather more in it, in material and psychological terms, for Kahlil than for Mary. We know that he was selfish and manipulative; we can guess that he was insecure. It is hard to avoid the conclusion that he knew he was on to a good thing, and made sure that it remained in place.

Since this chapter has largely been concerned with Gibran's love life and his narcissistic profile, it is not inappropriate to append a brief record of his epistolary relationship with May Ziadeh, even though this is not its correct chronological position. Gibran seems to have wanted to play down his relationship with May to Mary. He mentioned it only once, and then in an offhand fashion: in the context of talking about psychic experiences, he remarked that he once had a dream that a young Syrian woman he knew in Egypt was in great pain, and then he received a letter from her with news of some crisis she and her family had been going through.[72] He told Mary this story in July 1921, and said, apparently without naming May Ziadeh (although Mary was not always good at remembering foreign names), that this young Lebanese woman living in Egypt had written to him several times and that he had written to her too. This makes it sound as though their communication had recently begun, and as though very few letters had passed between them. As a matter of fact, however, they corresponded fitfully between 1912 and 1914, and then regularly from 1919 until Gibran's death in 1931. There was something about this correspondence that he didn't want Mary to know, or thought perhaps she would misunderstand.[73]

May Ziadeh's father was Lebanese, but her mother was Palestinian.

She was born Mary Ziadeh – another Mary in Gibran's life – on 11 February 1886, but moved with her family to Egypt in 1908, where she soon became a well-known writer and contributor to newspapers, and changed her name to May, which she felt was less ordinary. In time she came to host the chief literary salon of Cairo, and her fame spread throughout the Arab world – not only as a writer, but also as a champion of women's rights. In the 1930s, following the death of her parents and Gibran, she tried to kill herself and spent some time in an asylum in Lebanon, but she recovered and returned to Cairo, where she died in 1941.

She first came to Gibran's attention as a literary critic, though she knew Rihani, and it is not impossible that he had mentioned her to Gibran. In any case, on its publication in 1912 he sent her a review copy of *The Broken Wings*. This was the beginning of their correspondence – and they never met in the flesh: their relationship was mediated entirely by letters. At first the tone of their letters is what you might expect: they were both leading lights in the Arabic literary world, and they exchange views and comments on each other's work. In 1913 she acted as his proxy at a memorial conference on the eminent Lebanese writer Khalil Mutran; he sent a poem, 'The Poet from Baalbek', which she read out at the conference. The tone of Gibran's earliest letters to her is formal, grave and gracious. By 1919, however, soon after their correspondence had resumed after a five-year interval, a flirtatious spirit had crept in: in a letter of 7 February that year, for instance, he fantasizes about her smile. Usually, however, his love-making was more oblique: he tells her how he longs for her letters, and values the days when they arrive. He hints at her presence in his soul, brought there by their common love of beauty. They feel themselves to be kindred spirits – exiles in this world of pain and suffering – and they praise each other's work.

Gibran's letter to her of 25 July 1919 is a declaration of love:

My dear Miss May

You have been in my mind ever since I last wrote to you. I have spent long hours thinking of you, talking to you, endeavouring to discover your secrets, trying to unravel your mysteries . . .

You will naturally be surprised to hear me talk like this; I myself find it strange that I should feel this urge and this necessity to write to you . . . I have recently established [with you] a bond, abstract, delicate, firm, strange and unlike all other bonds in its nature and characteristics . . . Not a single one of the threads which form this bond was woven by the days and nights which measure time and intersperse the distance that separates the cradle from the grave. Not a single one of those threads was woven by past interests or future aspirations – for this bond has existed between two people who were brought together by neither the past nor the present, and who may not be united by the future, either.

In such a bond, May, in such a private emotion, in such a secret understanding, there exist dreams more exotic and more unfathomable than anything that surges in the human breast; dreams within dreams within dreams.

Such an understanding, May, is a deep and silent song which is heard in the stillness of the night; it transports us beyond the realms of day, beyond the realms of night, beyond time, beyond eternity.

Such an emotion, May, involves sharp pangs that will never disappear, but which are dear to us, and which we would not exchange, even if we had the chance, for any amount of glory or pleasure, known or imagined.

He then implores her to write to him and tell him if his feelings are reciprocated. Piecing together her response from snippets of Gibran's letters to her, it is clear that she was cross with him and accused him of being lost in a fantasy. Gibran fell into depression, and reiterated that she haunted his dreams and that he imagined them together all the time in the suprāsensible realms of truth and beauty. To May he used exactly the same language of her constant presence with him – so that she sees out of his eyes, he claims – that he had used years before with Josephine and Mary. Gradually his lengthy and passionate urging that he and May were special and were therefore made for each other – that only he could comfort and understand her loneliness, as she could his – undermined her defences. In the only one of her intimate later letters that has been translated into English, dating from 15 January 1924, he is her 'beloved' (as he also referred to her in his letters) and she fancifully and passionately wonders, on seeing Venus in the sky, whether this planet, under the aegis of the goddess of Love, is peopled by others like herself and Kahlil, 'who love and are filled with longing'. She goes on: 'Might it not be possible that Venus is like me and has her own Gibran – a distant, beautiful presence who is in reality very near . . . knowing [that a long time will pass] before she sees her loved one?' This, as I say, is from a letter dated 1924, but to judge from Gibran's letters to her, she had already softened and was returning Gibran's ethereal passion by 1921. One of Gibran's letters to her, which needs no linguistic translation, consisted simply of a heart pierced with a dagger.[74]

They were both courted in real life by people – real people with all their unsatisfactory and disappointing features. For both of them, this long-distance affair was far better. It was their secret, and Gibran was in ecstasy whenever one of her love letters to him arrived. His reticence to Mary about May is hardly surprising. Inevitably, given their extraordinary circumstances, he and May had occasional misunderstandings, but their love for each other remained steady and constant up to Gibran's death. In a letter of October 1923 he summed up their relationship: 'You live in me and I in you, you know this and I know it too.' The closest they ever got to physical contact was an exchange of photographs.

There is no doubt in my mind that Gibran's love for May Ziadeh was authentic: he had nothing to gain by it, and nothing to lose by not feeling or declaring it. The tone of the letters is that of a genuine lover. This love comes across as more real, because more passionate, than his love for Mary Haskell, and as more mature than his youthful infatuation with Josephine Peabody. Leaving aside his sexual affairs, it therefore counts as the single abiding love of Gibran's life – and yet it was with a woman he never met. Presumably he did not really want to meet her. Although in several of his letters he asked, rhetorically, when he would leave New York and return to the Middle East and meet his beloved May, it would surely not have been too problematic for him to at least pay a visit to Egypt, had he wanted to. It is hard to resist the conclusion that he was able to give his love to her, to pour out his feelings to her in letter after letter, *precisely because* she was so distant. She was safe. She would never know him as a real, flawed person.

I wrote earlier in this chapter that narcissistic people find it difficult to enter into a full relationship with another as a living, breathing person. May Ziadeh remained for Gibran a remote, spiritual being –

almost an angel rather than a human being. But Gibran was an intelligent man. Some part of his mind, at some time, must have said to him: 'This is crazy! This situation is absurd!' And so we gain a new insight into Gibran: it is very likely that throughout his life he was a deeply sad, deeply troubled person.

8

Friends and Enemies

In New York at the end of 1911 Gibran was close to breaking into a wider circle of influential friends and acquaintances, and on the brink of capping his success in the Arab world with recognition in America.[1] He had fallen in love with New York straight away, finding its energy and skyline invigorating.[2] Compared with Boston it had the energy of an arriviste, which the ambitious immigrant Gibran found congenial. It seemed a city of infinite possibility. Nothing symbolizes this better than the aggressive competition among the designers and builders of skyscrapers in Manhattan. The air was filled with the machine-gun chatter of riveters erecting enormous and stunning buildings.

Back in Boston Mary was doing her best to arrange an exhibition of Gibran's paintings and drawings, which he had left in Boston for this purpose. She made a three-pronged attack. She approached Fred Holland Day for help, talked to Mr and Mrs Copley Greene (who had met and admired Gibran and were members of the prestigious St Botolph Club, which held exhibitions) and invited Frances Keyes, who had the ear of Isabella Stewart Gardner, to come to the school to see Gibran's work. But Day never responded, the Copley Greenes had cooled, and Miss Keyes savagely criticized Gibran's work as lacking technical merit. When, after a few days, Mary summoned up the courage to tell him in detail what Miss Keyes had said, Gibran received the news with equanimity, and wrote back that in his opinion Miss Keyes was simply out of sympathy with the *kind* of work he did, and was using an attack on technique to disguise this lack of sympathy. Mary read his equanimity as a sign of his now unshakeable confidence in the Reality he was trying to express.[3]

In fact, though, Gibran may well have had other things on his mind. Throughout the summer and autumn he saw a great deal of Charlotte, Mary's best friend. They became very close indeed, and Gibran seems to have fallen in love with her – as, in fact, he admitted to Mary some years later.[4] Mary clearly *thought* something was going on at the time, because she worried about them in her diary (on and off in the summer and autumn of 1911). There was also an odd episode in February. Mary suffered a curious mixture of emotions over the portrait that Gibran painted that month of Charlotte. As the Gibrans put it, 'Her admiration [of the picture] was not based on critical judgment, but the fact that it was by him and of Charlotte enflamed her.'[5] And before Gibran left her rooms one evening, she made him kiss her in front of his picture of Charlotte. Did she want Charlotte to be looking on and approving their love, was she trying symbolically to show Charlotte that he was hers, or did she want Gibran to be aware that *she* was his, whereas Charlotte was not?

When Gibran was living in New York, and seeing Charlotte almost every day, Charlotte felt she had to calm Mary's fears: 'If he and I were the only two on the much-abused . . . desert island I could not feel him as a man.' The chemistry between them wasn't right, she explained.[6] So far, were it not for Gibran's 1915 confession that he had been in love with Charlotte, we might think nothing more about it. Mary, however, was convinced that Gibran was in love with Charlotte. In an extraordinary diary entry, written in the pages for 7–8 November 1911, she talks first about a mysterious other woman: 'From her, sex love is itself an added world of revelation. I have not that to give – she has.' She compares their two roles: she can give Gibran's work form, while the other woman can give him energy. She goes on: 'I make the tool for which she gives exercise. And I shall continue to look with joy at what the two together create . . . This is a door opened to him by the same Hand that has opened others . . . What is the allegiance that shall demand he reject it? None!' In other words, since they have broken off their engagement, she has no claim over him: the other woman can step into her shoes as his female counterpart and guide. At last we learn who this other woman is: 'C will feel she never knew complete union and wonder of the soul before, and K that he never realized how much power is in him as poet and painter. She will fill his thoughts as no woman ever yet did and reveal his own passion to himself.'

In her diary for 5 October, a month before this November entry, Mary had recorded that Gibran had told her how much his mind was filled with Charlotte.[7] This November entry was Mary's response: she courageously consigned Gibran to Charlotte, blessing their union, and even giving them permission to have sex. Three days later in her diary she wrote: 'Today came letters from C and K. No word yet of what I had in mind.' But there is no way of knowing what proposition she had put to them, or perhaps to one of them alone.

In fact, however, the love that Kahlil felt for Charlotte was never returned, so Mary's brave relinquishment of him was unnecessary. Two factors prevented Charlotte from returning his love. The first was 'chemistry'; as we have already seen, Charlotte did not feel that it was there, and later, during her first visit to New York, Mary recorded, 'C's not yet drawn [to Kahlil] other than Platonically, but I look for that in time. He needs to express affection – misses expression in her, no doubt.'[8] The second factor was that Charlotte never gave herself the time that Mary spoke of to be attracted to Gibran: a little later that month, December 1911, she fell head over heels in love with Amin Rihani, with whom she had a short-lived, passionate sexual affair.[9] During the affair with Rihani, far from seeing Gibran as a potential suitor, she paired him off with Mary, just as she was with Rihani, and dreamed that 'one of the four, or two of the four, or four of the four, may give birth to the Child who is to unite the East and the West by its Genius'.[10] And only a few months later, on 16 October, Charlotte married a young man called Gilbert Hirsch, with whom she remained apparently happily married for the rest of his short life. He died in 1926, she in 1954.

One of the strangest aspects of this whole situation is that it was all taking place at a time when Kahlil and Mary were still sustaining some kind of relationship themselves. They were no longer engaged to be married, but they were undecided whether or not to consummate their relationship sexually. Mary did not feel free: in contemplating or even trying to engineer a relationship between him and Charlotte, she was bravely facing up to what she felt she was a *fait accompli*. A measure of Kahlil's sense of freedom from her, however, is that he and Charlotte together imagined that Mary might marry someone else, a man called Harry Lorber.[11] The whole network of emotions between the three of them – and Rihani, as it turned out – reeks of almost incestuous intensity.

However, if Mary's fears about Charlotte came to nothing, other rumours were reaching her ears. Charlotte was convinced that Kahlil was a womanizer, and Mary remembered that Micheline had said the same about him in Paris. Charlotte warned Mary that however many terms of endearment Gibran used to her, he was saying the same things to other women, just as all men do. It occurred to Mary that Gibran had once said to her that it was possible for him to love seven women at once, and that sexual intercourse was no more than picking a flower.[12] So was there any truth in Charlotte's impressions? When she bluntly asked Gibran about it, he denied it vehemently. If Charlotte and Micheline – and Rihani and his friend Marie al-Khoury, he naïvely adds – think him a womanizer, he refrains from telling them they're wrong only because he is too fastidious to go into intimate details of his life with anyone. He blamed his relative ignorance of English for giving her a misleading impression. He admitted a number of affairs in the past, with older and more knowing women,[13] but none in New York in the present. He appealed to the volume of work he had created: did this leave him any time for romance? Although he saw a lot of women, and although women liked his work more than men, this didn't mean, he insisted, that he was having sex with all or any of them, though he admitted that he had had offers, and that he could find other women sexually attractive.[14]

If we are inclined to think that here Gibran is protesting too much, fuel can be added to the fire of our imaginations by considering the portrait of Gibran executed by Rose O'Neill in 1914. This shows quite a different side of Gibran from those he lets Mary see. O'Neill portrays him as sensuous, sexual, dangerously good-looking. It is not surprising that he never mentioned this portrait to Mary.

One of the issues at stake here is whether Gibran was lying when he told Mary that he had given up sex and was living a celibate life in New York from 1915 onwards. Even from within the journals there is some reason to doubt that he was entirely wholehearted about his self-imposed asceticism. Right from the start he left open the possibility that for all his efforts to sacrifice his sex-drive in order to create energy for his work, it might return, since he still had his youth.[15] In the same vein, in December 1922 he told her that he had no sexual relations with any woman, and would 'probably' continue not to. In July 1921, in the course of a conversation about sex with Mary, he remarked that creative people are always more highly sexed than others – and of course he always counted himself as extremely creative. There was also the peculiar occasion in 1922, a good eight years after there had been any kind of juice in their relationship, when he seemed to entertain the possibility that he and Mary might one day have physical sex, whereas at the moment they had a great deal of spiritual sex.[16] All these hint that his sex drive may not have been entirely dead, even if it was torpid.

From time to time in Mary's journals Gibran seems to be trying to convince her that people misunderstand him where sex is concerned. He told her, for instance, that because he was so interested in people, he listened with a peculiar intensity when they talked to him – and women often mistook this intensity for personal interest in them. Hence, he explained, he preferred male friends: they found it easier to be impersonal. Perhaps it is no wonder that women made this mistake, since on another occasion, when he and Mary had been talking about the models he used for his painting, he told her that he was always undressing people with his eyes. When Mary told him that a friend had written to her that she had met a young Syrian woman who knew Gibran 'very intimately', Gibran defensively said she must mean that the young woman knew his work. At much the same time he categorically told her, in passing, that he was not involved in any love affairs.[17] There are, however, supposed to be in existence some letters from Gibran to a young Syrian woman called Helena, dating from round about this time, inviting her to visit him, alone, in his studio.

There is also some additional circumstantial evidence. Hawi states with confidence, having interviewed people who knew Gibran at the time, that in his early years in New York he was having an affair with Marie al-Khoury, a wealthy Syrian who patronized Gibran, buying his paintings and helping him become established. In the oral tradition, she is portrayed as something of a calculating vamp, who moved lightly from an affair with Rihani to one with Gibran, and just as easily gave him up too. There is no hard evidence for an affair between her and Gibran, although in the nature of things it is unlikely that there would be. There is, however, a rumour of love letters from Gibran to her.[18] Then there is Witter Bynner's cavalier reminiscence, dating presumably from the later 1910s, before he left New York for Santa Fe, that Gibran's moods were brought on by his painting or making love.[19] And later, for the 1920s, there is a persistent rumour of an unnamed Manhattan jeweller's wife who insisted on having Gibran's letters to her buried with her.[20] This, however, may tell us more about the jeweller's wife than about Gibran. He was certainly surrounded by adoring women in the 1920s, but where there is any evidence, from letters between Gibran and Margaret Crofts, for instance, or Marie Meloney, he appears no more than polite and friendly.

Of course, even if Gibran was celibate, he may well have fallen in love. By the 1920s, I think that he had honestly given his heart to May Ziadeh, with whom of course he had no choice but to be celibate. But in a letter to her of 3 November 1920, speaking (as often in these letters) of himself in the third person, he said: 'What might I say of a man who is torn between two women: one weaving the hours of his waking out of his dreams; the other forming his dreams from the hours of his wakefulness?' This is one of the more obscure sentences in these often wistfully vague letters. But whichever of these two women is supposed to be May herself, another woman is unaccounted for.

In his biography Mikhail Naimy told a scurrilous story of Gibran in about 1930 succumbing to his loneliness and taking advantage of a young woman's near-worship of him to get her into bed with him. The scenario is all too familiar to us nowadays, in the 1990s, from tabloid stories of how gurus abuse their personal power. At first blush, the tale seems unbelievable. How would Naimy have come to hear of the affair? He himself presents Gibran as deeply ashamed of his behaviour, so it is hardly plausible that Gibran would have told him. However, there is a basis of truth to the tale. In 1930 Gibran *did* fall in love with a young woman called Gertrude Stern. Although there is no evidence of their having sex together, he did ask her to marry him. After Gibran's death, Stern was in touch with Naimy by letter, so that must be how he got wind of the story.[21]

The evidence is ambiguous, but seems to be enough to warrant remembering the saying that there is 'no smoke without fire'. At the very least, it seems certain that he was still capable of being tempted, and to that extent he gave Mary a misleading impression of his life in New York. When asked in the early 1980s about Gibran's love life, Dora, the wife of Ilya Abu Madi, Gibran's famous colleague in the Pen Club, who knew Gibran well in the 1920s, laughed and said, 'He wanted to marry them all!'[22] This seems an occasion when there is enough evidence for us to draw aside the veil of the myth and to counterbalance the lopsidedness of the image he projected to Mary Haskell, the chief source for his life, and so to state with some confidence that Gibran pursued an active love life in New York, which presumably led, on some occasions at least, to sexual conquest.

Gibran liked the image of himself as a lonely, ascetic, even tortured man. He called his studio in New York 'The Hermitage' and, especially as his role became transformed from that of melancholic Romantic to that of prophet, he projected himself to Mary and his other friends as an isolated seer, labouring away unheeded in his hermitage. He once told Mary, 'Sometimes I'm almost proud of my hermitness, my loneliness. I'm not accepted – that's all. I never have been and I never shall be. I just don't fit. I have suffered, and I am willing to suffer. I look for the worst and I am ready for the worst.' At another time he said, 'It really draws people to you to be real and remote.'[23] It is clear that he liked this image, and equated loneliness with his sense of being unique.

Charlotte's portrayal of him as a womanizer clashed directly with the image Gibran was attempting to portray of a lonely artist, caring only about his work and his mission to humankind. He deeply resented what he saw as her betrayal of him, and his love rapidly turned to intense dislike. From then on he never has a good thing to say about her (or about Micheline, for that matter). In fact, it is not clear whether after the late summer of 1912 they even *met* again properly – that is, apart from a fleeting encounter in 1914 at one of Gibran's exhibitions – when previously they had been seeing each other almost daily; the fact that she moved uptown to 529 East 77th Street had little to do with it.[24] Mary remained friends with her, and often stayed with her when she came to New York, but she could only ever record in her journals negative remarks from Gibran. Charlotte lacks the will to fulfil her potential, he says; she leads a limited life; she and her husband are childlike disciples of Freud. Once, developing the idea that human beings exist between two worlds, the conscious and the organic, he used Charlotte and Micheline as examples of people in whom the organic had conquered the conscious.[25] Micheline, he told Mary in 1914, he now found 'repellent', and though he still saw her occasionally, he felt that any time spent with her was wasted.[26] He freely admitted that Charlotte's idea of him as a womanizer was the cause of the split between them, but added as another reason that Charlotte had not been able to stand his criticisms of her work.[27]

Rihani suffered much the same fate. Gibran fell out with him too, although it is not clear when or why. They were still friends in May 1912, but after that it is impossible to tell from Gibran's references to him how close they are. The only extant letter from Gibran to Rihani after this date is a formal one from 1918, when they were colleagues on a committee. It is tempting to say that Gibran outgrew him: Rihani was his role model for a while, but as Gibran's role changed from that of angry young man to that of prophet, Rihani could no longer act as a paradigm. But this hypothesis does not explain the resentment Gibran apparently felt against Rihani. It seems plausible to suggest that Gibran resented the fact that the politically connected Rihani was chosen, along with Najib Diab, as representatives at the Arab Congress in Paris in 1913. Gibran expected to go himself, but having failed to be chosen he voiced dissatisfaction with the Congress – a dissatisfaction that may have been motivated by a personal grudge. Years later when, with typical lack of attention to reality, Gibran wanted to persuade Mary that he had never lost a friend in his life – 'Everybody I ever loved I love still' – he went on to explain that Rihani had never been his friend, but that even so, if Rihani came and apologized, he would welcome him back.[28] We do not know what he wanted Rihani to apologize for. That relations between them had soured is also shown by Rihani's somewhat caustic remark on Gibran's later success. He attributed it not to talent, but to the fact that Gibran chose commercial subjects and cultivated the acquaintance of publishers.[29]

*

But these storms were all in the future at the end of 1911. Mary came to New York for a Thanksgiving dinner in Charlotte's apartment. Of course, she couldn't wait to visit Gibran's studio and she has left us a breathlessly vivid impression of its interior.

Under the little black balcony a rose-and-gold-dust silvery rug on the small couch and walls of yellow – the yellow brocade and curtains from Paris – with the star-carved Christ's head – a hanging lamp – and marvels of old iridescent Syrian glass – one plate of it hanging up – and three small shelves of smaller pieces . . . Among them are a gold-gilt cup and saucer and a dark amber-golden bell-wine-glass left for K by his predecessors in the studio. A rug of deepest rose is near the door – night-rose – and this and his couch rug that seems sun itself are his own – sold him at cost by an old Syrian who has waited 16 or 17 years to know him and show love for him. 'May this,' said he of the couch-rug, 'be a joy to your eyes at morning and at evening.' It is royal – nothing more beautiful in museums . . . Three pictures he has . . . Charlotte lay like a fourth picture on the dark rug by the red-mouthed little stove . . . then K sat under the high window and read from *The Broken Wings* in Arabic . . . I never saw him so himself before.[30]

Even though Mary sometimes urged him to find himself a second room to live in, leaving the studio to be strictly a studio, he always remained in a single room, making the most of a few belongings, and did so even later in life, after acquiring some wealth. Although, as we have seen and shall continue to see, there is commonly a gap between the man and his philosophy, in the spareness of his surroundings he came closest to putting his ideas into practice.

What of the man himself? It is time to complement the pictures reproduced in this book with a description of some of his features that cannot be captured on film. Physically, he could appear slight and weak, liable to colds, flu and stomach upsets, or sturdy and compact. He was not tall – about five foot three or four – so that he and Mary must have made a slightly unusual couple, since she was taller than him. His build was slim: when healthy, he weighed about 140 pounds, but owing to his frequent bouts of ill health he was often closer to 130 pounds. His voice was quite high-pitched, and it broke relatively late in his teens. The moustache that is constant in the photographs from 1902 onwards was complemented by a trim beard for a while in the early 1920s. By 1917 his hair was grey at the temples, and in later life he wore spectacles for reading.[31] We should imagine him with a cigarette in his hands (he smoked heavily from his time in Paris onwards), and with a cup of thick Middle Eastern coffee by his side. His energy was often tense and nervous; he paced up and down the room while working, but took little proper exercise and generally ate sparingly. His movements were graceful. His face easily reflected his mood, changing from light to dark in an instant, and he had extraordinarily expressive eyes. His clothes in the 1910s were often of dull colours, but when in the 1920s he adopted the more cosmopolitan role success made natural to him, he occasionally wore lighter colours. At work in his studio, he wore Syrian clothes, but as the years went by Western suits became more his style.[32]

Joseph Gollomb met him in 1919, interviewing him for the *Evening Post*, and left the following impression. After contrasting him with Tagore, in the sense that Tagore looked like a typical mystic, whereas Gibran looked like 'a correctly dressed cosmopolitan of the western world', Gollomb goes on to say:

> His dark brows and moustache and somewhat curly hair above a good forehead; the clear brown eyes, thoughtful but never abstracted in expression; the sensibly tailored clothes, smart but not conspicuous – there seemed to me a chameleon-like ease of adaptiveness about him. In his studio in West 10th Street he looked a sensible denizen of Greenwich Village – for such there be. But had I seen him at a congress of economists, or in a Viennese café, or in his native Syria, I feel sure he would look equally in the picture in each instance. It is not a case of lack of individuality with him, but, on the contrary, an unusual common sense and sympathy which transcend differences and enable him to understand so well each environment in which he finds himself that he neither feels nor looks the stranger.[33]

He clearly gave an impression of intensity and this must have been one of the reasons for his immediate success in New York society. Quite a few people in New York, as we have seen, felt that society was on the brink of major change, and that the arts had a leading role to play in bringing about this change. There was also a great deal

1. *Fred Holland Day, the fin-de-siècle architect of Gibran's soul. The photograph was taken by Reginald Craigie in about 1900. It gives little indication of Day's pleasing eccentricities.*

2. *An 1892 photograph of Josephine Preston Peabody, Gibran's first love. She first met Gibran six years later, in 1898. It is easy to see why Gibran became so smitten with her.*

3. Mary Haskell (closer to the camera), Gibran's constant friend and editor, and nearly his lover, on a Sierra Club outing in the summer of 1910. Mikhail Naimy said of her: 'She was not a beautiful woman, but she laid her foot upon the earth as if she loved it.'

4. Charlotte Teller in 1909. A close friend of Mary Haskell, and another creative person whom Mary supported financially, her friendship with Gibran was soon to reach its most intense phase.

5. Micheline (Émilie Michel) in the early 1920s, when she was already ill with the crippling disease that was soon to kill her. She has put on weight, and suffered, but the young woman who bewitched Gibran fifteen years earlier may still be glimpsed.

6. Four eminent members of the Pen Club: (from left to right) Nasib 'Arida, Kahlil Gibran, 'Abd al-Masih Haddad and Mikhail Naimy. The photograph dates from 1920.

7. Jean Delville's 'Love of Souls' (1900) – a typical Symbolist painting which may well have influenced Gibran in style, theme and composition.

8. A self-portrait of 1914. The picture is actually half of a diptych, with a portrait of Mary Haskell as the other half. We should imagine Gibran working on the portraits during one of Mary's visits to New York.

9. A sensuous portrait of Gibran – the rake, the impassioned poet – by Rose Cecil O'Neill (of Kewpie Dolls fame), painted in 1914. Compare the more anodyne self-portrait on the facing page: the one is perhaps how he presented himself to Mary Haskell, the other how he was to his western New York friends.

10. This photograph of Gibran was taken in late 1930, a few months before his death, when his final illness had already taken hold of his body.

11. *A striking photograph of Gibran's large second studio at 51 West 10th Street, New York. Many famous pictures can be seen hanging on the walls. Judging by the pictures, I would date the photograph to about 1925.*

12. *An early oil painting by Gibran, 'The Head of Orpheus Floating down the River Hebrus to the Sea'. The theme is after Delville, the date is perhaps 1907.*

13. An untitled portrait of a woman with a death's head (1910). Gibran the Symbolist very often placed background and foreground portraits together in this way, and invariably with the more ethereal or mysterious figure in the background.

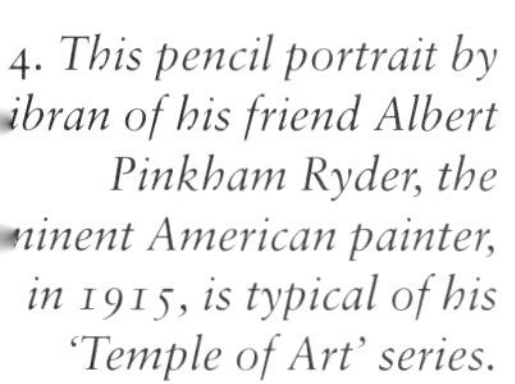

4. This pencil portrait by ibran of his friend Albert Pinkham Ryder, the ninent American painter, in 1915, is typical of his 'Temple of Art' series.

15. 'The Great Longing', a wash drawing from 1916, when Gibran was working hard to find recognition in New York as an artist. The centaur was a common figure at the time: half man, half beast, it represents our dual nature, with the lower part adhering to the earth and the higher part reaching for the stars.

16. 'The Heavenly Mother' (1920), an illustration for The Forerunner, *typical of the latest phase of Gibran's work as an artist. The lines are firmer, but the symbolism is still the same.*

of interest in alternative forms of religious expression, both Eastern and Western – especially spiritualism, the New Thought movement, Theosophy, Christian Science and the ideas of Swedenborg, Phineas Quimby and Warren Felt Evans. In Europe, George Ivanovich Gurdjieff was beginning to attract followers, and Aleister Crowley was beginning to attract notoriety; Yeats and Eliot were poised to unleash their mystical visions on the literary world.

These new religious movements shared certain common features (though of course not all of them had all the following beliefs): an Emersonian emphasis on self-reliance, rather than the creedal and priestly authority of organized churches; the belief that in essence human beings are divine; the view that evil is an illusion, not an active principle in the world; a de-emphasizing of faith in favour of the attempt of an individual to discover the cosmic laws of creation by himself or herself and in favour of an individual's direct experience of metaphysical levels of reality; a belief in reincarnation; a general vague optimism – a kind of Pollyanna spirit that ignored, in Jungian terms, the shadow side of things.

Gibran fitted into this New York context with consummate ease.[34] Here was a man who was apparently a master of two of the arts; he came from the East, which was beginning to be equated with a more spiritual approach to life;[35] he had the ability to generalize from almost any topic of conversation in an attempt to lay bare the underlying metaphysical realities. In short, he epitomized the artistic-religious side (rather than the political side, with which he was not in sympathy) of the imminent revolution and was warmly welcomed – even lionized and fêted – as one of its potential leaders. Before long his appointment diary was full, and he was an essential member of many a dinner-party or soirée. In his memoirs, the critic and author Edmund Wilson wrote:

Elinor Wylie's story of dinner at Mrs Simeon Ford's. Mercedes da Costa, Gibran the Persian [*sic*], etc. Great enthusiasm for Whitman: Whitman and Christ perhaps the two greatest people who ever lived. 'What poets do you like?' 'Why, Milton, for example –' 'Milton!!!' They cried with horror, turning to one another and saying: 'She says she likes Milton!' It had to be shouted at Mrs Ford, who was deaf; when she understood, she made a frightful grimace: 'Milton!' 'Why,' said someone to Elinor, 'I thought you were a *good* poet. You haven't been influenced by *Milton*!' 'Well, why should I be? You admire Jesus Christ, but you don't behave like him, do you?'[36]

Gibran sometimes complained to Mary about all the invitations he received, and about how many visitors wanted to come and see him in his studio.[37] Moreover, even as late as 1919, he claimed that it was tiring for him to have to talk at length in English. Nevertheless, one cannot help detecting a certain note of smugness as he drops the names of all the famous people he has met, some of whom he was able to draw for his Temple of Art series.[38] He was hungry for fame, and nothing is more pleasing to ambitious people than to be in the company of those whose ranks they aspire to join. So in his first years in New York, he plunged into the swim of things with zest. He told Mary that he found the 'New York technique' peculiar, but necessary – the technique of first checking out a person socially, and then deciding on the merits of his work. Many of the tea-parties and dinners he was invited to bored him, but some he enjoyed. He could be found in the houses of a number of society hostesses, whom he called 'matrons', including Mrs Julia Ellsworth Ford (whose husband Simeon owned a number of hotels), Mrs Bennett (the wife of a senator), Mrs Morten and Mrs Harden, both rich patronesses of the arts, Mrs Tiffany, and Rose O'Neill.

Once he felt himself to be established, he picked and chose with more discrimination. Mrs Ford remained a firm favourite. For many years, on Friday nights, she held a dinner for 'interesting' men, to which an occasional interesting woman, such as the dancer Ruth St Denis, might be invited. Gibran was a regular, along with the poet Witter Bynner, Tom Raymond (bibliophile mayor of Newark and an expert on Stephen Crane), the playwright Percy Mackaye, the painter Arthur B. Davies and the poet Howard Willard Cook. These dinners started in at least 1913, and were still being held as late as 1921.[39]

From 1918 onwards, he was also a frequent visitor at Mrs Corinne Roosevelt Robinson's, the sister of Theodore Roosevelt (whom he also met). Mrs Robinson was herself a well-published poet, with volumes to her credit such as *The Call of Brotherhood* (1912), *One Woman to Another* (1914) and *Service and Sacrifice* (1919). Of particular interest to us is her volume *Out of Nymph*, published in 1930. There is a letter from Gibran to her, thanking her for sending him a copy. It was a natural gift for her to give, for in one of its sections, 'Portraits', the book contains the following poem, entitled 'Kahlil Gibran, Poet and Prophet':

So sensitive that often Man
might fail to find
you, dear Gibran,
Unless the 'Prophet'
speaks, and then
You will be known of
women, men,
And even children,
for the word
The 'Prophet' speaks
All hearts has stirred,
Until in knowing
all things true,
Prophet – and Seer, we
shall know *you*!

There are also extant a number of other letters from Gibran to Mrs Robinson, which tell us a lot about his relation to all these society ladies. The tone of the letters is unfailingly polite, almost to the point of being obsequious. Some of the letters are carefully phrased responses to invitations to dinner, and to read a poem or two; or again, he thanks her for her kindness in having him to stay at her summer house, or in congratulating him on the appearance of a book. Thanking her for a brief stay in the country, he says, 'Would that I could have flutes for words to tell you how grateful I am for the three vast days you gave me at Henderson House. I have no flutes, nor strings; I have only words. Will you not, in your great graciousness, translate my words, even the unwritten ones, into that soundless language of the spirit?' On hearing that she was ill, he writes: 'It grieves beyond words to hear that you are ill. I feel, as all those who love you feel, that you are *the* one person in the world who should be always well that you may give the world that Rooseveltian quickening element, and make people think and act as they should rather than they do.' It is only really in his later letters to her that he appears to have acquired the confidence to address her in a less fawning tone.

The out-of-town season familiar from the novels of Edith Wharton, for instance, was still obligatory in the loftier circles of New York life, and Gibran accepted invitations to stay at the summer houses not only of Mrs Ford, but of other New York society ladies such as Mrs van Patten and Mrs Tison, and their Boston equivalents, Mrs Manning and Mrs Garland. The successful artist Rose O'Neill spent at least some of the money she made from her cartoon characters, the Kewpie Dolls, supporting other artists in their careers and keeping an open house in Washington Square, where Gibran was sometimes to be found.[40] In case anyone should wonder about the presence of all these women, it should be made clear that in the centres of high society in America at the time – especially Boston and New York – the women ruled the roost. They were the ones who issued the invitations and made the reputations. Unless you were a modern woman like Rose O'Neill, it was generally essential to have a wealthy husband, to add respectability and to finance the proceedings; but the glamour came from the ladies. It was a form of matriarchy.

Gibran could always charm the ladies. He had a ready and interesting opinion on most matters, but was also a good listener; he was soft-spoken and polite, and was a dab hand with a pencil. Even as late as 1918 he admits that, just as he had in Boston, he occasionally paid his way in society by giving his host or hostess a drawing, just as portraiture was always an incidental source of income.[41] There is a particularly telling anecdote about Gibran at a New York dinner in a letter from his friend Witter Bynner, written in 1941 in response to a query from a student about Gibran:

> Perhaps the best illustration I can give you of the man's personal quality is an episode which took place at the house of Mrs. Simeon Ford (Julia Ellsworth Ford) through whom I met him.
>
> One night at dinner there the maids failed to bring on one of the courses, and after a considerable wait and several bell ringings, Mrs. Ford rose and went to the pantry. There, behind a screen, stood two maids. When

reprimanded, one of them explained, 'But Mrs. Ford, how can we go about our business when Mr Gibran is talking? He sounds like Jesus.' And he did.[42]

Much the same impression comes across from another fascinating vignette, this one written by the Pulitzer-prize-winning poet and novelist Robert Hillyer in 1949. After talking about Gibran's philosophy and writings, he goes on:

Gibran himself I remember from the days before World War I when I was occasionally taken to his studio by friends. I recall the shadowy studio, the folders of drawings, and a small but dignified Levantine with luminous dark eyes and exquisite hands. I see him making some Turkish coffee with ritualistic care ... He spoke of the sacredness of the poet; and as I was a very young poet, nineteen to be exact, I squirmed and smiled with embarrassment, at which he fixed me with his profound gaze, and I felt too awkward and unholy for my high calling. At the insistence of someone present he recited two or three of his parables, which subsequently appeared in *The Prophet* ... My general memory is of a man who had devoted his life to Contemplation, to Peace, to Love, to the Life of the Soul, and the myriad forms of Beauty. That these virtues too often remain mere capitalized abstractions in his writing diminishes the power but not the timeliness of their presentation.[43]

But who were his Western friends? A number of names recur in Mary's journals and elsewhere – the Perrys (Ronald Perry was a sculptor), Howard Cook, Haniel Long (a very prolific poet), Adele Watson, Dr Beatrice Hinkle (a pioneering woman doctor and early psychotherapist) and others – but four men are worth singling out as his particular friends, on the grounds that their names occur most frequently in the journals and letters, and that they are treated with the most warmth. These are Witter Bynner, Tom Raymond, James Oppenheim and Albert Pinkham Ryder.

His relationship with the eminent Symbolist painter Albert Pinkham Ryder is fascinating. The visionary Ryder, born in 1847, was already an old man when Gibran came to New York, and was living as a virtual recluse in filthy surroundings. Wallpaper hung in long streamers from the ceilings, he never threw anything away, and there was dirt and dust everywhere. He slept on a piece of carpet on the floor, or on three chairs placed in a row. He was rarely seen out on the streets, but when he did emerge from his rooms, he was sometimes mistaken for a tramp, with his long, unkempt beard, frowning face and watery eyes.

Nevertheless, on one occasion in December 1914 he was recognized at an exhibition of some of Gibran's paintings. When asked what he thought of the work, he replied, 'He seems to mean it, at any rate. That's the main thing.' Gibran, who had long admired Ryder's work, was delighted, and determined to find a way to meet him. He decided to write a short prose-poem dedicated to Ryder, to attract him out of his lair. Lightly corrected by Mary, and privately published, this poem is Gibran's first published piece in the English language.[44] It is a blatant piece of flattery, addressing Ryder as a prophet as well as a poet, an inhabitant of the 'Giant-World', and so on. Astonishingly, this naïve plan worked, and Ryder agreed to meet Gibran, so that Gibran could present him with a copy of the poem.

The crotchety old man seems to have taken to Gibran, as much as he did to anyone. After the preliminary meeting, he agreed to sit for Gibran's Temple of Art series the very next day. Gibran was pleased with the drawing, and even more delighted with Ryder himself, whose lack of connection to the world he found stimulating. 'He is full . . . of that wonder that is the mark of the real and great ones,' he concluded.[45] This was in March 1915, but a few months later Ryder was in hospital; though guarded there and for the rest of his life by a Mrs Fitzpatrick, Gibran was apparently one of the very few people she allowed to visit. When Ryder went back to hospital, terminally, in March 1917, Gibran was a regular visitor. The old man died on 28 March.[46]

It is frustrating not to know more about the relationship between Gibran and Thomas Lynch Raymond, who is now chiefly remembered as a pioneering mayor of Newark. It is clear from the tone of Gibran's references to him, filtered mostly through Mary's journals, that he felt as close to Raymond as to any of his circle. They could talk to each other about anything. It is also clear that they corresponded, but none of this correspondence remains, to my knowledge. Raymond was only briefly married, but then divorced (and came to loathe women, according to Gibran),[47] and left no children. After his death in 1928, his book collection was sold and the rest of his belongings were presumably either scattered or destroyed. It was through him that Gibran met Rose O'Neill in 1914. Even in the thick of Newark city politics, Tom retained a bolt-hole in Greenwich Village, and remained a regular presence at Mrs Ford's dinners.[48]

The cases of Witter Bynner and James Oppenheim are interesting, because as well as having Gibran's comments on them in Mary's journals, a number of Gibran's letters to them have survived, which can act to confirm or refute the impression to be gained from the journals. Bynner – known as Hal to his friends – is nowadays best known for having bequeathed money for the Witter Bynner Foundation for Poetry, which operates out of Santa Fe, but in his time he was a very famous modernist lyric poet, with about thirty volumes of verse to his credit. Here is a short, untitled poem of his:

> All tempest
> Has
> Like a navel
> A hole in its middle
> Through which a gull may fly
> In silence.

Somewhat surprisingly, he appears only some half dozen times in Mary's journals.[49] I say that this is surprising, because the tone of Gibran's letters to him is exceptionally warm and open. After reading a number of Gibran's letters, one begins to get the distinct impression that most of them are carefully crafted. But the letters to Bynner are more relaxed and natural; they reveal a Gibran who is far less guarded than usual. Since Bynner was openly homosexual (he lived with Robert Hunt in New Mexico from the 1930s until Hunt's death in 1964), I did begin to wonder whether he and Gibran might conceivably have been attracted to each other in the 1910s – remembering also how close Gibran had been to Fred Holland Day, and that Tom Raymond too may well have been gay. Gibran's letters to Bynner address him as 'Beloved', exactly as he was addressing Mary at the same time; he says 'My love, with this [letter], goes to you' and 'I miss you badly', and so on and so forth. Unfortunately, there are no surviving letters from Bynner to Gibran. Bynner dedicated his 1922 play, *Cycle: A Play of War*, to Gibran,[50] and remembered him with affection in later letters, but that is all we have to go on from his end. It seems to me that Gibran's manner of addressing Bynner was unusually strong, even given the ways one might expect aesthetes in the 1910s and 1920s to have spoken to one another. The fact that Gibran's expressed attitude towards homosexuality veered from hostility to curiosity is neither here nor there, since there is so frequently a gulf on this topic between public attitude and private behaviour. However, I cannot see that there is enough evidence to suggest that they did actually have an affair. My impression of the scenario is that Kahlil knew Bynner was gay, and *for that reason* employed such strong terms of affection in his letters – not because he wanted to tease Witter, but in a safe flirtatious way, knowing that he could see how it felt to flirt with a homosexual without the worry of anything coming of it. My feeling – and it really is no more than a feeling – is that Gibran may well have been uncertain about his own heterosexuality, and relished the opportunity to test himself in this way.

James Oppenheim, whom Gibran met through Beatrice Hinkle (who was Oppenheim's analyst), was a Whitmanesque poet, the author of books such as *Monday Morning and Other Poems* (1909), *Songs for the New Age* (1914), *War and Laughter* (1916), *The Mystic Warrior* (1921) and *The Sea* (1924), as well as a number of novels. He is remembered nowadays as the editor of the literary journal *The Seven Arts*, which was his original connection with Gibran in that he invited Gibran to be one of its advisory editors. He was perhaps best known in New York in the 1910s, however, as the author of the song 'Bread and Roses', which was one of the anthems of the socialists.

If we had only Mary's journals, and did not know when Oppenheim was born, we might think that he was a young man embarking on a poetic career, whose faltering steps Gibran was able to guide on to the true path of artistic creativity. Only once in this record do the two men appear to meet as equals – and that is when Mary is present at a chance meeting in a restaurant, rather than hearing about Oppenheim from Kahlil behind his back, so to speak.[51] As a matter of fact, however, Oppenheim was much the same age as Gibran – a few months older – and had an impressive track record as a published poet. Interestingly, this comes across in Gibran's letters to him – that is, the letters reveal that Gibran's actual attitude towards Oppenheim was far more deferential than Gibran was telling Mary. By the 1920s they appear to have been able to meet as friends, as equals, but before that Gibran treated him, with perfect propriety, as one professional to another. The test case is this. In August 1916, Oppenheim asked Gibran to submit an idea for the cover of *The Seven Arts*. Gibran sent him a drawing of a hand with a flame rising out of it (one of his favourite images). Oppenheim was not happy with it, and sent it back with some criticisms. To Mary, Gibran complained that Oppenheim didn't understand his intentions; to Oppenheim he wrote: 'You are quite right. The hand was not strong enough in the first design, and the flame did not look like a flame. You see, I really do not know how to use pen and ink – and I cannot make a design to save my soul. However, I have just made another one, and I hope you will like it.'

This difference between the public and the private attitude Kahlil held towards his friends bedevilled his relationships. He was all politeness, smiles and warmth to them in person, but he privately thought himself their superior – and that is no basis for true friendship. Time and again in Mary's journals there are unequivocal glimpses of this attitude. Witter Bynner and the playwright Percy Mackaye went crazy over one of his poems – but he doesn't think they understood it properly. Arthur Davies is a divided personality, and morbid. Isadora Duncan he found trivial and uninteresting, even gross, though he acknowledges her greatness as a dancer and counts her greater even than Ruth St Denis. Arthur Farwell – an old friend of Mary, who proved to be a very useful contact when Gibran first went to New York – is a mindless person who comes to see him, Gibran says, for inspiration. Oppenheim comes to Gibran for suggestions and rewrites his poems according to what he says; Gibran describes him as his 'worshipper' and says he is trying to wean him off his small-minded political views. Percy Mackaye is dismissed as 'shabby, physically and spiritually' and a bore. He feels he taught Witter Bynner how to include a sense of the transcendental world in his work.[52] There may be some truth in some or all of these claims, but the arrogant exaggeration with which he speaks inclines us to take them with a hefty pinch of salt. At any rate, it is clear that these people could not be true friends – and there is more than a faint echo here of Kahlil's relationship to Mary, whom he could also treat with high-handed arrogance and at the same time as a kind of special disciple. It seems likely that he had no close friends among white Americans, and that therefore all his talk about loneliness is heartfelt. Once again, paradoxically, the person he was closest to was May Ziadeh – and she lived several thousand miles away.

What about his contacts with the Syrian community? As I have remarked, Gibran came back from Paris with a slightly higher degree of political awareness than he had had when he went there. This is reflected not so much in his Arabic writings from the beginning of the 1910s, which continue in much the same wistful, Romantic vein as before, but in some of his other activities. On returning from Paris, for instance, he joined the Golden Links Society (*Al-Halaqat al-Dhahabiyyah*), an international Syrian organization with US branches in both Boston and New York. The ostensible purpose of the society was the improvement of life for Syrians all around the world – which included their homeland, where improvement of life could mean taking a stand on Ottoman rule. Certainly this is how Gibran understood it, for, as we have seen, he gave a talk to the Boston branch in February 1911, recommending that Syria learn to think and act independently of the Ottoman Empire.[53] He even tried to approach the Muslim community in Syria, warning them, in an open letter, that the Ottomans were out to destroy Islam, and professing his heartfelt sympathy with Islam.[54] This is in keeping with his earlier Romantic politics, in which he takes the Ottomans to task on the grounds that they – and all humankind – are brothers, for attempting to oppress Syria,[55] but there is a harder edge to Gibran's political thinking now, because he also warns Syrians, both Muslim and Christian, that unless they work together their Ottoman masters would simply be replaced by new European ones.

In New York he was welcomed by the Syrians, not just as a famous writer, but also as a potential spokesman for their various causes. On 10 January 1914, for instance, a dinner was held in honour of his birthday; in 1916 a group of editors and writers presented him with a ruby ring, which he proudly wore on his index finger.[56] Gibran did his best to remain aloof from factions, but at the same time accepted invitations to address various Syrian audiences in the city.[57] His popularity among the Syrians grew in proportion to his involvement in their political causes, particularly Syrian nationalism.

His increased politicization shows more particularly in the increased number of times Syrian political matters occur in Mary's journals and in his letters to her.[58] Gibran was very excited, for instance, about the Italian declaration of war on Turkey in late September 1911, which he saw as opening up the possibility of the partition of the empire, and therefore the possibility of Syria's independence; he felt the same about the war between Turkey and the Balkan states in 1912.[59] When World War I broke out in 1914, Gibran eagerly lectured Mary on its potential significance for Syria, as well as discussing with her the rights and wrongs of 'Germanism' in general, which he saw as an inferior manifestation of the human spirit. Once this was swept away by the war, he believed, humankind would be in a position to evolve towards a larger, global consciousness.[60] He declares himself to be in favour of an Arab empire, which was the dream of Arab nationalists at the time, and he was longing to go to Syria to foster revolt against Turkey.[61] In a 1912 letter to Mary he powerfully denounces armchair pacifists who worry about the Balkan states having stirred up war, when the inhabitants of those states have suffered terribly under the Ottoman Empire during the 'hypocritical peace'.[62] In 1918 he wrote his famous poem 'Defeat, My Defeat' to encourage the Serbian rebels in Kosovo.

However, his general political views about Syria's future tend to be rather naïve. Typically those educated, as Gibran was, in the Catholic system in Syria were conditioned in favour of France.[63] In short, the French could do little wrong in Gibran's eyes, and this leads him to a distorted view of some events. For instance, he placed a great deal of confidence in the post-war Paris Conference, at which pro-French Lebanese were lobbying for French protection not just of Lebanon but even of Syria as a whole after the war. He argued, with extreme innocence, that it would be better for France to govern Syria than any other European country, because France had no Eastern empire and therefore less of an agenda.[64]

Equally, his attitude towards the war in general may be seen as rather naïve. While declaring himself to be on the whole not in favour of war, he completely swallowed the propaganda that this was 'the war to end all wars', and so supported the Allied war effort and followed the news with enthusiasm, believing that Allied victory over 'Germanism' would lead to unbroken peace thereafter, where diplomatic rather than armed solutions might be found to international problems.[65] As he says in the last lines of his poem 'The Giants', which was written during the war, 'Spring will come, but he who seeks spring without winter will never find it.' At the same time, he applauded the fact that the war had forced a change of consciousness on people: instead of thinking parochially, only about their local or national interests, they were now more aware of the world at large.[66]

His most overt quasi-political activity, which occurred later in the war, was fund-raising to try to help relieve the famine in Mount Lebanon. The situation in Mount Lebanon was dire: during the war, in one of the great forgotten horrors of the twentieth century, fully one-third of the Lebanese mountain population died of starvation – an estimated 100,000 people.[67] Gibran dedicated his royalties from *A Tear and a Smile* to the cause, and set about cajoling the immigrant population into remembering the suffering back in their native land. There is no doubt that he was well placed to undertake this activity, and as early as December 1914, before the need really arose, he was talking vaguely about doing it, if he could find the time.[68] As a well-known figurehead, he could act as a front man for an appeal – 'the bird that lays golden eggs', as he once cynically expressed his role[69] – and so he was made Secretary of the Syrian-Mount Lebanon Relief Committee when it was formed early in June 1916 under the chairmanship of Najib Malouf. It is to his credit that when the situation called for it, Gibran did find the time. In his poem 'Dead Are My People', written in 1916, he publicly lamented the fact that he was living in relative comfort in New York while his countrymen were dying by the thousand at home; also, as in another 1916 poem, 'In the Dark Night', he appealed (albeit in Arabic) to the West for help.[70]

He could talk the talk, but would he walk the walk? When the time came, he did. As well as working out of the committee's offices at 55 Broadway, Gibran also made trips to Boston and the Midwest to appeal for funds.[71] Not only that, but the Assistant Chairman of the Committee was Amin Rihani, so Gibran had to lay aside his personal differences to concentrate on the work. And in addition to his fund-raising activities, he also worked as English-language secretary for the Syrian-Mount Lebanon League of Liberation, which actively campaigned for autonomy for the Middle Eastern countries, and helped to organize the Syrian-Mount Lebanon Volunteer Committee, to advise Syrians resident in the United States on how to enter the French army so that they could play their part in the war. Nor was his contribution to this effort unimportant. In a tribute to Gibran published in 1929, Salloum Mokarzel recalled how once, when in the typical Syrian way deadlock had been reached because of the arguments of opposing factions, Gibran's emotional appeal to his fellow workers to remember the people starving at home brought them to their senses.[72]

Although the work exhausted him and damaged his frail health,[73] it also filled a gap in his life. He had been in danger of thinking too much in the abstract, without, as it were, getting his hands dirty. He seems to acknowledge this when he says to Mary, 'There was something wrong with me before I began to work for Syria in the War.'[74] But he was never sent to Paris or Egypt, as he occasionally hoped, nor did he ever quite get around to enlisting in the French army, which was an idea he toyed with to set an example to other Syrians in America.[75] Typically, he was always on the verge of some important move, without actually making it, just as he seems to have been on the margins of the important political groups (such as that surrounding his college friend, Ayub Tabet, now in exile in New York), without actually becoming deeply involved. His non-inclusion in the Arab Congress, which opened in Paris on 18 June 1913, he blamed on the fact that he was too much of an individualist, and he criticized the diplomatic and fatalist approach taken by the Syrian representatives, as opposed to the course of violent revolution.[76] This fantasy side of his political life reaches somewhat ridiculous proportions when he talks to Mary about the possibility of his being assassinated by Turkish agents because of his involvement in Arabic and Syrian nationalism.[77]

Considering Gibran's circles in New York in the 1910s can tell us quite a lot about his character. Briefly put, his Western friends were often socialists and pacifists, while his Eastern friends – especially Tabet and the League of Liberation – were belligerent nationalists.

In the summer of 1917, Oppenheim's *The Seven Arts* became one of the most important voices opposing the entry of the United States into World War I on 6 April that year. Now, Gibran was not without principles. He did not put on a pacifist face with Oppenheim and the rest, while retaining his belligerent stance in the Syrian community. It is clear that even among his Western friends he let his views on the war be known,[78] and since he was not entirely in favour of socialism (which he believed tends to seek the lowest common denominator, rather than bringing out the best in people), we may give him the benefit of the doubt and assume that he was also not afraid to let his socialist friends know his views.[79]

It is interesting that he remained at home in both worlds, despite the very obvious clash between them. In fact, the clash was so obvious that his Syrian friends urged him to withdraw from the advisory committee of *The Seven Arts*, most of whose members were known to be pacifists, as a gesture of solidarity with the Syrian cause which they all felt would be furthered by Allied victory in the war.[80] This situation points up clearly not only the tension in Gibran between the demands of the East and those of the West, which we have had occasion to note before, but also the fact that he was somewhat of a chameleon. He could be at home in most environments. He was a tepid socialist who, through Oppenheim, was on the margins of the New York radical circle that included John Reed, Emma Goldman, Henrietta Rodman, Rose Pastor Stokes and Randolph Bourne; he was a hawk surrounded by both fashionable and committed doves.

Whether one regards this as a sign of a strong or a weak character depends largely on one's own views. On the one hand, it could well be argued that Gibran could never have been a chameleon if he was fully and passionately committed to his beliefs and engaged in furthering them. From this point of view, his otherworldly etherealism will appear a weakness, an excuse for sitting on the fence. On the other hand, one might applaud his attempt to refer everything to higher principles, and to stick to his own metaphysical viewpoint despite all the pressures around him. It is not always easy or comfortable being neutral: both sides tend to treat you as an enemy. At a social level, Gibran avoided this danger through his charm. His winning ways could pour oil on troubled waters.

9

The Wordsmith

The comfortable but ultimately distancing routine of periodic contact with Mary in either New York or Boston continued throughout the 1910s. The flood of letters between them slowed to a stream by 1916 and then to a trickle by 1919. Typically, in the early days, she would write a long letter, asking about his work, praising the latest manifestations of it that she had seen, worrying about his health, telling him about her reading or the latest concerts and shows she had been to. Occasionally she urged holidays on him (at her expense) in New Hampshire, Vermont, California, or even the West Indies, which he would politely refuse; she offered him advice on practical matters such as health and insurance. She told him her travel arrangements, if she was coming to New York, and gave him news of Marianna, with whom she maintained a steady but formal relationship. On her summer trips to the west coast, she wrote long newsy letters full of her delight in the wilderness. Just as typically, these letters from her would receive a prompt but far more brief reply from Kahlil. By the end of 1919, the tone of the letters has become considerably less personal; the distance between them can be measured by the slightly stiff politeness of their communication.

While relishing the opportunities that New York offered, and preparing to seize them with both hands, Gibran did not immediately settle down. He had several sustained bouts of illness in 1912, culminating in the removal of six bad teeth in September, and both he and Mary were at least partly inclined to attribute his weakness to the smallness of his present studio. By the end of the year, with Mary's encouragement, he began looking for a larger one. In February 1913 the perfect opportunity arose – a larger room on the top floor of the same building at 51 West 10th Street, with tall windows high up one wall affording a generous amount of good daylight. The rent was $45 a month, and he would have to spend some money doing it up, but Mary was more than happy to finance both the immediate costs and the long-term commitment. On the first day of May, Gibran moved in and began the process of redecorating in his favourite muted colours. This was now 'the Hermitage', the studio where he would spend the rest of his life. He wrote to Mary in exultation: 'I am no longer in a cage. I [can] move about without touching the walls with my wings! . . . It is a sort of resurrection.'[1]

The move does seem to have done him good, at least in the sense that he entered a highly productive phase for the next few years. There is also a certain roundedness to his work at this period, in the sense that all its aspects interlock. Rather than vacillating between forms in both his writing and his painting, he knows what he wants to say, and is seeking ways to express it. There is a far higher degree of single-mindedness about his efforts. Commonly, for instance, a piece written in Arabic and destined for publication in one of the Arabic newspapers in New York or Cairo would then be translated (with Mary's help) and published in English in a magazine, and then later a book. At the same time, these pieces formed the backbone of his readings to both formal and informal gatherings in New York – formal ones such as the Poetry Society, and informal ones such as some soirée arranged by Mrs Robinson or one of his society acquaintances.

But what was it he was trying to express at this time? If we were left with only his paintings and writings, his concrete work, we would have to embark on the treacherous waters of interpreting self-confessedly vague and symbolic work. Fortunately, in her journals Mary preserved a number of remarks which together add up to a fascinating cosmology. These ideas are not always articulated clearly, and never form a coherent whole that one would want to call 'Gibranism' or whatever, but they are striking in their simplicity and originality.[2]

The earliest promise of Gibran's developed philosophy appears in his repeated insistence that the only important thing is Life itself. It – whatever 'it' may be – is all here now, and all we have to learn to do, if we want to penetrate the core of Reality, is learn to perceive it here and now. Hence – useful advice by any standard – 'We need to see each thing as if we had not seen it before, and live each moment as it really is, as a new moment.'[3] Gibran denied that there are realms so transcendental that they are unavailable to us; the deepest mysteries of the world are hidden within the world itself. 'There are no keys,' he told Mary on one occasion, 'because there are no doors. Here it is – Life – not locked away from us, but all around us.' Personal growth is simply the increase of sensitiveness, until finally there is nothing between oneself and reality, and one is conscious of, or feels, the totality of what is. This is possible because everything is interconnected. Everything is made out of the same elements, and so I have within me the stuff of and the means of understanding the smallest atom and the greatest star. This is of a piece with his earlier anticlerical promotion of personal religion: there is no need of priests when Life is all there is, and is right here to be appreciated in its entirety. And so he claims that God is right here now.[4]

At a personal level, then, it is possible to increase one's consciousness. However, there is a crucial impersonal element to such self-development. Here is the heart of Gibran's thought. We live in a hierarchical universe. Not only is there inorganic and organic life, but beyond organic life there are levels of more refined and simple matter – the human soul, the spirit of the earth as a whole, and finally God. The hierarchical nature of the universe means that the higher levels may well not perceive the lower levels: God perceives the human soul, but he may not notice anything lower than that.[5] All these layers are material, but at further and further degrees of refinement.

There is an evolutionary impulse to the totality, and to each of its parts: every level of reality wants to develop the next kind of consciousness and become simpler. The impersonal aspect of our self-development is that we are not really developing ourselves; rather, we are being used by the earth as a whole because an increase in human consciousness, which will lift humankind on to the next plane of its evolution, will simultaneously allow planetary consciousness to develop too. A step up for one level of life has a knock-on effect at all levels. In fact it is wrong to say that every level of reality wants to develop the next kind of consciousness: the wanting, the desire, comes from the level above it, not from itself. The ultimate desirer, as in Sufism, is God. God wants the Earth to become like him, and so the Earth – and we creatures of the Earth – grow towards God by the power of that desire.

This means that God too evolves. We will never achieve God-consciousness, because by the time we get to what is now God-consciousness, God himself will have moved on to further inconceivable levels. Apart from the basic broad levels of reality – God, planet, human soul, human body – there are lesser levels-within-levels. Thus the mind may use the body of an individual, just as the planet may use humankind as a whole. We are all used, willy-nilly, but more aware people (such as Gibran) know it, and submit to the forces working through them. This submission is all one can do in the face of the mighty powers involved. Smaller people are used by smaller forces: in a choice turn of phrase, Gibran once described certain people as having no personal reality, but being merely 'embodied points of view'; in Jungian terms we might say that they were possessed by an archetype. An important insight Gibran gained, but seems not always to have applied much to his own case, is that since development is always possible, we should not hold any views as final.

Somewhat oddly, alongside the principle that the higher level uses the lower level Gibran also maintained that the higher level is born out of the lower level. God is born from the Earth, as the soul is the child of the body. God is trying to use the Earth to express himself; on the Earth human beings are God's best material, so he uses us to enlarge himself and escape from the Earth. Similarly, our souls are potentially in us from birth. However, he leaves it unclear how the higher level grows out of the lower, except to say that it is the tendency of matter to expand. Perhaps he saw it, then, simply as an organic development. Certainly, at one point he told Mary that the Greater Self keeps on growing regardless of the actions of our lower selves, which may at best retard the growth a little.

The idea that God uses us humans as his means of development is extraordinary. It gives us a certain terrifying responsibility for God. Gibran could have used this to develop a whole ethics, in the sense that God's future development requires us to behave in certain ways (such as an environmental concern for the Earth), but there is no sign that he did so. However, he does grasp the nettle firmly in one respect: the implication of an evolving God is that God is not perfect, and Gibran is very firm about this. He describes perfection as a limitation, and therefore as something alien to God.

Every generation progresses, he claims, but there are also large-scale movements. The present generation is the summit of a 'mood' that started 6,000 years or more ago in ancient Egypt. So the wireless is the fruit of the word, and the railway is the consummation of beating a path between huts. A new sense of scale, gained perhaps by access to other planets beyond our own,[6] is what is needed to open up the next evolutionary leap for humanity as a whole. Meanwhile, those far-sighted beings at the cutting edge of the human race – poets, prophets, artists – allow themselves to draw out what is in the human subconscious or soul, so that it can express its own desire for evolution and thereby assist the evolution of the general mass of humanity. This is not aimless evolution, but progress towards perfection: contradicting his other statements about the undesirability of perfection, Gibran here maintains that God created the world full of imperfection so as to allow it to develop towards perfection. Perfection is God-consciousness, but since God is infinite and his own consciousness is developing too, we can never encompass the whole of God.

It is certain that Gibran developed this philosophy out of his reading and thinking, over a period of time, but he must have been delighted once it had formed in his mind, because he was able to tie up a lot of his other intuitive but disconnected views into the same cosmological bundle. So, for instance, pain and suffering is said to be necessary for new birth. Pain is, if you like, the pain of labour, the pain of developing into a further phase of evolutionary potential.[7] Or again, as we have already seen, poets and artists, who had always, naturally, been exalted in Gibran's thinking, now find their place as the very people who further the development of humanity by drawing out of its subconscious what it is seeking to express.[8] Perhaps most importantly, it provided Gibran with a broad philosophical rationale for his youthful Romantic emphasis on love. Love is now seen as an aspiration towards our own potential: we love what we may become. That is why we love Christ, for instance, or why a boy loves his father.[9]

Another of his cherished beliefs, reincarnation, becomes accommodated within this cosmology as follows. The soul is elementary and is therefore indestructible because there is nothing for it to be dissolved into. Like everything else in the universe, it desires its own perfection and that of the level of matter beneath it – in this case, the human body. It is the soul's striving for perfection that causes physical death. Presumably the idea here is that if the soul were content with the body (which is to say, if the body were perfect), it would have no need to shed one body in favour of another one further along the evolutionary scale.[10] Mary, however, was always sceptical about the survival of the personality, which Gibran confidently affirms. He ends up simply asserting the continuation of personality, basing this belief on his claimed experience of suprasensible presences surrounding us all the time.[11] He develops the notion that personality is the clothing of the soul, or is like a fine dust given off by the body, but that does not in itself take us any nearer to understanding how it can survive death, or why it should be reincarnated at all. In effect, he seems to want to say that it is *because* all is matter that nothing perishes: it simply transmutes into another form. But in the case of the soul this is to confuse transmutation with transmigration.[12]

So there are some difficulties with his cosmology, but nevertheless Gibran was excited by what he took to be his own original philosophy, and felt that he had found his message for humankind and one which had a genuine contribution to make. The idea that God evolves, he says, is going to change human thinking; as for the idea that soul is a higher form of matter, when he first announced it to Mary he added, as if to mark the occasion portentously, 'I believe that this is the first time this has been said on this planet.' It is such a dynamic concept, he said on another occasion, that even if ultimately it proved false it would still send us on to find what is true.[13]

For a biographer, one of the most interesting things about this cosmology and philosophy is how little it is directly expressed in Gibran's writings. Although he described his writing as 'imprisoning thoughts',[14] these are thoughts that he apparently chose to leave more or less free. They occur either as fragments or as the deep underlying structure of a work. In *The Madman*, for instance, the eponymous protagonist of the book addresses God with the words: 'My God, my aim and my fulfilment; I am thy yesterday and thou art my tomorrow.

I am thy root in the earth and thou art my flower in the sky, and together we grow before the face of the sun.' Or again, in *The Earth Gods*, we meet the idea that human beings are food for the gods. And in 'The Giants', he asserts: 'I am among those who believe in the Law of Evolution: I believe that ideal entities evolve, like brute beings, and that religions and governments are raised to higher planes.'[15] More broadly, the underlying message of *The Prophet*, he tells Mary on more than one occasion, is that we human beings are bigger than we think we are, that we can be infinite – a powerful idea which seized Gibran's mind at the same time that he was developing this evolutionary cosmology.[16]

In fact, it was his paintings rather than his writings which were the chief vehicles for this philosophy. In 1919, after the publication of *Twenty Drawings*, he planned another volume of pictures, on the theme of the soul's journey towards God.[17] Even though this book was never published, it is easy to detect in the extant paintings echoes of his cosmology. For instance, following William Blake, a higher spirit is likely to be depicted as a larger being looming behind us small mortals; or a device such as a figure with arms reaching out towards a larger being might represent an evolutionary aspiration. Often we see a group of figures: for instance, the earth mother and her children with the Great Spirit hovering over them all. This is how he attempts to communicate his philosophy by visual means.

Finally on this topic, it is surely no coincidence that Gibran developed this evolutionary philosophy while living in New York, in the grip of the city's energy. For at the heart of this energy was a sense of striving to overcome physical limitations – epitomized above all by the architecture of the skyscrapers and by the excitement surrounding aeroplane flights. That was why New York was so attractive to so many young writers and thinkers: it was a place where they could break the bounds and forge the future. That was why Freud's thought found such a ready market in New York: it seemed to offer a way to free oneself from inhibitions. One way or another, in New York Gibran was surrounded by growth and the prospect of growth; at some level his evolutionary philosophy is a reflection of this.

Gibran's fame in the Arab world continued to rise, with the publication in 1912 of *The Broken Wings* and with the continued appearance of incidental pieces in Arabic newspapers. In 1913 the newspaper *Al-Funun* (*The Arts*) was launched. The editor, Nasib 'Arida, was a personal friend of Gibran, and not only was he happy to publish his poems, prose-poems, parables and essays, but he also gave him a fairly free hand with regard to the layout and design of the paper, printed a number of his drawings, and allowed him to do some commissioning too. For the next few years of its sporadic career,[18] *Al-Funun* was to be the main vehicle for Gibran's Arabic work, as it was for other Lebanese immigrant writers in the States. It was in these pages over the next few years that Gibran began to publish the parables and Aesopian fables which, when translated, would become his first English book, *The Madman*.

Through *Al-Funun* Gibran came into contact with another immigrant writer, who was to become his closest friend. In 1913 Mikhail Naimy had been in the States for almost two years, after several years in the Theological Seminary in Poltava in the Ukraine (since he had been educated at the Russian school in his native village of Baskinta), but had largely avoided the New York scene. While studying law at Washington State University the 24-year-old Naimy was sent a copy of *The Broken Wings*, and he wrote a long review of it, in which he criticized the simplicity of the characterization and plot of the book, but nevertheless found that its formal features contained enough promise for him to use it as a springboard for a passionate appeal for a renaissance in Arabic literature.[19] The publication of this review by *Al-Funun* was the start of Naimy's long and illustrious career as a writer and critic.[20] Soon he not only became a regular contributor to *Al-Funun*, but also corresponded with Gibran, until he finally settled in New York in 1916.

In 1914 *A Tear and a Smile* was published by 'Arida, to Gibran's apparent regret. He felt that he had outgrown the early pieces that were included in this anthology, and described them as 'the unripe grapes of my vineyard'.[21] When 'Arida started to push for permission to collect and publish the poems, Gibran half-heartedly tried to put him off by saying:

The youth who wrote *A Tear and a Smile* has long since died and been buried in the valley of dreams. Why do you wish to exhume his remains?

Do as you like, but do not forget that the soul of that youth has been reincarnated in a man whose love for will and power is equal to his love for grace and beauty.[22]

We have already seen this harder edge in Gibran's war poems, and we will see more of it in his first English writing. In other respects, however, he had not changed: *A Tear and a Smile* came with a eulogistic introduction, supposedly written by 'Arida, but in fact written by Gibran himself.[23] It seems that for all his seeming diffidence about the book's publication, Gibran was still eager to make use of it as an opportunity for self-glorification. Moreover, this public assertion that he had grown out of the poems of *A Tear and a Smile* must be set against his private conversations with Mary, in which he shows considerably less dissatisfaction with them.

Al-Funun also provided the context for one of Gibran's more notorious public lies. When 'Arida asked him for biographical information to publish in the paper, Gibran gave it and 'Arida wrote it up in the September 1916 issue of the paper exactly as he was given it: 'Gibran was born in the year 1883 in Bsharri, Lebanon (though some say in Bombay, India) . . .' Nor did his biographical lies to 'Arida stop there. He awarded himself a degree from the École des Beaux-Arts in Paris and membership of the Union Internationale des Beaux-Arts et des Lettres. This boastful exaggeration of his student days in Paris at least has comprehensible motives, but what can he possibly have hoped to gain from the oblique reference to India? At first I thought that he must have been trying to cash in on the wave of Indophilia that was sweeping America in the wake of Rabindranath Tagore's triumphal visit in 1916, but *Al-Funun* went out only to the Arab populace, so that hypothesis will not do. It seems that he just wanted to cloak himself in the mystique of having a mysterious birth.[24]

Just as he felt he had moved on as a writer, so he also felt he was developing as an artist. Just as there were metaphorical hard edges to his writing, so there could be literal hard edges to his drawings. The blurred mistiness of his middle period gradually gave way to a greater sureness of line, just as the melancholic Romantic of his early Arabic poetry had given way to the Nietzschean rebel of the 1910s. As an artist, Gibran was still a Symbolist. He was full of praise for the latest European developments in art, and along with tens of thousands of others he visited the Armory Show in 1913 (while Mary visited it when it moved to Boston). He described the show as a 'declaration of independence',[25] but he remained fixed in his Symbolist groove. The main development in the 1910s is that he seems more sure of his ground – an increased certainty which I attribute to the development of his own personal philosophy, his message for humankind. In 1915 it was still common for any of his pencilled figures to be no more than an outline both surrounded by and containing swirling lines indicative of half-formed energies; but by 1918 these tentative swirlings have yielded to a more confident use of shading to give an impression of the contours of the body. At the same time a greater degree of overt symbolism enters the paintings, typically with smaller figures being embraced, perhaps, by larger figures. This is the sculptural style of painting and drawing familiar to readers of *The Madman*. From 1915 onwards Gibran was also beginning to work with wash drawings, in which an original pencil sketch is overlaid with a lightly coloured layer of transparent paint. He found this style particularly congenial, and it grew naturally into the watercolours for which he is most famous, because a number of them were included in his later books, such as *The Prophet*.[26]

However, he first received attention in New York when he was still a fully fledged Symbolist of the swirling mist school. In 1914, after a number of nibbles from other galleries, Mr Montross, an influential dealer whose gallery was well placed at 550 5th Avenue, promised him an exhibition. He liked the work and guaranteed a solo exhibition in December, a good month for shows. He also made the right kind of encouraging noises to feed Gibran's ambitions, saying that the exhibition would give New York a big surprise. Gibran and Mary felt sure that this was the breakthrough for which he had been waiting.[27] Now he would come to the wider attention of New York. His joyful letters to her were matched by the tone of her responses. Despite the fact that only a year previously he had described an exhibition as a trap,[28] when it came down to it this was no more than sour grapes. He worked throughout the summer, enduring the hot, heavy air of New York, and took only a three-week break in Boston, where he could continue to prepare for the show. As the time for the exhibition drew close his conversations with and letters to Mary were filled with news about his plans for the show. He found Montross's 25 per cent commission steep, but at the same time appreciated that his work could fetch a far greater price through this gallery than in most other outlets.

Some important details about the exhibition remain frustratingly elusive. The most authoritative figure for the number of pieces exhibited is forty-four – twenty-five paintings and nineteen heads from the Temple of Art series. However, it is quite unclear whether it was enough of a financial or critical success. Gibran cleared almost $5,000 after paying Montross's commission, and was able to invest at least some of this money. This was the equivalent of two years' income, no paltry sum. But it was apparently not enough to keep Montross interested in him and to want to put on another solo exhibition.[29] Although the exhibition, which ran from 14 to 30 December, was well attended, only five paintings were sold, and most of those went to people who were already within Gibran's circle of friends and acquaintances: Rose O'Neill bought one called 'The Great Solitude', the Mortens bought 'Nebula', Julia Ford bought 'Silence', and of the other two, one went to Cecilia Beaux, a portrait painter of Gibran's acquaintance, and the second to an otherwise unknown Mrs Gibson.[30]

While his friends paid him the compliment of buying his work, the critical reception was largely hostile. The *New York Times* spoke of 'cloudy visions of striving and unhappy humanity', the *Tribune* described him as a 'feeble Arthur Davies', the *Evening Post* talked of his 'foggy symbolism', and Henry McBride, the famous critic writing at that time for the *Sun*, damned Gibran's work with faint praise as 'earnest', and then, like the *Times* critic, went on to regret the apparent pessimism of the subject matter, where the blind seemed to be leading the blind towards unknown destinations. Only an old friend from Boston, Joseph Edgar Chamberlain, writing in the *Evening Mail*, and Charles H. Caffin in the *American*, were warmer. Indeed, Caffin's review is extremely complimentary: technically, the drawings are 'extraordinarily fine'; Gibran creates 'a world of original creation' – an elemental world 'as of vast forces, still inchoate, stirring in the womb of infinity', which symbolizes the world of the spirit; the exhibition is 'distinguished throughout by profoundness of purpose and feeling' and it 'avoids the banality of allegorical representation'.

Another old friend from Boston took the opportunity to stab Mary in the heart. Charlotte Teller Hirsch returned from Germany, where she had been living with her husband, in time to catch the opening of the exhibition. She wrote to Mary that she now utterly repudiated Orientalism in all its forms, as the 'sleeping sickness of the Universe'. She found Kahlil's pictures suffused with the Oriental spirit, but too weak and fuzzy to be as dangerous as that spirit could be, in her opinion. In another letter a couple of months later she described his work as 'supine', and claimed that like others of the East he refused to face up to the hard facts of life.[31] Charlotte had truly wedded herself to the craze for 'terrible honesty' that was beginning to sweep through New York, under the influence of Freud.[32]

Nevertheless, Gibran was clearly pleased with the exhibition. It had, after all, been well attended, and one of his main aims at this stage was simply to become better known. But he was to be disappointed if he hoped that it would lead to further exhibitions. In 1915, with Mary acting as his scout, he began to angle for a major show in Boston. The prestigious Boston Art Club, one of the foci of a society lady's life, agreed in January to host a show in May, but then changed its mind at the last minute. Gibran was in touch with them on 17 April to tell them that the pictures were all ready to be shipped, but he received a telegram by return abruptly cancelling the exhibition and promising a fuller explanation later, which seems never to have come.

Mary suggested the gallery of Doll and Richards, at 71 Newbury Street, as an alternative venue for a May show in Boston, but Gibran refused, saying that May was not a good month for exhibiting, and that his work was for a lifetime, so that minor setbacks were unimportant. What with one thing and another – the war, Gibran's involvement in the Relief Committee and a renewal of his rate of writing – it was February 1916 before there was a definite offer of another exhibition. This time the venue was the excellent Knoedler Gallery, at 556–558 5th Avenue, from 29 January to 10 February 1917 – and this time there *was* a follow-up exhibition in Boston, at Doll and Richards from 16 to 28 April.

By the time of these two exhibitions, Gibran was working entirely with small wash drawings. This represented a departure for him, since they were more representational and less symbolic. They remind one somewhat of watercolours by Rodin. A common figure in them is that of the centaur, representing our dual nature (earthbound and spiritual), but as usual Gibran concentrated on the naked human form. Forty of these wash drawings were shown at the Knoedler Gallery, and then thirty in Boston. Gibran had met Mr and Mrs Albert Sterner, who were employees of the Knoedler Gallery (as well as being, in Albert Sterner's case, at any rate, an artist in his own right), in November 1915. They admired his work and Gibran immediately began to talk about 'going over' to Knoedler's and leaving Montross, who still had one or two of his pictures on display. He claimed that the Sterners were completely bowled over by his work, and that Sterner now tried to paint just like him.[33] In any case, it is certain that the Sterners were impressed enough with the wash drawings to want to have them in Knoedler's, and to arrange a good exhibition for them. Gibran worked hard in conjunction with them, taking care over the frames and all aspects of the presentation of the drawings on the gallery's walls. The results were pleasing, and this time the *New York Times* was at least lukewarm. The critic acknowledged that many people would enjoy 'this spontaneous form of artistic expression', and whereas the wash drawings were rather too artificial for his taste, he called some of the ordinary drawings 'as solid and quiet as those of a good student before the atelier model'. In other words, competent stuff, if lacking in flair.

Once again, sales were disappointing, even though these smaller pieces were considerably cheaper than the paintings at the Montross exhibition. Only three were sold, and two of those went to acquaintances. Gibran blames these poor sales on Mrs Sterner herself, calling her 'a great blunderer', without explaining what he means, despite the fact that a few days earlier he had told Mary, when she came to New York to see the show, that the exhibition had done a great deal for him.[34] The Doll and Richards exhibition a couple of months later was no more of a commercial success, although the Boston critics were on the whole kinder than those in New York.

*

Each exhibition took months of planning, preparing and hoping. The returns must have seemed frustratingly small. Within his lifetime Gibran had only two further solo exhibitions, one of forty wash drawings in Boston at the Women's City Club, 10–31 January 1922, and another at his own studio in New York from January to March 1930.[35] He seems to have given up this method of acquiring fame and fortune. Knoedler's kept him on, however, and his name appears among twenty-eight other artists in an exhibition held there from 27 November to 16 December 1919, entitled 'Foreign and American Paintings'.

If success was not to come his way through his painting, it had to come through his writing. Oddly, the first widespread mention of his name in America at large came about by accident. Albert Pinkham Ryder's death in 1917 was followed by a wave of posthumous tributes to this American painter, the first of which, written by no less than Henry McBride, quoted the poem Gibran had written for Ryder. Newspapers across the country from Toledo to Chicago picked up the ball and ran with it. In the ephemeral world of journalism, this was scarcely enough to make him a household name, but it was a kind of brief recognition. When Rodin died later in the year, on 17 November, Gibran tried the same thing again, and wrote an elaborate homage in English (with Mary's help). Although he submitted it to several magazines, there is no record of its being published.

Far more important was his association with James Oppenheim's magazine *The Seven Arts*. The magazine was widely acclaimed in literary circles; as well as attracting a prestigious list of authors, Oppenheim had gathered together an impressive advisory board, including (apart from Gibran himself) from the literary world Robert Frost, Louis Untermeyer and the historian and critic Edna Kenton, and from the musical world David Mannes and Robert Edmond Jones. Waldo Frank and Van Wyck Brooks were Oppenheim's associate editors. Apart from regular contributions by Gibran and the other advisers,[36] *The Seven Arts* was to publish Sherwood Anderson, D. H. Lawrence, Eugene O'Neill, Theodore Dreiser, John Dos Passos, H. L. Mencken, Bertrand Russell and a number of other luminaries. This was a publication with an extremely high profile, and Gibran's success in the English-speaking world owes far more to his association with it than to any other single source, as he recognized. He told Mary that the publication of his work in the magazine had done a great deal for him, and that he was now as famous in New York as he had been in Syria fifteen years before.[37] The magazine collapsed in October 1917, having started only the previous year, when Annette Rankin caved in to public pressure and withdrew her financial support in the face of the growing unpopularity of the magazine's pacifist stance. But in its short life it had given Gibran just the platform he needed for entry into the literary life of New York.[38]

The Seven Arts also furthered Gibran's career in a more obvious fashion. In their issue for March 1917, with the memory of the Knoedler exhibition still fresh in readers' minds, they ran an adulatory essay by Alice Raphael on 'The Art of Kahlil Gibran'. In this essay (which was reprinted in 1919 as the introduction to the book *Twenty Drawings*) she claimed that Gibran's work was hard to categorize, because he stood on the borderline between East and West, between symbolism and representation, and between sculpture and painting. She commended the work for the universal meanings it managed to convey, and argued that the roots of the paintings lay in 'those truths which are fundamental for all ages and all experience'. This was nothing short of an encomium. Everything was coming together for Gibran at once; he was riding the crest of a wave. On 25 February 1917, he even had his drawing of John Masefield published in the *New York Times* magazine. The fact that he had his own phone installed in the studio at the beginning of 1917, rather than sharing the one common to the building, is both a symbol of his increasing prestige and an indication of his availability, at least to the Syrian community for his committee work, which continued even after the end of the war.[39]

One crucial means of publicity to which Gibran was introduced as a result of his association with the magazine and its literati was that of poetry readings. He soon became a popular figure for readings at the Poetry Society or the MacDowell Club where, usually in company with one or more other poets reading their work, he would try out the parables that would become *The Madman* and *The Forerunner*, and then later the 'Counsels' that would become *The Prophet*. One such evening, for instance, was advertised by the MacDowell Club as follows: 'Tuesday evening, December Second [1919] at half past eight o'clock, the Committee on Literature announces readings of Kahlil

Gibran's Parables and of Witter Bynner's Canticles by the authors.' Not only could Gibran use these evenings as a way of assessing the English-speaking world's reaction to his English pieces, but they served the important purpose of building up an eager market for his books as they appeared.

There are one or two amusing stories about these readings. The first concerns Mrs Corinne Roosevelt Robinson. The first time she came across Gibran was at a Poetry Society evening in March 1915 at which he read, among other pieces, the parable which came to be called 'The Greater Sea' in *The Madman*, in which Gibran imagines himself and his soul looking for a private place to bathe in the great sea. Everywhere they went, however, they found the place occupied by some representative of mankind's foibles – the pessimist who throws pinches of salt into the sea, the optimist who throws in handfuls of sugar, the philanthropist who picks up dead fish and returns them to the sea, the mystic who traces his shadow in the sand and then does it all over again when the sea erases the traces, the idealist who scoops up the sea-foam and puts it carefully into an alabaster bowl, the so-called realist who listens to the sea in a shell while turning his back on the sea itself, the puritan who buries his head in the sand by the sea. There is nowhere for the soul to expose herself, so they leave the great sea and go in search of the Greater Sea. When Mrs Robinson heard this parable, she leapt to her feet in high dudgeon and denounced it as negative and destructive. 'We must not encourage such a spirit in our literature,' she said. 'It is contrary to all our forms of morality and true beauty.'[40] Subsequently she came to know and like Kahlil, and became one of his truest supporters and patrons.

Another story concerns Rose Pastor Stokes, the tireless socialist campaigner who admired Russian communism and called for violent revolution in America. She was married to James Graham Phelps Stokes, dubbed by the *New York Times* on 23 October 1910 'the richest socialist in the world'. In April 1920 at the MacDowell Club Gibran read, among other pieces, the parable which was to become 'The Plutocrat' in *The Forerunner*:

In my wanderings I once saw upon an island a man-headed, iron-hoofed monster who ate of the earth and drank of the sea incessantly. And for a long while I watched him. Then I approached him and said, 'Have you never enough; is your hunger never satisfied and your thirst never quenched?'

And he answered saying, 'Yes, I am satisfied, nay, I am weary of eating and drinking; but I am afraid that tomorrow there will be no more earth to eat and no more sea to drink.'

Apparently, the audience greeted this with dead silence – which was then broken by the solitary clapping of Rose Pastor Stokes.[41]

Gibran's acquaintance with Rose Pastor Stokes went back a few years and perfectly illustrates the importance to his career and public profile of these poetry readings. In 1917 and 1918 Stokes was involved in setting up a series of concerts in the States for the blind Russian baritone Vladimir Resnikoff, whose singing of his motherland's folk songs was said to reveal the soul of Russia. One such concert was at the Little Theatre in New York. A two-sided flyer was produced to promote the concert, starting, 'Would you have revealed to you the soul of a people?', and continuing with quotes from favourable reviews of an earlier concert. The back of the flyer was devoted to a testimonial from Kahlil Gibran, described (with imperfect accuracy) as 'the visiting Eastern poet and painter who himself, last winter, made so deep an impression upon the Poetry Society of America'. There is no need to quote the whole of the testimonial. Suffice it to say that Gibran saw Resnikoff, like himself, as one 'whose art is not an expression but a longing for the Unknown'.[42] But the point is that Gibran had come to the public's attention, and was the kind of person Stokes might invite to contribute such a testimonial, because of his readings at the Poetry Society. This shows clearly the potential such readings had to make or break a career. They made Gibran.[43] He was even courted in 1919 and the 1920s by the famous Pond's Lecture Agency, which had arranged tours for, among others, Mark Twain, Matthew Arnold and Sir Arthur Conan Doyle. However, not only was Gibran reluctant to undertake the kind of tiring tour of the western states that they were proposing, but the agency itself had to close for a while due to financial problems, and so the tour never took place.[44]

So from 1915 onwards, in the sphere of writing, Gibran was working chiefly with the parable or wisdom story, which he used to express his dissatisfaction with the state of the world. There were a few years of transition from 1913 onwards, when he was writing in both his earlier and later moods simultaneously, despite the considerable differences in tone. So on the one hand in 1913 he wrote 'The Poet', a typical Romantic piece in which he both mourns and celebrates the poet's lot as a stranger in this strange land. On the other hand, he also wrote 'Satan', in which a priest stops (after considerably more hesitation than the Good Samaritan displayed) to help a wounded traveller on the road. The wounded man turns out to be Satan, who argues not only that without sin, born of Satan, the priest would be out of a job, but also that sin and evil permeate the very fabric of society. He wins the priest over, and the priest saves the life of Satan. This new Nietzschean bitterness – even savagery – continues in 1915 with poems and stories such as 'The Grave-digger' and 'My Countrymen'. In the former, living people are condemned as walking dead,[45] and in the latter he fiercely attacks the complacency of the Lebanese, in particular their tendency to praise his poems while refusing to put into practice any of his recommendations. 'I see your weakness,' he says, 'and my soul trembles with disgust.' At the same time, however, tales such as 'Honeyed Poison' and 'Behind the Garment', which belong to this period, could have been written years before, with their theme of love outside marriage, as could 'At the Door of the Temple', which celebrates Love. The Romantic bitterness of the angry young man resurfaces in 'The Storm' (one of Gibran's most successful poems, which was reprinted all over the Near East), which I have already summarized in another context.[46] Other Arabic poems and prose-poems from this period tell of Jesus' alienation in a world which has forgotten his teachings, and of how urban civilization is like a zoo, where people have all the bad points of animals, but none of their good points.

The parables which make up *The Madman* – usually written first in Arabic and then translated into English – are generally in harmony with this bitter tone, though the mood is muted by the obliqueness of the parable form, which at its most extreme can leave the reader guessing what precisely the author meant to convey. The concept of the book is that each of the parables is supposed to be spoken by a so-called madman, who of course is really more sane and keen-sighted than the rest of us. He is simply someone who has lost or shed the masks which normally enable us to live comfortably in the society of others. Gibran had an interest in the notion of lunacy and on more than one occasion regaled Mary with fanciful stories of lunatics he had met in his childhood and youth in Lebanon, where the treatment of insanity was medieval. The point of the stories is generally that Kahlil felt a certain affinity with the crazy wisdom of these so-called lunatics. Think of Yuhanna the Madman in *Nymphs of the Valley*: even in those early days Gibran was making a madman his alter ego.[47] As early as 1911, Gibran was considering a whole book with the title *The Madman*, but it seems that at this stage the book was conceived of as an Arabic play. Later it became a vehicle for collecting prose-poems and short stories. It was only with the rise of his interest in writing parables that the book settled into its final form.[48]

We have already glanced at a few of the parables from *The Madman*, but perhaps not enough to convey the tone of the book. Within its pages we meet a mother and a daughter who are all smiles and pleasantries during their waking hours, but when they meet each other at night as sleepwalkers they curse each other and reveal their mutual hatred. We meet people who befriend others only for their masks, without any knowledge of the true selves underneath. Others have such a superficial understanding of the Bible that they have literally plucked out their eyes and cut off their right hands; these are the inhabitants of the ironically titled 'Blessed City'. Children grow up to conform to society's lies and to forget about the true blessedness of the paradise from which they came. In society, madness is regarded as wisdom and wisdom as madness; for those who are duped by society's norms, a perfect world is one in which every event is circumscribed and regulated.

There are themes here that are reminiscent of the Gibran of *Nymphs of the Valley* and *Spirits Rebellious*. What is new is partly the irony of the parable form, which lends his tirade against social convention an added bitterness, and partly the universality of his criticism, which is no longer confined to reflections on Syrian society. This means that we hear less of Gibran's sympathy for the oppressed, and more of the other side of the coin – his contempt for authority. The madman himself is considered mad because he stands outside society, and we are to think, of course, that this is a better place to be. 'To be the only sane man among fools is to appear as the only fool among sane men.'[49] There are redeeming features to the bleak picture Gibran gives us in *The Madman*, but they are no more than glimpses. In 'The Greater Sea', for instance, paraphrased a little earlier, we hear at least that there *is* a Greater Sea – a more ideal world beyond this one, just as in 'The Astronomer' it is clear that the blind astronomer sees an immaterial world greater and more glorious than this one; but we are given few clues as to how to get there, apart from the idea that we have to transcend society's rules and the limitations of our own natures. In 'The Grave-digger' we are told that if we could laugh at ourselves and at society, that would be a good start.[50] Self-transcendence, evolution towards a divine state, is possible for us human beings – so much of Gibran's process philosophy underlies the book – but he leaves us no clear signposts or methodology.

Gibran was aware of the bitterness of *The Madman*. He claimed that the purpose of the book was to destroy illusions and proclaim Life, and added that it was personal to him: 'I am becoming like my madman,' he told Mary once, in that he felt impatient with people, wanted to hurt them, and could not abide what they said.[51] This mood had been on him for a long time. Even in 1911, looking forward to the publication of *The Broken Wings*, he complained that it was coming out when he had already outgrown it: 'I don't want to write of love. I feel like struggle, like crushing things.'[52] When it came down to it, however, he implied that rather than writing out of a savage whim, he was working to a programme: this book would destroy illusions, while the next book would concentrate more on human potential, once the ground had been cleared, so to speak, by *The Madman*.[53]

The book was essentially complete by the middle of 1917. The way had been prepared by publication of many of the parables in both the Arabic press,[54] and in *The Seven Arts*, and by public readings at the Poetry Society and elsewhere. All that remained was to find a publisher. Early in 1918 he sent it to two publishers – first William Morrow of the publishing company Frederick A. Stokes, and then Macmillan – but they both rejected it.[55] Then in May he heard that a young publisher called Alfred Knopf, who was already establishing a reputation for taking literary work seriously, while also achieving good sales, was interested in the book, to which his attention had been drawn by Gibran's friends – especially Oppenheim and Bynner. In June Gibran met Knopf, and the contract was signed on 20 June. So began a working relationship which lasted the rest of Gibran's life. The firm of Alfred A. Knopf, Inc., remains the American publisher of Gibran's English-language books.

The relationship between Gibran and Knopf never developed into a proper friendship, although Gibran went round to his house for dinner or tea once or twice. In fact, most of Gibran's dealings over the publication of his books were with Knopf's wife Blanche, rather than with the man himself. Gibran was basically happy with the way the books were published, while grumbling from time to time about the high prices Knopf put on them, and about occasional delays to their publication, but ultimately he found him too commercial to become one of his friends. He started off by singing his praises, describing him as a 'sweet being' and commending him for being open to suggestions, but by 1922 he was describing him as greedy, and by 1924 he told Mary that he avoided meeting him as much as possible, since success had spoiled him.[56] The extant letters between Gibran and the firm – chiefly, as I've said, to and from Blanche Knopf – never get far from formality.

The Madman was published in October 1918. The publicity flyer produced to advertise the book is notorious. It prominently printed a testimonial from Auguste Rodin (now conveniently dead) to the effect that Gibran was 'the William Blake of the twentieth century' and that 'the world should expect much from this poet-painter of Lebanon'. However, it is now generally accepted that this quotation was a figment of Gibran's imagination, 'invented by him . . . more in the spirit of promotion than of truth', as the Gibrans delicately put it.[57] We have by now seen so many cases of Gibran's lying that there is no need for further comment on this incident.

As a publicity idea, however, it worked extremely well. It catalysed Gibran's career in the same way that Emerson's famous letter to Whitman had catapulted him into the limelight. Nearly all the reviewers made use of the Rodin quotation in the course of their reviews. The reviewer in *The Dial*, for instance, said: 'It is not strange that Rodin should have hoped much of this Arabian poet. For in those parables and poems which Gibran has given us in English he curiously seems to express what Rodin did with marble and clay.' The *Sun* and the *Evening Post* gave favourable reviews; the *Sun* had chosen Howard Cook, a friend of Gibran, as the reviewer. *The Dial* and *The Nation* were more reserved, expressing doubts about the suitability of the book as fare for Western tastes. While the reviewer in *The Dial* sat on the fence, the critic in *The Nation* went so far as to talk about the book's 'exotic perversity' and insisted: 'East is East and West is West, and Tagore has not really succeeded in bridging the chasm between them, nor do we think that Gibran will do so.' Harriet Monroe, in *Poetry*, found the book pompous and tedious, and described the author as a 'journeyman poet' rather than a 'true son of the muses'.

One index of the critical reception of *The Madman* is that a couple of pieces from it – 'The Fox' and 'Said a Blade of Grass' – had already made it into an anthology of contemporary poetry only a year after its publication. And the compiler of the anthology, Marguerite Wilkinson, had this to say:

> Not very remote [from one of the Biblical Psalms] in spirit and in structure are a number of poems by poets of the Far East who are now writing in our language. Kahlil Gibran is writing poems and parables that have an individual music, a naïve charm and distinction and a structural symmetry based on symbol, contrast, repetition and parallelism . . . The poetry of Kahlil Gibran . . . is almost entirely a poetry of symbolism. His poems are parables, not designs in rhyme, rhythm or imagery, although his rhythms are clear and pleasing. In his book *The Madman*, we have the best parables that can be found in contemporary poetry. And each may be interpreted according to the whimsy of the reader.[58]

By the time *The Madman* was published, Kahlil was already working on a new set of parables, which would in due course become *The Forerunner*. In between, in 1919, two further books came out. *Al-Mawakib* (*The Procession*) was originally due to be published at more or less the same time as *The Madman*, but a government restriction on stocks of the kind of heavy paper needed for the high-quality production Gibran was after delayed things until March the next year, when it was published by Mir'at al-Gharb, with an introduction by the publisher, Nasib ʿArida, and accompanied by eight drawings by Gibran. The book consists of a number of short epigrammatic poems on themes such as the soul, death, love, happiness, religion, the illusory world; each theme is first treated in a few stanzas by an aged 'sage', whose words are then responded to by a 'youth', who caps many of his responses with a carefree refrain: 'Give me the flute and let me sing, and through my soul let music ring!' It is a lyrical poem – and indeed, Gibran told Mary that on two occasions it was actually sung.[59]

The Procession was Gibran's summer book. The bulk of it was written while staying at Cohasset on the Massachusetts coast in the summers of 1917 and 1918, though the drawings were done in between, in New York.[60] However, the tone of it is not entirely light and sunny. The sage is deeply pessimistic about the evil of the majority of humanity, insists on the brevity and sorrow of life, and on the futility of what passes for religion, stresses the criminality of the power-possessing members of society and the speciousness of the so-called social virtues; true love passes unrecognized by most people or is unwelcome to society; happiness is fleeting, and life is harsh, with only death to look forward to as a release from care. The sage is a man bound and worn down by urban civilization, trapped in dualities (good and evil, death and life, etc.), while the youth represents the freedom of natural life in the field and the forest, symbols which here take the place of the Greater Sea in *The Madman* and stand for the Absolute. He denies all the sage's gloom and attempts to replace it with a joyful picture of life lived without encumbrances, in unity and innocence.

The poem is simply a study in contrasts: it is impossible to say whether either the sage or the youth is victorious over the other – or, from a biographical point of view, which of these two sides of the author's character is predominant at this time. What is interesting is that there are two marked changes relative to the tone of *The Madman*. In the first place, the sage is not so much bitter as resigned; in the second place, Gibran is now prepared to give equal space to the voice of freedom, joy and love. Gibran was pleased with *The Procession* and described it to Mary as the best poem he had written.[61]

The drawings in the book are good examples of Gibran's work at the time. In one, for instance, a youth – the youth of the poem – walks forward confidently, with a calm smile on his face and head held high, while an angelic figure hovers vaguely in support behind him, and the rest of mankind, portrayed on a diminutive scale compared to the size of the youth and the angel, follow in his train with heads bowed down towards the ground. The drawing accompanying the passage on justice represents human justice as a powerful man deliberately weighing down the scales to the detriment of the diminutive human figure crouched in the other pan of the scales, while all around men and women circle endlessly in grief, seeming to search for true justice.

The other book to come out in 1919 was *Twenty Drawings*, which is exactly as the title implies. Published by Knopf, with Alice Raphael's *Seven Arts* essay reprinted as an introduction, it displays twenty of Gibran's wash drawings. A number of these drawings are not particularly good; they seem crude and unfinished. For instance, in 'The Burden', a rather muscular nude woman carries a baby on her shoulder. Behind her are giant-size helping hands, offering support for her burden; but the hands end at the wrists and fade away into a few pencil marks on the page, almost as if Gibran was idly doodling. 'Innermost' shows us a *Penseur*-like figure, wrapped up in himself – but there is even a small sketch of the same or a similar figure on the same page, as if Gibran was uncertain which was the best pose for his model. Three of the drawings have titles which evoke natural phenomena – 'The Waterfall', 'The Mountain' and 'The Rock'. Each of these drawings shows groups of naked bodies clustered together and vaguely forming the requisite shape, though in the case of 'The Mountain' it requires considerable charity to see the resulting shape as mountainous.

Sales of the book were never impressive; in fact, it is the only one of Gibran's Western-published books ever to have gone out of print. Nor did it receive much critical attention at the time. The only reviewer, Glen Mullin, writing in *The Nation*, was ambivalent. On the one hand, he found the work derivative – like a second-rate Rodin or a 'tepid' Blake – and was disappointed that some of the drawings seemed too tentative to have been worth publishing. On the other hand, he praised the delicate, flexible handling of line, the 'feminine sweetness of touch and conception', and concluded: 'The chief discovery that can be squeezed out of Gibran's symbolical offerings is that the soul of man, if not yet free of the beast, is yearning upward towards hopeful release. Gibran's message is not one of arcane transcendencies, but one of graceful emotional exposition of form. There his work is valuable and secure.'

Mullin also criticized Alice Raphael's essay for praising Gibran's mastery of symbolism, which he found Gibran's weakest point: he complains that the drawings lack the cosmic sweep of Blake and tend towards self-conscious sentimentalism. He rightly says that the symbols come across as 'titular' – that is, that it looks as though Gibran completed a drawing and then tacked on a symbolic title as an afterthought. Unlike Blake's paintings, each of Gibran's drawings could bear some other title. So, for instance, 'The Great Aloneness' just shows a woman resting, and 'Toward the Infinite' has an awkward, lumpy female head straining forward. These are my examples, not Mullin's, but his criticism is sound, because that is exactly how Gibran described his method to Mary: he doodles, lets something emerge on the paper, and then sees what it is that has emerged; at another time he paints a whole lot of pictures, some for *The Prophet* and some for 'poems yet unwritten', as Mary puts it.[62] Another sound point Mullin made was to take Raphael to task for making Gibran out to stand at the crossroads of East and West; on the contrary, Mullin said, there is nothing in these drawings which could not be found in other Western artists.

The Forerunner, published in 1920, is a bit of a hybrid. On the one hand, it continues the trend towards concentrating less on the negative aspects of life and more on our potential for living a greater life. In this sense, the book acts as a bridge between *The Madman* and *The Prophet*.[63] On the other hand, there are pieces in it that are so slight as to be more or less meaningless and insignificant. It is a very short book, but even so it is hard to resist the impression that some of these pieces were included just to pad it out, rather than because they belonged there in any thematic sense. This impression is corroborated by the lack of enthusiasm and pride accompanying the composition of the pieces, and by the fact that it had a far shorter gestation than any of his other books. The earliest mention of it is in July 1919, and the book was published in October 1920, complete with five drawings.

Whereas while working on *The Madman* he said that he could not make parables, but had to wait for them to come to him, the speed with which he composed the bulk of *The Forerunner* in the summer of 1919 indicates a different way of working. Gibran still presents each parable to Mary for checking, but there is less excitement on his part for the project. She also notes her own reactions less commonly, although when he read her 'War and the Small Nations' and 'The Dying Man and the Vulture' she was moved to tears, and she adored the wash drawings in it and 'The Last Watch', the undeniably powerful epilogue to the book. Otherwise, she tactfully said that what he left unsaid in the book was better than what was said. One feels that this book is a pot-boiler for him, while he was having difficulty finishing off *The Prophet*.[64]

The book was originally to be called *The Lonely Man*, continuing Gibran's interest in outsider figures, but *The Forerunner* is a far stronger title.[65] The architecture of the book is looser than that of *The Madman*, but since the book starts by introducing us to the character 'the Forerunner' and ends with a moving speech by him, it is probable that all the parables and poems in between are supposed to be spoken by him. As opposed to the 'Lonely Man', the Forerunner is also a far more optimistic figure. Not only is the name meant to convey that there is a part of each of us which, as it were, reaches out beyond ourselves to greater possibilities, but also in his closing speech the Forerunner lists various types of human being, along with their weaknesses and sins, and expressly says that he loves each of them, for all their limitations. The Forerunner undoubtedly speaks for Gibran himself when he says that even while denouncing them, he loved them in his heart; that they cluster around him, listening for his words of wisdom; that he feels there is a new, better dawn breaking for all of them. Here Gibran is announcing a change of mood: gone is the bitterness of past years; he will now write from the love for humankind that he always felt underneath all harsh and cruel words. Mary recognized that this section of the book, 'The Last Watch', was personal in this way, and thanked him for it.[66]

This greater optimism is also reflected in some of the pieces included in the book. In the poem 'Out of My Deeper Heart', for instance, the heart is envisaged as a bird that develops from a swallow to a lark, then an eagle, then a spring cloud, and finally merges with the starry sky. In 'Beyond My Solitude' the poet is still imprisoned, but knows that there are places for him to go, and knows that he has to slay his 'burdened selves' in order to make the transcendental leap. Likewise, in 'The Greater Self' a king realizes that even more significant than the trappings of majesty is his naked, true self, and in 'Other Seas' a fish speaks of greater oceans beyond the one known to fish.

To me, what is important about *The Forerunner* is that Gibran seems for the first time not just to point to the greater realms of whose existence he was convinced, but also to indicate some means of getting there (slaying one's lesser selves) and to show a willingness to apply the lesson to himself. He has been held back by his pride and disdain for others. He also acknowledged the same faults in person to Mary, telling her that what hindered his progress was the inheritance from his father's side of the family of anger and vanity and caring for fame. He clearly announced a change of consciousness, saying twice within the space of a few months that he had been self-centred and self-absorbed, and is 'humiliated' by the realization of how he used to regard himself as a man apart, with a gulf set between himself and ordinary mortals.[67] But he confidently asserts that now he loves people better and that recognition of these faults will lessen their hold over him.

If only it were so! People say that such recognition is half the battle, but everyone knows from experience how easy it is to backslide into a bad habit one has in theory forsworn. Gibran comes closer when he says elsewhere that if he could only accept his flaws they would disappear.[68] But there is little sign that the post-*Forerunner* Gibran was any less narcissistic than he had been before. If there is less concern with fame, that is because he has acquired it by now, and so can afford to smile at his youthful yearning. He speaks with comfortable pomposity, for instance, about how stupid it is to feel bitter because one isn't accepted or appreciated – but this is late in 1922, when such sentiments could come easily to him.[69] Where the specific issue of feeling that there is a gulf between himself and the rest of humanity is concerned, it is not easy to accept his assertion that he has left all that behind and is now a more humble person, when not very much later, in the midst of the messianic phase that I have already noted as a feature of the 1920s, he says, 'Some of us are conscious for the race . . . It is not the collective that makes the steps for the race, but the few, the minority – and I'm counting myself in with the few. The few make history.'[70]

The reviews of *The Forerunner*, such as they were, were unkind. Oddly, *The Bookman* (December 1920) found in the book 'the exotic fancy and mysticism of the East'. This had already become a meaningless cliché for reviewers of Gibran's books: there is really nothing peculiarly Eastern about *The Forerunner*; it is true that the parable form had commonly been used in Arabic literature, but Gibran's models might just as well have been Aesop or some of the short allegorical prose pieces in Ernest Dowson's 1899 book *Decorations*, or parable-like poems in Stephen Crane's *The Black Riders and Other Lines*. Even the reviewer in *The Dial* (which, as one of Gibran's own publishers, might have been expected to look after its own) was lukewarm, speaking of the 'manufactured mysticism of Tagore' and of the 'dreamy' paintings. Isidor Schneider, writing in *Poetry*, was more thoughtful. He spoke of Gibran's tendency to preach and went on: 'The form . . . gives an irritating finality to the content, which a world grown skeptical is tempted to snub. There is in the book neither the stark authenticity of prophecy, nor the beautiful crystallizations of a creative imagination. What we have here is pompous dramatizations of only half-individualized platitudes.'

These hard words resound with highbrow contempt, but Gibran was trying to speak to everyman, not the high literati. In any case, he was scornful of critics. He told Witter Bynner – who repeated the somewhat opaque *mot* in his article on Gibran – that 'They praise us when they should explain us, and they dissect us when they should reflect us. And they are so peevish!'[71] Nevertheless, he must have been disappointed with the book's critical reception. It was not his fault if the world had 'grown skeptical', and for the first time he had made an effort in print to resolve his own cynicism. Anyone, however slightly narcissistic, likes such efforts not to go unnoticed. Despite the book's poor critical reception, however, sales were at least satisfactory, so Gibran and Knopf had that consolation.

So ended a productive and dynamic period for Gibran, with books and paintings flowing from him, recognition coming his way to the degree that he always thought he deserved, and – let us not forget – his love for May Ziadeh blossoming in the background. And all this time the book that he always knew was going to be the best and most important thing he had written was taking shape.

10

The Pen Club

By 1916, the Hermitage had become a meeting-place for Syrian literati and writers living in New York. 'Arida and some others had temporarily revived *Al-Funun*, and Mikhail Naimy came to live in New York, since it was so obviously the place to be for an aspiring Arabic writer and critic in the States. The intellectuals who worked for or contributed to *Al-Funun* – chiefly 'Arida, 'Abd al-Masih Haddad, Najib Diab, Elias Sabagh and Wadi' Bahut – began to meet at Gibran's studio once a week in the evening. One day in April they all decided to form a society, which would meet once a fortnight in one room or another.[1] In the June issue of *Al-Funun* several of them displayed their affiliation to this society by writing '*al-Rabita al-Qalamiyya*', 'the Pen Club', after their names.

Nothing very much came of this immediately. Everyone was too distracted by the war, and as long as *Al-Funun* was in existence there was no particular need for further identification: this group of writers was recognizable enough simply by the fact that they were regular contributors to the paper. However, when *Al-Funun* was finally laid to rest in 1919, the impulse to organize and co-operate was again felt as urgent. The services *Al-Funun* had provided were to continue to break new ground in Arabic literature, and to give a high profile in particular to the Arab immigrant writers in the States – the Mahjar writers, as they have come to be called, *mahjar* meaning 'place of immigration'. Gibran and his fellow Arabic literati in New York wanted these services to continue.

An instrument was ready to hand, because one of their number, Haddad, had for some years been the publisher of a magazine called *As-Sa'ih* (*The Traveller*), and he was more than happy for it to attempt to fill the void left by the demise of *Al-Funun*. Later, those who also wrote in English used the pages of *The Syrian World*, the first English-language magazine for Arabs, started in 1927. But it was no longer enough just to have an instrument. These people were crusaders, and so in April 1920 the Pen Club was resuscitated and put on a more formal footing.

Mikhail Naimy recorded the minutes of the first meeting:

On the evening of April 20, 1920, at an entertainment given by the publisher of *As-Sayeh* and his brothers at their home, the discussion arose as to what the Syrian writers in New York could do to lift Arabic literature from the quagmire of stagnation and imitation, and to infuse a new life into its veins so as to make of it an active force in the building up of the Arab nations. It was suggested that an organization be created to band the writers together and to unify their efforts in the service of the Arabic language and its literature. The suggestion was met with warm approval by all the poets and the writers present, viz. Gibran K. Gibran, Nasseeb Arida, William Catzeflis, Rasheed Ayoub, Abdul-Maseeh Haddad, Nadra Haddad, Mikhail Naimy. The time not permitting to work out details and by-laws, Gibran invited the company to spend the evening of April 28 at his studio.[2]

The formality of the language is a measure of how seriously they took themselves. In the talk not just of Arabic literature but of Arab nationalism, there are interesting echoes. In 1847 Nasif al-Yasiji and Butrus al-Bustani, the two men chiefly responsible for reviving Arabic literature (both Syrian Christians), founded in Beirut the Society of Arts and Sciences, which met weekly throughout its five-year history for the reading of papers by members. The society was a vital element in the development of education in the Arab world, which, as we have seen, was in turn crucial for the rise of Arab nationalism. Christians themselves, the members of the Pen Club would have been aware of their noble precedent.

And so on 28 April 1920, at Gibran's studio, the Pen Club (commonly called simply 'Arrabitah', an Anglicization of the first part of its Arabic name) was formally launched. Gibran was elected President, and Naimy Secretary. The number of active members, who were called 'workers', was limited to ten; they were the ones with the right to use the Club's name as a badge on their work. The Pen Club manifesto was drafted shortly afterwards. It includes the following stirring words, in which it would surely be accurate to detect some of Gibran's ideas and rhythms:

> Not everything that parades as literature is literature; nor is every rimester a poet. The literature we esteem as worthy of the name is that only which draws its nourishment from Life's soil and light and air . . . And the man of letters is he who is endowed with more than the average mortal's share of sensitiveness and taste, and the power of estimation and penetration together with the talent of expressing clearly and beautifully whatever imprints Life's constant waves leave upon his soul.

And they took as their motto a verse from the Hadith: 'How wonderful the treasures beneath God's throne which only poets' tongues can unlock.'

The members of the Pen Club met with more or less regularity from 1920 until Gibran's death in 1931. He was the heart and centre of the group, as well as its most famous member, and with his death the life went out of it for the others, as constructive argument degenerated into futile strife. Throughout the 1920s they met not so much to plan campaigns – there was no need for that, because as individuals they were all committed writers anyway – but to exchange ideas and to encourage one another's efforts. Particularly important in their campaign was Haddad's programme of starting each year with a special issue of *As-Sa'ih* to which every Pen Club worker felt compelled to contribute. These special issues were eagerly awaited throughout the Arabic-speaking world, and many of the articles and poems written by Gibran and his fellow workers were widely reprinted in the Near East. 'Thus,' as Naimy says, 'the name of "Arrabitah" spread wide and far, becoming tantamount to renaissance, to rejuvenation in the minds of the younger generations, and to iconoclasm and hot-headed rebellion in the eyes of older and more conservative ones.'[3] In fact, however, this programme of publication, including anthologies of the workers' writings, proved impossible to sustain, and after about 1925 the Pen Club became a purely social and convivial group.

For a while, though, Gibran had found the perfect channel for his rebellious spirit, and it is clear from all accounts that he put a lot of energy into keeping the group together, co-ordinating its efforts and fund-raising.[4] At a personal level, the fame of the group as a whole also went a long way towards increasing his already high profile in the Arabic world, so he was well repaid for his time and work. We should imagine him in these years dividing his time between his own personal work and working for the Pen Club. However, he is less overtly involved in political or quasi-political work now: in 1920 he wrote the prose-poem 'Your Lebanon and Mine' as a kind of political farewell, having told Mary the year before, 'Perhaps the best form of fighting is in painting pictures and writing poetry.'[5] In this poem he contrasts 'his' Lebanon, the land of beautiful valleys and mountains, of peace and simple lifestyles, with the modern Lebanon of political and sectarian fighting:

> What will *you* leave for Lebanon and her sons a hundred years from today? Tell me, what will you leave for the future save pretence, falsehood, and stupidity?
>
> Truly I say to you that the olive sapling planted by the villager at the foot of the mountain in Lebanon will outlast your deeds and achievements. And the wooden plough drawn by two oxen over the terraces of Lebanon outglories your hopes and ambitions.

And so on; there is much more in the same vein. The poem became a *cause célèbre* in the East, especially because, to Gibran's delight, it was censored in some newspapers, presumably on the grounds that it betrayed the cause of Arab nationalism.[6]

He still met frequently with his American friends and took one or two breaks a year at the summer houses of those of them who were rich enough to own one. We should picture him working on a new 'Counsel' for *The Prophet*, or a picture or poem for Scofield Thayer's magazine *The Dial*, which became his main non-Arabic outlet after the collapse of *The Seven Arts*.[7] There were many letters for him to write, on business matters and in response to questions from admirers around the world; but in the quiet of the night, alone in his studio, he wrote love letters to May Ziadeh in Egypt by candlelight, with only the sound of the occasional hoof beats filtering through the heavy black velvet curtains of his studio.[8]

By now we have covered the period within which Gibran did most of his Arabic writing, and he has begun to write in English too, under Mary's tutelage. In the early 1920s, recognizing that after the war the Near East was wide open to Western influence, he wrote a series of essays warning his fellow Arabs against slavish imitation of the worst of Western culture,[9] but generally, in the 1920s, he wrote less in Arabic. English became his chosen medium. His first English books met, as we have seen, with a mixed critical reception. It may help, at this point, since we have reached the end, effectively, of Gibran's Arabic writing, to pause and place his work within some kind of context. The reason for introducing a discussion of context at this stage is because of the danger to which I drew attention in the Preface. It is inevitable that, as I quote or refer to snippets of Gibran's work, the reader will read them with eyes conditioned by his or her own contemporary context. So it is in order to offset this conditioning, to try to replace it with a picture of Gibran's own context, that we need this discussion now.

On a freezing day in the middle of March 1996 I turned off the deserted streets of the quiet Chicago suburb of Evanston, where a howling northerly gale had driven all but the most determined off the streets and the temperature down well into double figures below zero. The waters of Lake Michigan were grey and whipped up into savage breakers. It was so cold that occasionally, as the waves crashed on to the shore, the spray would freeze and form fantastic ice sculptures. I turned aside from the biting storm into the peace of Northwestern University Library – there being few students around that week – and found my way down to the basement, into the newspaper microtext department. But there I encountered another storm, no less bitter in its way.

It so happened that the first three pieces I read that day, the first day of my library research in the States, were all relatively modern, written in the 1970s and 1980s. Jonathan Yardley, writing in the *Washington Post*, reported on a heated debate in Congress over whether or not to support the erection of a monument to Gibran in the capital city. Yardley does not disguise his own opinion about this. He describes Gibran as the 'patron saint of calendar and greeting-card copywriters', a favourite of ladies' Wednesday afternoon tea clubs, a something-for-everyone philosopher. 'What a thrill it is,' Yardley goes on, 'to know that thanks to the farsightedness of those who speak for America in Congress, visitors to this capital city will be able to pause in reverence before monuments to the greatest of all Americans: Washington, Jefferson, Lincoln, Gibran.'

Whereas the main weapon in Yardley's arsenal is sarcasm, Stefan Kanfer has a choicer turn of phrase. In an article entitled 'But Is It Not Strange That Even Elephants Will Yield – and That *The Prophet* Is Still Popular?' he asserts that Gibran's writing is 'limp, mucid hooey . . . *Also Sprach Zarathustra* written in mauve icing on a cake of halvah . . . a patented blend of emptiness and pretension'. He cannot even pay Gibran the back-handed compliment of being a charlatan: he charges him with too much naïveté for that. His beliefs are 'infantile, but authentic'. He is a 'candy metaphysician', a purveyor of 'aesthetics for imbeciles'; and so on and so forth.[10] At least he gets the colour of the icing right: I have argued that Gibran was a product, to a large extent, of the fantasy of Fred Holland Day, who was in turn a purveyor of the values of the 1890s, otherwise known as the Mauve Decade.

This is strong stuff, and can be paralleled elsewhere.[11] The third piece I read was an interview by John Cooley in *The Christian Science Monitor* with Mikhail Naimy, the close friend and colleague of Gibran, and who was by then an old and very respected man. In the course of the interview, Naimy has this to say about himself and Gibran:

> Both of us looked beyond the immediate moment. We both believed that man is destined to unfold the tremendous powers latent within him and to reach, at the end, a full recognition of his divinity. We both believed in reincarnation and in the magic power of the word if properly used – and also in that of all the arts. But the arts must reveal not only the outer beauty of things, but also their inner reality . . . He always avoided the trite, the commonplace or the trivial.

Well, both sides cannot be right. Either he avoided the trite and the trivial, or he is the patron saint of the trite and the trivial; either his aesthetics is for imbeciles or Naimy must be misrepresenting Gibran's aesthetics. Part of the difficulty is caused by the unreflectiveness of Gibran's English writing. It all seems to have a purpose, but we are never told what that purpose is. There appears to be a unity of vision, but we are never perfectly sure if we are looking in the same direction as the author, because he teases us with open-ended tales, paradox and ambiguous endings. This is in fact the chief difference between his English and his Arabic writing: his Arabic work wears its philosophy on its sleeve. It may be somewhat repetitious – especially in those aspects that make up the 'angry young man' syndrome – but you know exactly what Gibran is trying to communicate. In English, however, Gibran concentrated on honing pithy sayings and wise homilies, without necessarily making plain the thinking that had led him to those conclusions.

Let me confess a certain sympathy with Kanfer's and Yardley's points of view, even if not for the nasty way they express it.[12] I think that Gibran can descend into platitude and that it is dishonest of his devotees not to admit it. Such a descent is simply a danger inherent in the kind of writing he was undertaking in English, which treads a narrow line between profundity and banality. Gibran once told Mary, 'I have just one rule in writing – to say it the simplest way I can.'[13] Simplicity of expression runs the risk of appearing naïve and banal. In any case, it is unfair of Kanfer and his fellows to quote only a few sentences, choosing those it is easy to mock. We all have our bad days. One of the dullest art exhibitions I have ever been to was of Picasso's later works, and Walt Whitman veers wildly between sublimity and turgidity. *Timon of Athens* is not *Hamlet*.

Besides, in so far as the accusation of writing platitudes is an accusation of unoriginality, it strikes me as rather hollow. In the first place, true originality, as opposed to reformulation, is so rare that 99 per cent of our thinkers are open to the same charge. In the second place, the modern Western desire for originality easily slides into approval of change for change's sake, without any real progress – like the futile motions of the Red Queen in *Alice Through the Looking-Glass*. For the ancients, to borrow from a predecessor or from the stock of common wisdom was a sign of respect. And why should one not recognize in the thought of another one's own deeply held beliefs?

'It is no more according to Plato than according to me,' said Emerson.[14] So yes, it is true that others have celebrated love as Gibran did, have expressed suffering and talked of the Higher Self and so on; but that is not enough to condemn his work. And it remains the undeniable fact that his books outsell all the others and therefore must strike a chord somewhere in the human heart.

Another way to give Gibran's work a bad press is to compare it with contemporary works of literature. The years of his main books, between *The Madman* and *The Prophet*, are peppered with books by Willa Cather, F. Scott Fitzgerald, James Joyce, Herman Hesse, D. H. Lawrence and many other bright names. Still, perhaps this is to compare chalk with cheese: Gibran was not writing literary fiction, but poetic religious philosophy. But the point is taken: *sub specie aeternitatis* Gibran's work may not come out well – though some of it has lasted pretty well so far.

Fashions change, and the vantage-point of eternity may not be the only place from which to judge Gibran's work. It is at least as relevant to judge his writing from within its setting. We have seen that Gibran was strongly influenced, as both an artist and a writer, by a stream of thought we may fairly call platonizing. This stream has many tributaries: Plato himself, but especially the Neoplatonists; the Romantics; Swedenborg; the New England Transcendentalists such as Emerson and Thoreau; Eastern religious philosophy, as purveyed by the Transcendentalists or taken neat; post-Romantic essayists such as Maurice Maeterlinck and Francis Grierson; the aesthetic movements of the Pre-Raphaelites and Decadents; the Theosophy of Madame Blavatsky; the Symbolists.

Although it is fair to say that Gibran came pretty much at the end of this stream, it was still a vital and very potent force. It casually occurs in the conversations of 'modern' women such as Mary Haskell and Charlotte Teller; we have seen how certain New York literary circles – the ones to which Gibran belonged and which Don Marquis mercilessly satirized in *Hermione* – met regularly to discuss such philosophies and phenomena. What happens if Gibran is judged within *this* context? What might he have been trying to achieve?

Gibran always thought of himself as a poet. This is most evident in the patently autobiographical tone of many of his pieces dealing with poetry. On occasion, his view of himself as primarily a poet can lead him to make almost inane assertions, such as: 'Better a poor thought, musically said, than a good thought in bad form.'[15] Now, there is a recurring attitude towards poetry and poets, expressed variously by various of the literary participators in the platonizing stream. For instance, in his essay 'The Poet', published in 1844, Emerson says:

> The poet . . . stands among partial men for the complete man, and apprises us not of his wealth, but of the common wealth . . . The poet is . . . the man without impediment, who sees and handles that which others dream of, traverses the whole scale of experience, and is representative of man, in virtue of being the largest power to receive and to impart . . . The signs and credentials of the poet are that he announces that which no man foretold. He is the true and only doctor; he knows and he tells; he is the only teller of news, for he was present and privy to the appearance which he describes.

And so on; it is not a short essay, and there is plenty more in the same vein. An important thread in the essay is the notion that there is at least a single such 'true poet' for each generation, to reveal something new and therefore assist the evolution of mankind.[16] For Shelley, in *The Defence of Poetry*, the poet is overtly a prophet, who not only 'beholds intensely the present as it is', but also 'participates in the eternal, the infinite, and the one', and recreates the world anew in his poetry for himself and for us lesser mortals.

In short, the poet feels, knows and experiences more than the rest of us. This may make him either a solitary, escaping to the margins of society, a voice crying in the wilderness, or a teacher, illuminating us about the higher realms with which he is familiar and we are not. In either case, the poet is little short of a prophet. In the French Symbolist school the aim was to arrange words or images according to their capacity to suggest fleeting experience, so that poetry or painting behaves exactly like music, and evokes an impression which is as close as possible to the artist's intention. 'True artists are the most religious of men,' Auguste Rodin once asserted. It is explicit in the statements of the thinkers of the Symbolist school that the poet is a priest or a prophet, one who knows the law of correspondences and can find exactly the right word for the right occasion to transport his reader or listener into another world of experience. 'It [the symbol] constitutes a correspondence between our perception of matter and the eternal truths of a spiritual order,' Henri Dorra says, in introducing Baudelaire's poem 'Correspondances', which contains the lovely notion of 'long echoes that mingle in the distance in a profound tenebrous unity'.[17] It is no coincidence that many of the Symbolists were steeped in Platonism or Kabbalah: for Mallarmé, the most reflective of the school, to speak of a flower was to speak of an ideal flower. 'The essence of Symbolism is its insistence on a world of ideal beauty, and its conviction that this is realized through art.'[18]

The cause of this idea was taken up as a crusade in some quarters. For Walt Whitman 'aesthetic appreciation was crucial for the human spirit in an increasingly materialistic age'; poetry has a religious purpose and the ideal poet will some day replace the priest.[19] And consider the manifesto of *The Knight Errant*, one of the magazines produced by Fred Holland Day's circle in Boston:

> It is no longer to strive against the Paynim in the Holy Land, to contend with ravening dragons, to succour forlorn ladies in distress that he [the knight errant] is called to action, but rather to war against the Paynims of realism in art, to assail the dragon of materialism, and the fierce dragon of mammonism, to ride for the succour of forlorn hopes and the restoration of forgotten ideals . . . The cause remains: false ideals, truths oppressed, idealism quite forgot, the realm of the imagination lost . . . One by one in this last night, the beautiful things have disappeared, until at last, in a world grown old and ugly, men, forced to find some excuse for the peculiarity of their environment, have discredited even beauty itself, find it childish, unworthy and – unscientific.

So in the first issue of the magazine (1891), Ralph Adams Cram spoke of a new literary renaissance and cited Wagner, William Morris, Walter Pater and others as its prophets. Not many years later, in his weird but rather wonderful novel *Jurgen* (1919), James Branch Cabell took up the fight against the land, or mind-set, he calls 'Philistia'.

Gibran, ever the Symbolist, expressly took on the role of poet-as-prophet.[20] This is clear not just from the autobiographical flavour of his writings about the work of poetry, but also from his anti-rationalist streak, which shows up in, for instance, 'The Scholar and the Poet' in *The Forerunner* and in his constant affirmation of inspiration over intellectual understanding. Not only did close friends such as Josephine and Mary think of him as a prophet, but to others, such as the liberal minister Robert Norwood, he was explicitly known as both a poet and a prophet. As Claude Bragdon said, 'Three words describe him: *artist, poet, prophet*, though they should be only one word, but this the English language fails to furnish forth.'[21] Once, in an overt equation of the artist and the prophet, Gibran described Christ as an artist, because, as Mary put it in her journal, 'he studied and perceived the soul of life and expressed it in perfect form in his stories and sayings.' The artist or poet, Gibran claimed on more than one occasion, expresses what is latent in the collective subconscious of the human race: this is his special gift, his role as diviner. According to the evolutionary philosophy which we saw Gibran developing in the last chapter, Life is always trying to express itself better and more fully; it is the artist's job to assist that expression. The poet is, as it were, the most refined sense the Earth or Life has of its own potential.[22] More than once in these entries the role of the poet or prophet in reminding people of what they already know in seed form is explicitly taken by Gibran himself, and he sometimes claims that he paints in a 'dreamlike' or 'floating' state which makes his work divination or prophecy. The book *The Prophet* is, of course, Gibran's most explicit identification with the role, because Almustafa the Prophet is a mouthpiece for Gibran's ideas; like the Madman and the Forerunner before him, the Prophet authoritatively declares Gibran's vision of life. In talking about the book Gibran told Mary that everything a person writes or paints is a picture or story of his own inner self, the implication of which is that the Prophet is Gibran's alter ego.[23] Elsewhere Gibran claims that whereas Nietzsche spoke for the next 300 years, he – Gibran – speaks for the next 600. Then, finally, there is his certainty, which infuses Mary's reports of his conversations with her, that he is bringing a new message for mankind.[24]

This conviction grew throughout the 1910s and culminated in the almost messianic role he seems occasionally to have slipped into in the 1920s.[25] The distinction is to a certain extent artificial, since there is plenty of overlap between the two, but it is possible to detect an evolution within Gibran's role-playing from that of wounded, melancholic Romantic (the role he played best with Josephine Peabody and in his early Arabic writings) to that of Prophet. A considerable boost to this change of role was provided by Gibran's development of his evolutionary cosmology, which I summarized in the last chapter. At any rate, his letters at the time to Mary not infrequently speak of a feeling of being infused with the spirit of God, of spending all his time in the presence of God, and so on.[26] He was elated by his discoveries, and was sure that he had found his purpose in the world – one which justified all the long years of apprenticeship through suffering. He felt that a great gulf had opened up between himself and the rest of the world.[27]

New York too was an important factor. Not only was there the immeasurable effect of the magic of its energy, but Gibran determined to make the most of the opportunities there, and expressly decided to change role. He wrote to Mary that he wanted to be his own man, no longer the exotic Easterner (which was the part he had played to the hilt in Boston, and which blended perfectly with that of melancholic Romantic).[28] And once he had found his way around New York life, the confidence he gained as a result of his increasing fame and success was another crucial factor in his adoption of an elevated role. As well as being a well-known figure in the Arab world, he was making important contacts among Americans, contacts which would undoubtedly lead in due course to publication in English. At the same time, Mary and his circle of friends in New York were giving him immense amounts of positive feedback, supporting his high self-regard. We have seen to what extent Mary and others came to see him as a messiah-like figure. Conclusive confirmation that he had a religious message to bring to the world came from the way liberal Christian ministers took to his readings and began to use his words or his pictures in their sermons and invite him to read in their churches.[29] By the end of 1920, he is saying things like: 'I want to be a teacher. I want to give themselves to people [*sic*]. I want to wake their consciousness to what I know that it can know.'[30]

In his published writings too, Gibran sometimes identifies the true poet and the true prophet.[31] One of the aphorisms in *Sand and Foam* states, 'There lies a green field between the scholar and the poet; should the scholar cross it, he becomes a wise man; should the poet cross it, he becomes a prophet.' Like much of *Sand and Foam*, this is rather opaque, but a saying quoted in Mary's journals illuminates it: 'The difference between a prophet and a poet is that the prophet lives what he teaches, and the poet does not.'[32] The 'green field', then, is life, with which a scholar has to engage to become wise, and the poet has to engage to become a prophet.[33] Gibran certainly felt that *he* had engaged in life – in fact, that he had had a hard life, full of suffering and personal tragedy. In short, he thought that he had evolved from a mere poet to a fully fledged prophet–poet.

Echoing Shelley's claim that the poet can articulate the platonic realms which the rest of us perceive only dimly, if at all, Gibran has the Prophet say, 'I only speak to you in words of that which you yourselves know in thought. And what is word knowledge but a shadow of wordless knowledge?'[34] With an unusual choice of metaphor he once told Mary that the difference between an ordinary poet, a great poet, and a very great poet is that the first, coming into a room full of ashes, would mould them into form, while the second would bring ashes from other rooms to contribute to the form he makes, but the third would dig beneath the ashes to find the fire which had caused the ashes in the first place, so that his images would be burning with the underlying fire.[35] Echoing Emerson's claim that the poet has access to something common and universal, Gibran has the Prophet say, 'I teach you your larger self, which contains all men.'[36] But it is in the nature of his English writing, which concentrates on parables and homilies, that the theme is likely to occur more in his earlier Arabic writing. In a poem called simply 'Poet', Gibran writes:

> A ring connecting this world to the next. A sweet spring from which thirsty souls draw water. A firmly planted tree on the bank of the river of beauty, on which grow ripe fruits sought by ravenous hearts . . . An angel whom the gods dispatched to teach the people divine things. A radiant light that the darkness does not vanquish and the bushel does not hide.[37]

And the poem goes on to emphasize how this breadth of vision is bound to make the poet misunderstood by common people. The loneliness of the poet, and his consequent longing for death, when he will be removed from misunderstanding and prejudice, recur in two other pieces, 'The Lonely Poet' and 'A Poet's Death Is His Life'.[38] Again, in the prose-poem 'A Poet's Voice', he says:

> The power of charity sows deep in my heart, and I reap and gather the wheat in bundles and give them to the hungry.
> My soul gives life to the grapevine and I press its bunches and give juice to the thirsty.
> Heaven fills my lamp with oil and I place it at my window to direct the stranger through the dark . . .
> Humans are divided into different clans and tribes, and belong to countries and towns. But I find myself a stranger to all communities and belong to no settlement. The universe is my country and the human family is my tribe.[39]

And just as the poet is a stranger in a strange land, so too in *The Procession* is the prophet:

> He is a stranger to this life,
> Stranger to those who praise or blame,
> For he upholds the Torch of Truth,
> Although devoured by the flame.[40]

In short, one way or another, in this vital respect – what a poet's job is, and by inference what his own job is – Gibran places himself squarely within the platonizing tradition. Even his perception of the loneliness of the poet finds its echo in the notorious deliberate aloofness of some of the French Symbolist poets, especially Gérard de Nerval, Rimbaud and Mallarmé. As well as considering his work *sub specie aeternitatis* or by comparing it to that of others, then, we should also consider it on its own terms. This does not entail the impossible question, 'How successful was Gibran at revealing eternal verities?' Who could be qualified to answer such a question? Nor do I want to undertake an aesthetic assessment of his poetry (which is best left to Arab scholars, since most of his actual poetry was written in Arabic). All I want to ask is: 'How successful was Gibran, in his writing, in uniting the roles of poet and prophet?' In case that question too reduces to a consideration of his success in transmitting eternal verities, let us look at it from the point of view of his audience. How has his work come to be perceived? Here we come across a curious and ironic paradox. While explicitly taking on the role of poet-cum-prophet in his lifetime, his reputation in the years after his death has undergone a bifurcation: in the English-speaking world he is known chiefly as a prophet, while in the Arabic-speaking world he is known chiefly as a poet.

His reputation in the English-speaking world is easily dealt with. Any bookshop in the UK which stocks his books will put them in their 'New Age' or 'Mind, Body, Spirit' or even 'Esoteric' section. In the States, where floor space is at less of a premium and stocks are larger, one may occasionally – but only very occasionally – find his books in the poetry or Middle East department as well, but again they are more likely to be found exclusively among the New Age books. Ask almost anyone in the English-speaking world whether they have heard of Gibran and they will recognize him as the author of *The Prophet*. In the States, as of April 1996, *The Prophet* had sold over 9,000,000 copies since publication, and still sells at a very healthy rate; in the rest of the English-speaking world, apart from the USA, about another 25,000 copies are still sold every year. Those of his other books which are still available reach only a fraction of the sales of *The Prophet*. In other words, in the English-speaking world he is known more or less exclusively as the author of *The Prophet*, and therefore as a purveyor of spiritual teaching.

This will be our only opportunity to consider the reception and influence of his Arabic writing, so we need to be somewhat more thorough. There are numerous indications that even from the outset his writing was more eagerly appreciated in the Arab world than his English works were at first in the English-speaking world.[41] He became known as 'the Syrian Shelley' and some of his books sold very well indeed, by the standards of the Arabic-speaking world.[42] His short pieces for newspapers and magazines were eagerly awaited and much reproduced. As we have seen, he was greatly in demand in the Arab expatriate community in the United States; he was invited to speak at their clubs and was a regular contributor to their newspapers from a relatively early age. And in general his written work brought him considerable status in the Arab-American community; he became their figurehead and, to some extent, their mouthpiece.[43] However, it is also clear that in literary terms he was not perceived as *unique*, as he tends to be in the English-speaking world nowadays, but as part of a movement. He was the most famous part, perhaps, and received the most attention, but he was not alone. In order to come to a true assessment of his contribution to Arabic literature, therefore, we should place him within the context of what was happening in the world of Arabic letters.

It is hard for Westerners to realize, if they have not looked into the subject, how easy it was for Arabic literature to become fossilized. In fact, it remains the case today that, to an ultra-orthodox Muslim, only words and grammatical forms found in the Koran are permissible. Likewise, over the centuries only certain verse-forms had become recognized as acceptable within the canon of classical Arabic literature and, if they wanted to be read, poets simply did not work outside these forms.

Arabic writers were not working entirely in a vacuum, however. There was a revivalist tradition extending back some fifty or sixty years before Gibran's life to great writers such as Nasif al-Yasiji and Butrus al-Bustani. Poets were aware of trends in Western poetry and, since there was a long and rich tradition of love poetry in the Arabic language, they were particularly attracted by English Romantic poetry. Under this influence, a slight loosening of the strictures is noticeable by the end of the nineteenth century, in the work, for instance, of Khalil Mutran, a Lebanese poet who lived from 1872 to 1949 and allowed a greater degree of subjectivity into his poems than had previously been the norm; as with the English Romantics, what the poet himself feels starts to gain prominence. This trend was continued in Egypt by several contemporaries of Mutran, such as 'Abd al-Rahman Shukri, Ibrahim 'Abd al-Qadir al-Mazini and 'Abbas Mahmud al-'Aqqad, the main members of the so-called Diwan school, although the impression their poetry gives is that they were applying method rather than following the dictates of inspiration.

However, it was not until Arab intellectuals began to emigrate, particularly to the United States, that the changes became wholesale and heartfelt. And here Gibran does become important. He, Naimy and others constitute a distinct expatriate school, which centred on the Pen Club in New York. Through the pages of *Al-Funun* and its other chosen organs, the Mahjar school, as it is known, became a force to be reckoned with in the Arab literary world. Its other leading members included Nasib 'Arida, Rashid Ayyub, Nudra Haddad and, most importantly, Ilya Abu Madi, who joined the Pen Club in 1921. Madi is considered to have written some of the finest Romantic poetry in Arabic, and is the most widely read of the expatriate poets. From New York their influence spread back to the Arab world and by now has profoundly affected many branches of literature, from poetry to the development of the novel and of short stories. They initiated the Romantic revolution in Arabic literature.[44]

Based as they were in the USA, they gained a greater freedom from the approved canons of literary taste in Beirut, Damascus and Cairo. They allowed themselves to experiment, to alter verse-forms, to use more than one metre within a single poem, and to borrow widely from Western literature. They used more everyday language, and allowed themselves to draw their characters from real life rather than from tradition or high-flown imagination. William Catzeflis, treasurer and founder-member of the Pen Club, described the iconoclastic spirit of the northern *émigrés* as follows: 'If the meaning or beauty of a thought requires the breaking of a rule, break it; if there is no known word to express your idea, borrow or invent one; if syntax stands in the way of a needed or useful expression, away with syntax.'[45]

The development of the prose-poem was central. A prose-poem may be defined as prose with a touch of the imaginative, prose infused with poetic emotion and rhythm, but which definitely does not conform to strict standards of metre and rhyme. The Mahjar poets were heavily influenced in this respect by the rhythms of the Bible, whether in its English versions or as translated into Arabic,[46] and by the free verse of Walt Whitman (who was himself not at all averse to Biblical cadences). Amin Rihani, a pioneer of Arabic prose-poetry, was consciously imitating Whitman. Gibran and Rihani would both also have been aware, especially from their time in Paris, of the free verse of the French Symbolist poets, which, in *Against*

Nature, Joris-Karl Huysmans, at any rate, describes as prose-poetry and accords a penetrating analysis.[47] The whole modern Arabic free-verse movement of the 1950s may safely be said to have been impossible without the prose-poetic experiments of Rihani and Gibran.

The scholar and historian of Arabic literature, Salma Jayyusi, sums the situation up as follows:

> It was very early in the century and at the hands of al-Raihani and then Gibran that the possibility of a poem written in prose was suggested and given initial form, although with them it never reached a truly mature stage. Arabic poetry at this time, i.e. during the first and second decades of this century, was showing signs of restlessness with the more or less settled norms of neo-Classicism. All over the Arab world there were attempts at change in the diction, subject matter and form of poetry. In Egypt, the failure of such attempts at innovation was due to a limited talent and lack of intuitive guidance . . . The Mahjar attempts at innovation were much more successful despite a weaker linguistic basis in the two leading writers, al-Raihani and Gibran. A keen intuition, a well-guided talent, a basically different outlook coloured by a persistent foreign cultural influence all helped to release the stream of creativity in these men. A movement of innovation and literary adventure, unequalled in the rest of the Arab world, was launched.[48]

The revolution the Mahjar initiated, or in which they participated, was to change the emphasis of Arabic poetry, in terms of both form and content, from craftsmanship to inspiration. They echoed Mallarmé's challenging cry: 'Where is inspiration? Where the unforeseen?'[49] Now, it will already be clear from this brief synopsis of the Mahjar context within which Gibran was working that he was not unique. The Diwan school were experimenting too; Rihani pioneered prose-poems before Gibran (though with less imagination and emotive force); Naimy was a greater champion of reform in Arabic literature. This is an important point, worth repeating; because Gibran is by far the best known Arab poet in the English-speaking West, the only one to have achieved a real breakthrough, there is a danger of thinking that he was somehow an isolated phenomenon. But not only were there others doing much the same, they were often, it must be said, doing it just as well. Gibran's poem *Al-Mawakib* (*The Procession*), for instance, in which he fostered the revolution of employing more than one metre within a single poem, is not reckoned to be great poetry. 'As a poem it is less than inspired, and is merely a repetition in verse form of much of what the author had said previously in his more original and attractive prose works.'[50]

In his Arabic works Gibran did undertake a degree of experimentation with language. He felt he could not fully express himself in the inherited rhythms of classical Arabic verse; he allowed himself more lyrical and emotionally charged conjunctions of words, and colloquial forms of expression, which irritated conservative critics in the Arab world.[51] Paradox, rhetorical questioning, parallelism, repetition, near synonyms, antithesis and polar pairs such as life and death, day and night, are also used to arouse the reader's feelings. One of the main ways in which he sought to express emotion was through imagery. The senses have their 'songs'; a kiss is 'a goblet filled by the gods from the fountain of love'; slavery 'kneels in blind imitation of tradition'; religion is 'a well-tilled field, planted and watered by desire'; eyes grow heavy with 'the wine of years'; and so on and so forth. Some of his most common symbols are wings, the sea, night and day, the forest. What is interesting about Gibran's use of imagery is that he draws mainly on familiar images – images which successfully convey precisely the feeling the author wants, but which do not rely on arcane vocabulary to do so. He is, in all his writing, accessible to any reader. Another common but less original way in which he arouses the reader's feelings is by liberally sprinkling his pieces with emotionally charged abstract words such as 'beauty', 'love', 'justice'. These are often personified, or made particular, by a judicious use of imagery and adjective.

On the down side, one occasionally feels, in his early Arabic works, that he piles too many images and adjectives on top of one another, unable, as it were, to stem the flow of his creativity or the desire to communicate; and his attempts to arouse genuine emotion are often dragged down, perhaps by a failure of nerve, into the realm of sentiment. Both these faults are a result of his intention to keep his writing, even when prose, in a highly poetic vein. On examining successive drafts of *The Broken Wings*, Hawi discovered that he had systematically set about eliminating 'every last shred of the prosaic'.[52] Both his themes and his images are repeated so often that they can lose their force, and the didacticism which also mars much of his English writing (because both prophets and angry young men preach) can grate on one's sensibilities, for all that it is a traditional Romantic ploy. Characters are rarely differentiated; all speak in much the same high-flown tone of voice, which is clearly Gibran's voice. While his poetry and prose-poetry is often good, it is rarely great.

Most of these features of his Arabic style, the bad as well as the good, were influential on the Romantic movement in Arabic literature. Gibran's chief literary importance, however, lies not so much in his poetic or prose-poetic experiments with *form*, as in the *content* of his works, and particularly his early Arabic prose works. His exposure to Western culture gave him a strong and enduring taste for personal freedom in both religion and politics. His early Arabic works, as we have already seen, are shot through with these themes, passionately and forcefully presented – the themes of anticlericalism and of the value of the simple life as opposed to the corruption of civilization and urban culture, the spiritual theme of the soul's separate existence and reincarnation, the possibility of human beings achieving a kind of mystical union with the world of nature, his description of the poet as a despised and lonely prophet, the themes of love and sorrow and despair. These ideas and themes, all of which can be paralleled in the Western Romantics and most of which were already present in Arabic literature before Gibran,[53] had a strong influence on his Mahjar and Pen-Club colleagues. And even though Rihani pioneered protest before Gibran, it was to Gibran rather than Rihani that the Mahjar poets and writers looked for inspiration, because of his greater imaginative sweep. They were often more talented poets and writers than he was, but the revolution they initiated would have been impossible without the input of his ideas and adventurous experimentation. One of the Mahjar, ʿAbd al-Masih Haddad, described meeting and talking to Gibran as 'like the awakening of spring in a barren land'.[54]

So far in this book the East–West dichotomy has figured in Gibran's life in a number of ways. He seems never to have been sure to which hemisphere he belonged, with the result that he felt uncomfortable in both, and played out parts in both rather than letting himself settle and be at sufficient ease somewhere to be himself. For instance, even while making himself out to his Western friends to be the scion of a wealthy and noble family, he was portraying himself in his Arabic writings as a poor and humble poet. Whatever it takes to fulfil his ambitions and find a niche of fame from which to laugh at his insecurity, Gibran will do it.

The Romantic fusion of poet and prophet was undoubtedly Gibran's best opportunity for bringing East and West together, and he grasped it well. Of all the parts he played, that of poet–prophet was perhaps the most congenial. He took to it like a duck to water, and his 'exotic' Eastern origins helped him all the way. But history was to cheat him even of this reconciliation. In the end, and with unfortunate irony, the man who, more than anyone, perfected that fusion of poetry and prophecy which the platonizing Romantics and Symbolists had so desired, finds himself pulled apart on precisely these poles. 'With [the Arabic language] he triumphed over the mind, with English over the heart.'[55] In the English-speaking world he is known only as a prophet; his work is considered popular but not literary, and has had no discernible impact on any major writer or movement in the English language. He has not even founded a school of philosophy – Gibranism, or whatever. In the Arabic-speaking world, however, the opposite is true. Even though his English books have been translated into Arabic, they have not received the attention or success the Western world has given them; he is unknown as a prophet, yet has had a considerable, if oblique, effect on literature. Even if we accept the scholarly assessment of his poetry as not of the first rank, he remains of vital importance. He was the right person in the right place at the right time to bridge the gap between Western and Arabic literature in terms of both form and content. He was also the right person at the right time to bridge the gap as an Eastern prophet speaking with tantalizing clarity to the West. But subsequently he has become, once again, the Gibran of multiple personalities.[56]

11

The Prophet

In Europe World War I brought to a sudden end a way of life that many had assumed to be permanent and God-given. The war was no less of a watershed in American cultural history, but its effects were less focused. Much of the adrenaline rush of modernism was exhausted in the emotion and banality of war. The United States emerged relatively unscathed and in a position to corner a number of world markets while Europe struggled to recover, with the result that the country as a whole entered a period of material prosperity. One of the effects of this was the corruption of the sense of imminent revolution, epitomized in 1913 by the Armory Show and the Paterson Strike Pageant, while the sense of joy that underlay it had become bogged down in the mud of the trenches. The new generation was more hard-boiled than its predecessors, because the first thing the war destroyed was idealism: there was nothing moral about this war. One of the ideals to suffer was the dream of a creative conjunction of poetry and politics – the notion that politics has a transcendent purpose and that poetry can bring about a social revolution. There is less of such talk in the 1920s: the war brought people down to earth and drove a wedge between the two activities.

Along with its illusions, the new generation lost a great many of its inhibitions. The end of the war released a huge amount of energy. What were people to do with it? The answer was not far to seek, because wartime had cast its usual spell and loosened the hold of the moral code. Flappers smoked and drank, when previously polite women had done neither in public, and certainly had not got drunk; young men and women petted in the backs of automobiles, which for the first time gave them the freedom to escape easily from their parents' orbit. Rising hemlines, short hair covered with cloche hats (in imitation, conscious or unconscious, of the helmets of the trenches), lipstick and rouge, flesh-coloured stockings rolled down – these were only the outward manifestations of a new freedom compounded of the remnants of the revolutionary energy of the 1910s, the suffragette movement, and the Freudian or pseudo-Freudian view that loss of sexual inhibitions, bringing it all out into the open, was good for the soul. Sex became so available a commodity in New York that, except around Times Square, streetwalkers were driven indoors.

This was the era of the Fitzgeralds ('Scott is a novelist and Zelda is a novelty,' said Ring Lardner), of Djuna Barnes ('I spent all summer looking for a night to go with that night-gown'), of Hemingway and O'Neill, Dorothy Parker and Duke Ellington. This was the era of speakeasies, ragtime, Florenz Ziegfeld's *Follies*, all-night parties and the café society, where beauties such as Belle Gifford and Edna St Vincent Millay had languid affairs – in Millay's case with either sex – with casual ennui, borne along on a tide of jazz. It was the first age of the cult of youth, ushered in by Randolph Bourne's 1913 book *Youth and Life*, which sang the praises of youth for the authenticity of its vision and for its natural impulse towards 'self-expression', one of the buzz-words of the time. The cult of youth found its popular peak ten years later in Gertrude Atherton's famous novel *Black Oxen*, in which the heroine finds a potion that enables her to recapture her lost youth.

These were selfish, hedonistic times, compared with the idealism of the Liberal Club and the years immediately preceding the Great War. A saying which encapsulates this aspect of the 1920s is attributed to the penniless, eccentric Baroness Elsa von Freytag von Loringhoven, who shaved her head and lacquered it bright vermilion, and was once arrested for the indecency of her clothes. 'I wouldn't lift a leg for humanity,' she said. Inevitably, when values change so quickly, the change wasn't permanent and even the most vociferous champions of the new order became disillusioned and fell into cynicism and anomie. Fitzgerald, in *The Crack-up*, memorably summed up the aura of the times with the phrase 'glamor and loneliness'.[1] Gertrude Stein, the 'high priestess of abstract modernism',[2] called them 'the lost generation', and the label stuck.

Our sources for Gibran's thoughts, feelings and activities in the 1920s are pitifully thin. On the face of it, Barbara Young's biography offers the best prospect of such information, since in 1925 she became his secretary and amanuensis and worshipper, while retaining her career as an accomplished and well-published poet; but the book is derivative and uncritical. We will never know quite what he thought about the corrupt ways of the Harding administration, or about the 1925 trial of John Scopes in Dayton, Tennessee, on the issue of whether it was legal to teach the doctrine of evolution in schools. How did he react to the deification of Lindbergh for making the first solo flight across the Atlantic? Did he learn Mah Jong, try his hand at a crossword puzzle, go to see Houdini? Did he express his usual philosophical sorrow at the rise of gangsterism and racketeering, or at the great Wall Street Crash of 1929? What – to bring matters close to home – did he think of the increasing success and fame of his Pen Club colleagues, Rihani, Madi and Naimy, which threatened for a while to eclipse his own?

The main reason for the gaps in our knowledge of Gibran's life in the 1920s is the increasing distance between him and Mary Haskell. They saw each other less often and wrote fewer letters, an increasing proportion of the letters being mainly or merely about editorial matters. At the end of 1921 Mary's older cousin Louise died and she spent her Christmas vacation in Savannah, Georgia, with the elderly widower, Jacob Florance Minis. Florance, an imposing figure with a white military moustache, asked her to move down south and become his companion. Throughout much of 1922, when she and Kahlil met, a great deal of their conversation revolved around the question of whether she should give up her career (of which she was tired) and move south. By September she had decided to make the break, and so early in 1923, with no great fanfare of farewells on either side between her and Kahlil, she retired to the peace, humidity and elegant charm of Savannah. After Boston the slower pace of life must have been heaven; on 7 May 1926 she put her stay there on a permanent basis by marrying her 'uncle'. Minis was elderly, petulant and somewhat hypochondriac. He demanded Mary's time and attention, and was jealous of her relationship with Kahlil.[3] When she worked on Kahlil's books and wrote to him, she had to do so furtively; she used the coded initials 'C.J.' to refer to him in her diaries, and once 'J. Grinch'.[4] All this, naturally, meant that sustaining their friendship at even a fraction of its former intensity was impossible. It also presumably spelled the end of their financial arrangement; in any case, with book advances and royalties, fees from lecturing and reading, illustrating books of poetry such as Madeline Mason-Manheim's 1925 *Hill Fragments*,[5] and the sale of pictures – especially, these days, commissioned portraits[6] – Kahlil was undoubtedly better off than he had been, and could dispense with Mary's patronage.

So there are solid enough reasons for the thinness of our knowledge of Gibran's life in the 1920s. However, it is also not impossible that it is a true reflection of the fact that, for a number of reasons, there was less happening in his life. In the first place, he had arrived. He no longer had to thrust himself forward, but coasted along, surrounded by his own adoring coterie, and keeping up only with a few familiar friends like the Robinsons.[7] His exalted position as the Prophet of New York did not come without a cost in isolation and loneliness, however. Having clothed himself in this mythical persona, which had evolved gradually over the years out of the melancholy Romantic image foisted on him by Fred Holland Day, he now found people could only see the clothing, not the man underneath.[8] And so he withdrew somewhat from New York society. This withdrawal should be measured not so much by, say, the frequency with which he went out to the theatre or a restaurant with friends, for that continued unabated,[9] but by the decreasing variety of people that he chose to see and be seen with.

Likewise, ostensibly often for reasons of health, he spent longer and longer periods away from New York, sometimes months at a time (ten months in 1929, three months in 1922, another three months in 1930), staying either with friends in the countryside or with Marianna in Boston or on the Massachusetts coast. There may have been sound health reasons for some of these trips, but it is hard to imagine the Gibran of the 1910s allowing himself so much time off work. Again, he had arrived, so he was doing less.[10] More than once he told Mary that he had renounced the feeling that he had to be producing work to justify his existence. In a 1924 letter to her he said that he was working only a little every day, and felt released, as if from prison.[11]

It is undoubtedly true that he was ill quite a lot in the 1920s. His first real scare came in 1921 when, still aged only thirty-eight, he suffered from palpitations or an irregular over-fast heartbeat. Despite the fact that he alerted all his friends to his condition, doctors could find nothing organically wrong with him, and merely advised him against overwork and stress. But there were recurrent bouts of illness every year, and he reached the point where he never felt completely well, though he told Mary that he had learned to master pain with his mind.[12] So here is another reason he was leading a quieter, less eventful life.

Finally, it is also clear that he was out of step with the times. In *The Crack-up* Scott Fitzgerald wrote, 'Society, even in small cities, now dined in separate chambers, and the sober table learned about the gay table only from hearsay. There were very few people left at the sober table.'[13] Gibran definitely sided, at least in public, with the sober table. He made himself out to be prudish about sex at a time when sex was all the rage; he not infrequently complained to Mary that people seemed to have become sex-mad.[14] When irony was *de rigueur*, he pursued his own brand of sincerity; while the smart set displayed cynicism, he continued to preach engagement in the pleasures and pains of life; in an era when the new science of advertising was peddling envy, credibility and appearance, he purveyed what he saw as reality. As a small but telling instance of his being out of harmony with the 1920s, consider his comments on the new fad for cosmetics: he told Mary that any woman wearing make-up had loose morals, and that was why men did not like make-up on a woman, because they could not respect such women.[15] Likewise, in an age addicted to progress, he was opposed to it. He told Barbara Young once, for example, that he would like to unmake the aeroplane and the 'hell of machinery'.[16] It is not so much that the 1920s passed Gibran by, but that he withdrew from them. In a 1925 letter to May Ziadeh he describes New York as an awful place, and there is sincerity in his claim that only the golden chains he had forged for himself kept him there.[17] In many respects he was a fish out of water. Up till now it has been possible to read him as a man of his times, a Romantic in an age sympathetic to Romanticism; but Romanticism was definitely out of vogue in the 1920s.

However, whereas in most respects Gibran's life in the 1920s was somewhat tangential to the mainstream, it did intersect more fully at certain points, particularly those relating to his private life. In the first place, he had always enjoyed going to the theatre, and there was an explosion of theatres in New York in the 1920s. On average an incredible 225 plays were produced each year of the decade.[18] So I'm sure we can imagine him, with more money and leisure on his hands, going often to the theatre, perhaps on his own, or more likely with a select band of friends. Once in 1923 Mary saw him at the theatre when he did not know she was there. He made up a fourth with Edgar Speyer and two ladies, and she noticed not only how he was not afraid to show his emotions in public, when he was moved by the play, but also how in the interval his companions would hang on his words, as he responded to some question of theirs. This undoubtedly gives us a valid snapshot of an aspect of Gibran's life in the 1920s.

However, two other points at which Gibran's life intersected with popular movements in the 1920s are considerably less placid. One of the results of the prosperity of the Coolidge years was a widespread property boom. Although this was most marked in Florida, where prices went crazy until a couple of hurricanes rudely demonstrated that the south-east was not quite the paradise on earth the brochures had been claiming, the feeling in other parts of the country as well was that property made a sound investment. Gibran was caught by this bullish mood. In May 1924 he went halves with a Boston friend, Faris Malouf, in laying out $24,000 as a down-payment on two conjoining brownstones at 409 and 411 Marlborough Street, Boston, just a couple of blocks south of the Charles River. Together the two houses had a large number of rooms, and the plan was to renovate the buildings and then hire them out to some suitable organization. Things went well at first. A Miss Quimby and a Miss Fowler approached the partners and offered to lease the buildings for ten years for their Fenway Business Women's Club, provided that Gibran and Malouf made certain repairs and alterations in order to bring it into line with their requirements. Gibran and Malouf were already stretched by the $40,000 mortgage they had had to take out to acquire the building, and the renovation work was not going to be cheap, but the prospect of a guaranteed steady income, which would more than cover their repayments, kept them hopeful for the future.

The rest of the affair can be tracked through Kahlil's letters to Mary. He told her the good news about the Misses Quimby and Fowler in September, calling it 'a fat piece of good luck', and estimating his and Malouf's profit as about $12,000 a year. By October, however, he is starting to sound desperate: the workmen are in the building, so there is no going back, but he needs to raise more money urgently, because the renovation work is going to cost $12,000, which he and Malouf don't have, and there are outstanding bills already. The lease signed with the Fenway Business Women's Club was unsecured, and so no one will lend them the money they need. He feels he is out of his depth and asks Mary what he should do. She responded to the message between the lines and sent him a cheque to cover the most urgent bills, keeping all this, of course, perfectly secret from Florance. She suggested that he might use some of his pictures as collateral on a loan, and asked him to keep all the accounts for her to look over when she was in Boston later that month.

When it came down to it, however, she again covered his immediate debts, to the tune of a little over $6,000, and sent him the money in tranches, as she was able surreptitiously to raise it. For all his gratitude, Gibran was mortified by the fact that he had been forced to turn to her; he confessed to her that he had been greedy and stupid. By the beginning of December, with the immediate worries behind him thanks to Mary's largesse, a brighter tone enters his letters. Malouf seems to be able to raise the money to cover his portion of the bills and debts, and they are confident in the future of the buildings with the Misses Quimby and Fowler.

But they were counting chickens. In the New Year of 1925 Miss Quimby and Miss Fowler told the partners that to their deep regret they were not able to raise enough support for their proposed club to make it viable for them to lease the buildings. The whole deck of cards collapsed around Gibran's ears. In February the banks moved in to repossess the buildings. Gibran was not ruined financially – he had a little salted away in other savings accounts with Syrian friends in Boston – but he had lost the majority of his capital. Mary told him to be philosophical, on the grounds that money loss still leaves the soul intact. But there is no doubt that Gibran suffered deeply, not just from the financial loss, but from the blow to his self-esteem, at having his greed and stupidity revealed to him, and potentially to the world at large, although he managed to keep the business a secret from most people. In May he looked back on the whole affair as a 'long, dark winter'.[19] The champion of poverty had been caught by greed.

Four years later, when he joined his cousin Assaf George in a similar venture, the outlay was far more modest and the whole enterprise more secure; they bought two houses at 180–182 Broadway, not far from Tyler Street, where Marianna was still living. This was considered to be a safety net for Marianna, but in the event she didn't need it, because in 1930 Gibran bought her a house of her own in the Boston suburb of Jamaica Plain. The Broadway houses presumably remained in Assaf George's hands after Gibran's death; at any rate, we hear no more about them. In 1928 Gibran, through Assaf George, also investigated the possibility of buying an old monastery near Bsharri called Mar Sarkis, or the monastery of St Sergius.[20] More about this later, but it does look as though he was at last planning to put his money where his mouth was, as the saying goes, and translate into action the longing for Lebanon he so often expressed in his letters.

The other aspect of his life in the 1920s to be covered in this context is the fact that in his later years Gibran was an alcoholic. Here the greatest gap opens up between the man and the myth, between the prophet persona he had adopted and promulgated through his writings and the actual, miserable human being underneath. To my mind, since, as I have said before, we do reasonably require prophets to live the kind of life they preach, the gap is wide enough to cast a serious shadow over the integrity of the message he was trying to put across in his writings.

It was Mikhail Naimy's biography which broke the news when it was published in Arabic in 1934. For many years after the publication of his biography, many of Gibran's Arabic acquaintances were inclined to think that Naimy had exaggerated. Gibran was known within the Arab community in New York as a heavy social drinker, as were several members of the Pen Club,[21] but they could not believe that he was actually an alcoholic. But there turned out to be independent witnesses. The

Gibrans revealed in their biography, first published in 1974, that by 1928 Gibran was peppering his letters to his sister with requests for arak – large quantities of arak. They also told the story of how in 1930 a visitor, Idella Purnell Stone, brought a Chilean poet Gabriela Mistral to visit Gibran, whom she admired greatly from his writings. 'Because of her eager, child-like faith,' Stone wrote in a 1950 review of Naimy's biography, 'I did not mention . . . that during the course of the evening when her prophet excused himself for a moment and stepped behind an oriental screen, it was to take a swig out of a bottle which, in the unfortunately arranged mirror, didn't look like a medicine bottle!'[22]

A final piece of evidence was not available to the Gibrans. In a 1941 letter his old friend Witter Bynner wrote, 'And it is a sorrow to remember that at the end, caught by a fatal disease, he withdrew into isolation in his studio and assuagement through drink.'[23] This is not the most accurate of letters, because in the next sentence Bynner claims that Gibran had been locked in his studio dead for a day or two before his body was discovered, which is entirely false. Nevertheless, his testimony about Gibran's drinking is telling. It is impressively objective testimony when one considers that Bynner was extremely unlikely to have read Naimy's biography, which was at that date available only in Arabic (not one of Bynner's languages), and so must have heard about Gibran's drinking from friends back in New York. In fact, one of his sources may well have been Idella Purnell Stone, who was a friend of his. After her visit to Gibran she must have written to Bynner, expressing some of her concerns, because there is a letter back from him to her in which he says, 'I am glad you had at least one pleasant interview with Kahlil, but I am sorry that you encountered, the second time, one of his bad moods. I know them well. They usually mean, not that he is drunk, but that he is painting or making love.'[24]

Quite when Gibran started drinking heavily is not clear. He had always enjoyed the odd glass of wine when eating out,[25] but there is no sign of heavy drinking until later. The testimonies cited above are from late in the 1920s, but we should also consider the nature of the illness from which he was suffering even earlier. At the beginning of 1929 one of the main problems was a painful enlargement of the liver.[26] Now, although in the advanced stages of alcoholism a shrunken liver is most likely, in its earlier stages the liver may well become enlarged. The rate of enlargement varies from patient to patient, but if we attribute Gibran's liver problem to his drinking, we could go on to say that this showed that he had been drinking heavily for at least two or three years previously. This would push his dependence on alcohol back to 1926, but in all likelihood his heavy drinking started considerably earlier. Mikhail Naimy told his nephew Nadeem Naimy that Gibran was a daily drinker for many years.

Charitably, we may be inclined to adopt Bynner's line and say that Gibran started drinking heavily in order to anaesthetize himself from the pain of whatever disease it was that had a hold of his body; but, in fact, there is no real reason why we should think this, rather than that he simply had a weakness for drink – and even that the drinking was the cause of the illness, rather than the other way round. There is a rumour that written in Arabic on one of his paintings owned by Marie al-Khoury was the line: 'Do not blame a person for drinking lest he is trying to forget something more serious than drinking.'[27] Even if this story is true, it is undatable, and so can tell us nothing about when Gibran started drinking; all the same, it is interesting that the line talks of 'forgetting' rather than 'anaesthetizing'. As an alcoholic in literary New York in the 1920s, Gibran was in good company: Ann Douglas lists no fewer than thirty-two of his contemporaries in the New York of the 1920s who were alcoholics, a list that includes Thurber, Hemingway, O'Neill, Dorothy Parker, Hart Crane, Fitzgerald and Sinclair Lewis.

Now, this was of course the Prohibition era; the Eighteenth Amendment came into effect on 16 January 1920.[28] However,

> Prohibition . . . was a joke in most of urban America, but in New York it was an all-out full-scale farce. Seven thousand arrests for alcohol possession or drinking in New York City between 1921 and 1923 (when enforcement was more or less openly abandoned) resulted in only seventeen convictions; observers estimated the number of illegal speak-easies, dives, and drugstores as somewhere between a monstrous 32,000 and an unbelievable 100,000 . . . Some people during Prohibition, playing on John Winthrop's famous words about the 'city on a hill', called New York the 'City on a Still'.[29]

Alcohol flowed from illegal stills in the city and the countryside, or from across the border in Canada; there were far too few Prohibition agents, and the police were invariably in the pay of the bootleggers, since they enjoyed a drink as much as the next man. There were maybe 20,000 speakeasies in Manhattan alone, ranging from 'clip joints' run by criminals to brownstones disguised as clubs. Perhaps we should add to our picture of Gibran and have him seated in a speakeasy late at night with a whisky in front of him on the table, but my impression is that he drank alone in his studio, or in the private company of a few friends. His arak was made in illegal stills in the back streets of Boston and brought to New York by trusted family members. It seems that, as was the case with his disastrous 1924 attempt at becoming a property landlord, he wanted to keep his darker secrets hidden from his New York peers. That kind of reputation could only damage his exalted position in the city.

There is some slight evidence that in the 1920s Gibran himself was aware of the gap between the man and the myth, and was disappointed in himself. This added, no doubt, to the unhappiness and narcissistic self-hatred of which we have previously seen some signs. It is not surprising that there is only slight evidence for this, because these are the man's deepest secrets. Nor is it surprising that what little evidence there is should stem from the 1920s, when his position and self-estimation had become so exalted that any gap would be more noticeable.

In the first place, and most importantly, this is the context of the story told in the Overture to this book, when Gibran admitted to Mikhail Naimy that he felt he was a 'false alarm'.[30] Another incident, dating from 1929, reeks of the emotional instability and confessional mode of drunkenness. On the day after a huge Syrian banquet in his honour, there was a more private celebration of his forty-sixth birthday, at the studio of his friend, the great Mexican painter José Clemente Orozco. Over a dozen people were present, mainly from two artistic circles – the Delphic group and the New York Craftsman's Poetry Group. Belle Baker, who was well known in New York as a reader of Gibran's work, read extracts from *The Prophet*, *Lazarus* and *Jesus, the Son of Man*, while Gibran himself read from *The Madman* and *The Forerunner*. It was a convivial, cosmopolitan evening – but as it progressed Gibran became more and more emotional, until he rushed weeping from the room. Alma Reed, the writer who has preserved the story, followed him out and he confessed to her, and to Orozco a moment later, his feelings of inadequacy. He told them that he was no longer working well, and had lost the creative spark which had vitalized him in the late 1910s. There he was, apparently at the height of his power – but it was all a sham, because he had no power left.[31] This was close to the truth: a lot of Gibran's work in the 1920s is actually old work rehashed. Perhaps he was comparing himself with his Pen Club colleagues Rihani, Naimy and Madi, whose stars were shining very brightly. Naimy was capable of getting some of his poems published in the *New York Times* in 1928; Rihani was by now an established poet and political commentator at home and abroad, and his important political work, *Maker of Modern Arabia*, was published in 1928; Madi's *Al-Jadawil* (*The Brooks*), which many critics regard as the seminal book of Arabic Romantic poetry, was published in 1927.

It may seem strange to say that Gibran was working less in the 1920s. After all, look at the books that were published: *The Prophet* (1923), *Al-Bada'i' wa-'t-tara'if* (*The Beautiful and the Rare* or, as Gibran preferred, rather prosaically, *Best Things and Masterpieces*, also 1923), *Sand and Foam* (1926), *Kalimat Jibran* (*Spiritual Sayings*, 1927), *Jesus, the Son of Man* (1928), *Al-Sanabil* (*The Spikes of Grain*, 1929), and *The Earth Gods* (1931). Even after his death two further books were waiting to be published: *The Wanderer* (1932) and *The Garden of the Prophet* (1933). But in fact a lot of this was old work and a couple of these books are extremely short; however, the main decrease in his work rate was that he was painting less, except to illustrate his books or make money.

Al-Bada'i' wa-'t-tara'if and *Al-Sanabil* are no more than anthologies of earlier work. The first, *Best Things and Masterpieces*, Gibran seems to have found more of a nuisance than something of which he could be proud. In this case, the anthology appears to have contained some new pieces as well as old ones; and as with other anthologies he felt that he had to rework every old piece, and that was 'labour, not creation'.[32] The only thing that was engaging his interest at the time was

The Prophet. *Best Things and Masterpieces* contains some interesting work, but nothing that is not recognizably in the whimsical style already familiar from the rest of his Arabic work. Apart from 'Your Lebanon and Mine',[33] for instance, there is the odd story 'A Ship in the Mist',[34] in which a young man is haunted by a ghostly woman, a modest succubus, who is his true love, but deserts him the minute he leaves the shores of Lebanon on a scientific mission to Venice – at exactly the same time that the daughter of the man he is visiting dies. When the protagonist of the story visits the girl's deathbed, he finds to his horror that she is the exact image of his ghostly wife. Then there is the prose-poem 'My Soul is Heavy Laden with its Fruits', in which Gibran complains that for all the riches he has to offer, there is no one to appreciate them enough to lighten the load of his artistic burden; it is better to be poor and free, he insists, than rich and imprisoned by one's riches. These two are enough to assure us that, as far as his Arabic writing is concerned, Gibran has not moved on.

Spikes of Grain is merely an honorific – an anthology of his Arabic work collated by friends, published by friends, and presented to him in 1929 in recognition of his services to Arabic literature – but *Kalimat Jibran* (literally *Words of Gibran*, but translated into English as *Spiritual Sayings*) is more interesting. Gibran always had a ready facility with pithy sayings. This is evident time and again from Mary's journals, and is one reason, no doubt, why he was in such demand in New York society: on any topic that came up Gibran would not only have an opinion, but would more often than not express himself with brevity and an impression of profundity. Some of the shorter parables in books like *The Madman* are little more than aphorisms anyway, and it is possible to see *The Prophet* as strings of aphorisms stitched together by the structure of the Prophet's homilies.

Gibran was aware that this was a strong suit for him. He was no academic philosopher; he had no desire or ability to construct lengthy or logically coherent arguments justifying his points of view. In 1915, when he was developing his fragmentary evolutionary philosophy, he suggested to Mary: 'Perhaps all that can be written about it is just little sayings', and gave a few examples: 'The soul is the highest form of matter' and 'The highest in man is the lowest in God.'[35] The idea of writing sayings, even if not to elucidate this philosophy, seems to have taken root, to bloom from 1920 onwards in a torrent of them, which (as usual) were often published first in Arabic in some newspaper, in groups of perhaps twelve to twenty sayings, and then translated into English for *The Dial* or *The Syrian World*.[36] Occasionally he toyed with the idea of presenting them within some over-arching context, as the parables in *The Madman* are supposed to be told by the Madman. The two ideas that occurred to him on this were either to write a kind of follow-up to *The Prophet*, in which people would reminisce about the Prophet, and thereby mention numbers of 'his' shorter sayings, or to write a book provisionally called *The Way of the Seven Days*, in which he and a stranger are on a journey to the Holy City, and on the first day the stranger comes out with all kinds of bitter aphorisms, but gradually, day by day as they approach the Holy City, the sayings become less and less bitter, more and more cosmic . . . and then the stranger dies on reaching Mecca.[37]

In the event, however, and probably because the sayings were occurring to him randomly, he abandoned any idea of grouping them together by theme or spokesman, and just presented them as grapeshot. There is no unifying theme to *Spiritual Sayings*, nor is there any sign of the evolutionary philosophy. It is just a collection of aphorisms, like those of La Rochefoucauld, say, or Novalis. Typical examples include: 'Our worst fault is our preoccupation with the faults of others'; 'When affection withers, it intellectualizes'; 'Show me your mother's face; I will tell you who you are'; 'Trading is thieving unless it is barter.' These are typical in the sense that the tone is predominantly ethical, and that they represent the average length of a maxim. Some are full of insight, others are fairly ordinary.

Gibran was still writing occasional pieces for the Arabic newspapers,[38] and his relationship with the Syrian community both at home and abroad remained solid. A sign of his identification as a spokesman for Syria was that in 1925 he was invited by Syud Hossain, a well-known authority and lecturer on Middle Eastern politics, to join the board of the New Orient Society in New York and to become one of the regular contributors to their quarterly magazine, *The New Orient*, with Hossain as editor. This was another prestigious post, equivalent in its way to his position on the advisory board of *The Seven Arts* in the 1910s, except with a more international flavour. Through the board of the New Orient Society he rubbed shoulders – literally, or on the pages of the magazine – not only with old friends such as Julia Ellsworth Ford and Witter Bynner, but also with Mahatma Gandhi, Annie Besant, Ananda Coomaraswamy, Bertrand Russell, Claude Bragdon, George Russell (A.E.) and H. G. Wells, as well as others whose names have not lasted the years so well.[39] The aim of the magazine was to bring East and West together 'in intellectual and spiritual comradeship', emphasizing what is common to the heritage of humankind the world over, 'which alone may serve as the foundation for an enduring and enlightened fellowship among the nations'.[40] The magazine was unfortunately short-lived, but for a while it provided Gibran with a congenial medium in which to reproduce a number of short poems of varying quality, and some drawings too. His drawing 'The Blind Poet', in the July–September 1925 issue of the magazine, is particularly fine: the poet, Christ-like in appearance, is cradled in the arms of a beautiful, caped, peaceful Madonna-like figure. The picture accompanies a poem with the same title.

In 1927, though without any official capacity, he was close to the organizers of the magazine *The Syrian World*. Edited by Salloum Mokarzel, this was the first English-language magazine for the now considerably Westernized first wave of Syrian immigrants and their children. Apart from Gibran, regular contributors included Rihani, Naimy and Philip Hitti. Here was the next convenient outlet for ongoing work – some new parables which would later be included in *The Wanderer*, the short sayings and aphorisms he was still working with these days. Just as importantly, it was on the opening page of the first issue of *The Syrian World* in July 1927 that Gibran published his famous address 'To Young Americans of Syrian Origin', in which he urged his target audience to be proud of both their Western and their Eastern heritage, and to draw on both in working for the future of their adopted land. The full text was reprinted by the journal for framing and circulated widely among the Syrian immigrant population. Gibran was explicitly lending his support to the magazine's largely unsuccessful call for the unification of all Syrian immigrants, whatever their sect or religion.

Perhaps the most interesting Arabic piece Gibran wrote in the 1920s was the one-act play *Iram Dhat al-'Imad* (*Iram, City of Lofty Pillars*), which was reprinted in *Best Things and Masterpieces*. A scholar, Najib Rahmé, comes in search of a spiritual being, Aminah al-'Alawiyah, to ask about her visit to the mythical city Iram. After learning something about her mortal history from Zain Abedin, a Sufi mystic who is associated with Aminah, the lady herself appears. Of course, Najib learns more than he bargained for: in addition to hearing something about Iram (which turns out to be a state of mind, instantly accessible if one is in the right state), he is told about the relation of the soul and the body, of the unity of all religions, of the spiritual oneness of all things; Aminah teaches him that he contains all creation within himself and that nothing perishes (which means not only that he will be reincarnated, but that we are always surrounded by invisible spiritual beings); and she insists on the importance of faith and the imagination as a supplement to the scientific senses. This is Gibran's most overtly mystical piece of writing, and he used it to express a number of his most cherished beliefs. It is a pity it is not more widely known, because it could act as accessible background reading for those who want to understand some of the thinking behind his more famous works, particularly *The Prophet*.[41]

Turning from his Arabic writing to his publications with Knopf,[42] the first book that demands our attention is, at last, *The Prophet*. Gibran always knew that this was the most important book of his life, and this certainty is reflected not just in overt statements to that effect,[43] but in the number of times the book crops up in Mary's journals and in the letters that passed between them.[44] Rather than sitting down and writing actively, forcing the words to come, Gibran took many years over the book, waiting always for particular moments of inspiration. In an interview after the publication of the book he was asked how he came to write it. 'Did I write it?' he replied. 'It wrote me.'[45] But he also had Mary check every phase of the work: the finished form of *The Prophet* owes quite a bit to her invisible hand. Even after the whole book was written, they worked together in May 1922 on the 'spacing' of the sentences (taking the Book of Job as their model), and of course she read the proofs.[46]

Gibran acknowledged her help, telling her that she had shaped his English more than anyone else. Her influence on the finished form of

all Gibran's English books should not be underestimated. In June 1918, for instance, Gibran wrote the counsel 'On Reason and Passion'. Mary's input consisted not just in spelling and punctuation corrections, but also in suggestions for alternative words and whole phrases. She was always cautious and deferent – she always left the final decision up to Kahlil – but her judgement was good. Where Gibran had written 'you would but drift or be at a standstill in mid-sea', she suggested 'you will but toss and drift or else be held at a standstill in mid-sea', which still isn't exactly what was finally adopted and printed in the book, but is a lot better than the original. In the very next sentence, Gibran had written 'passion, when unhindered, is a power that seeks its own destruction' while being uncertain whether 'power' or 'flame' was the right word here. Mary suggested either 'a flame that burns to its own destruction' or 'a power that rages to its own destruction'. As readers of the book know, Gibran adopted the former. From the pages of her journals or of her letters examples could be found to illustrate her work on almost any of Gibran's English books, but let this example stand to make the biographical point: Gibran needed Mary Haskell to improve his English. She was the perfect sympathetic editor, and without her help his impact on the English world might well have been considerably less.

Through the pages of her journals, we can track something of the long gestation of *The Prophet*. In the first place, it was not always called *The Prophet*. She refers to it mainly as *Counsels* or *The Commonwealth*. Under one or another of these titles, fragments of what was to become *The Prophet* begin to be reflected in her journal as early as 1912, though it is not until 1915 or 1916 that he clearly had a single book in mind rather than two.[47] However, Gibran was later to claim that he first dreamt of the book, and drafted a version of it, when he was a child in Lebanon.[48] Be that as it may, the structure of the book – the prophet delivering counsels as he is on the point of leaving an island where he has been in exile – was in place by 1912. Then the book is mentioned from time to time in Mary's journal entries, until by 1919 it had evolved into its present form, after an intense spring in 1918 when sixteen of the counsels were written. By 1919 its title has definitely become *The Prophet*, with the term 'counsels' being reserved for the various sections of it – the counsel on work, for instance. In 1919 he became distracted by work on *The Forerunner*, but then there was another intense phase in the summer of 1920, when most of the remaining counsels were written. After that, work on the book slowed down, partly for reasons of illness and creative fatigue, though perhaps he was mulling it over in the back of his mind. Later he was to say that he kept the finished manuscript for four years before delivering it to the publisher, because 'I wanted to be very sure that every word of it was the very best I had to offer.'[49] At any rate, the book was certainly more or less finished by the end of 1921, although some tinkering was still going on in 1922, and there were some illustrations to be painted. Knopf accepted the book – indeed, he had been waiting for it for some time – and it was published in September 1923. No doubt Gibran wanted the book published in September, because it is in the month of Ielool, or September, that the book is set.

In *The Prophet*, Almustafa the Prophet is about to embark on a journey by ship out of exile in the city of Orphalese and back at last to his native country. Before he leaves, the people of Orphalese gather round him to hear his last words of wisdom. In all he delivers twenty-six counsels on topics ranging from religion to eating and drinking.[50] It has been said that Almustafa's desire to return to his native land expresses Gibran's own longing to return to Lebanon from New York, and that may be true, although there are also symbolic overtones to the idea of returning to one's homeland from a place of limitations. In any case, it is undeniable (although Gibran used modestly to attempt to deny it) that Almustafa, the 'chosen one', is Gibran's alter ego, and Nadeem Naimy rightly talks about a fusion at this stage of Gibran's writing career between his homesickness for Lebanon and his poetic longing for a metaphysical homeland.[51]

Few of its readers know that the book was originally intended as the first of a trilogy. Roughly speaking (Gibran himself was not entirely clear on this), if the first book covered the large topics of human life – birth, death, religion, marriage, love, children, work, and so on – broadly under the rubric of man's relationship to man, the second book was to cover man's relationship to nature, and the third man's relationship to the divine. Once he summarized the difference between the first two books by saying that if the message of *The Prophet* was that all is well, the message of the second book would be that all is beautiful.[52] But Gibran himself sometimes got muddled about the contents of the various books: he once told Mary that he would cover both silence and beauty in the second book, and she had to remind him that he had already written a counsel on beauty for *The Prophet*.[53] After the publication of *The Prophet*, however, Gibran's interest in completing the trilogy waned, but at the time of his death he was working on the second book, *The Garden of the Prophet*. After his death this was edited by Barbara Young, and published posthumously. All that remains of the third book, *The Death of the Prophet*, is a fragment revealing the nature of Almustafa's death: 'And he shall return to the City of Orphalese, and they shall stone him in the market-place, even unto death; and he shall call every stone a blessed name.'[54]

By any standards, *The Prophet* is a remarkable book. The statistics of its publishing history reflect something of this. Knopf can have had no high expectations when he accepted the book for publication, given the far from outstanding sales of Gibran's previous English-language books. But Gibran was convinced that the book would do well, and told Knopf so.[55] He had already tried out a number of sections of the book on various audiences, at poetry societies and so on, and had met with a favourable response.[56] Knopf printed 1,500 and these sold out quickly; but that was no big deal. The next year sales doubled; and the year after that they doubled again. News of the book was getting around by word of mouth. Even during the Depression in the 1930s the book held steady at around 13,000 copies a year. In 1944 it sold 60,000 copies. Since the late 1950s, in North America alone, where the book became a kind of underground bible on the college campuses, the book has sold at a phenomenal rate. In some years it was, or was nearly, Knopf's best seller, and it always did well. In 1957 it passed the million mark; by 1965 it had sold 2.5 million, by 1970 four million. At times, in both the 1960s and 1970s, *The Prophet* was selling in the States at the rate of about 5,000 copies a week – not bad for a 50-year-old book! By now it has sold an astonishing nine million copies in North America alone. That is not counting the UK market, or the twenty or so foreign languages into which it has been translated. Now, of course, it is even available on the Internet, and there is talk of a major Hollywood film.[57]

The Prophet has often been criticized as platitudinous, over-sentimental and trite. These are the arrogant criticisms of elitist and hard-hearted intellectuals. The sales figures alone show that the book continues to fulfil an urgent need in people. It strikes a chord, responds to something deep. In our present rather secular age, many people turn to *The Prophet* for succour and spiritual sustenance at times of crisis, or to supplement or stand in for the liturgy of marriage and funeral services. Traditionalists may deplore this, but some measure of spiritual sustenance is better than none. It is expressed in clear, simple words, rather than complexities. Where is the harm in that? Maybe its language only enables it to cut through the superficial layers of the associative mind and penetrate to some deeper part of the mind, or to the heart.

Gibran wrote it this way on purpose. He was aware of the dangers. Even at the eleventh hour, late in 1922, he and Mary read it through to each other one last time, to make sure that it wasn't too 'preachy', as she expressed it in her journal.[58] And as early in the book's gestation as September 1914 he explained to Mary his policy as regards the style of writing: 'I do not explain or discuss. It is just said – with authority. Analysis does not live and it is not delicious to us.' He also deliberately made it short (as are all his books), believing that the best books – the 'reallest' books, as he put it – are short.[59]

The form of the book – but no more than the form – is lifted from Nietzsche. In *Thus Spake Zarathustra* Nietzsche made a prophet his mouthpiece, and it is clear that Zarathustra too is in exile from his homeland, which is also an island, just as in *The Prophet*. Zarathustra dispenses wisdom to the people in much the same way as Almustafa, and in the same pithy way addresses matters topic by topic. But what about the content of the book? What is it that strikes such a chord in so many people? Not long before the book's publication Gibran said that its message was very simple: 'You are far greater than you know, and all is well.'[60] It is clear, then, that the evolution away from Gibran's earlier deep pessimism about the unpleasantness of the world and the futility of people's lives has been completed. The faint promises of *The Madman* and the greater optimism of *The Forerunner* have been fulfilled.[61] The message of *The Prophet* is light, confident and optimistic, and this is undoubtedly the first aspect of the book that appeals to people.

However, there are also profundities in the book; it obviously contains the fruit of years of thought on deep matters relevant to human life. Since by choice Gibran wrote down only the fruit, without any of the reasoning which led him to these conclusions, the ideas can strike with considerable force. In fact, that is the book's main feature. Gibran never claimed that the ideas it contains are particularly new, but he did claim to be expressing them well and forcefully, in a way that would appeal to people and would make them think.[62]

The philosophy of *The Prophet* is hard to pin down, but this may not be a bad thing. If it were not the case, the book would be more limited; it would lose its ability to speak to large numbers of people. It seems that Gibran always intended this. For instance, when talking to Mary about the counsel on crime and punishment, he told her that he could write volumes on the subject, but wanted to leave things open for 'the reader to have his or her say too'.[63] Gibran is trying to communicate something of 'the mysterious' (as the philosopher Ludwig Wittgenstein called it), and that, by definition, is not directly accessible to verbal delineation. 'If these be vague words,' he has the Prophet say, 'then seek not to clear them.'[64] Hence Gibran should be described as a poet as much as a philosopher – he certainly thought of himself as such – since it is the poet's job to communicate 'the mysterious', by means of the feelings and emotions his or her words arouse in the reader. Good poets manage to do so without crossing the narrow dividing-line between the mysterious and the incoherent.

Nevertheless, something can be said about 'the mysterious' as Gibran perceived it in *The Prophet*. We human beings are bound in an utterly degrading fashion to the world by its man-made laws and so-called civilization, but we can free ourselves, and become our Greater Selves, by allowing love into our hearts. Love is the essence of God in man. The path of love is not easy, however, since it causes as much pain as joy – but pain is 'the bitter potion by which the physician within you heals your sick self', and 'the deeper that sorrow carves into your being, the more joy you can contain'.[65] Only through this path of love can a human being hope to fulfil his or her potential, which is nothing less than divinity. The freedom to live with perfect virtue, while withholding judgement on others, in the actual realization that life is one and infinite is the gift of the mysterious to the person who has attained self-realization. And what is perhaps most important is that this freedom is accessible to us here and now. This is reminiscent of his constant belief: 'There are no keys, for there are no doors. Here it is – Life – not locked away from us, but all around us.'[66] This freedom, however, does not seem to involve breaking free of the wheel of incarnation, as it would in Buddhist doctrine, for instance. At any rate, assuming that Almustafa is a perfectly realized being, he still expects to be reincarnated: 'A little while . . . and another woman shall bear me.'[67] Reincarnation remains, as always, a firm belief of Gibran.

Privately, the book was immediately very well received; Kahlil told Mary that he had been overwhelmed with letters even by the end of November 1923.[68] But it is Mary's own prophetic assessment of the book that will strike a chord with many readers:

> This book will be held as one of the treasures of English literature. And in our darkness and in our weakness we will open it, to find ourselves again and the heaven and earth within ourselves. Generations will not exhaust it, but instead generation after generation will find in the book what they would fain be, and it will be better and better loved as men grow riper and riper. It is the most loving book ever written . . . More and more will love you as years go by, long, long after your body is dust.[69]

With hindsight, it is surprising how little review attention the book received – but then the reviewers were not to know how famous a book it would become. Marjorie Seiffert's review in *Poetry*, headed 'Foreign Food', is a tired piece, criticizing the book in terms reminiscent of reviews of others of Gibran's books, as too oriental for 'the robust hunger of the occidental spirit'. Though she acknowledges that the book may find favour with 'restless and unsatisfied spirits', in her view Eastern philosophy is a means of escape from facing up to the realities of the world. And so the book as a whole 'lacks vigor'; its rhythms are charming, but ultimately monotonous; the best that can be said for it is that certain passages have beauty, and that certain lines are insightful. *The Bookman* speaks in similar terms, contrasting East and West.[70] On the other hand, the Chicago *Evening Post* praised the book as a 'little Bible', filled with truth, and congratulated Gibran on having the courage to be an idealist in a cynical age. But that was about it: that *The Prophet* came into the world with a whimper, not a bang, must stand as one of the greatest ever underestimations by the literary community of the importance of a book to the reading public.[71]

The next book to be published was *Sand and Foam*. This is no more than a collection of sayings, exactly like *Spiritual Sayings*, but in English rather than Arabic. However, it is at least a *different* collection of sayings. The 322 sayings (there were 289 in *Spiritual Sayings*) are accompanied by seven illustrations painted by Gibran, and each of the sayings is separated from its neighbours by a floral decoration also from Gibran's pen. The tone of the aphorisms is very much the same as those of *Spiritual Sayings*: 'Love and doubt have never been on speaking terms'; 'Fame is the shadow of passion standing in the light'; 'What we long for and cannot attain is dearer than what we have already attained'; 'Poetry is a deal of joy and pain and wonder, with a dash of the dictionary.' The tone is that of *The Prophet* rather than *The Madman*, and is too anodyne for one to read into it any biographical pointers. At any rate, since Mary Haskell had worked with Gibran on a number of sayings, the book should certainly not be read as 'a forsaken hermit's graffiti', testifying to his loneliness after she deserted him and moved down south.[72]

Again, the book's private reception outstripped the impression it made on the critics. The anonymous reviewer in the New York *Herald Tribune* dipped his pen in acid:

> This book of aphorisms is justly titled. One does not look for flowers among the sands. One tries vainly to lay hands upon foam. Mr Gibran's speech is as arid as the former and as tenuous as the second. There are pages which dully display moth-eaten observations . . . There are pages of intolerable nonsense . . . Mr Gibran's illustrations . . . are scarcely more interesting than his remarks. They remind one of a bad dream of Arthur Davies after an afternoon with the murals of Puvis de Chavannes.

The London *Times Literary Supplement* regretted Gibran's 'preference for the inarticulate to the articulate'. Barbara Young, however, naturally gave the book a rave review for *The Syrian World*.

Jesus, the Son of Man was the longest book Gibran wrote. Whereas all the other books we have so far looked at in the 1920s were more or less left over from the 1910s, *Jesus, the Son of Man* was written from scratch, from November 1926 to December 1927, when he sent it off to Mary for checking.[73] It was published late in October 1928. The fact that Gibran's longest book was devoted to Jesus might occasion some surprise. He may have been brought up in the Catholic faith, but with his belief in reincarnation, and his attraction to pagan pantheism, he was hardly orthodox. He even believed, as we have seen, in the ideal unity of all religions, and in a talk delivered to Mary Haskell's school in January 1919 he developed this idea as follows: at the time of Jesus, and thanks to Jesus, people became aware of the unity of God; at the time of the Renaissance, people became aware of the unity of the earth; now, in the twentieth century, people were becoming aware of the unity of humankind. In the future Gibran looked forward to an era when all three – God, the earth and humankind – might be seen as a unity.[74]

In Gibran's eyes, the Church – and especially the Maronite Church in Lebanon – was co-operating with the worldly power of governments to oppress the poor. This insight was decisive for Gibran, and (until his funeral, over which he had no control) he never again resumed his links with organized religion in any form, and indeed in his writings recommended a form of personal, non-clerical religion, in which each person is responsible for her own relationship with God. Despite all this, the person of Christ, and his original teachings as expounded in the Gospels, remained strong sources of inspiration for Gibran throughout his life. Mary Haskell's journals are littered with paraphrased conversations between the two of them on Christ or his teachings, and in particular with references to the recurrence of the figure of Christ in Kahlil's dreams. The first such dream occurred when he was 12 years old, on the ship across the Atlantic to America in 1895, and the last recorded one is in May 1923 – but we have no reason to believe that they stopped just when Mary's journals stopped. Typically, in the dreams Christ and Gibran meet in a rural setting in Lebanon; they may exchange gifts – cherries, some cress – but few words. The dreams always stress Christ's humanity – the dust on his feet, the colour of his hair, that kind of thing – as well as communicating something of his glory. Afterwards Gibran always retained a strong impression of his face – so much so that the head of Christ is a very common subject in his drawings. His and Mary's conversations on the subject add very little, beyond confirming that Gibran always thought that Christ was the greatest teacher who had ever walked the earth, and was commonly misunderstood. The only time the discussion tips over into strangeness is when Gibran tells Mary that he knows a great many parables which did not make it into the Gospels, because he has often talked with him.[75] Presumably he means that he has talked to him in his dreams, so this shows us that he takes these dreams to be true apparitions.[76]

Some of his earliest and most powerful stories also reveal his perennial fascination with Christ – think, for instance, of 'Yuhanna the Madman' or 'Khalil the Heretic', both distinctly Christ-like figures. These two stories show how important the *teaching* of Christ was for Gibran, even if he rejected the institution of the Church. Other writings elaborate the theme that if Jesus were to come back and witness what the Church had done in his name, he would be surprised, at the least, and even appalled. The situation is pithily summed up in a few words in *Sand and Foam*:

> Once every hundred years Jesus of Nazareth meets Jesus of the Christian in a garden among the hills of Lebanon, and they talk long. And each time Jesus of Nazareth goes away saying to Jesus of the Christian, 'My friend, I fear we shall never, never agree.'[77]

Another theme that crops up, though more rarely, in Gibran's early writings, is the insistence that for all his meekness and passivity, Jesus was far from weak. He was, in Gibran's eyes, closer to the model of the Nietzschean superman. This is from 'The Crucified':[78]

> For centuries Humanity has been worshipping weakness in the person of the Saviour. The Nazarene was not weak! He was strong and is strong! But the people refuse to heed the true meaning of strength.
>
> Jesus never lived a life of fear, nor did He die suffering or complaining. He lived as a leader: He was crucified as a crusader: He died with a heroism that frightened His killers and tormentors.

Jesus was not a bird with broken wings. He was a raging tempest who broke all crooked wings . . . Free and brave and daring He was. He defied all despots and oppressors . . .

Both these themes, and plenty more (including controversial re-interpretations of both the Sermon on the Mount and the Lord's Prayer), recur in *Jesus, the Son of Man.* Through the ingenious device of imagining what Jesus' contemporaries might have said about him – of 'straining' Jesus through the eyes of his contemporaries, as Claude Bragdon put it[79] – Gibran portrays Jesus as a multi-faceted being, with almost as many sides as there were people to see him. Drawing sometimes on Biblical characters and stories, and sometimes on his own imagination, Gibran shows Jesus as a mirror of people's strengths and weaknesses. Most of the characters in the book are favourably inclined to Jesus, but some are hostile: this too enables Gibran to bring out further dimensions of Jesus' nature. Above all, Gibran locates Jesus in everyday surroundings, showing his essential humanity. The book was the fulfilment of an old promise, dating back to 1909, when after discovering Ernest Renan in Paris Gibran wrote to Mary that he wanted to portray the life of Christ as no one had before; and in October 1911 he told Mary that he wanted to work on Christ because he loved him, and disagreed with conventional views and representations about him.[80] It is clear that he was strongly influenced by Renan's controversial *La Vie de Jésus.* Renan, who as an archaeologist had explored the mountains of Lebanon, attempted to undermine the supernatural aspects of Christ's life and teachings and stress his essential humanity, as Maeterlinck did too, in *Wisdom and Destiny.*

Throughout his life, whether he was writing in Arabic or in English, Gibran's work was influenced by the rhythms and cadences of the Bible, so that, given its subject matter, *Jesus, the Son of Man* reads almost as a new, apocryphal gospel. As some reviewers were quick to point out, this is not a work of scholarship; there is no historical evidence for all the characters in Gibran's book saying or thinking what he has them say or think about Christ. It is a work of artistic imagination, and it should be read only as such. Most reviewers – and this book received more reviews than any of his others –

appreciated this, and gave the book favourable, or even rave reviews.[81] After *The Prophet*, it is the book of Gibran that achieves the best sales.

Gibran's interest in Christ and Christian themes at this time shows also in two slim and slight one-act plays he wrote in English late in the 1920s, *Lazarus and His Beloved* and *The Blind*.[82] Neither of these was published in his lifetime, although as we have seen *Lazarus* was available for readings in certain contexts. Gibran was perennially interested in writing plays. Apart from *Iram Dhat al-'Imad* (*Iram, City of Lofty Pillars*), at which we have already glanced, another short Arabic play was *Assilban*, written at much the same time early in the 1920s. He uses this slight offering to bang some familiar drums – the unfortunate Westernization of Lebanon, the true artist's contempt for wealth and isolation from the norms of society.[83]

Lazarus is another piece whose concept had occurred to Gibran a long time before he actually got round to writing it. Mary Haskell recorded the outline of an Arabic poem about Lazarus in 1914, but it first appears as a completed work, in English, in 1926.[84] The scene is set in Lazarus' house in Bethany, on the day after Jesus' crucifixion. Mary, Martha and their mother are waiting for Lazarus to return from the hills. Also present, though never heard by any of the mortal characters, is the Madman, who comments dryly on the proceedings, in an attempt to inject a cosmic dimension into the drama. When Lazarus returns, he tells Mary – clearly his favourite sister, and the one whose mind is more attuned to Gibranesque metaphysics – that he has been with his beloved, an invisible spirit reminiscent of the spirit-wife of the Arabic poem 'A Ship in the Mist'. Lazarus is closer to the spirit world because of his famous brush with death; hence he longs again for death, because it is the giver of insight and wisdom. In fact, his wisdom is such that he identifies himself with Jesus, and, on hearing that Jesus has risen from the dead, he leaves to take up his role as Jesus' counterpart, and even to be crucified.

The Christ-like figure in *The Blind* is a blind musician called David Rugby; again, the Madman is on hand to guide our thinking. The plot of the play is that Rugby is married to an older woman, whose daughter, Anna, his step-daughter, is devoted to him because, for all his blindness, he is the only man in the world who can see. His blindness has given him wisdom, tenderness and the ability to love. Helen, the mother, is an irritable woman, who fails to understand her husband and her daughter. She has a lover, called Kingdon, to whom she can complain that she is trapped in the house of the blind. Rugby walks in on them and though of course he cannot see Kingdon, he senses a presence in the room. He calls Anna into the room, and asks her who else is there. Shocked, but retaining a noble presence of mind, she tells him that there is nobody there – that they are the only two real people in the room, in the world. Rugby in a sense exorcizes the room, and Kingdon and Helen both leave. Rugby and Anna are alone. Through suffering, and through Anna's nobility, Rugby has attained a wider understanding.

The Earth Gods was published just a few weeks before Gibran's death, in March 1931. By 1929 or 1930 he was too ill to put in any sustained work, so it will come as no surprise to find that this is another book which was actually written a long time previously. In June 1915 Kahlil exultantly told Mary, 'I've just begun a big thing in English . . . It's going to be a play, with a prologue. And the prologue is what I'm writing it for. The prologue is the big thing.' Mary goes on to say that he has already written fifteen pages of the prologue, which has three gods talking on a mountain. The first god is weary of his life as a god and desires an end to it, while the second relishes every second of his power over man, and the third simply delights in the singing and dancing of a young man and a young woman in the valley below the mountain where the three gods sit. Because this is a pretty fair synopsis of *The Earth Gods* as it was finally published in 1931; because Gibran continued to add pages in 1915 and 1916; and because the finished text made perhaps only forty hand-written pages, it is clear that in 1930 Gibran was tired, and was content to submit what was, substantially, old work to Knopf for publication. Even in 1915 he considered publishing what he and Mary called 'The Prologue' or 'The Three Gods' separately, without the play to which it was originally conceived as the prologue.[85] In fact, if it is to be identified with the poem Mary at one point calls 'The Three Giants', it is clear that there was a complete version by 1916, because it was read out to Oppenheim then.[86] And so there is little mention of the poem after 1916; Gibran obviously laid it aside as a more or less finished piece.[87]

Mary and he had worked together on it in 1915 and 1916, so it is the only one of his English-language books whose final pre-publication stages she was not involved in: the first she heard about it, apparently, is when she received a copy in March 1931.[88]

Knowing the history of the poem is crucial for any developmental study of Gibran's literary output. Hawi, for instance, is puzzled to find so gloomy a book occurring so late in Gibran's *oeuvre*, and has no choice but to say that it 'heralds the return of darkness to his mind'.[89] In fact, though, it was written well within Gibran's bitter period, and so from that perspective it is less surprising to find that the first two gods reveal something of the bitter cynicism of the old man in *The Procession*, while the youngest god is equivalent to the young man in *The Procession*. In essence, the three gods are genuine archetypes, representing the gods we each enthrone in us, since every person is motivated by the desire for either power or delight or intellectual understanding. Since *The Earth Gods* was at least drafted before *The Procession*, we could say that *The Procession* is a simplification of *The Earth Gods* from three voices down to two.

Gibran did not live long enough to see whether and how favourably *The Earth Gods* was reviewed. This was perhaps just as well. No doubt he revised the book before publication, as he always did with all his old work, but critics are generally astute enough to recognize tired work. The book received hardly any attention. William Rose Benet in the *Saturday Review of Literature* found that the poem lacked both rhythm and rhetorical force, but acknowledged a few 'incidental beauties',[90] while the anonymous reviewer in the New York *Herald Tribune* more or less dismissed the text as an imitation of Blake's prophetic books, and the paintings and drawings also as pale reflections of Blake. The wheel has turned full circle, because this reviewer begins by quoting Knopf's standard publicity angle, the old fake Rodin quote about Gibran being the Blake of the twentieth century. The lie which had helped to launch his career in the English-speaking literary world was now being cast back in his teeth. When this had happened before in a review, it had been with some passion;[91] now the response is weary, in response to a dying man's last gasp. *The Earth Gods* and *The Wanderer* are tired work. If he had but known it, Gibran's bid for immortality had already succeeded; if he had known how wildly successful *The Prophet* was to become, he might not have risked tarnishing his literary reputation with these other works.

12

Death and After

On a flying visit to New York in May 1928, Mary Haskell found the opportunity to break away from her husband and visit Kahlil. She must have been shocked by his appearance. He was only 45 years old, and in her memory he was still the slim young man she had loved. But contemporary photographs from the end of the 1920s show him looking pasty and bloated, grey-haired and weary. She had no idea that he had been an alcoholic for some years. By November 1930, however, his bloated body was rapidly wasting, in the manner which is typical of advanced alcoholism. There is a family tradition that he knew he was terminally ill, and awaited death with fortitude, even refusing a potentially life-saving operation.[1] But there is no other evidence that he appreciated how ill he was; indeed, in a 1930 letter to May Ziadeh he said that if only he could overcome his writer's block, he could get well again: 'I am a small volcano whose opening has been closed. If I were able today to write something great and beautiful, I would be completely cured.' And in another letter from much the same time, to his friend Felix Farris, he talks about returning to Lebanon as soon as he is better.[2] Of course, he may be dissembling, but it is just as likely that he did not know how ill he was. It is common for alcoholics to deny both their primary illness and any of its secondary effects.

By March 1931, he was spending most of his time in bed, too weak to get up, and tended by Anna Johansen, the female half of the building's caretaking team, who had cleaned Gibran's room and brought his breakfast in the mornings since 1924. On Thursday 9 April, four days after Easter, Barbara Young made her daily phone call to his studio, and something about the sound of his voice worried her. She went round and found that Mrs Johansen had already alerted an old neighbour of Gibran, Mrs Leonobel Jacobs, who had sent for a doctor. After examining Gibran, the doctor, who did not consider him an emergency case, booked him in to St Vincent's Hospital, on the corner of 7th Avenue and 12th Street, for the next day. On Friday morning he was considerably worse, but he managed to whisper to Barbara Young, 'Don't be troubled. All is well.'[3] But Barbara was neither consoled nor convinced, and she sent a telegram to Marianna in Boston, telling her to come at once. Later in the day she also telephoned the office of *The Syrian World*.

Gibran lapsed into a coma in the early afternoon. By the time Mikhail Naimy arrived at the hospital, there were four women at vigil outside the dying man's room on the third floor – Barbara Young, Adele Watson (a constant friend since Gibran's arrival in New York), Marie Meloney, and Leonobel Jacobs. Salloum Mokarzel and a Maronite priest, Francis Wakim, had also visited, but left, seeing that there was nothing they could do. Wakim apparently had tried shouting Gibran's name, to penetrate his coma, but it was no good. Naimy joined the four distraught women, and together they waited for what the doctors told them was inevitable. Before Gibran had lapsed into unconsciousness, a nun had asked him if he was a Catholic and would like to receive the last rites, and he told her no.

Naimy spent some time in the room listening to his old friend's rattling breathing and reflecting on their times together and Gibran's greatness. Marianna hurried by train from Boston and arrived at the hospital at eight in the evening, in great distress bordering on hysteria, calling on friends and doctors alike to save her brother's life. But both prayers and medicine were vain. Kahlil Gibran never recovered consciousness and he died, aged 48, at 10.55 at night, on Friday, 10 April 1931.

Following an autopsy, the official hospital report stated that the cause of death was 'Cirrhosis of the liver with incipient tuberculosis in one of the lungs'. A great deal has been made of this incipient tuberculosis – which has even grown to incipient cancer in some accounts – but nothing incipient kills people. Gibran died of the effects of cirrhosis of the liver, and that, as everyone knows, is most commonly brought on by heavy drinking. Cirrhosis of the liver is not a killer in itself, but it leads either to internal bleeding or to a weakening of the body due to the inability of the liver to cope with toxins, and eventually to a coma from which the patient never recovers. In Gibran's case the cirrhosis clearly had the second of these two possible effects. He was another victim of the Prohibition era and, on some analyses of alcoholism, of the failure to fulfil his spiritual quest.[4]

Alcoholism is, of course, self-destructive; in a sense, Gibran had always courted death. The loss of his sister, half-brother and mother at an early age had presumably touched him deeply, and on top of this there was his Romantic conditioning from Fred Holland Day. For the Romantics, death was no great evil, but a release from the sorrows of this world, and an awakening into a greater life. Just as Sleep and Death were siblings in the ancient world, so some Romantics went so far as to portray Beauty and Death as 'two sisters equally terrible, equally fertile, with the same aura of mystery and the same secret'.[5] In the same mode Gibran once commented to Mary how death highlights the face,[6] and he wrote a poem called 'The Beauty of Death'. There was no doubt that he had experienced pain in his life, especially through those early deaths in the family, but he still had to choose to wear this sorrow all his life and develop it into a Romantic philosophy, in which death becomes an 'inexplicable blessing'. In an early letter to Mary from Paris he told her that he was in love with death.[7]

In his Arabic poetry, Gibran spoke of death as the release of the poet back to his 'celestial homeland',[8] and wrote a poem entitled 'A Poet's Death Is His Life'. Although in *The Prophet* he insists that there is really no such thing as death – that death and life are part of the same continuum – in actual fact he seems to acknowledge that death is a great change, and at times to desire the utter change that only death can bring. There is an obvious tension here with his public philosophy, which stressed the omnipresence of life and the need to immerse oneself in it. Perhaps he felt that for poets and prophets, 'ethereal' people like himself, the normal rules were broken:

> And death on earth, to son of earth
> Is final, but to him who is
> Ethereal, it is but the start
> Of triumph certain to be his.[9]

Or, as the poem 'Two Wishes' suggests, perhaps death releases into eternity only those who have spent their lives seeking eternity.

One of the benefits of death for himself, in his own view, was that it would reveal the meaning and structure of life.[10] In a 1928 letter to May Ziadeh,[11] Gibran spoke of his longing for death – a longing which was checked only by recalling that he still had work to do on this earth. Nevertheless, he was consistently opposed to suicide, while respecting a person's decision to take his own life if that was genuinely the best solution to his problems.[12] However, it is hardly going too far to see his alcoholism as a kind of unconscious and prolonged suicide – a translation of the fey Romantic longing for death into harsh reality.

No one except Marianna knew of Mary Haskell's existence, or at least of how important she had been to Kahlil. The next day, Marianna had the presence of mind to send her a telegram with the news of his death, and of the imminent transport of the body to Boston. Mary caught the next available train for Boston.

Gibran would have been flattered at all the fuss that was being made of him after his death. Over the weekend his body lay in state in the Universal Funeral Parlor on Lexington Avenue, where, according to *The Syrian World*, 'hundreds filed by in reverence and grief in a continual stream'.[13] On Monday Marianna took the coffin to Boston for burial, accompanied by close friends of Gibran from the Syrian community, and by Barbara Young. The story was also receiving attention in some serious newspapers. On the Saturday, 11 April, the *New York Times* had given him a reasonable obituary, littered with the usual inaccuracies, and over the next few months they would follow some of the post-mortem circus with articles on 25 July and 20 September. Later in the week the New York *Sun* gave him the headline 'A Seer Departed', while for the Ohio *Penitentiary News*, his death was a front-page story on the 18th.

Further tributes followed in the succeeding weeks. On 29 April an old Boston acquaintance of Gibran, Charles Fleischer, organized a remembrance at the Roerich Museum in New York, at which he, Claude Bragdon, Salloum Mokarzel and Syud Hossain delivered brief eulogistic speeches, while Mikhail Naimy and Barbara Young read farewell poems, and selections from Gibran's books were read. One of Gibran's poems had been set to music, and was sung, and 'some touching Oriental music' was played on the oud. Over 200 people, 'representative of the city's best intellectual element', attended the remembrance.[14] Four weeks later, on 24 May, the Syrian communities of New York and Boston held their own memorial meetings in Brooklyn and the South End of Boston, where 1,000 people congregated in the Municipal Building.

Meanwhile, on arriving in Boston Marianna was upset again because word had got around that Gibran had refused the last rites. When Father Wakim had arrived at the hospital, he must have wanted to administer the last rites (as a priest can to an unconscious person), but one of the nuns had presumably told Wakim of Gibran's rejection of these rites, and under these circumstances he was not able to carry out the sacrament. Father Wakim apparently then warned the church authorities in Boston. So Marianna was uncertain whether her brother would be allowed a proper Catholic funeral. Father Stephen al-Douaihy of the church of Our Lady of the Cedars at 78 Tyler Street, next to one of the tenement houses where Marianna had lived, assured her that he would. Indeed, there was nothing stopping him burying Gibran according to Catholic ceremony; as long as a person is a baptized Catholic, he can be buried according to Roman rites. Besides, Father al-Douaihy and Gibran were personal friends, and had enjoyed many a discussion during Gibran's visits to Boston.[15] After posing at the station for a formal photograph, with Gibran's coffin draped in both the Lebanese and American flags, Marianna and the rest of the followers escorted the body to the Syrian Ladies Club at 44 West Newton Street, where it was again laid out for public display, and again 'interminable lines of weeping beings from every walk of life . . . passed through the long room'.[16]

When Mary Haskell arrived later that day, Monday, 13 April, she went round to Marianna's and Marianna took her to the Club to see the body. Then the two of them joined a number of other old friends from Boston and New York for a 'last supper' for Gibran.[17] For the first time, Mary met all those friends Gibran had kept her from – Mikhail Naimy, Najib Diab, Nasib 'Arida and others – along with his Boston relatives and some of the coterie of adoring New York ladies, including Barbara Young and Gertrude Stern.[18] One wonders whether Mary at last realized why Gibran had so consistently kept her apart from his Arab friends. On the one hand, they were all gifted people, and Gibran did not want rivals for her patronage; on the other hand, they could easily have exposed to her his lies about his childhood, for instance. They knew perfectly well that Gibran was not the scion of a wealthy and privileged family. Lies always lead to complications: having told so many lies to his Western friends, Gibran was forced to keep them totally apart from his Arabic friends. In his life it was certainly true that East was East and West was West, and that never the twain should meet.

The next day hundreds of people from the Syrian ghetto followed the coffin on its journey from the Ladies Club to the church in Tyler Street, where Gibran was buried in a simple but emotional Mass, during which a number of people spoke in honour of their friend.[19] The burial of a person is rarely the end. In Gibran's case, the repercussions of his death would reverberate for many decades. Mary and Marianna returned to New York later in the week to undertake the process of sorting out Gibran's affairs. The nightmare that followed had two main strands. One was Barbara Young, and the other was Gibran's will.

The problem with Barbara Young was that she refused to let go. Circumstances came to her aid, because although the will clearly left Mary Haskell in charge of his paintings and so on, it was too hard for Mary to manage the estate from Savannah, so, while at first patiently enduring Barbara's weaknesses, she relied on her to be her proxy in New York. Barbara took the opportunity to lay claim to quite a number of his paintings and personal belongings, which she said he had given her or promised her while he was alive. Her grasping attitude was doubtless aggravated by plain jealousy, because when she came to tidy up the studio, she uncovered all Mary's letters to him. Barbara had not known of Mary's existence before the funeral, and certainly had no idea how close she had been to her beloved prophet.

In the first place, she wanted to destroy all the letters and journals relating to Mary's relationship with Gibran. Fortunately, on her first visit to the studio Mary had gone equipped with two large suitcases, and had locked away all that was personal to her – the journals and letters (not only hers to him, but his to her too, which she must have left in Kahlil's keeping when she went down south to live with Florance Minis). The Gibrans are certainly right to see this move from Barbara as part of her attempted apotheosis of Gibran; she was reluctant for there to be any extant record which revealed his all-too-human side. She established herself in the studio and set it up as a kind of shrine, lit with thirty-five candles. This attempted apotheosis climaxed in her biography, a short draft of which was published later in 1931. This, in the form of the eventual full biography, which was published in 1945, was all the biographical information that was available on Gibran in English for almost thirty years, and has left indelible marks of inaccuracy and adulation on the record.

Second, she directly interfered in the editing process of *The Wanderer*. At the time of Gibran's death Mary was editing his draft of the book. In fact, her last letter to him was a brief note, dated 6 April 1931: 'Ever so happy with *The Wanderer* – and will return it as soon as I possibly can.' Everything looked straightforward; this was their familiar editing routine. It must have been a shock for her to receive Marianna's telegram only a week later. Mary continued to edit the book, and eventually sent it off for Barbara to check before giving it to Knopf. But Barbara undid all the work that Mary had done, and the book was published with hardly any of her input. Barbara explained to Mary that she had in many cases restored 'the words of the blessed one'.[20]

As a third example of her influence, consider her association with Andrew Ghareeb, the young man who translated *Prose Poems*, published by Knopf in 1934, and for a long time the only available translation for the English-speaking world of some of Gibran's Arabic work. Barbara encouraged Ghareeb and wrote the foreword to the book. However, Gibran did not like Ghareeb's translations. There is a letter from Marie Meloney to Gibran, when she was the editor of the *Herald Tribune*'s Sunday Magazine, saying that Ghareeb had sent her some of his translations for publication, and asking him whether these were authorized translations. Gibran's reply was unequivocal:

'I do not like them!'[21] Ironically, then – and perhaps due to her ignorance of Arabic – Barbara caused to be perpetuated a version of Gibran's work for which he would rather not have been remembered.

Gibran's will proved so problematic that it has been cited in a textbook on copyright law in the States.[22] The most recent will that was found, superseding two dating from 1911 and 1913 which were in Mary's possession,[23] left any money and securities held by Edgar Speyer (the poetess Leonora's husband) to Marianna, who also received the forty shares of the 51 West 10th Street Studio Association, which represented Gibran's stake in the building. These shares had been left in a safe deposit box in the Bank of Manhattan Trust Company, located at 31 Union Square. Another New York bank held two accounts, the money from which Gibran instructed Marianna to take to Bsharri to 'spend upon charities'. Everything found in his studio after his death ('pictures, books, objects of art, etcetra' [*sic*]) was to go to Mary Haskell Mines [*sic*], with the instruction that she should send to Bsharri anything she didn't want to keep. Interestingly, there is no mention of money left in Boston; it looks as though in 1930 Gibran had organized his affairs, withdrawing money from his friends in Boston, and entrusting it all to Edgar Speyer.

So far, so good. The problems arose with the details of his royalties. The will stated: 'The royalties of my copyrights, which copyrights I understand can be extended upon request by my heirs for an additional period of twenty-eight years after my death, are to go to my home town.' Squabbles broke out immediately after Gibran's death. Some people refused to believe that Gibran had left the money from his accounts to Bsharri, let alone the royalties (which they were perhaps inclined to overlook, since at the time no great amounts were involved).[24] But no other will was ever found, and this one had been properly witnessed and lodged with Speyer in March 1930, while a spare copy was given by Gibran to Marianna.

Interestingly, it seems to have been Marianna – quiet, retiring Marianna – who stirred up the worst trouble. There is a letter to her dated 8 May 1931 from William Saxe, Gibran's lawyer, in which he raised the possibility of her contesting the will. He estimated Gibran's estate to be worth $40,000, a not inconsiderable sum, especially after the Wall Street Crash. Was Saxe raising this possibility of his own accord, or had Marianna asked him about it? At any rate Marianna certainly chose in the end to contest the will, although she waited until the renewal of copyright was due, twenty-eight years after the original publication of the books – presumably, then, first in 1946, when copyright in *The Madman* would have come up for renewal. Until then she was content for the ever-increasing money from Gibran's royalties to go to the 'National Committee of Gibran' in Bsharri, which had been formed to cope with the influx of money following their famous son's death.

The problem was that American copyright law anticipated one of two situations: either a will would have been drawn up, naming an executor, or no will would have been drawn up, in which case the next of kin would automatically be entitled to the royalties. But here was a case where a will had been drawn up, but without naming an executor. Under US law, if the author was dead at the time of renewal of copyright, the renewal went to 'the widow . . . or children of the author, if the author be not living, or if such author, widow . . . or children be not living, then the author's executors, or in the absence of a will, his next of kin, shall be entitled to a renewal and extension of the copyright'. In other words, the law was established to look after the interests of a dead author's widow and children. This did not apply in Gibran's case, so it was a contest between his literary executors or his next of kin. Although Gibran did not name any executor, 'both the trial and the appellate court before which the case came held for the Lebanese townfolk on the ground that the copyright law gives the renewal copyrights to the next of kin only in the absence of a will'.[25] Marianna lost the case.

This was not the end of the matter, however. Faced with Marianna's suit, the people of Bsharri had hired a lawyer, George Shiya, to handle their case in the American courts. The fee Shiya negotiated with them was an astonishing 25 per cent of all future royalties on the books. After they had won the case, the naïve townfolk of Bsharri hired another lawyer to take Shiya to court over the contract. They fought Shiya all the way up to the Supreme Court, but of course the contract was all legal and above board, and so they lost the case. And that is how George Shiya, and now, after his death, his seven heirs, come to be paid 25 per cent of the royalties in the States on *The Prophet*, *The Madman*, and all the other books which Gibran had written at the time of his death and which were therefore included in the terms of his will.

In a moment of whimsy, Gibran had willed his royalties to Bsharri. No doubt his conscious motives were good and honourable, but I cannot help remembering all his lies about the privileged background he claimed to his American friends. Perhaps, unconsciously, he was redeeming these lies retrospectively. Now there would be Gibran money in Bsharri. At first, Bsharri was suitably grateful, but as the years rolled by and profits from *The Prophet* increased, greed took the place of gratitude. By the early 1950s, the sums involved were quite substantial. Corruption set in, and only about 20 per cent of the money coming in was actually used for the charitable and investment purposes the Bsharri committee had intended; the rest was disappearing, presumably into people's pockets. Moreover, membership of the Bsharri committee administering the funds pouring in from Knopf suddenly became a route to political power in the town as a whole, in the sense that 'Any goatherd who sought assistance from the estate became politically indebted to the member who sponsored him . . . Soon families split apart in the clamor to win a committee position. Age-old feuds gained new fury, and at least two deaths resulted. Ultimately the two largest families . . . set up rival committees.'[26]

Under these circumstances, Knopf had no choice but to withhold the royalties. The situation carried on until 1967, by which time the royalties were worth an estimated $300,000 a year. At this point the Lebanese government stepped in, dissolved the two rival committees, and took control itself for a few years, until in 1971 a new local committee was established, with two members from each of the two rival clans, and one additional member from the non-aligned residents of the town. Peace returned to the town, Knopf released the royalties, and the money began to be used for its proper purposes – to fund scholarships, to build a music school, to tend to Gibran's tomb, things like that. However, rumours of some corruption persist, and it remains the case that it is hard to see where the substantial sums involved end up. Since the funding of scholarships and so on has ended, the only acknowledged expense is the upkeep of the Gibran Museum in Bsharri. Even allowing for the considerable expenses entailed by this (especially in the thorough refurbishment and modernization undertaken in the early 1990s), it seems likely that money is quietly accumulating somewhere. It is to be hoped that it will in due course be released for some appropriate purpose.

So for many years the legacy of Gibran's sentimental will was tension and chaos. To return to 1931, at first, as I have said, the people of Bsharri were sensible of the honour Gibran had done them, and were happy to fall in with suggestions from America – probably from Mary via William Saxe – that a shrine or museum be established in Bsharri, containing not only Gibran's body, but also most of the items from his studio. Mary and Kahlil had spoken as far back as 1913 about his being buried in Lebanon,[27] and so she now pushed for the fulfilment of this dream. She had personally asked Marianna soon after Gibran's death to take his body to Bsharri, but Marianna was slow off the mark, and it took a telegram from Bsharri at the end of April to provoke some action.

By June the arrangements were made. Marianna was to go to Lebanon, accompanied by her cousins, with her brother's body and $1,000 of the charity money. And so on 23 July Gibran's body was exhumed and the casket was escorted by a long line of cars to Providence, Rhode Island, where it was loaded, in a fine drizzle, on to the liner *Sinaia*. As the *New York Times* reported: 'Before the coffin was placed on board the ship services were held at the pier in the presence of more than 200 Lebanese from New York, Boston, Providence and Fall River. Gibran was eulogized in English and Arabic by a number of speakers and a wreath from the 700 Lebanese living in Providence was placed at the base of the casket.'[28]

Four weeks later, the ship docked in Beirut, and the round of ceremonies began all over again, this time on an even more impressive and exotic scale.[29] The casket was met at the dock by an official delegation headed by the Minister of the Interior and the Minister of Education, who solemnly pinned a fine arts decoration, as decreed by the government, on the casket. The coffin was draped in the Lebanese flag and escorted to the Maronite Cathedral of St George, where

Archbishop Ignatius Mobarak received the body. In the evening, Charles Dabbas, the President of the Republic, officiated at the government reception in Gibran's honour. After a day and night in the cathedral, watched over by an honour guard of 300 young men from the Bsharri region, the bier was taken in procession along the coast and up to Bsharri, a journey of some eighty miles. At every town and village people lined the road to spectate and honour their dead compatriot. Eventually the road was clogged with over 200 cars and 100 horsemen. Salloum Mokarzel, who had received a report from Lebanon, told the *Times*:

> At various stages along the road young men, in colorful native costumes, engaged in spirited sword-play before the slowly-moving hearse. Others followed singing martial songs or improvising eulogies for the dead. At a town near Gebail, the ancient Byblus and the seat of worship of the Syrian goddess Astarte, a company of maidens came out to meet the body. They wore loose flowing robes and their long hair fell in heavy waves over their shoulders. They also sang the praise of Gibran, but they did so in the sense of one who is living, welcoming him as 'the beautiful bridegroom of our dreams', and scattered roses along the road before him and perfume upon his casket.

The last word on all this pomp and display – 'more like a triumphal entry than a funeral'[30] – belongs to Rose O'Neill. Writing at Christmas to her friends and former members of her 'court', Birger and Matta Lie in Norway, she enclosed a clipping of the report from the *Times* and said, 'Isn't this charming about the young men in native dress engaging in sword-play before the hearse? How Kahlil would have loved that.' Gibran had sought all his life for fame and recognition; he was certainly getting more than his fair share after his death. But he would also have been amused by all the religious ceremonies, since he had never been a churchgoer, and indeed had spent much of his life inveighing against priests and all they stood for.

His body had so far lain in state in New York, travelled by train to Boston, and lain in state again there, before being buried at the church of Our Lady of the Cedars; it had been exhumed, transported across the seas to Lebanon, rested again in the cathedral there, and escorted along the dusty road up to the mountains, back to Bsharri. Even then he had not reached the end of his journey. His body was due to stay in the church of St John in Bsharri, but only until his tomb was completed. The chosen site was the ancient monastery of Mar Sarkis, which Gibran had set his heart on acquiring a few years before his death. By the beginning of 1932, Marianna had succeeded in buying the abandoned monastery, and work began on turning it into a shrine and museum to Gibran. That is now where his body lies. Few corpses can have been so disturbed in the first year after death. All this posthumous movement is a perfect symbol for his own restlessness, never knowing who he was, crucified on the dichotomies of East and West, man and myth, and striving always to find himself – or perhaps to forget – by work and more work.

His final resting-place, to Western eyes, used to be over-ornate and gaudy. One disillusioned American visitor in the 1970s said, 'A lot of romantics are going to hate this, but they might as well know the truth: Kahlil Gibran is buried in a gift shop.'[31] However, recent work has restored a measure of decorum to the place. The sixteenth-century monastery is cool inside, and the visitor moves from cell to cell, each of which is now filled with the best collection in the world of Gibran's paintings. In addition, there are bookshelves preserving his library, and display cases with notebooks, manuscripts, and *objets* from his New York studio.

The casket lies downstairs, in a cave hewn out of the rock. The narrow opening is obscured by a naturalistic abstract sculpture, which looks as though it has been made out of the roots of a cedar (one of the few remaining groves of the famous Cedars of Lebanon is situated near by); nevertheless, it appears that the casket is empty, since one can see through a crack in it, right through to the wall behind. At some point, then, someone has taken it upon themselves to remove Gibran's body, while pretending to visitors that he is still buried there. Plainly artificial small stalagmites and stalactites adorn the floor and ceiling around the coffin, cheapening the effect. Above the opening is a niche with a small statue of a madonna and child, presumably taken from the New York studio. An Arabic inscription reads: 'The house of Gibran, 1931'. To the right another Arabic inscription on a wooden plaque reads: 'A word I want to be written on my tomb: I am alive like you and I am standing now at your side, so close your eyes and look around, and you will see me in front of you.' Elsewhere in the cavernous room are a few artefacts from the studio – his bed, and a couple of easels, for instance – and a wonderful old Armenian tapestry, an altarpiece that used to hang on one of the walls of the Hermitage.

Barbara Young certainly visited Bsharri and Gibran's tomb. There is no record that Mary Haskell ever did, but I like to think of her, after Florance's death in 1936, making the long pilgrimage east and pausing for an hour or two in the cool of the old monastery, reflecting on the past – on all that was and might have been.

So Gibran's physical life was at an end, but, as everyone knows, he has joined the ranks of those few writers whose work not only survives their death, but goes on for generation after generation, always attracting fresh readers. There are signs now, at the end of the 1990s, of a renewed interest in Gibran and his work. This shows not just in an upturn in book sales, but in the more rounded approach that is being taken to Gibran. Whereas previously, speaking generally, the West knew him only as the author of *The Prophet*, and whereas his Arabic works had been poorly translated, there are good new translations of his early works which will introduce that whole neglected side of Gibran to new generations of readers. At the same time, the pace of exhibitions of his paintings and drawings seems to be accelerating. Paintings of his were included in an American bicentennial exhibition at the National Portrait Gallery, Washington, called 'Abroad in America: Visitors to the New Nation', and in a major exhibition of American Symbolists which was held in 1979 at New York University's Grey Art Gallery and the Spencer Museum of Art at the University of Kansas. Ten years later several of his works were included in a show called 'Lebanon: The Artists' View', which was put on in both London and Paris, and in the same year there was a solo retrospective, from 25 May to 24 June 1989 in New York's Baghoomian Gallery, consisting of fifty-two of his paintings and drawings on loan from the Telfair Museum in Savannah; this exhibition was entitled simply 'Kahlil Gibran: Paintings and Drawings 1905–1930'. Although hardly any of Gibran's works are on permanent display at the Telfair Museum, they brought them out of the basement in 1994 for an exhibition entitled 'To Discover Beauty: The Art of Kahlil Gibran'. Finally, there was another major exhibition, again of works on loan from Savannah, in 1995 at the Detroit Institute of Arts, called 'Speak to Us of Beauty: The Paintings and Drawings of Kahlil Gibran'. As I write, there is talk of a grand affair in Paris late in 1998, with paintings from both Bsharri and Savannah represented.

From another perspective, there are also a few signs that Gibran is beginning to attract scholarly attention. In the early 1970s Professor Suheil Bushrui organized two international conferences on Gibran in Beirut (the first, in 1970, with the then aged Mikhail Naimy as the guest of honour), and there is a notice posted on the Web as I write, in 1997, of another such conference, again organized by Bushrui, who is now at the University of Maryland. The two most recent translators of Gibran's Arabic works are both university scholars, and discussions of Gibran have featured in a number of recent textbooks on the history of Arabic literature.

This is all to the good. In Chapter 10 I wrote of the irony that Gibran, who tried in his lifetime to unite the roles of poet and prophet, had been pulled apart by historical circumstances until he was known as a poet in the East and a prophet in the West. But perhaps these indications of a more rounded approach to Gibran in the West will go some way towards healing the breach, until he is once again recognized as both a poet and a prophet.[32]

Who buys Gibran's books? As I travelled around the American libraries during my research for this book, curious librarians would ask me what I was working on. On hearing that I was writing a life of Gibran, and that his books continued to sell, a typical response was: 'Yes, well, there are a lot of teenagers about.' It is a common perception, perhaps correct, that the main market for Gibran's books are young people, followed by those who are buying for a special occasion such as a sentimental birthday gift, or for a text to be read out at a wedding or funeral.

Knopf himself had no answer to the question. His response was: 'It must be a cult, but I have never met any of its members. I haven't met five people who have read Gibran.'[33] This is certainly dissimulation, because even in the 1920s he was publishing authors such as Bynner and Bragdon who were among Gibran's friends and readers. Still, the interesting point is that the books remain cult classics, even if they are too popular to be described as underground. They sell entirely by word of mouth. The only time Knopf tried advertising *The Prophet*, in the late 1920s, he found that sales fell a little. He never tried it again.[34]

Let's assume, for the sake of argument, that the main market for the books – which means, of course, largely for *The Prophet* – is a teenage and student market. What does that tell us about the book's appeal? Has it endured because it consists of palatable platitudes, or is there something about it that calls to the depths of the reader? It is important first to make the point that if the book's usual purchasers are young, that does not automatically tell us that this is a book to be lightly dismissed, as is often assumed. The editors of *The Seven Arts* and *The Dial* were not fools. They did not publish Gibran because they had a spare half page they needed to fill up. They published him because they considered him good – and not even 'good of his kind', because there are no others quite like him. The same people who were publishing early T. S. Eliot, e. e. cummings, Robert Frost and so on, were also publishing Gibran. Two conclusions immediately follow from this. First, if nowadays Gibran provokes highbrow contempt, that contempt must be qualified by the recognition that it is the product of fashion, and that in his own day Gibran was acceptable in the highest ranks of literature. Second, it suggests that Gibran needs looking at again, with fresh, uncynical eyes – eyes that are still open to the distant views of a spiritual quest, and have not yet become, or have resisted becoming dimmed by the burden of mortgages and the daily grind. The essence of Gibran's later evolutionary thought was, in Bragdon's words, that there is 'nothing higher than the human'.[35] We have Greater Selves and, by the force of God's evolutionary desire, the ability to grow into those Greater Selves. The Nietzschean or Romantic idea that we are bigger than we normally suppose may appeal to those, like teenagers, who are full of themselves, but perhaps more people need to acquire a taste of that fullness in order to glimpse their potential and not accept the mediocrity of their lives.

In *The House of Mirth*, Edith Wharton has Selden say, 'Why do we call all our generous ideas illusions, and the mean ones truths?'[36]

Gibran's reputation has undoubtedly suffered from this kind of hard-hearted cynicism, which runs the risk of being too glib, too quickly dismissive. His appeal is precisely that he offers simplicity in a world of complexity. If this appeals to fresh eyes and ears, who is to say that they are wrong? Higher orders of generality are always simpler than lower orders of specificity. What is wrong, in a complex world, in drawing attention to the simpler levels? His ideas may end up as comforting placebos, but any ideas can suffer that fate. For instance, there are plenty of Christians around who believe that they don't have to work on themselves at all because Christ died on the cross for them; their idleness does not nullify Christ's message. Besides, an idea is a comforting placebo only if it is adopted so wholeheartedly that any discomfort is ignored or overlooked in a thorough denial of the shadow side of life; but there is no evidence that Gibran is read like that, rather than just as someone who offers periodic refreshment in a grim world and confirms the validity of one's youthful, anti-materialistic, spiritual yearnings.

Gibran is charged, above all, with being sentimental and vague. Let's spend a little time on each of these charges, trying to separate them out, although they are interconnected. In both cases, I find good and bad points in Gibran's work. In other words, in both cases he should not be dismissed out of hand. The charge of sentimentalism – obviously in the sense of mawkishness – is brought forward, in the first place, by those who have read only *The Prophet* and have conveniently ignored the rest of his work, some of which has far harder edges. However, there is no doubt that Gibran can be sentimental. In my opinion, this is a result of his standing in the Romantic tradition, without having either the technical abilities or the profundity of experience of the great Romantics. Reading Keats or Wordsworth or Shelley, you feel they know what they are talking about, that they are not just expressing literary commonplaces, and this lifts much of their work out of the slough of sentimentalism and into the refined air of deep emotion. As I have said more than once, Gibran seems to have *assumed* his Romanticism, although it came on top of a naturally sensitive character and some painful experiences, and he lacks the greatness of talent that might have redeemed this pose and transformed it into great literature.

Underlying all sentimentalism, however, is simply the fact that a writer expresses himself or herself emotionally, speaks from the heart to others' hearts. Hard cynicism runs the risk of valuing the head to the exclusion of the heart. 'When Life does not find a singer to sing her heart,' Gibran said in *Sand and Foam*, 'she produces a philosopher to speak her mind.'[37] And it is obvious which of the two he both preferred and identified with: he was interested only in appealing to the heart, and so to judge him by the head may be to miss the point altogether. 'Thinking is always the stumbling stone to poetry.'[38] This is where the fresh eyes come in. If Gibran wrote simply and clearly, believing that experiences were in themselves simple, then perhaps we need to respond by peeling back a few layers of rationality and opening ourselves up to some emotional food. Teenagers, and those in emotionally vulnerable situations (such as at weddings and funerals), tend to have that ability to respond from the heart more than others.

As for vagueness, Gibran was accused of this even in his own lifetime, by his friends.[39] But vagueness can be a strength as well as a weakness. Words that some people might be inclined to call vague may simply be an attempt to capture an order of abstraction or generality that defies ordinary language. And so Gibran himself came to embrace and justify his vagueness, when in *The Prophet* he has Almustafa say, 'If these be vague words, then seek not to clear them. Vague and nebulous is the beginning of all things, but not their end. And I fain would have you remember me as a beginning.'[40] Vagueness is also a result of a writer not explaining himself, but that too may not be desirable in every type of writing. In academic philosophy, of course we have a right to expect the writer to dot every 'i' and footnote every 't', but the same does not go for many types of religious or spiritual writing. As soon as a writer starts to explain himself – as soon as the words 'but' and 'because' and 'if . . . then' appear – he is appealing to the associative and rational mind of the reader, asking it to wake up and agree with what is being said. But it is in the nature of the rational mind that, once awoken, it will also find things to disagree with and ways to argue its case. And so there is a type of spiritual and poetic writing which simply speaks with authority, and does not enter into argument. All the argument, as it were, has taken place in silence, before pen is put to paper. Every sacred scripture of every religion in the world is of this type, and so is most poetry, and sacred scripture and poetry were Gibran's models. 'Inspiration will always sing; inspiration will never explain.'[41] He believed, and his closest friends encouraged him to believe, that he was a prophet, with an inspired message for humankind.

So there can be considerable strength in vagueness, properly used, and provided it is shored up by genuine experience which has been assayed by hard argument. But now to qualify this approval, consider the following assertion from Arthur Symons: 'All art hates the vague; not the mysterious, but the vague; two opposites very commonly confused, as the secret with the obscure, the infinite with the indefinite.'[42] Symons is right, and from this point of view we can say that Gibran does occasionally fall into the trap of failing to distinguish the mysterious and the vague, the infinite and the indefinite. There is a difference between the elusiveness of the *Tao Te Ching*, for example, and that of some of Gibran's parables. Great works of scripture briefly draw aside the veil and remind us of what we always knew; Gibran too often veils what he is trying to reveal. Moreover, in so far as he appeals entirely to the feelings, one might want to challenge him, as any relativist, to explain what part an external, objective moral code might play, on top of being 'true to one's own feelings'. As Gibran's contemporary, the novelist James Huneker, says, 'Without dogma a religion is like a body without skeleton.'[43]

Gibran came at the tail end of a long Romantic and platonizing tradition in Western literature, whose ideas and doctrines he absorbed in his youth and retailed in his maturity, without having anything particularly new to add and without having enough technical flair to rise, more than a few times, to passages of great power. From this perspective his work may be judged unsatisfying and derivative, but at the same time it is important to acknowledge his gifts. He undeniably has the ability to remind his readers of something. Ultimately, very few books, by their very nature, can be more than such triggers. Gibran's great strength is that he can enable people to remember not to sweep the extraordinary under the carpet and ignore it, and can send them off on a possibly lifelong quest to expand the glimpses he offers into full and meaningful reality.

Gibran's appeal lies in presenting things pithily, clearly and simply enough to strike a chord in those who remain open to his message. That is why any attempt to summarize his thought – even the cursory attempts I have made in this book, as we came across his various works – feel slightly dishonest.[44] They are, to a degree, attempts to fit a square peg into a round hole, because the appeal of Gibran lies chiefly in his aphoristic style, where each saying strikes the reader atomistically, without forming part of a coherent body of thought. Nevertheless, if I had to encapsulate Gibran's message in a single sentence, I would draw on his own words. In 1925, in the letter to Witter Bynner (dated 14 April 1925) which Bynner then paraphrased in his article, Gibran told him that in the East his message – Gibranism – was taken to be 'freedom in all things'. In Gibran's earlier writings he preached political and social freedom; by the time of *The Prophet* he preaches metaphysical freedom. There is no harm in offering glimpses of freedom. Even if we were to agree with Gibran's critics that his writings are sentimental and trite, this would remain the case. And it needs to be noted that the only people who think there is harm in a message of freedom are those who would imprison us.

Talk of his message of freedom introduces another fascinating facet of Gibran's afterlife. Even a superficial analysis of the sales figures of his books shows that he sold extraordinarily well in the West in the 1960s and 1970s. The 1960s, in particular, were a time when talk of freedom was in the air, and when every hippie was said to have a copy of *The Prophet* in his or her rucksack. There are two lines of speculation I would like to pursue here. The first involves what we might call 'cultural resonance', and the second concerns the actual degree to which Gibran may have influenced the counterculture of the 1960s and subsequent decades.

The idea of cultural resonance goes something like this. In so far as Gibran was writing in the late 1910s and early 1920s, it is at least curious to note that he was surrounded by a youth culture which was devoted to hedonism and freedom from what were perceived as outdated and authoritarian mores. They flaunted their difference with outlandish forms of clothing and hairstyles, and had their own music, dances and subcultural jargon, to which the 'older generation' was not privy. Their search for meaning involved the use of drugs (alcohol, in particular, but also hashish) and a strong emphasis on self-expression and sexual promiscuity. All this inevitably reminds us of the hippie period – that is, strictly, about 1967 to 1969, though some historians allow a few years of latitude either side. Of course, there were a number of differences between the two periods. In particular, the young people in the 1920s were not opposed to rationality and materialistic technocracy in the way that particularly characterizes the late 1960s. It is hard to imagine Scott Fitzgerald and his crowd attempting the quintessential gesture of the hippies and the New Left – the exorcism and levitation of the White House in 1967. In fact, the young set in the 1920s were all in favour of technological progress. Nevertheless, the parallels are marked. If Gibran absorbed something of that longing for freedom and reflected it in his books, it is hardly surprising that his sales were so outstanding in the late 1960s.

However, his sales continued strong in the 1970s and very healthy in the 1980s. As far as these decades, and beyond, are concerned, Gibran's popularity should be seen less in terms of any resonance between his personal narcissism and the apparent narcissism of this era,[45] than by the fact that, growing out of the hippie years, the 1970s and the next decades saw the growth of the New Age movement. Gibran had Almustafa say, 'Remember me as a beginning . . .'. I think it is arguable that Gibran was one of the founding fathers of the New Age.

The easiest way to argue this is to pick out the chief features of the New Age and see how they correspond to 'Gibranism'.[46] As Heelas and others have demonstrated, the New Age is less of a disorganized mishmash than is usually supposed. While it is not exactly unified, it is a matrix connected by certain beliefs. Most New Age groups would agree with the majority, probably all, of the following: mundane life reflects and is imbued with spiritual life; human beings have higher, spiritual selves which can, and should, operate as their main centres; there is more to the world than meets the eye, or indeed all the other senses, however highly enhanced by scientific instruments; the purpose of all existence is to bring love and enlightenment into existence; all religions are expressions of the same inner reality (and hence rigid dogma and a priesthood may be unnecessary); everyone is free to choose his or her own spiritual path; all life is interconnected; we are jointly responsible for the state of ourselves and our environment; we are now at a time – the New Age – when fundamental change is taking place, and things are evolving towards a more spiritual future.

As will be obvious by this stage of the book, there is nothing here that could not have been lifted from the pages of one or another of Gibran's books, or from their implicit philosophy. The New Age shares both the evolutionary strengths and the humanistic weaknesses of Gibran's thought. In case this seems almost too obvious to have needed stating, I should explain that Gibran is constantly overlooked in this context. In her best-selling book *The Aquarian Conspiracy*, for instance, Marilyn Ferguson elicited the support of large numbers of predecessors to the spiritual and scientific paradigm shift she was exploring, from Meister Eckhart and the Transcendentalists through to H. G. Wells, Pierre Teilhard de Chardin and Alfred Korzybski. But there is never a mention of Kahlil Gibran. Hanegraaff's painstaking analysis of the historical roots of the New Age also overlooks Gibran. But to repeat: his books have so far sold about 10 million copies in English alone. They must have left some imprint on people's minds.

I suggest that Gibran has been one of the hidden influences on the New Age, via the 1960s and early 1970s, when his sales peaked. It is always difficult to say what exactly causes any wide-scale movement such as hippiedom or the New Age. Roszac narrows the influences on what he calls the 'Aquarian Frontier' down to six main headings – but each has up to twenty subheadings under it.[47] However, there is little doubt in my mind that Gibran's role was to parlay into readily accessible symbols the basic message of the Romantics and Transcendentalists who chiefly influenced him – Blake, Nietzsche, Rousseau, Maeterlinck, Carpenter, Emerson, Whitman – and transmit this in an easily digestible form to future generations. I cannot say that without him the New Age movement would not have arisen, but it is, I think, safe to say that he has had an enormous influence on it.

If I am right, Gibran becomes an important historical figure, because – contrary to what many observers would like to believe – the New Age movement is in some sense here to stay. Few of the people who were hippies in the late 1960s and early 1970s are still hippies. To some degree they have 'sold out' – to some degree, but not always entirely. These people are now in their forties and fifties; many of them are in positions of power and authority in their societies; they have not forgotten all the values they absorbed at the time. The New Age has already made fundamental changes: complementary medicine is no longer 'alternative' and healthcare practices will never be the same again; our attitude towards the environment has changed for good; quality of growth is now considered just as important in some quarters as quantity; sustainability is seen as promising more for the future than exploitation; the management of businesses is in the process of shifting away from impersonal and heavy-handed authoritarianism; there is a marked decline in traditional forms of worship and religious expression. In all likelihood, we should expect further changes along these lines in other walks of life.

If even some of this revolution is a legacy of Gibran, it reveals a new dimension to the man's creativity. He was creative not just in terms of the amount of work he did in his lifetime, but also in the sense that he sowed seeds for the future. Yet he was, in his lifetime, I have suggested, in many ways a difficult, even unlikeable man. As well as being charismatic, intelligent, talented, the sort of person others admired and looked to for leadership, he was also a consummate liar, abusive to Mary Haskell, arrogant, narcissistic, mock-modest, self-indulgent and weak, with an inability to distinguish fantasy from reality.

While I was writing this book, two images above all kept recurring to me. The first is of Gibran alone in the Hermitage, staring up at the stars through the telescope he bought in 1921.[48] He had a fascination with astronomy – a hunger Mary used to feed with books on the subject and, to cap it all, with a fragment of meteorite, which Gibran would clutch in bed at night.[49] This is the image of a sad and lonely man, who does not feel at all at home in this world. He has transformed his loneliness into a gospel of aloneness, calling it 'the fundamental reality' and 'the source of all richness'.[50] For all his affirmations of the sacredness of Life, one feels that the freedom he found in what he called 'planetary consciousness' was actually the freedom of detachment from the complexities of the real world. Close to the start of this book I asked what the core was around which Gibran's masks cohered. We are now in a position to see that, at bottom, he was a lonely, frightened individual, adrift in a foreign world, desperately seeking shelter in his work, in mother figures, in his masks, and finally in alcoholism.

The second image is more complex. As I have mentioned, in his childhood Gibran suffered a bad accident. Here is his voice through Mary Haskell's journal for 30 June 1915:

> When I was ten or eleven years old, I was in a monastery one day with another boy – a cousin, a little older. We were walking along a high place that fell off more than a thousand feet. The path had a hand rail, but it had weakened and path and rail and all fell with us, and we rolled probably one hundred and fifty yards in the landslide. My cousin fractured his leg, and I got several wounds and cuts in the head down to the skull, and injured my shoulder. The shoulder healed crooked – too high, and too far forward. So they pulled it apart again and strapped me to a cross . . . and I stayed strapped to that cross forty days.

The boy who would one day have messianic delusions, and who would independently remind his close friends, Mary Haskell and Witter Bynner, of Christ was strapped to a *cross* – and *for forty days*! It is a powerful coincidence, and even if one wants to dismiss it as a false or exaggerated memory, it is a striking image. In my mind the two arms of the cross came to symbolize either or both of the dichotomies 'East and West' and 'Man and Myth'. Gibran never knew who he was: he found a home in the West as an exotic Easterner, and became famous in the East for vilifying Eastern customs from a vantage point gained as a result of reading Western Romantics. He adopted a persona at an early age and identified with it so thoroughly that it becomes virtually impossible to find the man beneath the myth. Moreover, since the role he chose to play was that of poet–prophet, it proved hard to live up to. To my mind, then, Gibran was crucified on these dichotomies. We have seen occasional signs that he was, underneath it all, a deeply unhappy and unsatisfied man – his peculiar relationship with May Ziadeh, his alcoholism, his admission to Mikhail Naimy that he was failing to live up to his own projected image. Gibran was not a perfect man, and that is a failing in a guru. But though he may have suffered secretly, spreadeagled on the cross of these polarities, though he may finally have burnt himself out within the fire of the tension created by them, his failure to reconcile them was a source of strength as well as of suffering. Polarity creates energy, which Gibran, ever restless, poured into his work. If only we could all turn our problems and complexes into sources of creative energy! Gibran was creative enough, I have suggested, even to have influenced further generations, and not necessarily in harmful ways. He was not a bad man, and so the question of justifying ends by means does not arise. He was simply a troubled man, who could not live up to the ideal of being a prophet, and could not endure the reality of being a human being. He wrote his own epitaph in *Sand and Foam*:[51] 'Even the most winged spirit cannot escape physical necessity.'

Notes and References

Most of the abbreviations used in these notes are self-explanatory. When an author has only a single book mentioned in the bibliography, that book is referred to by the author's name alone. When an author has more than one book mentioned in the bibliography, that book is referred to by the author's name and, in parentheses, the date of the relevant book.

Only one book is referred to consistently by a cipher abbreviation: *KGLW* is *Kahlil Gibran: His Life and World*, by Jean and Kahlil Gibran.

The following abbreviations are relevant to the letters and journals that are the staples of a biography:

KG = Kahlil Gibran
MH = Mary Haskell
JP = Josephine Peabody
CT = Charlotte Teller
MZ = May Ziadeh

For the most part, the editions of books referred to are as in the bibliography. However, there are so many different editions of Gibran's actual works that I should specify which I have actually used in each case, since the pagination in these notes may not exactly correspond to that of the editions on any given reader's shelf. Here they are, in alphabetical order:

The Beloved (White Cloud Press, 1994)
The Blind, see *Lazarus and His Beloved*
Broken Wings, trs. Anthony Ferris (as in *A Second Treasury of Kahlil Gibran*, Mandarin, 1992)
The Broken Wings, trs. Juan Cole (White Cloud Press, 1998)
The Earth Gods (Knopf, 1979)
The Forerunner (as in *The Voice of Kahlil Gibran*, Penguin Arkana, 1995)
The Garden of the Prophet (Penguin Arkana, 1996)
Gibran: Love Letters (Oneworld Publications, 1995)
Jesus, the Son of Man (Oneworld Publications, 1993)

Lazarus and His Beloved and *The Blind* (Westminster Press, 1981)
The Madman (Knopf, 1966)
Nymphs of the Valley (Knopf, 1961)
The Procession (Arab-American Press, 1947)
The Prophet (Penguin Arkana, 1992)
Prose Poems (Knopf, 1945)
Sand and Foam (Knopf, 1993)
A Self-portrait (as in *A Second Treasury of Kahlil Gibran*, Mandarin, 1992)
Spirit Brides (White Cloud Press, 1993)
Spiritual Sayings (Carol Publishing, 1990)
The Storm (White Cloud Press, 1993)
A Tear and a Smile (Knopf, 1992)
Thoughts and Meditations (as in *A Second Treasury of Kahlil Gibran*, Mandarin, 1992)
A Treasury of Kahlil Gibran (single-volume Mandarin paperback edition, 1991)
The Vision (White Cloud Press, 1994)
The Voice of the Master (as in *A Second Treasury of Kahlil Gibran*, Mandarin, 1992)
The Wanderer (The Kahlil Gibran Pocket Library, Knopf, 1995)

1 From East to West

1 In May 1908 Gibran told his friend Mary Haskell that he made about 300 friends on the boat during the trip to America. This is sheer fantasy, even if as a young boy he could charm without being able to speak the others' languages.

2 James, p. 66.

3 Hanna (1973), p. 27, n. 3.

4 *KGLW*, p. 23.

5 Reference no. M237 38-39/643. Incidentally, the Rhamés and their compatriots on the ship are clearly marked as 'Syrians', which makes a nonsense of the denial (by Alixa Naff, for instance, at pp. 108, 252) that US immigration recognized such a category before 1899.

6 KG to JP, 6 Jan. 1906.

7 *KGLW*, p. 25.

8 The location is now used more generally: in 1979 the Lebanese army added an inscription, but not because they were an invading or passing army. Most of the older inscriptions are now worn to illegibility by the combination of the sea air and modern pollution: a major road has been tunnelled through the rock under the site of most of the inscriptions.

9 Nowadays there are about 1 million Maronites and 100,000 Druze, but there are also other Christian sects, and about the same number of Muslims as Christians in the country.
10 Awareness of religious roots remains high in Lebanon even today. One of the problems hindering unification in the country is that people assess their identity first in terms of their family or village of origin, second in terms of their religion, and only third in terms of the country itself.
11 Churchill, p. 42. Note that Colonel Churchill had lived in Syria for ten years, and was speaking as an eyewitness.
12 It should go without saying that the 1860 massacres, apparently forgotten, were suddenly remembered in the aftermath of the most recent outbreak of sectarian and religious violence in 1975.
13 Of course, there is an irony in missionaries feeling they had to come to Lebanon at all, since so many of the population were already Christians.
14 Salibi (1965), p. 140.
15 Antonius, p. 13.
16 *The Independent*, 30 April 1907, p. 1010.
17 Cole, p. 3.
18 As reflected, for example, in the article 'Syrians in the United States', *Literary Digest*, 3 May 1919, p. 43. If this article is typical, the motive for attributing to immigrants the desire to escape from political persecution in the old country is to boost the putative freedom of the new country. However, the scholarly book by Philip and Joseph Kayal also tries to reinstate this motive.
19 Among several items in the bibliography, see especially the excellent book by Alixa Naff, and Gregory Orfalea's *Before the Flames*.
20 Orfalea, *op. cit.* (1988), pp. 77–8.
21 Naff, p. 281.
22 *KGLW*, chapter 1, *passim*. The Kahlil Gibran who is the co-author of this book is the son of Gibran's first cousin. His co-author, Jean Gibran, is his wife.
23 Bragdon, p. 140. Similarly, Gibran seems to have given Fred Holland Day the idea that his father was a sheikh (JP Journal, 12 Dec. 1898).
24 MH Journal, 7 Dec. 1910, 21 Jan. 1911, 24 March 1911, 5 June 1911, 2 Dec. 1911, 2 Sept. 1914, 4 Sept. 1914, 11 April 1915, 24 Aug. 1915, 25 Aug. 1915, 19 Sept. 1915, 14 Nov. 1915, 26–28 Dec. 1917, 24 March 1918, 1 Sept. 1918, 30 Sept. 1922, 2 Jan. 1923. The muleteer story is from Naimy (1950), pp. 22–3. Perhaps there is a greater degree of honesty in an apparently casual remark Kahlil once made to Mary to the effect that childhood is rarely happy, partly because a child is envious of other children's things (MH Journal, 12 Aug. 1921). This is not the voice of one whose privileged childhood made him the object of envy, rather than subject to it.

25 MH Journal, 31 Aug. 1914; compare 19 Sept. 1915: 'There are many things in me that I don't want any human beings to know.' He hated curiosity about himself, sympathy and pity, and held that those who understand a person enslave something in that person (KG to MH, 8 July 1914, 8 March 1922).
26 MH Journal, 21 Jan. 1911, 6 April 1911, 2 Dec. 1911, 14 Nov. 1915.
27 Young, p. 7. Gibran always loved storms, and they recur frequently in the sources for his life: see e.g. KG to MH, 14 Aug. 1912, 1 March 1914, 24 May 1914; MH Journal, 10 June 1911, 11 May 1915, 30 July 1917, 10 Sept. 1917, 31 Aug. 1920, 14 Jan. 1922, 26 May 1924.
28 Young, chapter 1, *passim*; Naimy (1950), chapter 1, *passim*; MH Journal, 26 Feb. 1911, 1 March 1911, 25 Aug. 1915, 27 Aug. 1915. Young, chapter 16, has further whimsical tales of his childhood.
29 MH Journal, 25 Aug. 1915.
30 Hawi, p. 84, based on interviews with people who claim to have known Gibran as a child.
31 MH Journal, 23 July 1916.
32 MH Journal, 2 Dec. 1911, 31 Aug.–1 Sept. 1918.
33 Hawi, p. 83. With typical exaggeration, Gibran claims that her father was a bishop (MH Journal, 25 Aug. 1915).
34 MH Journal, 3 Nov. 1915, 3 Sept. 1920.
35 MH Journal, 25 Aug. 1915, 19 Sept. 1915.
36 Physically Gibran took after his slight mother rather than his more robust father. His voice broke late, and as a grown man, even when healthy (and he often was not), he weighed only about 140 lb and could not outrun Mary Haskell – though she was, admittedly, a hearty outdoor type (MH Journal, 17 March 1911, 7 Sept. 1912, 30 Aug. 1914).
37 'He doesn't possess an idea: the idea possesses him. His mother always knew that of him.' MH Journal, 1 June 1912.
38 KG to MZ, n.d., 1928. This is a curious, probably unwitting, echo of the nineteenth-century American feminist reformer Henry Blackwell, who said, 'All that I am, I owe to women.' However, once, to Mary Haskell, Gibran added his father as the third major influence on his life, as well as his mother and her – his father because 'he fought me and called out the fighter in me' (MH Journal, 16 June 1923).

2 Beautiful Dreamer

1 The population was 351,000 in 1880 and 561,000 in 1900. Boston at the time of the Gibrans' arrival was vying with St Louis for the position of fourth largest city in the States, after New York, Chicago and Philadelphia.

2 The fire raged uncontrolled from 9 to 10 November 1872 and destroyed 60 acres of the city.
3 The quote is from *The American Scene*, p. 173.
4 Thus Silas Lapham, the eponymous arriviste hero of William Dean Howells's novel, 'bought very cheap of a terrified gentleman of good extraction who had discovered too late that the South End was not the thing, and who in the eagerness of his flight to the Back Bay threw in his carpets and shades for almost nothing' (*The Rise of Silas Lapham*, p. 24, Penguin edition).
5 Mary Antin, *The Provincial Land* (Boston, 1912). See also Mikhail Naimy (1950), p. 29, for another description of the squalor of the district.
6 This attitude is particularly manifest in a report published by the Associated Charities of Boston in 1899, referring to the Syrian immigrants: 'Every time a kind-hearted individual buys of a Syrian something he does not want – or gives food, clothing, or money for doctors' bills without investigating the case – he encourages begging, lying, idleness, neglect, exposure . . . The desire to appear poor encourages a mode of living which is alike unhealthful physically and morally . . . They overcrowd tenements to avoid high rents, and dirt and squalor are their companions' (pp. 56–7).
7 Howe, p. 382.
8 In 'Slavery', from *The Storm*, translated by John Walbridge (p. 40).
9 The origin of the name 'Assad' is unknown. It is unlikely to be a baptismal name. Perhaps a friend called Assad brought him along to the school for his first day, and the registrar got muddled. Later, Quincy School was sold to the Chinese community for the nominal sum of $1 and it is now the Administrative and Educational Center for the Chinese American Civic Association. It still has the unmistakable aura of a school building inside.
10 MH Journal, 27 Aug. 1915, 23 July 1916, 12 July 1921.
11 Much later, biting the hand that fed him, Gibran expressed disapproval of the Settlement Houses for their Americanization of the Syrians: MH Journal, 19 May 1922.
12 Jussim, p. 38.
13 Parrish, p. 9.
14 Elbert Hubbard, *The Philistine* 6 (Jan. 1898), p. 41.
15 For the manifesto of *The Knight Errant*, which was really no more than William Morris's *Hobby Horse* transposed to American soil, see p. 227. *The Mahogany Tree* published, among others, a young undergraduate from the University of Nebraska called Willa Cather.
16 The description is from Le Gallienne, p. 71.
17 Parrish, p. 49.
18 In a letter to her friend Agnes Clarke dated 24 June 1896, Louise Guiney, who as a firm Christian always kept slightly aloof from at least these occult activities of the Visionists, described Cram as 'a mad agitator for "dead

issues"'; three years later, writing to Herbert Clarke on 23 June 1899, she said, 'Poor old R. Cram has been making a DONK of himself, since he became "Prior" of the No. American Cycle of the Order of the White Rose.' Despite her close friendship with Day during the 1890s, after moving to England she looked back on him as 'rather a crank' (letter to Strickland Gibson, 12 Aug. 1912).

19 In a letter to writer Stephen Parrish, Day's doctor, Conrad Wesselhöft, described Day during this phase: 'Swathed in blankets pinned with meticulous care about his wrists, he reclined in bed both winter and summer, hibernating muscularly but with his mind alert. Surrounded by ingenious gadgets and movable bedside bookshelves, he reduced physical efforts to the minimum. Nursed, nourished and waited on by devoted attendants, his scholarly accomplishments were comparable to the perpetual egg-laying of a queen bee. His great exertion of the day was a trip to the bathroom.' Quoted by Parrish, p. 324.

20 Jussim, p. 8.

21 MIT Press edition, p. 305.

22 Le Gallienne, pp. 129, 156–7.

23 Wilson (1931), p. 2.

24 See e.g. pp. 91, 226.

25 Quoted by Chiari, p. 25.

26 Wilson (1931), p. 21. See, in particular, the articles by W. B. Yeats in the bibliography.

27 He was apparently a solemn, unsmiling child at the time: MH Journal, 21 April 1916.

28 Adams, p. 13 (Penguin edition).

29 Chiefly by Hawi and Ditelberg. Ditelberg's thesis is marred by too narrow a definition of what constitutes an 'influence' on Gibran. He limits himself to only those books which Gibran is known to have read, and is too eager to belittle the influence of Eastern writers on Gibran. But Gibran undoubtedly read widely in Eastern literature as well, not only during his college days in Beirut, but also beforehand, since these writers' works circulated within the Arab ghettos. Moreover, even where we cannot be certain that Gibran had read any complete work by, say, Nietzsche, we should not overlook the way Arabic journals and papers carried articles summarizing the views of important European thinkers.

30 Letter to Herbert Clarke dated 12 Oct. 1897.

31 William Dana Orcutt, 'Frederick Holland Day', *Publishers Weekly* 125 (6 Jan. 1934), p. 54.

32 MH Journal, appendix to 7 Sept. 1912.

33 MH Journal, 27 Jan. 1911, 14 Feb. 1911, 10 March 1911, 17 March 1911, 1 June 1912, 10 June 1912, 7 Sept. 1912, 27 Dec. 1912, 28 Dec. 1912, 6 April

1913, 30 Aug. 1914, 23 April 1916, 10 Sept. 1917, 12 July 1921, 8 Aug. 1921, 9 Sept. 1921, 8 March 1922, 21 April 1922, 12 May 1922, 12 Nov. 1922, 29 May 1924, 18 June 1924; KG to MH, 29 April 1909, 10 Nov. 1909, 6 Oct. 1915; letter to Anthony Bashir, 10 Nov. 1925, cited in *KGLW*, pp. 431–2. His short appreciative essays on al-Farid, Avicenna and al-Ghazali are translated by Sheban.

34 KG to MH, 23 June 1909, 8 Feb. 1912, 26 Jan. 1913, 16 May 1913, 8 Feb. 1914; MH Journal, 20 Dec. 1912, 26 June 1913, 30 Aug. 1913, 26 April 1914, 5 June 1915, 4 Aug. 1919, 30 Dec. 1919, 17 April 1920, 6 Jan. 1921, 22 July 1921, 9 Sept. 1921, 30 Sept. 1922; KG to MZ, 17 Jan. 1924.

35 MH Journal, 6 April 1913, cf. 31 Dec. 1914.

36 See e.g. *Iolaus* (privately printed, 1902), *Homogenic Love* (Manchester: The Labour Press Society, 1894), *An Unknown People* (London: no publisher named, 1897). Later, see *The Intermediate Sex: A Study of Some Transitional Types of Men and Women* (New York: Mitchell Kennerley, 1912) and *Intermediate Types among Primitive Folk* (New York: Mitchell Kennerley, 1921).

37 See e.g. three of a series of pamphlets published in Manchester by The Labour Press Society in 1894: *Sex-Love*, *Marriage* and *Woman*. Some of these pamphlets were collected together and published in America in 1903 (Chicago: Charles H. Kerr and Co.) under the title *Love's Coming of Age*.

38 MH Journal, 9 June 1911, 2 Sept. 1914, 4 Sept. 1914, 19 Dec. 1914, 31 Dec. 1914, 23 July 1916, 11 Nov. 1917, 12 Jan. 1918, 1 Sept. 1918, 14 April 1919, 14 Nov. 1919; KG to MH, 4 Nov. 1913. Typically, however, Gibran chops and changes about women's suffrage. On 9 June 1911 Mary records him as being against it, but on 7 June 1915 she paraphrased his views as: 'I don't care whether women vote or not – or how soon – because that is a mere detail. But I care very much for feminism because that is a great new movement in the race.' However, two days later they have a curiously modern argument, with her claiming and him denying that rape is far more common than is usually recognized. See also 10 Nov. 1917. On 15 Dec. 1914, the *Buffalo Times* carried an article about Gibran with the heading: 'Set Womankind Free and There'll be No War, Says Oriental Painter, Born on Mt. Lebanon'.

39 In this paragraph I focus on broad themes; each of these authors also gave Gibran various isolated images which occur from time to time in his works.

40 On the publication of *The Prophet* in 1923, Louise Guiney, friend to them both, wrote to Day and asked: 'Why isn't the book dedicated to you?'

41 W. D. Orcutt, as note 31.

42 Louise Guiney to Fred Holland Day, 10 Jan. 1919. Quoted by Jussim, p. 117, with regard to what she calls Gibran's 'bloated ego'.

43 See *KGLW*, p. 427.

44 MH Journal, 27 Aug. 1915.
45 JP Journal, 8 Dec. 1898.
46 Curiously, it seems that Mary Haskell owned a copy of this edition of Maeterlinck. Gibran recognized it on her shelves: MH Journal, 21 April 1922.
47 This is not to say that he got on particularly well with the Perrys, who probably remained somewhat aloof. At any rate, when they coincided at an exhibition in 1914, he studiously avoided them: MH Journal, 28 Dec. 1914.
48 '[He said that] it seemed to him, when he looked at me, that we had known each other long, long, many years before.' JP Journal, 17 Nov. 1902.
49 MH Diary, March–April 1912. Mikhail Naimy's account (1950, pp. 29–40) is a fanciful representation of the affair.
50 In the short story 'The Storm', he has a character say: 'There is nothing in the West that you can consider superior except yet another manifestation of empty delusion' (John Walbridge's translation, p. 21). The idea that neither is better than the other recurs at MH Journal, 26 Feb. 1911; but the superiority of the East to the West in certain important respects – chiefly aesthetic and spiritual – is a recurrent theme: MH Journal, 7 Sept. 1912, 30 Aug. 1914, 6 April 1915, 5 June 1915, 9 June 1915, 4 Aug. 1919, 14 Aug. 1919, 22 July 1921, 29 July 1921, 31 Dec. 1922. But this is not a naïve preference for the East simply *qua* East (a view for which he gently criticized Pierre Loti: KG to MH, 29 Sept. 1912, 22 Oct. 1912); it is subsumed under the preference for things aesthetic and spiritual.
51 Letter to Day, 10 Sept. 1898.
52 MH Journal, 30 Dec. 1919.

3 A Smile and a Tear

1 The old building has long been demolished, but the school still exists (with its name also translated into French as Collège de la Sagesse, School of Wisdom) in a large, plain building in the Achrafiyya district of East Beirut.
2 MH Journal, 14 April 1919.
3 MH Journal, 23 July 1916.
4 Hawi, p. 86.
5 For alternative titles, see Hawi, p. 87, n. 4.
6 Huwayyik was also born in 1883 – which sits awkwardly with Gibran's claim to have been the baby of the class by some eighteen months (MH Journal, 11 Nov. 1917). His uncle, Elias Huwayyik, was to play an important role in Lebanon's struggle for independence after the First World War: see Akarli, p. 176.
7 MH Journal, 5 June 1912.

8 MH Journal, 19 April 1911, 23 July 1916.
9 MH Journal, 19 April 1911.
10 MH Journal, 24 March 1911.
11 MH Journal, 26 and 28 Dec. 1917. However, along with his attempt to whitewash his father and reinvent himself as the product of a privileged childhood, he also gave out more charitable interpretations of his father's behaviour: 'Father opposed my writing and painting, though he was a lover of the fine arts. He probably knew that the life of an artist involves much suffering and wanted to spare me' (MH Journal, 25 Aug. 1915).
12 *KGLW*, p. 85.
13 JP Journal, 8 Dec. 1898; see also 12 Dec. 1898.
14 JP Journal, 17 Nov. 1902.
15 The authors of *KGLW* claim to reproduce the letter 'with all of its errors' (p. 80). In fact, a comparison with the original reveals almost forty places where they have inaccurately copied the letter. The envelope for the letter was addressed in another, neater hand than Gibran's immature handwriting; perhaps he enlisted the help of one of the teachers at the college.
16 MH Journal, 16 Sept. 1911; the revision was perhaps undertaken during his years in Paris (MH Journal, 7–8 Dec. 1918). Of the two translations available, the one by Juan Cole is far better than the other. Curiously, there exists a third, unpublished translation among Mary Haskell's papers, which may well be the most authentic, in the sense that it may have been approved by Gibran himself. It reads well. However, we do not know who the translator was, or when it came into Mary's possession. It contains pen corrections in a hand that is neither hers nor Gibran's. All we can say is that it predates 1952, because Mary has dated her jottings on it.
17 The phrase 'broken wings' apparently originated with Kahlil's mother. Once, when he was young, she maternally described him as an angel and asked to feel his wings. She touched his shoulder-blades and, probably in a reference to the childhood accident in which he broke his shoulder (see p. 292), said 'Broken wings!' (MH Journal, 20 April 1920).
18 Gibran was not an innovator with this call for female emancipation: for instance, Nu'man Abduh al-Qasatli of Damascus (1854–1920) had written in 1880 a book called *Al-Fatat al-Amina wa Ummuha* (*The Faithful Maiden and Her Mother*) which was strongly critical of social conventions that led to the victimization of young women, especially in denying them the right to marry for love. Gibrin's countryman Butrus al-Bustani had stood up for women as early as 1849, and the Egyptian Qasim Amin, who died in 1908, spent much of his life fighting for equality for women.
19 Gibran's constant belief in reincarnation may originally stem from contact with the Druze.
20 Hawi, pp. 87–8; Glass, p. 316.

21 pp. 97–100 (London: George Allen, 1898). Maeterlinck argues that everyone suffers, but that certain sages render their suffering harmless by accepting it.

22 Given what we have seen of Gibran's deteriorating relationship with his father, it is interesting to see how often in these early works the father is used as a symbol of tyranny: it is he who tries to force women to ignore the dictates of love and conform to society's false norms.

23 See, for instance, 'Decayed Teeth' in *Thoughts and Meditations*; 'Your Lebanon and Mine' in *Spiritual Sayings*; 'My Countrymen' in *A Treasury of Kahlil Gibran.*

24 A good short article on Gibran's love for his homeland is 'Gibran and the Cedars', by Suheil Bushrui, printed in Bushrui and Gotch (eds).

25 Translated by Suheil Bushrui, from his anthology *An Introduction to Kahlil Gibran.*

26 See the quotation from the unknown young Syrian on p. 20.

27 Particularly the Egyptian writer Rifaʿa Badawi Rafiʿ al-Tahtawi (1801–73), and Faris al-Shidyaq (1801–87), who was Lebanese. It is also interesting to note that the first piece of European fiction translated into Arabic was al-Tahtawi's translation of Fénelon's *Les Aventures de Télémaque* – an overt attack on despotism. This tradition was built into Arabic fiction from the start. Faransis (Francis) Marrash (1836–73) continued the tradition by writing Rousseauistic tales with themes such as the contrast between natural freedom and social convention.

28 *Towards Democracy*, privately printed, 1883, p. 31. There is a strong echo of Walt Whitman's 'The Song of the Open Road'.

29 Gibran was not alone in promulgating these ideas or in using experimental forms such as the short story to express them. In particular, his friend, colleague and fellow Romantic Amin Rihani had published a novella in New York just two years before *Nymphs of the Valley* in which the same vehemently anti-clerical attitude can be found. In this novella, *Al-Mukari wa al-Kahin* (*The Muleteer and the Priest*), an illiterate muleteer, who has come to hate the priesthood, finds himself alone in a railway carriage with a priest. They fall into a discussion which becomes an argument. The priest strikes the muleteer on the cheek, but the muleteer, Christ-like, turns the other cheek and launches a critical attack developing the contrast between the Church and the actual teachings of Christ. The priest is converted, and spends the rest of his life working for the poor and the oppressed. It is obvious how this story resonates with 'Yuhanna the Madman' or 'Khalil the Heretic' – and also with Voltaire's anticlericalism, another European influence which had been absorbed by an earlier generation of Arabic writers.

30 Dedalus edition, p. 220.

31 Ostle (1992), 'The Literature of the *Mahjar*', p. 213.

32 Compare Richard Hovey's and Bliss Carman's three volumes of *Songs from Vagabondia*, which celebrate social rebels and outcasts as agents of change and destroyers of bourgeois and Victorian values. The first two of these volumes were published by Copeland and Day, so Gibran was certainly aware of them.

33 Translated by Anthony Ferris in *A Treasury of Kahlil Gibran*, p. 269.

34 MH Journal, 3 Sept. 1913, 9 June 1915, 14 Sept. 1920. This view seems to be confirmed by a letter Gibran wrote to his cousin N'oula on 15 March 1908, in which he says that the Arab world has actually been *friendly* towards him for the last three years (i.e. since the publication of *Nymphs of the Valley*), but that he was beginning to be described as a heretic then, in 1908. Perhaps in the same loose sense of the term, Huwayyik talks of Amin Rihani as having been excommunicated (Huwayyik, p. 164). Barbara Young, whose biography is always uncritical and often derivative, of course accepts the story of excommunication, and since her biography was for many years the only one available in English, the tale spread throughout the introductions and prefaces to editions of Gibran's works.

35 Letter to N'oula Gibran, 15 March 1908 (*A Self-portrait*, p. 28).

36 *A Self-portrait*, pp. 17–18. The editor of this collection of Gibran's letters first dated this letter to 1904, and that is still how it appears in print; but see Hawi, p. 89, n. 1.

37 MH Diary, 4 May 1908.

38 Oddly, there was another 'young widow' in Gibran's life in his youth, called Marthe M. (MH Journal, 16 June, 1923); but this is a unique mention and there is no way of knowing what kind of relationship is implied, or who the woman was.

39 MH Journal, 7 June 1915, 12 March 1922, 21 Jan. 1923. In a letter to May Ziadeh, dated 9 Nov. 1919, he claims to have visited Alexandria in the summer of 1903. Since we know that he was in Boston in the summer of 1903, then this is either a mistake or a misprint in the edition of his translated letters (*Gibran: Love Letters*, p. 21). Assuming that it should read '1902', then he may have stopped off in Egypt as well as Athens on his way to France.

40 MH Journal, 25 Aug. 1915; on 12 March 1922 he also claimed to have a diamond to sell during his later trip to Paris.

41 (1950), p. 57.

42 MH Journal, 10 March 1914. Gibran himself told Mary Haskell that he heard the news from the Syrian consul in Paris, who was (of course) a personal friend of the family. But this account is not entirely incompatible with Marianna's, since the consul could have been the one to show him the paper.

4 She

1 KG to JP, 10 Dec. 1902.
2 A sketch of a female figure entitled 'Consolation', drawn in January 1903, was based on Josephine. The idea of Woman as *Consolatrix* infuses a great deal of Romantic literature. See e.g. D'Annunzio's *The Child of Pleasure*, p. 177 (Dedalus edition): 'To a man of culture, Donna Maria Ferrès was the Ideal Woman . . . the perfect *Consolatrix*, the friend who can hold out both comfort and pardon.'
3 Letter dated 29 March 1903.
4 Later, Gibran implied that the family's debts at this period were in the region of $30,000 – an incredible amount for those days (MH Journal, 11 April 1915). Whatever the debt, it seems safest to assume that it could be repaid simply by selling Peter's business when the time came.
5 MH Journal, 10 March 1914 – a reminiscence of Marianna Gibran.
6 KG to JP, 17 Feb. 1903. Four days later he writes of being 'released' for a few hours to come and visit her.
7 It can be found among Mary Haskell's papers in Chapel Hill: Box 22, folder 145. Dated 29 Nov. 1905, it seems – though it is phrased in very ambiguous language – to be gently telling him off at a time of some strain between them.
8 JP Journal, 16 Nov. 1902, 13 Sept. 1903.
9 JP Journal, 9 May 1903.
10 For example, 12 June 1904: 'There is one thing very plain. The only thing in the world that makes me feel rich is to spend myself richly in the effort to share Beauty.'
11 JP Journal, 17 Nov. 1902.
12 JP Journal, 16 Nov. 1902, 17 Nov. 1902, 21 Nov. 1902, 24 Nov. 1902, 22 Dec. 1902, 21 Feb. 1903, 13 March 1903, 24 March 1903.
13 Contrast this picture with the one Gibran gave Mary Haskell: '"Just think,"' says Gibran arrogantly in her journal for 6 Sept. 1914, '"for 5 years I used to go and see her twice a week! She was writing her best things then – and tho' I was only 18 I say frankly that I believed I influenced her work." "Did you love her?" "Yes." "And she you?" "Yes, I think she loved me first. You see, she was a woman and I was a youth."' On another occasion he told Mary that Josephine was vain about her beauty (MH Journal, 1 June 1924).
14 In an end-note to his short monograph (1984), Gregory Orfalea writes: 'A personal letter to the author from Kahlil Gibran, the poet's cousin and most recent biographer (with his wife, Jean) states: ". . . I suspect Josephine Peabody and Gibran were intimate."' And that by 'intimate' Gibran here

meant 'sexually intimate' is shown by the next sentence in the letter: 'I am 100 per cent certain that there was an affair between him and an enormously attractive Boston musician whose letters turned up after our book's publication.' In the Gibrans' book, however, their raciest description of the relationship terms it 'a pleasant dalliance with an exotic youth' (*KGLW*, p. 122). On the affair between Gibran and the 'enormously attractive Boston musician', see pp. 101–2.

15 Letter dated 8 February 1903.

16 Ridge (1959), p. 11.

17 John Walbridge's translation, in *The Beloved*, p. 19.

18 This is the piece called 'A Vision' on pp. 30–31 of Nahmad's translation *A Tear and a Smile*, and called 'Vision' on pp. 233–4 of Ferris's *A Treasury of Kahlil Gibran*. It is not 'A Vision' from pp. 38–41 of Nahmad, which is the same as 'Vision' on pp. 92–5 of Juan Cole's *The Vision*; nor again is it 'The Vision' on pp. 6–8 of Cole's *The Vision*, which is the same as 'Vision' on pp. 61–3 of Ferris's *Thoughts and Meditations*, and as 'Revelation' on pp. 12–15 of Andrew Ghareeb's *Prose Poems*. Is that clear?

19 Very little work indeed has been done on clarifying the exact chronology of Gibran's Arabic pieces; even when we know when something was first published, it is of course possible that it might have been written some time before publication. Gibran's gestation periods were often lengthy. So there are hazards when attempting to date his work. For convenience, then, along with other writers on Gibran, I mean by his 'early works' the Arabic pieces translated especially in Nahmad's collection *A Tear and a Smile*, and in Ferris's *A Treasury of Kahlil Gibran*. Other anthologies are also worth consulting, and may well contain better translations, but these two are the most thorough.

20 KG to MH, 21 Jan. 1912.

21 MH Journal, 17 Sept. 1920.

22 Nahmad, *A Tear and a Smile*, p. 3.

23 ibid., p. 23.

24 ibid., p. 24.

25 ibid., p. 76.

26 ibid., p. 80.

27 Although *Falsafat al-Din wa al-Tadayyun* was probably drafted at around this period, the idea of establishing some kind of ideal community in Lebanon was still occurring to Gibran as late as 1923, when he told Mary Haskell of his dream of buying 400 acres there and creating a model agricultural community (MH Journal, 29 May 1923).

28 'The Voice of the Poet', in *The Vision*, pp. 19 ff. ('A Poet's Voice', Nahmad, pp. 189 ff.); Hawi, p. 161.

29 See further Chapter 10, pp. 227–31, on Gibran's view of the poet.

30 It is probably in this context that we should view his giving Day and others the impression that his background in Syria was noble: see p. 24.
31 See p. 36.
32 Compare, for instance, Gibran's 'Good Friday: A Study', with the head at the centre of Moreau's 'L'Apparition' (1876), or Gibran's close studies of heads with those of Redon (such as 'Closed Eyes', 1890), or Gibran's deliberate use of indistinctness with that of Carrière.
33 Compare, perhaps, the way Redon, in 'La Tentation de Saint-Antoine' (1896) positions the devil behind St Anthony in half-formed obscurity, a device already used by Arnold Böcklin in 'Self-portrait with Death Playing the Fiddle' (1872).
34 Apart from painting, see e.g. Honoré de Balzac, *Séraphita*, p. 33 (Dedalus edition); 'I retain, *of that world seen through veils and mists*, a ringing echo like the remembrance of departed pain . . .' (my italics).
35 These words could of course also represent Symbolist literature as well as art; on Symbolist literature, see pp. 226–7. The quote is from Redon's *À Soi-Même*, in Elizabeth Gilmore Holt (ed.), p. 496. The excerpt from this in Holt's book, or in Dorra (pp. 54–6), is worth reading *in toto*. It perfectly encapsulates the aims Gibran set himself as an artist throughout his life.
36 *The Child of Pleasure*, p. 26 (Dedalus edition).
37 On the relativism assumed by Symbolism, see pp. 39–40.
38 Even Josephine noted in her diary that the new moon would be conjunct with Jupiter in Gemini for her wedding to Lionel Marks; and in her diary for 11 Jan. 1906 she notes: 'In the evening K. [her quasi-Arabic symbol for K.] here; and some talk of things occult.' Apart from a wary interest in séances and spiritualism, Mary was an expert graphologist, and used to study the envelopes of letters she received before reading the letters, in order to get some idea of the condition of the writer: see e.g. MH to KG, 10 Feb. 1912, 15 Nov. 1913.
39 MH to KG, 7 Dec. 1913. English Walling was married to her sister Frederika.
40 MH Journal, 30 July 1917, 12 March 1922.
41 MH Journal, 7 Dec. 1910.
42 She described herself as plain, and Gibran's close friend Mikhail Naimy once said of her: 'She was not a beautiful woman, but she laid her foot upon the earth as if she loved it' (quoted by Chapin). See also the description in Naimy (1950), pp. 64–5 (however, this is vitiated by the fact that Naimy admits, p. 236, that he met Mary for the first time in 1931). She obviously exuded the kind of sexuality that attracted both men and women: we know of several male suitors, and on one occasion, before admitting to Kahlil that she had had a lesbian affair, she talks of another woman who was in love with her (MH Journal, 19 Dec. 1914).
43 MH Journal, 12 March 1922.

44 George Santayana, *The Last Puritan*, p. 50 (MIT edition).
45 MH Journal, 25 Dec. 1912.

5 City of Light

1 *KGLW*, p. 141.
2 This virtual repetition of letters is a trait of Gibran we have noted before (p. 77). In fact, he must sometimes have kept draft letters, because the first paragraph of a letter he wrote to Josephine on his birthday in 1908 is repeated almost verbatim a year later in a letter he wrote to Mary on his birthday in 1909. This habit of his detracts from the personal tone he attempts to convey in his letters: they are to a certain extent poses or productions. Nevertheless, he recognizes that letters – especially love letters – should be 'direct and simple' (MH Journal, 23 June 1923).
3 JP Journal, 26 Nov. 1904.
4 MH Journal, 21 April 1916; Young, p. 68. Mary, however, deeply regretted all the lost work: MH to KG, 2 Oct. 1914.
5 Nadeem Naimy (1985), p. 37. See also Mikhail Naimy (1950), p. 55.
6 Hawi, p. 245.
7 The suggestion that Kahlil did not reply to his invitation occurs in *KGLW*, p. 151.
8 She played singularly little part in Gibran's subsequent life. After she became famous, Mary once teasingly suggested that Gibran should draw her for the series of famous writers and artists he was preparing (MH Journal, 6 April 1911), and they met socially in New York in February 1914 (JP Diary, 24–28 Feb. 1914).
9 Only rarely, however, do we catch a glimpse of these other friends in the 1900s. For instance, in a letter written in March 1919 by an old friend of Gibran, one D. Weston Eliot, who was attempting to renew a lapsed fifteen-year-old acquaintance, Eliot reminds Gibran that they were introduced by a mutual friend called Burton Clark, and later in the letter he says: 'Do you remember going to the Whitings in Tower Hill, Wayland, and having a camp-fire supper. I have forgotten the artist chap we both knew there and you came with him' [*sic*]. So there are four friends of Gibran we know nothing else about: Eliot, Burton Clark, the Whitings, and the 'artist chap'.
10 See also the note in Hanna's dissertation to the effect that Kahlil Gibran the younger refused both her and a certain Professor Randall of the Lilly Library of Indiana University access to Gibran material. Similar stories also circulate by word of mouth among the Gibran fraternity. This is deeply distressing. I would not say, however, that it has been a serious impediment to my research, since their own book is pretty thorough on the details of

Gibran's life. All the more reason, then, why it seems unnecessary for them to have forbidden me and other researchers access to the material. If there is something to hide – in the Barrie letters, for instance – they could simply not have shown these offending articles to me; the world and I would have been none the wiser.

11 To Mary's distress, some years later Charlotte interpreted their friendship as a sublimated love-affair: MH Journal, 26 April 1914. But then New York was warming up to its frenzied admiration of all things Freudian (see Douglas, pp. 122–9), which Sherwood Anderson memorably summed up by saying, 'It was a time when it was well for a man to be somewhat guarded in the remarks he made, [and] what he did with his hands.'

12 The dedication reads: 'To the soul that embraced my soul, to the heart that poured its secrets into my own heart, to the hand that kindled the flame of my emotions, I dedicate this book.' In 1908, who could this refer to? Micheline seems the best bet, with Gertrude Barrie as runner-up, and Josephine third.

13 MH Journal, 10 May 1908.

14 Mary had a business partner, Sarah M. Dean, at the school from 1906 to 1912.

15 For much of the next fifteen years of Gibran's life, there is suddenly a wealth of material. Throughout the most intense phase of the relationship between Kahlil and Mary Haskell, they were often meeting, and Mary was keeping a thorough record of their meetings. In addition, they were writing to each other with great frequency: over 600 letters are extant. The forty or so volumes of Mary's diaries and journals constitute an extraordinary document. Its value lies not just in the light it sheds on her relationship with and feelings for Gibran, and on the details of his life, but, more widely, as a testimonial to the inner world of a woman of the times. They await discovery by some social historian of the period.

The diaries are mainly written in minute handwriting with a thin-nibbed pen, using the kind of shorthand and abbreviations one might expect. As her relationship with Kahlil became more intense, her diary entries began to get longer and longer, sometimes occupying several weeks of a diary. She therefore turned to journals, which at first were used, as Josephine's were, to supplement and run parallel to the diaries. The journals were written either after her meetings with Gibran, or sometimes even during their meetings, since they contain numerous pencil sketches by him. Up until about 1914 or 1915 they are journals about quite a bit of Mary's non-school life – that is, they contain her thoughts about and conversations with others, not just Gibran; gradually, however, they become devoted entirely to Gibran. They range from disjointed notes, scribbled in haste just as she recalled them, and sometimes blocked in later, to polished passages of sharp perception and almost lyrical prose. Sometimes it is clear – especially in the later journals, when their relationship was less intense – that she left several days between their meeting and her recording of it, and she herself occasionally says that she is remembering no more than the gist of the conversation. Generally, however, they can be relied on as an accurate paraphrase, though not necessarily a verbatim report, of their talks.

The often polished nature of the journal entries is both their strength and their weakness, for as well as providing a clear record they also embellish: Gibran's English, for instance, was never as good as she makes out, especially in the earlier years of their relationship. But she was aware that she was recording the life and sayings of someone she regarded as a master – a saint of some kind – and she wanted the record to do justice to him. She was also aware that the journals might some time see the light of day: once in a while, when recording a gossipy conversation, she leaves blank the names of the people they talked about. This too shows that they are a polished record.

The other weakness of the wealth of material on Gibran offered by Mary's journals and by the letters that passed between them is that they completely swamp all other sources of information, which are pitifully thin. So we see Gibran largely through Mary's eyes, and we see him as he projected himself to her. Their letters record a great many details about Gibran's life, but they invariably have the same flavour. For the biographer who is already faced with a subject who hid behind mythical screens, the problems are only compounded.

16 This was his 24th birthday. She was 33 years old and was already going grey. She noted in her diary for 10 March 1907: 'Kerosene on hair to stop falling and greyness.'

17 Letter dated 28 Jan. 1908.

18 MH Diary, 27 March 1908.

19 *A Self-portrait*, pp. 22–5.

20 Letter to MH dated 30 April 1908.

21 In April 1914, Micheline was living in New York, as was Gibran, but they rarely met. Gibran spoke to Mary about his boyish infatuation with her: MH Journal, 26 April 1914.

22 For both of these episodes, see Hawi, pp. 93–6, 103.

23 For instance, according to Huwayyik (p. 69) Gibran had never visited Athens – but see p. 72.

24 See pp. 69–70.

25 MH Journal, 3 Sept. 1913, 14 Sept. 1920.

26 MH Journal, 2 Jan. 1923.

27 MH Journal, 7–8 Dec. 1918.

28 p. 123.

29 MH Journal, 2 Sept. 1914, 7–8 Dec. 1918, 12 March 1922.

30 Hawi, p. 99, on the results of an interview with Huwayyik.
31 Especially Americans: in *The Last Puritan: A Memoir in the Form of a Novel*, George Santayana recalled: 'There were many such Americans *de luxe* in my generation who prolonged their youth at the *École des Beaux-Arts* or at Julian's, confident of personally restoring the age of Pericles' (p. 12, MIT edition).
32 There seems no good reason to doubt Gibran's word on this, but curiously the Centre historique des Archives nationales in Paris, which has the records of the Académie Julian, can find no trace of Gibran's name. It seems possible, then, that he never formally registered as a student, although he could still have attended classes.
33 Huwayyik, p. 181.
34 KG to MH, 19 Dec. 1909.
35 Compare two letters to Amin Goryeb, the first dated 12 Feb. 1908, the second 28 March 1908. Both can be read in *A Self-portrait*.
36 KG to MH, 19 Dec. 1909, 8 Jan. 1910; MH Journal, 26 April 1916. On his poverty in Paris, see e.g. MH Journal, 7–8 Dec. 1918 (where he claims to have lived on a diet of bread, cheese and eggs), 12 March 1922.
37 See pp. 145, 209. The Huwayyik reference is p. 180, and the KG to MH letters are 7 Feb. 1909 (which has been stolen from its file in the library of the Southern Historical Collection of the University of North Carolina in Chapel Hill, and is now available in full only on pp. 21–2 of Otto's collection) and 17 April 1909.
38 The notice is reproduced in some detail in *KGLW*, pp. 183–4.
39 KG to MH, 29 April 1909.
40 MH Journal, 10 March 1911.
41 KG to MH, 10 Nov. 1909, 19 Dec. 1909, 29 March 1910.
42 KG to MH, 10 May 1910.
43 MH Journal, 7–8 Dec. 1918. In her journal for 14 Sept. 1920, the 'delegation' has become a 'cousin' who offers him any post he wants. By the same token I also find implausible the idea that even at a later date, in 1928, he was offered a post in the government of Lebanon, which was by then a new, but not yet independent, parliamentary democracy. It is Barbara Young who tells us the story (p. 125); the Gibrans are inclined to give it some credence (p. 389), because by then his friend Ayub Tabet was a political power in Lebanon. Gibran could have acted as a cultural figurehead, but surely not as an active politician.
44 KG to MH, 5 June 1910.
45 MH Journal, 25 Aug. 1915, 12 March 1922.
46 MH Journal, 12 March 1922.

6 The Beacon of Fame

1 When Day visited Gibran's new studio, to Gibran's delight it met with his approval (MH Journal, 21 Feb. 1911).
2 Penguin edition, p. 44.
3 Letter to MH, 10–11 May 1910.
4 MH Diary, 10 Dec. 1910. She remembered the phrase, because it recurs in her journal years later on 20 June 1915.
5 MH Journal, 22–24 June 1912.
6 MH Journal, 12 Jan. 1911, 28 Jan. 1911; Diary, 28 Jan. 1911, 22 Feb. 1911.
7 MH Diary, 28 Jan. 1911; Journal, 1 March 1911.
8 MH Diary, 3 Feb. 1911.
9 MH Journal, 19 Feb. 1911. In an extant letter Charlotte refers to the marriage plans and says, 'Nothing can come between you two – nor indeed between us three – for the union is so established upon the plane of the spirit' (CT to MH, 5 March 1911).
10 MH Journal, 1 March 1911.
11 MH Diary, 1 March 1911, 30 March 1911, 1 April 1911; Journal, 10 March 1911, 17 March 1911, 15 April 1911.
12 MH Diary, 14 April 1911, 15 April 1911, 18 April 1911, 19 April 1911; Journal, 15 April 1911, 17 April 1911.
13 MH Journal, 15 April 1911, 17 April 1911.
14 Various entries in MH Journal, 10 April 1915 to 30 Dec. 1915; MH to KG, 18 April 1915, mid-July 1915; KG to MH, 2 Aug. 1915. Another extended conversation in which he analysed the early months of their relationship and told her how much she had hurt him occurred on 12 March 1922. See also MH Journal, 1 Sept. 1913, 26 April 1916, 7–8 Dec. 1918. His final recorded comment on this is rather more gracious: he claims that the shock helped him to burn away the 'little things' in him and focus on the larger issues (MH Journal, 23 June 1923; see 26–28 Dec. 1922 and also 20 Aug. 1920).
15 MH Journal, 17 March 1911.
16 MH Diary, 29 March 1911. For his part, he thought that 'Rose Sleeves' marked the end of his 'cowardly' attitude towards colour (MH Journal, 28 March 1911).
17 MH Journal, 22 Feb. 1911, 6 April 1911.
18 MH Journal, 28 March 1911.
19 MH Journal, 22 Feb. 1911.
20 MH Diary, 22 Feb. 1911, 3 March 1911, 8 March 1911, 19 April 1911; Journal, 22 Feb. 1911, 12 April 1911, 30 Dec. 1915.
21 Even in Paris, Gibran still felt himself to be a suffering soul: see his letter from there to his cousin N'oula in *A Self-portrait*, pp. 35–6.

22 *A Self-portrait*, pp. 36–7.
23 MH Journal, 6 April 1911.
24 *A Self-portrait*, p. 32.
25 American artists were also represented, but were outclassed by those from Europe, who included Ingres, Delacroix, Degas, Renoir, Manet, Cézanne, Van Gogh, Gauguin, Matisse, Redon, Picasso, Picabia, Duchamp, Seurat, Toulouse-Lautrec and Augustus John.
26 Richwine, p. 40.
27 To express his views about the mixture of art and radical politics in the famous magazine *The Masses*, one unkind reviewer composed a piece of doggerel verse: 'They draw nude women for *The Masses* / Thick, fat, ungainly lasses – / How does that help the working classes?'
28 Green, p. 21, see also pp. 228–9.
29 *The Book of Khalid* was, according to Gibran (MH Journal, 2 Jan. 1912), autobiographical. It is partly the story of an immigrant's journey to and first experiences in the States, and is partly also reminiscent of *The Broken Wings*. It and Rihani's other English works show that he had a better grasp of the English language than Gibran ever achieved; his poems come across as harder than Gibran's, with less lyricism in them. He was a model for Gibran in two important ways: as a pioneer of protest and, with regard to *The Book of Khalid* in particular, in writing about Arab experiences in English – that is, for an international audience. Rihani was, in general, a pioneer in almost every field later explored by Gibran and his fellow Mahjar writers, and yet he failed to perfect any of the literary genres in which he experimented.
30 Letter to MH, 1 May 1911.
31 Letter to MH, 5–7 May 1911. His next talk was on 19 May, with the subject 'Self-reliance'. The political tenor of the titles is noteworthy.
32 *A Self-portrait*, p. 53.
33 MH Journal, 3 June 1911, 11 April 1915.
34 He died twenty years later in April 1931, while she in fact lived to be over ninety, and died on 9 October 1964. On 23 July 1916, with even greater accuracy, he told her, 'You will see 80 years or more, but I think I shall live only 15, possible [*sic*] 17 years longer.' Also on 14 Sept. 1920 she records his prophecy that she would outlive him, but he is not always so accurate: on 2 Jan. 1923 he said that he felt he would live to be old, and on 29 March 1921 that he had no idea how long he would live. Most wildly, he tells her that it has several times been foretold that he will die on a burning ship (MH Journal, 12 April 1911).
35 MH Diary, 9 Oct. 1911, 11 Oct. 1911.
36 MH Journal, 2 Oct. 1911.
37 MH Journal, 29 Sept. 1911; see also her diary for 3 Oct. 1911. It is certainly true that Mary's interpretations of his paintings can be very insightful

and sympathetic. Here – because more brief – I quote another, of 'Two Crosses', which Gibran gave her on 11 October 1911: 'On the bare heights in a storm glow one crucified is hanging, half his length against the sky. But we see no cross – only the arms stretched into the air and the helpless feet. And at those feet has fallen another sufferer – spent, despairing. Her cross too is invisible. Crucified and erect, the man can see far and from afar be seen. But now he is looking only down at her – and his eyes and kind face are filled with her, sunk under her load on the deaf earth and except for him unseen and unutterably alone.' It is not at all unlikely that Mary was reading this painting partly as a parable of her and Gibran. At any rate, she certainly saw him as a crucified figure, both in terms of his suffering and of his Christ-like nature, and would be pleased to have him look down at her at his feet. Gibran himself saw the two figures as representing two types of suffering, perhaps even in the same person – the suffering of being laid low and the suffering of being raised high.

7 Mother Mary

1 She continues to rave over his paintings, though. For instance: 'Then K.G. brought out one of the most glorious things ever done by hand and brush of man – a Hand; *the* Hand' (MH Journal, 24 March 1918). Or: 'To praise them would be like complimenting works of God. We wonder at them and we love them . . . Yes, something else too: we obey them' (MH Journal, 18 Sept. 1915).
2 The quoted passages are from the journals for 6 April 1911, 28 Jan. 1912, an appendix to Sept. 1912, 23 June 1913, 29 Aug. 1913, 19 Dec. 1914, 20 June 1915, 30 June 1915, 25 Aug. 1915. Other general expressions of adulation occur throughout her letters and journals, with too great a frequency to cite.
3 See pp. 126–7.
4 MH Journal, 19 Sept. 1915.
5 Another example: she was dissatisfied with a couple of the pictures in his book *Twenty Drawings* (which in truth are not all good), and he ticked her off for failing to recognize the universal form in them: MH Journal, 27 Dec. 1919.
6 MH Journal, 23 June 1913.
7 MH Journal, 30 Aug. 1914.
8 MH Journal, 27 Dec. 1912, 6 Sept. 1914, 25 Aug. 1920, 19 May 1922; once he even admitted that he found it impossible to adjust to other people, and had to get them to adjust to him (MH Journal, 29 March 1921).
9 MH Journal, 28 June 1915.

10 MH Journal, 27–28 June 1912, 25 June 1913, 30 Aug. 1913, 4 Sept. 1914, 20 June 1915; MH to KG, 27 May 1912.

11 Mary and Kahlil were products of their times in the way they spoke about coloured people and, especially, Jews, of whom Gibran was not very fond, particularly when the Zionist movement began to target Palestine as their preferred homeland.

12 MH Journal, 3 April 1912, 30 Aug. 1914, 31 Aug. 1914, 26 Dec. 1915, 24 March 1918, 11 Sept. 1922, 30 Sept. 1922, 16 June 1923.

13 MH Journal, 9 Nov. 1912.

14 For instance, MH Diary, 12 Oct. 1911; Journal, 15 June 1912, 6 April 1913, 9 June 1915, 28 June 1915.

15 See pp. 110–11.

16 See p. 110.

17 See *KGLW*, p. 383.

18 On books: MH Journal, 14 Nov. 1915, 10 Sept. 1917, 11 Nov. 1917, 4 Aug. 1919, 30 Dec. 1919. On lobster: 21 April 1920.

19 MH Journal, 7–8 Dec. 1918, 8 March 1922.

20 MH Journal, 1 June 1924; more ambiguously, 'I may lie to man and to myself, but I won't lie to God' (MH Journal, 8 Nov. 1919).

21 A couple of times he prefaced his self-assessing remarks by assuring Mary that he was not boasting (MH Journal, 27 Jan. 1911, 30 July 1917), but she also caught him once or twice fishing for compliments (MH Journal, 20 June 1915, 2 Jan. 1918).

22 MH Journal, 27 Dec. 1914. Unacknowledged by either Mary or Kahlil, the saying is a slightly misremembered quote from Emerson: 'When half-gods go, the gods arrive.' Davies briefly caught the craze for Cubism after the Armory Show, but was basically a Symbolist painter, and there are easily discernible similarities between his work and Gibran's – but there is more earthiness, life and reality to Davies's work. He comes closest to Gibran, perhaps, in 'Gates of Paradise', 'Sleep' and 'Crescendo'.

23 MH Journal, 28 March 1911, 28 June 1915, 24 Aug. 1915, 13 Nov. 1915, 28 Dec. 1915, 25 April 1916, 30 July 1917, 2 Jan. 1918.

24 MH Journal, 9 June 1915.

25 MH Journal, 12 Jan. 1918, 5 Feb. 1921, 12 Jan. 1922.

26 MH Journal, 8 Feb. 1921, 12 Aug. 1921, 30 Aug. 1921, 16 June 1922.

27 e.g. MH Journal, 11 June 1915, 22 March 1918.

28 MH Journal, 20 June 1915, 12 July 1921.

29 MH Journal, 3 April 1912, 18 April 1920, 12 May 1922; *Sand and Foam*, p. 85. Similarly about the book that was to become *The Earth Gods* on 20 June 1915, and about Christ living his principles, on 10 Sept. 1920 and 30 Sept. 1922.

30 *Spiritual Sayings*, p. 54.

31 MH Journal, 31 Dec. 1922.

32 Jacoby, p. 87.
33 MH Journal, 25 Aug. 1920; *The Syrian World*, April 1931, p. 30. On 30 June 1915 he comments that he finds it a nuisance that people just come up to him on trains and in museums and start talking to him. It didn't take him long in New York to begin to acquire disciples (MH Journal, 31 Nov. 1911); see also the opinion of his friends on his worth compared with that of Arthur Davies, quoted on p. 146. His good friend Thomas Raymond, the mayor of Newark, NJ, once wrote him a letter beginning: 'Dearest Kahlil and Great Master' (MH Journal, 29 Dec. 1914). And Gibran describes James Oppenheim as a 'worshipper' of his (MH Journal, 21–22 July 1916).
34 MH Journal, 12 July 1921; similar sentiments in a letter to Corinne Roosevelt Robinson, 21 Nov. 1918. Mary's loving and perceptive comment on this aspect of his personality is that he loves praise because it is 'reassurance about your yet unproved self' (MH to KG, 2 Feb. 1915).
35 Apart from her frequent comments on his tiredness, insomnia and bouts of depression, and on his prodigious output, see MH Journal, 15 June 1912, 3 June 1915, 26 Dec. 1915, 30 July 1917, 28 Dec. 1917, 30 July 1919, 22 May 1920, 27 Aug. 1920, 8 Feb. 1921. In 1921 he made some effort to relax, fearing that he had a weak heart (MH Journal, 29 March 1921, 19 April 1921, 12 July 1921), but by 25 May 1922 he seems to be hyperactive again, since he says that hyperactivity like his is a disease.
36 e.g. MH Journal, 9 Jan. 1918, 30 Sept. 1922; KG to MH, 13 Dec. 1914, 28 Jan. 1915, 26 Feb. 1922.
37 MH Journal, 5 Feb. 1921.
38 MH Journal, 19 Sept. 1915, 9 May 1917, 28 April 1922.
39 MH Journal, 14 Nov. 1914; see also 2 Dec. 1911, 1 June 1912, 30 June 1915, 26 June 1916 ('I am beginning to feel that many thousands love me'). In 1915 he wrote that he now values praise not for its own sake, but because it spurs him on to greater efforts (KG to MH, 28 Jan. 1915, with her reply, 2 Feb. 1915). On 18 Dec. 1920 he told Mary that he had renounced his vain desire for fame, but Mikhail Naimy claimed that Gibran was always upset by adverse criticism and flattered by the slightest praise (1950, p. 103).
40 MH Journal, 30 July 1919.
41 MH Journal, 30 Dec. 1919; see also 6 Sept. 1914. Against the background of all this blatant desire for approbation, it is disingenuous of Gibran to have written to his friend May Ziadeh on 11 June 1919 that he found all the praise he received in the West tiresome (*Gibran: Love Letters*, pp. 13–14).
42 MH Journal, 3 Dec. 1911 (Kahlil described sexual intercourse as a 'feast, shared by two'), 23 June 1913, 15 Nov. 1914, 9 June 1915, 28 Dec. 1915 (anti-Freud), 5 Oct. 1916 (anti-Freud), 9 May 1917, 30 July 1917, 5 Feb. 1921, 29 March 1921 (anti-Freud), 14 July 1921, 5 Aug. 1921, 8 March 1922, 21 April 1922, 28 April 1922, 16 May 1922, 16 June 1923, 18 June 1924. If it

seems strange that sex should recur as a topic so often in their conversations, it should be remembered that this was an era of sexual reformism, leading in the 1920s to considerable promiscuity. Gibran was in favour of a degree of sexual liberation, but felt that people were becoming too obsessed by it.

43 Mary had already talked obscurely about it in her diary for 11 Jan. 1912, but there is no sign that they had talked about it openly between themselves.

44 MH Diary, 19–20 Feb. 1912.

45 MH to KG, 8 March 1912; KG to MH, 10 March 1912. Otherwise, all the material in this and the next few paragraphs is from Mary's extraordinary March-to-April diary entry.

46 MH Journal, 12 March 1922. On 14 Nov. 1915 he told her that people in the Middle East believe that every poet has a female spirit guide who is his real mate, whether or not he has a living, breathing wife. Since he often told Mary that she inspired his work, we can conclude that he wanted to turn Mary into his spirit guide.

47 She had persuaded herself of this by repeatedly telling her diary that age was the barrier: apart from other occasions already noted in this and the last chapter, see MH Diary, 17 Jan. 1912, 20 Jan. 1912.

48 MH Journal, 27–28 June 1912.

49 She kept this promise, although she had to wait longer than she expected to do so. However, when she did eventually marry her elderly 'uncle', Florance Minis, in 1921, it *was* purely for companionship.

50 MH Journal, 3 April 1912, 7 Sept. 1912; Diary, 7–9 Sept. 1912, 9 Nov. 1912. However, she continued to tease herself with the idea of their possibly getting married until as late as December 1913 (MH Journal, 21 Dec. 1913).

51 e.g. MH Journal, 26–27 Aug. 1912.

52 MH Journal, 30 April 1913, 1 Sept. 1913, 2 Sept. 1913. However, this visit of hers to New York at the end of August and the beginning of September 1913 was particularly turbulent and quarrelsome.

53 On the Armory Show, see p. 133.

54 MH Journal, 3 Sept. 1913.

55 MH Journal, 11 Jan. 1914.

56 MH Journal, 26 April 1914, 20 June 1914. This reasoning recurs as late as 12 March 1922, when Kahlil gave Mary a frank analysis of their relationship over the years.

57 KG to MH, 23 July 1914.

58 MH Journal, 31 Aug. 1914. She had just come back from her usual vigorous vacation. Previously, Kahlil had complained when she put on weight: MH Diary, 9 Nov. 1912.

59 We know little about the more intimate details of Mary's anatomy; but her bust size was 36 (MH to KG, 27 Jan. 1912).

60 MH Journal, 20 Dec. 1914.
61 MH Journal, 29 Dec. 1914, 31 Dec. 1914.
62 MH Journal, 3 June 1915.
63 MH Journal, 28 June 1915. She records a similar conversation in her journal for 28 Dec. 1915. He had warned her the previous year that he was growing distant from the 'physical side of relations' (MH Journal, 19 Dec. 1914), though this turned out to be premature since only ten days later he said, 'My sex feeling is stronger than it was a year ago.'
64 MH Journal, 11 April 1915, 28 Dec. 1915, 12 March 1922. Strangely, on this last date he also held out the possibility that he and Mary might one day have physical sex without it being destructive of their relationship. On spiritual progeny, see also Young, pp. 131–2.
65 MH Journal, appendix to 7 Sept. 1912, 11 Jan. 1914, 30 July 1917.
66 MH Journal, 1 June 1912.
67 See p. 146.
68 Mary quite often notes, although she is naturally inclined to forgive it, that he seems distant or distracted when she is there: he does not always give her his full attention, and does not always want her there. MH Diary, 9 Sept. 1912, 5 Oct. 1912; Journal, 26 June 1913, 31 Aug. 1914, 15 Nov. 1914, 11 April 1915, 3 June 1915, 20 June 1915, 5 Oct. 1916, 30 July 1917, 26–28 Dec. 1917, 12 Jan. 1918. After this date their relationship was not such that she would mind, or note, that he didn't really want her there. In her 1913 diary, which is used for a solid journal-like entry from the page for 1 Jan. until the page for 12 April, she recalls that he seemed almost glad when she was leaving after her visit to New York in Sept. 1912. By Aug. 1915, when she is in New York, she visits him in the evenings only, leaving his days free for work, whereas previously they had spent whole days together.
69 MH Diary, Jan.–April 1913; Journal, 6 June 1911, 6 April 1913, 26 June 1913, 31 Aug. 1913, 1 Sept. 1913, 3 Sept. 1913, 21 Sept. 1913, 21 Dec. 1913, 26 April 1914, 27 Aug. 1915, 13 Nov. 1915, 9 Nov. 1919, 12 March 1922; KG to MH, 30 April 1913, 16 March 1915, 18 April 1915, 10 Feb. 1916. It is also clear that Mary had to economize herself in order to afford her support of Gibran and her other charges: see *KGLW*, p. 249. Gibran also kept money for her as a tax dodge, to deplete her bank account so that the tax man would not know of its existence: MH to KG, 18 April 1917. It is possible that the two unspecified amounts of money in the record belong to this category, rather than to that of gifts from her to him.
70 KG to MH, 19 Dec. 1913. This is just one among many such suggestions of closeness-despite-distance.
71 MH Diary, 28 May–28 June 1912, Jan.–April 1913; Journal, 7 Oct. 1911, 15 June 1912, 6 April 1913, 31 Aug. 1914, 6 Sept. 1914, 9 June 1915, 3 Jan. 1921, and numerous letters (perhaps especially KG to MH, 3 May 1914).

72 The letter Gibran wrote to May Ziadeh after his dream is translated on p. 55 of *Gibran: Love Letters*.
73 Thirty-seven letters are translated in *Gibran: Love Letters*; a few more may be found in *A Self-portrait*, and the draft of a letter is quoted in *KGLW*, pp. 368–9. All these letters are from Gibran to Ziadeh; her letters to him exist, but her family do not wish at this time to release them, and only a few have been published in Arabic.
74 Sherfan (1971), p. 32.

8 Friends and Enemies

1 In a letter to Mary of 12 Dec. 1912, he acknowledges this threshold: 'It seems as though the nice people of New York are begining [*sic*] to know of my being somebody!'
2 MH Journal, 1 June 1911, 19 Dec. 1914, 27 Dec. 1914, 24 March 1918, 24 April 1921. Even when Gibran suffered pangs of nostalgia for the Middle East, he still described the bonds that tied him to New York as 'golden chains' (KG to MZ, 21 May 1921).
3 MH to KG, 18 Oct. 1911, 25 Oct. 1911, 28 Oct. 1911, 3 Nov. 1911; KG to MH, 29 Oct. 1911.
4 MH Journal, 6 April 1915; see also MH Journal, 7 April 1912, where, when she said he should find other women his own age, and not be in love with an older woman such as she was, he says words to the effect of: 'You mean other women to follow the love I had for Charlotte.'
5 *KGLW*, p. 202.
6 CT to MH, 18 Oct. 1911.
7 MH Diary, 5 Oct. 1911.
8 MH Diary, 2 Dec. 1911.
9 Mary talks somewhat primly about Charlotte's 'sex-fever' for Rihani, and even Charlotte later admitted that they were 'slaves and servants to the flesh'. The affair was fitful, and all over by May 1912: MH Diary, May 1912; CT to MH, 13 Jan. 1912, 1 March 1912, 21 May 1912; KG to MH, 6 Jan. 1912, 18 Feb. 1912.
10 CT to MH, 13 Dec. 1911.
11 MH Journal, 11 April 1915.
12 MH Diary, 16–28 May 1912.
13 This is another lie, though not one that Mary could have detected. Gertrude Barrie was only two years older than Kahlil, so in her case at least it is hardly fair to portray himself as an innocent abroad.
14 MH Diary, March–April 1912, May–June 1912; Journal, 3 April 1912, 29 Dec. 1912, 20 June 1914, 26–28 Dec. 1922.

15 MH Journal, 28 June 1915.
16 MH Journal, 14 July 1921, 12 March 1922, 26–28 Dec. 1922.
17 MH Journal, 29 Aug. 1913, 30 Aug. 1913, 4 Sept. 1914, 7 June 1915, 30 July 1917, 1 Sept. 1918, 7 Aug. 1919, 10 Sept. 1920, 5 Feb. 1921, 19 July 1921. In the 1920s the apparent interest he showed in people made women want to use his shoulder to cry on, and to confess the lovelessness of their marriages (MH Journal, 22 May 1920, 7 Sept. 1920, 18 Dec. 1920, 16 May 1922, 26–28 Dec. 1922). This in turn leads to his explaining several times to Mary his views on marriage, which are basically that couples should make friendship the basis of their marriage, have separate rooms, and generally give each other more space (MH Journal, 11 Nov. 1917, 24 April 1921, 16 May 1922, 26–28 Dec. 1922, 26 May 1923, 21 May 1924). The heart of all this is contained in the celebrated passage on marriage in *The Prophet*.
18 Hawi, pp. 103, 104, 108, 183. See also Mikhail Naimy (1950), p. 143, with his oblique reference to 'a Lebanese lady in New York' whom Gibran permitted to 'share his bed'. The rumour about the love letters is retailed in Sheban (reprinted in Sherfan (ed.), *A Third Treasury of Kahlil Gibran*, p. 77).
19 Kraft (ed.) (1981), p. 92.
20 'The Prophet's Profits', *Time*, 13 Aug. 1965.
21 Mikhail Naimy (1950), pp. 216–21; *KGLW*, pp. 432–3.
22 Orfalea (1984), p. 38.
23 MH Journal, 28 Dec. 1915, 6 Sept. 1914; see also 12 Jan. 1914, 3 June 1915, 9 June 1915, 11 June 1915, 24 Aug. 1915, 18 Sept. 1915, 23 April 1916, 5 Oct. 1916, 2 Jan. 1918, 12 July 1921, 8 March 1922, 12 Nov. 1922; KG to MH, 8 Oct. 1913, 5 April 1914. A letter to May Ziadeh on 9 May 1922 is almost a paean to loneliness. But of course some of this loneliness was self-imposed, since he refused to allow anyone near him (see Chapter 1, n. 25); moreover, he often resented the interruptions to his work schedule caused by visitors (MH Journal, 3 April 1912, 23 April 1916, 30 July 1917, 4 Aug. 1919). Mary once described his attitude towards such visitors as 'sour' (Journal, 24 March 1918).
24 The last recorded meeting between Kahlil and Charlotte is when he and Mary went for dinner in Sept. 1912 (MH Journal, 7 Sept. 1912).
25 MH Journal, 1 June 1912, 30 June 1915, 21 April 1916, 23 July 1916. On 29 May 1924 Mary mentions that they talked about Charlotte, but she deliberately doesn't write down what was said.
26 MH Journal, 20 June 1914; for a typical passing reference to a visit from her, see e.g. KG to MH, 21 Jan. 1914.
27 MH Diary, 28 May–29 June 1912; Journal, 31 May 1912, 27 Aug. 1915.
28 MH Journal, 29 May 1924.
29 Huwayyik, p. 170.
30 MH Journal, 31 Nov. 1911.

31 To May Ziadeh, whom he never met, he implied that he went grey at the temples six years later (KG to MZ, 2 Dec. 1923). Contrast his frank acknowledgement of the fact to Mikhail Naimy, to whom he could hardly deny it: *A Self-portrait*, p. 64.

32 MH Diary, 26 Dec. 1910; Journal, 27 Jan. 1911, 17 March 1911, 6 April 1911, 2 Dec. 1911, 2 Jan. 1912, 12 June 1912, appendix to 7 Sept. 1912, 28 Dec. 1912, 22 June 1913, 26 June 1913, 30 June 1915, 26 April 1916, 5 Oct. 1916, 10 Sept. 1917, 4 Aug. 1919, 14 July 1921, 12 Aug. 1921, 12 May 1922, 16 June 1922, 1 June 1924; KG to MZ, 3 Nov. 1920, 2 Dec. 1923, 26 Feb. 1924; Young, p. 126; Bragdon, p. 146.

33 Joseph Gollomb, *Evening Post*, 29 March 1919; Reed, p. 103, corroborates Gibran's cosmopolitan, chameleon-like appearance.

34 I do not mean to imply that Gibran subscribed to any of these beliefs. He was critical of some aspects of spiritualism, while embracing particularly its views on reincarnation and telepathy, was opposed to Rosicrucianism, and also was suspicious of palmistry and astrology (which was highly esteemed by the Theosophical school): MH Journal, 15 June 1912, 26 April 1916, 10 Sept. 1917, 28 Dec. 1915; on telepathy see also KG to MH, 5 June 1910.

35 There was also a general interest in things oriental. Witness, for instance, the success of Ruth St Denis's early dance-shows *Rahda* (1906) and *Egypta* (1910), and the fascination with the discovery of Tutankhamun's tomb in 1922. It is not surprising that Gibran and Ruth St Denis ('the mother of modern dance') should have got on when they met: at the root of her method was the belief that behind each physical gesture lies an emotional or spiritual dimension, which it was her job to express. She was, then, a Gibran of dance, and she said that his works inspired her. When Gibran drew her in 1914 she was at the height of her powers and success. He caught her in a typical pose – supple, graceful, and with bare feet.

36 This delightful snapshot, taken in 1921, is from *The Twenties*, p. 115. And by an odd coincidence we can confirm that Gibran didn't like Milton, because he told Mary so: MH Journal, 26 May 1924.

37 e.g. KG to MH, 18 March 1912; MH Journal, 20 April 1920.

38 Famous people Gibran met in the 1910s include: Carl Jung, Ruth St Denis, Isadora Duncan, Richard Le Gallienne, Rose O'Neill, Bainbridge Colby (a former Secretary of State), John Masefield, Frank Harris, Rabindranath Tagore, Abdul Baha (the founder of the religion Baha'ism), Amy Lowell, Rose Pastor Stokes, Lionel Barrymore, Lord Dunsanay, Edward Markham, Pierre Loti (the only writer apart from Victor Hugo to have been granted a state funeral in France), Anton Bojer, Sarah Bernhardt, Padraic Colum (prolific poet, playwright, essayist, novelist).

39 Mrs Ford herself had aspirations as a writer. Apart from a volume of poetry, *Snickerty Snick* (1919), she contributed, for instance, to the July 1926

issue of *The New Orient* an article entitled 'Akhnaton: Pharaoh and Prophet'. Concrete results of these dinners: Bynner's dedication of a play to Gibran (see note 50), Mackaye's use of Gibran's portrait as the frontispiece to his masque *St Louis*, and Cook's dedication of a volume of poetry to Gibran.

40 She invented the name 'Zanzos' for the alternative world she hoped her artistic friends would enter through the doors of her Washington Square house.

41 MH Journal, 31 Aug.–1 Sept. 1918. Mary's journals from 1912 to 1922, and the letters that passed between them, are mines of information about Gibran's social life in New York.

42 Kraft (ed.) (1981), p. 167.

43 Robert Hillyer, *New York Times Book Review*, 3 April 1949.

44 It is only about 250 words long. It is reproduced in full in *KGLW*, p. 280. Mary sent a long letter, 12 Jan. 1915, with numerous suggestions for improvement, but Gibran accepted only her grammatical corrections.

45 MH Journal, 11 April 1915; KG to MH, 28 Jan. 1915, 9 Feb. 1915, 14 March 1915.

46 MH Journal, 27 Aug. 1915, 21 April 1916, 9 May 1917, 20 April 1920, 12 Aug. 1921; KG to MH, 6 Aug. 1915.

47 This is a guess, but I imagine that Raymond was a repressed homosexual (unlike Bynner, who didn't repress it). He hated women, and had some very delicate habits, such as his hobby of making cut-out silhouettes of English churches.

48 MH Journal, 10 Jan. 1914, 26 April 1914, 20 Dec. 1914, 29 Dec. 1914, 24 Aug. 1915, 30 July 1917; KG to MH, 12 Sept. 1913, 8 March 1914, 19 April 1914, 30 Sept. 1918.

49 MH Journal, 3 June 1915, 23 July 1916, 22 March 1918, 24 March 1918, 29 July 1921, 8 March 1922.

50 The dedication is appropriate because the fast-paced, one-act play looks back on the actions of a Prussian officer, Friedrich, in Syria during the war – especially his rape of a young Syrian girl, whose father returns to take his vengeance. Bynner also wrote the entry about Gibran in *The Borzoi: Being a Sort of Record of Ten Years' Publishing*, which was a tribute to Knopf and his Borzoi imprint – but this tells us nothing about what Bynner really thought of Gibran, because we happen to have the letter of 14 April 1925 in which Gibran fed Bynner all the information, which Bynner simply rewrote in his way for the book.

51 MH Journal, 21–22 July 1916, 26 Aug. 1916, 3 Feb. 1917, 27 July 1917, 10 Nov. 1917, 12 June 1919, 3 Jan. 1921.

52 MH Journal, 3 Sept. 1913, 6 April 1915, 6 June 1915, 30 Dec. 1915, 21–22 July 1916, 3 Feb. 1917, 30 July 1917, 10 Nov. 1917, 31 Aug. 1918, 3 Jan. 1921, 6 Jan. 1921, 8 March 1922, 16 June 1923.

53 After Gibran's departure from Boston, the Boston branch of the Golden Links Society apparently began to disintegrate. Gibran attributed this to his absence: MH Journal, 29 Sept. 1911. He addressed the society again on 13 June 1912, urging them not to get caught on the superficial aspects of American life.
54 Hawi, pp. 157–8; *KGLW*, p. 290. This 'Open Letter to Islam' was published in *Al-Funun* in Nov. 1913, and was followed by an unsigned article entitled 'The Beginning of Revolution', in *As-Sa'ih*, 9 March 1914, which again argued that a prerequisite for revolution in Syria was co-operation between the various religions and sects.
55 See 'The Voice of the Poet' in *The Vision* (= 'A Poet's Voice' in *A Treasury of Kahlil Gibran* and *A Tear and a Smile*).
56 MH Journal, 10 Jan. 1914, 21 April 1916. On his popularity in the Syrian community, see also 28 Dec. 1915.
57 MH Journal, 4 Sept. 1914, 30 July 1917, 10 Sept. 1917.
58 He also comments occasionally on American politics, but invariably in a rather vague fashion. He quite often compares Roosevelt with Wilson, for instance, in Roosevelt's favour, because of the different spirits the two men represent, rather than because of their policies. See e.g. MH Journal, 26 April 1916, 3 Feb. 1917, 9 May 1917, 10 Nov. 1917, 30 Dec. 1919. The naïveté of the level of discussion Mary and Kahlil achieve about American politics is best exemplified in the journal for 26–28 Dec. 1917, when Mary suggested that America was Syria's best hope because any future American president would be a good man and wouldn't let bad things happen to Syria.
59 MH Journal, 29 Sept. 1911, 7 April 1912; KG to MH, 5 Nov. 1912. See also his pleasure in the revolution in Yemen (MH Journal, 17 March 1911). Gibran's hopes were only partially fulfilled: the Italian victory over the Ottomans in Tripolitania (Libya) did result in the Turkish loss of that country, at least.
60 MH Journal, 30 Aug. 1914, 20 Dec. 1914, 20 June 1915; KG to MH, 1 Nov. 1914, 17 Nov. 1918. See also his similar remarks following the abdication of the Czar in March 1916: KG to MH, 18 March 1916.
61 MH Journal, 30 Aug. 1914, 14 Nov. 1914. Round about this time he drafted a play on the subject of Syrian independence, but it was never finished (Hawi, p. 109).
62 KG to MH, 22 Oct. 1912.
63 As Gibran admitted: MH Journal, 9 Nov. 1919.
64 MH Journal, 8 Nov. 1919. This represents a slight change of view from before the war, when he had favoured English over French protection of Syria (MH Journal, 30 Aug. 1914).
65 MH Journal, 27 Dec. 1914, 27 July 1917.
66 KG to MH, 20 Aug. 1914, 20 Sept. 1914, 26 Feb. 1918. In letters to her

written on 21 Jan. 1918 and 5 Feb. 1918, he gives as a symptom of this welcome change of consciousness Americans' greater receptivity to his poetry!

67 Some eyewitness accounts in Orfalea (1988), pp. 66–71. Gibran rightly blamed the Turks for the famine (MH Journal, 21–22 July 1916, 26 Aug. 1916, 5 Oct. 1916, 26–28 Dec. 1917, 31 Aug.–1 Sept. 1918, 30 July 1919; KG to MH, 29 June 1916, 22 Aug. 1916). Although the British and French were blockading the Syrian coast as a whole, as part of their anti-Turkish moves, there was no actual starvation in coastal towns such as Beirut; the famine in the mountains arose because the Turks were preventing any grain getting through. With the help of the US government, the Relief Committee shipped money, food and medicines in mid-November 1916: KG to MH, 5 Nov. 1916; MH to KG, 12 Nov. 1916. After the war the US government sent a great deal of financial aid to Syria, which by then was more or less colonized. It was divided into three Occupied Enemy Territory Administrations – the south (i.e. Palestine), under Great Britain, the east (i.e. the interior of Syria), under Arab administration, and the west (i.e. coastal Syria and Lebanon), under France, as Gibran had wished.

68 MH Journal, 31 Dec. 1914.

69 MH Journal, 5 Oct. 1916.

70 A letter to Mary describing the suffering in Mount Lebanon led her to suggest that he donate $400 out of the money he was holding for her; he felt that was too much, because his main target was the Syrians in America and he didn't want them to think they need do nothing because white Americans would do it all. In the end, he gave $150 in her name, but she insisted on his giving the other $250 as well, and got her school also to raise money for the fund.

71 MH Journal, 26 Aug. 1916, 9 May 1917, 26–28 Dec. 1917, 31 Dec. 1917, 30 July 1919. He also sacrificed his usual summer vacation out of town: 'It is so hot that even one's most distant self becomes weary! And yet I must stay here and work for my stricken people' (KG to Oppenheim, 12 July 1916).

72 *The Syrian World*, Feb. 1929, pp. 32–3.

73 As a child he had suffered a bad fall which broke his left shoulder (MH Journal, 30 June 1915, 20 April 1920), and now this weak left side became partially paralysed, as a result, Gibran says, of a nervous breakdown (letter to Witter Bynner, Sept. 1916). After electrical treatment in New York, Gibran retreated with Marianna to Cohasset, a village on the coast south of Boston where he liked to spend the summer, and bathed his weak side in the sun until he was better – and striped with a sun-tanned left side and a paler 'wright' side.

74 MH Journal, 30 July 1917.

75 KG to MH, 10 June 1913; MH Journal, 29 Dec. 1914, 9 May 1917, 30 July 1917, 10 Nov. 1917, 26–28 Dec. 1917. He could not join the American army, as Mikhail Naimy did, presumably because he was not an American

citizen; although he thought about becoming one in 1910 and 1911, during the period of his engagement to Mary, there is no record of his having actually done so. This was not unusual: by 1930, only some 62 per cent of Syrian immigrants had taken US citizenship (Naff, p. 255).

76 KG to MH, 10 June 1913, 10 July 1913, 14 Oct. 1917, 31 Oct. 1917; MH Journal, 22 June 1913. KG to Witter Bynner, 15 March 1918. It is certainly true that the Arab Congress achieved little in terms of the devolution of Syria, although they won a few minor concessions from the Young Turks.

77 KG to MH, 8 March 1914; MH Journal, 26–28 Dec. 1917. There were certainly assassinations and executions within Syria, but none that I know of outside of it. As a result of the harsh executions in 1915, 6 May is still known in Syria and Lebanon as 'Martyrs' Day'.

78 MH Journal, 6 Sept. 1914 (he argued in favour of the war at a dinner party), 27 July 1917, 31 Aug.–1 Sept. 1918 (where Gibran says that Bynner has 'lapsed' back to pacifism after having been converted by Gibran to his stance on the war). Gibran believed that pacifism was not a natural state for man, whose 'ill-at-easiness' is bound to find some outlet (KG to MH, 16 May 1912). Every part of the world is in conflict with its surroundings; conflict is natural, and so human warfare is natural too; every struggle is a struggle for life, not death (KG to MH, 14 Oct. 1914).

79 For Gibran on socialism, see the references in Chapter 2, note 38.

80 MH Journal, 27 July 1917; see also 23 July 1916.

9 The Wordsmith

1 KG to MH, 16 May 1913; see also various letters between them from Dec. 1912 to April 1913.

2 The most important journal entries are as follows: 25 Dec. 1912, 6 April 1913, 26 June 1913, 26 April 1914, 6 Sept. 1914, 27 Dec. 1914, 11 April 1915, 20 June 1915, 24 Aug. 1915, 25 Aug. 1915, 19 Sept. 1915, 26 Dec. 1915, 28 Dec. 1915, 30 Dec. 1915, 21 April 1916, 23 April 1916, 23 July 1916, 11 Nov. 1916, 9 May 1917, 11 Nov. 1917, 12 Jan. 1918, 22 March 1918, 7 Dec. 1918, 9/12 June 1919, 22 May 1920, 19 July 1921; and three important letters are KG to MH, 30 Jan. 1916, 10 Feb. 1916, 3 Jan. 1917. What I have called Gibran's 'cosmology' is also discussed by Ghougassian, pp. 380 ff.

3 MH Journal, 2 Jan. 1923; see also 22 May 1920.

4 MH Journal, 24 Aug. 1915.

5 Contra MH Journal, 31 Dec. 1922: 'God is everything and everywhere.'

6 This is a remarkably far-sighted vision, given that there were people even in the 1950s who were still denying the possibility of space travel.

7 e.g. MH Journal, 3 Sept. 1920.

8 See e.g. MH Journal, 26 July 1921.
9 MH Journal, 25 Aug. 1915, 28 Dec. 1915, 21 April 1916, 12 Jan. 1918.
10 MH Journal, 21 April 1916.
11 MH Journal, 11 April 1915, 26 Dec. 1915. For Mary's disbelief, see e.g. MH Journal, 3 Feb. 1917; MH to KG, 27 Jan. 1912.
12 MH Journal, 26 April 1914, 7–8 Dec. 1918, 9 Nov. 1919.
13 MH Journal, 24 Aug. 1915, 19 Sept. 1915, 23 April 1916; KG to MH, 30 Jan. 1916.
14 KG to MH, 3 May 1912.
15 *The Madman*, p. 10; *The Earth Gods*, pp. 12-13; 'The Giants', in *Thoughts and Meditations*, pp. 98–9.
16 KG to MH, 1 March 1916.
17 MH Journal, 8 Nov. 1919. It seems that Knopf was encouraging him in this plan (MH Journal, 14 April 1919); since it never came to fruition, it may be that the discouraging sales of *Twenty Drawings* gave Knopf cold feet.
18 It foundered in 1914, was revived in 1916 (Mikhail Naimy came to New York to help), but it soon died again; there was one last unsuccessful effort to resuscitate it in 1919.
19 This was not the first time the book had been hailed as heralding such a renaissance. Some Arabic reviewers said much the same in 1912: KG to MH, 6 May 1912. Gibran claimed to have been aware while writing it that it was a departure for Arabic literature: MH Journal, 1 June 1912.
20 For summaries of Naimy's career, see Nadeem Naimy (1985) and Orfalea (1984). Both these books also contain summaries of Rihani's career as a writer.
21 KG to MZ, 28 Jan. 1920.
22 Quoted in Hawi, p. 184, and Naimy (1950), p. 126.
23 See Hawi, p. 184.
24 Oddly, in some quarters the lie seems to have taken root – unless this is just ignorance: in her book on Amy Lowell, when recording the meeting between Lowell and Gibran at a dinner party at Mrs Ford's in March 1919, Jean Gould describes him as 'the famous Indian poet'.
25 KG to MH, 16 May 1913.
26 However, this is not to say that he concentrated entirely on a single medium. In a letter to May Ziadeh on 3 Nov. 1920, for instance, he talks about some large oil paintings he is doing.
27 A measure of their confidence is that they concocted a plan to make an anonymous offer, through Montross, of one of Gibran's paintings to the Metropolitan Museum (MH to KG, 20 Nov. 1914; MH Journal, 19 Dec. 1914). The museum refused the offer (MH Journal, 28 Dec. 1914). After Gibran's death, however, they accepted Mary's gift of five paintings

and drawings – portraits of Albert Ryder and John Masefield, 'Toward the Infinite', 'I Have Come Down the Ages', and 'The Life Circle', from *Jesus, The Son of Man*.

28 MH Journal, 29 Aug. 1913.

29 Typically, Gibran claimed not that Montross didn't want to exhibit his pictures again, but that he had gone off Montross, as being too grasping and commercial: MH Journal, 13 Nov. 1915.

30 The Mortens, Rose O'Neill and Julia Ford were already owners of other Gibrans.

31 CT to MH, 25 Dec. 1914, 28 Feb. 1915. When Charlotte read *The Madman*, she found it 'autoerotic' (letter to MH, 23 Dec. 1918).

32 See also her letter to Mary cited in Chapter 5, note 11. The phrase 'terrible honesty', coined by Raymond Chandler, gave Ann Douglas the title of her wonderful book about 1920s New York.

33 MH Journal, 13 Nov. 1915, 26 Dec. 1915, 12 Jan. 1918.

34 KG to MH, 11 Feb. 1917; MH Journal, 3 Feb. 1917.

35 In November 1919, some of his wash drawings were on display in St Mark's Church, in the Bowery, where Gibran was friendly with the priest, William Norman Guthrie. But this hardly counts as an official exhibition. MH Journal, 8 Nov. 1919. After Gibran's death, Guthrie and St Mark's remained extraordinarily faithful to Gibran, and put on an annual adaptation of *The Prophet* as a religious drama (Young, p. 33). On the 1922 Boston exhibition, see KG to MH, 6 Oct. 1921, and MH Journal, 9 Jan. 1922. The rooms were all wrong and the show was generally disappointing. He was also close to an exhibition in London in 1922, but decided against it: KG to MH, 27 March 1922.

36 For instance, the first four issues contained five of Gibran's parables.

37 MH Journal, 3 Feb. 1917.

38 A perceptive reviewer – 'W.S.B.' – of *The Madman* in the Boston *Evening Transcript* for 25 Jan. 1919 considered that Gibran had been 'introduced to us in the pages of Mr. Oppenheim's magazine, *The Seven Arts*'.

39 KG to MH, 31 Jan. 1917. For committee work after the war, see KG to MH, 18 Oct. 1918, 27 Nov. 1918, 4 Nov. 1919.

40 KG to MH, 14 March 1915. Mikhail Naimy (1950, p. 140) reports another occasion, in 1916 or 1917, when Gibran was hissed off the stage of the Poetry Society after reading 'Night and the Madman', but I have not been able to verify this story.

41 MH Journal, 20 April 1920.

42 Resnikoff died of tuberculosis early in 1920. Gibran met him once or twice, but is probably exaggerating when he tells Mary that Resnikoff 'loved him' (MH Journal, 17 April 1920). It is interesting to see Gibran helping out a socialist – the concerts were sometimes used as socialist fund-raisers – since,

as we have seen, he was not entirely in sympathy with their aims or philosophy.
43 We hear about his reading or lecturing to the Poetry Society from time to time in the letters and journals: KG to MH, 28 Jan. 1918, 5 Feb. 1918, 26 Feb. 1918, 10 March 1918, 11 June 1918; KG to Witter Bynner, 15 March 1918; MH Journal, 9 Jan. 1918, 22 March 1918. Another lecture on art and literature, East and West, was delivered to some club at Columbia University (MH Journal, 23 July 1916), and one on Syria in Newark (KG to MH, 28 Jan. 1918). He would also read his poetry to more informal gatherings – at Mrs Robinson's, for instance.
44 MH Journal, 30 Dec. 1919, 17 April 1920, 20 Aug. 1920, 18 Dec. 1920, 5 Feb. 1921. This last approach by Pond's was for a one-off reading in New York, but Gibran again refused, on the grounds that he didn't want to produce stuff 'to order'. We hear no more about Pond's after that, which may be due to the sketchiness of our sources for Gibran's life in the 1920s, but may also be due to Pond's simply giving up on him.
45 The metaphor occurs as early as 1910 in a letter from Gibran to Rihani, dated 11 Nov. 1910.
46 See p. 69.
47 MH Journal, 11 June 1915, 13 Nov. 1915, 30 Dec. 1919. In a 1921 letter to Mikhail Naimy, Gibran explicitly identified himself as mad, and called on 'Mischa' to join him in this state (*A Self-portrait*, pp. 61–2). In July 1916 Gibran outlined to Mary a long poem he was planning to write, but apparently never got around to, which again had a 'madman' as the central character (MH Journal, 21–22 July 1916).
48 Mentions in the journals: 19 Jan. 1911 (diary), 29 March 1911, 10 June 1911, 12 June 1912, 29 Aug. 1913, 30 Aug. 1914, 31 Aug. 1914, 2 Sept. 1914, 4 Sept. 1914, 6 Sept. 1914, 10 April 1915, 3 June 1915, 7 June 1915, 11 June 1915, 20 June 1915, 13 Nov. 1915, 21 April 1916, 5 Oct. 1916, 3 Feb. 1917, 10 Sept. 1917, 11 Nov. 1917, 12 Jan. 1918, 22 March 1918. Mentions in letters (either KG to MH or MH to KG): 21 Sept. 1913 (when Kahlil first recruited Mary to be his English-language editor for the book), 10 May 1916, 14 May 1916, 3 Jan. 1917, 12 Jan. 1917, 15 Jan. 1917, 14 Oct. 1917, 20 Oct. 1917, 31 Oct. 1917, 5 Feb. 1918. All these letters are concerned with Mary's editing of various parables. The following letters concern the book's publication: 29 May 1918, 21 June 1918, 11 July 1918, 8 Aug. 1918, 30 Sept. 1918, 18 Oct. 1918. Three letters mention reviews: 17 Dec. 1918, 21 Jan. 1919, 23 Jan. 1919.
49 Nadeem Naimy (1975), p. 61.
50 Note that this English 'Grave-digger' is not the same as the earlier Arabic 'Grave-digger', which was included in *The Tempests*.
51 MH Journal, 30 Aug. 1914, 6 Sept. 1914, 21 April 1916, 31 Aug. 1918.
52 MH Journal, 10 June 1911.
53 MH Journal, 6 Sept. 1914.

54 A few of the fables are in fact traditional Lebanese tales: Hawi, p. 275.
55 KG to Witter Bynner, 15 March 1918. Assuming that one thing would have led to another, and that either of these publishing houses could have ended up with *The Prophet*, they must have regretted rejecting this first English book.
56 KG to MH, 29 May 1918, 11 June 1918, 21 June 1918, 30 Sept. 1918, 18 Oct. 1918; MH Journal, 31 Aug. 1918, 9 June 1919, 24 April 1921, 16 May 1922, 26 May 1924.
57 *KGLW*, p. 325.
58 Wilkinson, pp. 27, 95.
59 Once in New York, in Gibran's presence, and the other time in Cairo: MH Journal, 17 April 1920, 22 May 1920.
60 KG to MH, 11 July 1918, 8 Aug. 1918, 26 Aug. 1918; MH Journal, 10 Sept. 1917.
61 MH Journal, 10 Nov. 1917.
62 MH Journal, 26 April 1916, 6 Jan. 1918, 11 Sept. 1922; see also 18 Sept. 1915.
63 Gibran himself said, 'There is a sort of promise of the Prophet in the farewell of *The Forerunner*' (MH Journal, 30 May 1922).
64 They worked together on various of the parables when they met (MH Journal, 30 July 1919, 6 Aug. 1919, 7 Aug. 1919, 14 Aug. 1919, 8 Nov. 1919, 30 Dec. 1919, 17 April 1920) and by post (MH to KG, early June 1918; KG to MH, 7 May 1919). The comment about the spoken and the unspoken is reflected in a letter from KG to MH, 26 Oct. 1920. At much the same time Gibran was also revising some of his Arabic pieces for an anthology which was to be published in Cairo. *Al-'Awasif* (*The Tempests*) contains the poems whose largely bitter nature has been summarized on p. 206. MH Journal, 9/12 June 1919, 30 July 1919.
65 KG to MZ, 9 Nov. 1919. Mikhail Naimy may be right in thinking that the title was taken from Nietzsche (1950, p. 124).
66 MH to KG, 25 April 1920.
67 MH Journal, 18 April 1920, 18 Dec. 1920, 5 Feb. 1921.
68 MH Journal, 30 Sept. 1922.
69 MH Journal, 19 Nov. 1922.
70 MH Journal, 28 April 1922. On the messianic phase, see p. 147.
71 See also MH Journal, 30 Dec. 1919: critics write only for themselves.

10 The Pen Club

1 MH Journal, 23 April 1916.
2 Mikhail Naimy (1950), pp. 154–5.

3 Mikhail Naimy (1950), p. 157.
4 See e.g. Hawi, p. 114, and various letters to Naimy in *A Self-portrait*, and in the appendix to Naimy's biography. On fund-raising, see MH Journal, 7 Sept. 1920. In fact the Club was financed largely by a single man, the Lebanese immigrant philanthropist Salim Malouk, a linen importer with a shop on 5th Avenue.
5 MH Journal, 27 Feb. 1919, 27 Aug. 1920.
6 MH Journal, 18 Dec. 1920, 5 Aug. 1921. Translation by Ferris in *Spiritual Sayings*.
7 In the issue for April 1920, for instance, there are two of his wash drawings. Both are rather bad, but they are in good company: there are pieces by W. B. Yeats, Witter Bynner, Edmund Wilson, Hart Crane, Djuna Barnes and Van Wyck Brooks, and a reproduction of 'Clair de Lune' by Cézanne. *The Dial* was originally a Transcendentalist magazine, edited first by Margaret Fuller, and then by Emerson and Thoreau.
8 He refurbished the studio in shades of grey in the spring of 1917, and then again in the summer of 1920: MH Journal, 9 May 1917, 13 Nov. 1920. Along with other residents of the studio building, he also became a part-owner of it in 1920, apparently with the help of Mary's generosity: KG to MH, 11 May 1920. Nevertheless, later he once regretted not having had more money at the time of the buy-out, so as to gain the controlling vote in the building: MH Journal, 31 Dec. 1922. Typically, he gives himself the credit for initiating the buy-out: MH Journal, 17 April 1920. The studio was repainted again in 1924 and 1929: MH Journal, 21 May 1924; KG to MH, 8 Nov. 1929.
9 See also MH Journal, 31 Dec. 1922. In many respects his warnings went unheeded. Local dress largely gave way to Western clothing; thousands of cars roared down roads that had previously seen nothing more noisy than a donkey; the race for purchasing Western munitions was on.
10 The title of Kanfer's article is bewildering, until it is recognized as a partial quote from *Sand and Foam*: 'Worms will turn; but is it not strange that even elephants will yield?' (p. 57).
11 See Greenfeld, Beidler ('pretentious bombast, homogenized religiosity, vapid metaphysics'), Moosa ('puerile emotionalism', in the introduction to Huwayyik, p. 44), or Williams's talk of Gibran's diffuse sentimentalism. The popular teenage comic *Mad* once parodied Gibran as 'Kahlil Gibrish'.
12 Correspondents in the 16 July 1972 issue of the *New York Times* magazine, responding to Kanfer's piece, included Kathleen Smith, who pointed out that 'cleverness is not truth, nor bitchiness journalism', and Charles Stinson of the Department of Religion at Dartmouth College, who rightly said: '[Gibran's] continuing popularity calls for a critical – and civilized – analysis' rather than 'the literary equivalent of a street mugging'.
13 MH Journal, 20 Aug. 1920.

14 *The Complete Works of Ralph Waldo Emerson*, ed. Edward Waldo Emerson (Boston: Houghton Mifflin, 1903–12), vol. 9, p. 193. His essay 'Quotation and Originality' should also be read in this context.
15 MH Journal, 21 April 1916.
16 The essay occupies pp. 241–65 of *The Portable Emerson*, ed. Carl Bode and Malcolm Cowley (New York: Penguin Books, 1946).
17 Dorra, p. 9.
18 Bowra (1943), p. 6.
19 Reynolds, pp. 133, 252, 257, 263; the quote paraphrases Whitman's address to the Brooklyn Art Union on 31 March 1851.
20 It is interesting that the Arabic word for 'poet', *sha'er*, is related to the verb 'to feel': a poet is a sensitive soul, more receptive to subtle influences than the rest of us. This undoubtedly paved the way for Gibran's adoption of the role of united poet and prophet.
21 Norwood: *The Syrian World*, April 1931, p. 35; Bragdon: *Merely Players*, p. 140.
22 MH Journal, 5 June 1915, 21 April 1916, 26 April 1916, 23 July 1916, 27 July 1917, 7–8 Dec. 1918, 4 Aug. 1919, 18 April 1920, 21 April 1920, 8 Jan. 1921, 30 Sept. 1922.
23 MH Journal, 6 May 1918. Mary agreed that the 'hermit poet' of *The Prophet* was a perfect delineation of Gibran himself: MH Journal, 6 May 1918, 23 June 1923. On 30 August 1921, she says simply, 'How absolutely the Prophet is Kahlil,' though noting that he denies it. The Forerunner, another of Gibran's alter egos, is also likened to a prophet in the closing pages of the book.
24 For instance, MH Journal, 27 Jan. 1911, 10 March 1911, 30 Aug. 1913.
25 See p. 147.
26 KG to MH, 30 Jan. 1916, 10 Feb. 1916, 1 March 1916.
27 KG to MH, 9 April 1916; MH Journal, 9 June 1915.
28 KG to MH, 21 Jan. 1914.
29 See KG to MH, 11 Jan. 1915, 4 May 1919, 18 Dec. 1920; MH Journal, 13 Nov. 1915. However, it is to be hoped that Gibran could recognize the fact that it was only a few modernist ministers – the kind who were inclined to embrace Baha'ism (see MH Journal, 31 March 1921, for Baha'ism at St Mark's, the main New York church to adopt Gibran) and for whom God was 'a sort of oblong blur' (a priest quoted in Frederick Allen, p. 167) – who were open to his message.
30 KG to MH, 18 Dec. 1920. Likewise, on 25 Aug. that year he told Mary that spreading consciousness was his career.
31 The *true* poet only: 'Poetry is a flash of lightning; it becomes mere composition when it is an arrangement of words' (*Spiritual Sayings*, p. 32).
32 *Sand and Foam*, p. 64; MH Journal, 30 Sept. 1922; see also 30 Dec. 1919.

33 See also the stories 'Poets' and 'The Scholar and the Poet', both in *The Forerunner*.
34 Penguin edition, p. 112.
35 MH Journal, 6 April 1913.
36 *The Garden of the Prophet*, p. 60. On the universality of the poet's perception, see also 'The Voice of the Poet', best translated in Juan Cole's collection *The Vision*, pp. 19–26.
37 Juan Cole's translation, *The Vision*, p. 79.
38 All three pieces may be found in Anthony Ferris's collection *A Treasury of Kahlil Gibran*. The poem, part of which I have quoted, is translated by Juan Cole in *The Vision*, and by H. M. Nahmad in *A Tear and a Smile* (which also contains 'The Poet's Death Is His Life'). 'The Lonely Poet' is also translated as 'The Poet' in Andrew Ghareeb's collection *Prose Poems*, and as 'The Poet' again in John Walbridge's collection *The Storm*.
39 From *A Treasury of Kahlil Gibran*, p. 3.
40 Kheirallah, p. 30.
41 Not that he was without his critics in the Arabic-speaking world. He once famously said to them, 'Your saying that you do not understand me is a compliment which I do not deserve, and an insult which you do not deserve.'
42 MH Journal, 6 April 1913, 30 Aug. 1914.
43 In the context of considering his impact on Arabic literature, it is curious that in a letter written in 1941 (Kraft, 1981, pp. 166–7), Witter Bynner, describing how he came to introduce Gibran to the publisher Alfred A. Knopf, says: 'He was already an established writer, in fact a living classic in Arabic.' But since Bynner did not read Arabic, it is not clear how he reached this hyperbolic conclusion. Perhaps Gibran himself gave him that impression! It certainly seems to have been current publicity material: a reviewer in the Boston *Evening Transcript* for 25 Jan. 1919 claims that in the Arab world Gibran is considered 'the genius of the epoch'.
44 Philip Hitti, writing in a series of tributes to Gibran in *The Syrian World* for February 1929, naturally attributed the influence to Gibran alone rather than the Mahjar school in general: 'The influence which Gibran exercises in modern Arabic literature can be measured, in a way, not only by the multitude of people who have been benefited by reading him, but also by the big crop of would-be Gibrans, quasi-Gibrans and Gibran-imitators who have in recent years, mushroom-like, sprung up and flourished all over the Arabic-speaking world.'
45 From his introduction to Kheirallah's translation.
46 In Gibran's case, the influence of the Bible may be divided between the parables of the New Testament, affecting his parables and homilies, and the poetry of some of the Old Testament books, such as Job, Isaiah and Jeremiah, affecting his devotional language and incantational rhythms.

47 Penguin edition, pp. 198–9; Dover edition, pp. 185–6.
48 Jayyusi, p. 85.
49 See Dorra, p. 141.
50 Ostle in Hourani and Shehadi (eds), p. 212.
51 He himself was aware of his originality in this respect. He told Mary that he hated being constrained by language, and even as a child was always looking for his own way of expressing himself. He claimed to have coined new words and invented new rhythms which other writers then imitated. MH Journal, 6 Sept. 1914, 17 Sept. 1920, 3 Jan. 1921, 2 Jan. 1923. Interestingly, when Gibran and other *émigré* writers are accused of making 'mistakes' in their Arabic (as by Khemiri [in Khemiri and Kampffmeyer]), 'mistakes' means 'neologisms' and 'grammatical licence'; such was the hold of tradition on Arabic writing and criticism.
52 Hawi, p. 247.
53 See especially Chapter 3, notes 18, 27 and 29.
54 Hawi, p. 113. It should be noted that, naturally, not all Arab critics have celebrated the Romantic revolution in their literature and Gibran's part in it. In his own lifetime, on top of the official disapproval of his works by the Church and State authorities, he was constantly attacked by the influential Lebanese literary periodical *Al-Mashriq*. Posthumously, Eugene Paul Nasser, in particular, took Gibran to task for his vaporous form and transcendental content, his 'cold abstractions of Love and Life', and so on. See the extracts in Orfalea and Elmusa (eds), pp. 152–60, from Nasser's 'A Disputation with Kahlil Gibran'.
55 From Amin Rihani, 'Gibran', excerpts from which are translated in Orfalea and Elmusa (eds).
56 Given the extent of the influence of Walt Whitman on Gibran's style (on which see especially Suhail Hanna's article 'Gibran and Whitman'), it is a historical curiosity that Oscar Wilde deconstructed Whitman in exactly the same terms, and judged that he 'would be recalled as a philosopher-prophet but not as a poet' (Reynolds, p. 539).

11 The Prophet

1 p. 29.
2 Douglas, p. 70.
3 MH Diary, 20 May 1925, 1 Sept. 1925. Even after Gibran's funeral she returned to find Florance 'perfectly unsmiling': MH Diary, 21 April 1931.
4 'C.J.': e.g. MH Diary, 30 April 1928; 'J. Grinch': MH Diary, 10 May 1926. In 1930 she also started to use an extraordinary and uncrackable code in her diary. Strange ciphers begin to appear in her entry for 12 July, consisting

of letters and numerals, such as 'L1'. The letters used are L, Ph, P, Sp and C. The numbers increase over the days, and the ciphers accumulate until the entry for 5 Aug., for instance, reads: 4L-67-Ph7-P3'. Fortunately she left for posterity a later pencilled comment that these ciphers refer in some way to her work on 'K. Gibran's mss'. What she doesn't tell us is which manuscripts. The Gibrans suggest (*KGLW*, p. 396) that she was working on *The Earth Gods*, which was due to be published in 1931. It is certainly possible that she did work on *The Earth Gods*, but the Gibrans fail to take into account the fact that there are 108 such coded entries between 12 July and 2 Nov. 1930, and *The Earth Gods* is so short that it cannot have taken her so much time to edit; note also that she says 'mss' not 'ms' in the singular. Moreover, the coded entries resume in 1931, after Gibran's death, from 18 July almost daily until 26 October, and then again for a week from 16–22 May 1932. She was working on *The Wanderer* then. She says in her diary that she started work on that book on 24 April 1931, not in July. Since there are plenty of pencilled remarks on the extant letters and journals, my guess is that they are what she was rereading and editing, but I cannot crack the code, and I remain far from sure, especially since at least some of the journals were in Gibran's studio in New York in 1930, where Mary found them on 18 April 1931, and packed them up for sending to Savannah. Perhaps she was working on a portion of them in 1930, and the rest afterwards. But why the variety of letters, L, Ph, and so on? They appear to refer to a variety of works.

5 Published by Brentano's with a preface by no less than Arthur Symons, Gibran would have appreciated the optimistic and metaphysical style of the poems. He contributed a frontispiece of pale figures ascending winding steps and beckoning to encourage others to rise from cavernous depths to the light, and four further paintings: 'Silence', 'Compensation', 'Loneliness' and 'Life Answers'.

6 See e.g. MH Journal, 26 May 1923. His books were quite commonly being translated into foreign languages these days too.

7 Others died (like Raymond in 1928) or moved away (like Bynner in 1922).

8 Young, p. 129. A measure of his position in New York society is that in both 1925 and 1929 there were big celebrations of his birthday, the first held by his American friends (KG to MZ, 12 Jan. 1925), the second by the Syrians. This was a huge banquet, nominally in honour of his achievements in literature, but coincidentally on the evening before his birthday; it was commemorated with a special issue of *The Syrian World*, which reprinted the address given by the eminent academic Philip K. Hitti, as well as a poem by Barbara Young and a tribute to Gibran's compassion by Salloum Mokarzel.

9 e.g. MH Journal, 29 May 1923: 'I dine out oftener than alone.'

10 Trips out of New York: KG to MZ, 11 Jan. 1921, 21 May 1921, 1–3 Dec. 1923; KG to MH, 6 Oct. 1921, 20 Oct. 1921, 7 Aug. 1923, 4 Sept. 1924, 25 Aug. 1925, 16 May 1929; MH Journal, 14 April 1922, 16 June 1922, 11 Sept. 1922, 26 May 1923, 21 May 1924; Mikhail Naimy (1950), pp. 168 ff.

11 KG to MH, 22 April 1924; see also MH Journal, 29 March 1921, 21 Nov. 1922. He was reading little, too (MH Journal, 20 Dec. 1919). Late in 1929, he told Mary that his 'responsibilities in the East' were over, the implication being that he would now have to spend less time in Boston: KG to MH, 8 Nov. 1929. This is the letter in which he came up with the *mot* chosen for his memorial plaque in Copley Square, Boston (see p. 132): 'It was in my heart to help a little because I was helped much, and I am glad of it all.' In the original letter, however, he goes on to complain that he has found it hard work: 'The next time I shall measure, and measure well, the distance between my desire and my ability, and I shall not walk save in clear light.'

12 MH Journal, 12 Nov. 1922. There is plenty of evidence from journals and letters for Gibran's failing health in the 1920s.

13 p. 18.

14 See the references on sex in Chapter 7, note 42.

15 MH Journal, 20 May 1920.

16 Young, pp. 26–7. The 'hell of machinery' is due, presumably, to the fact that 'When man invents a machine, he runs it; then the machines begin to run him, and he becomes the slave of his slave' (*Spiritual Sayings*, p. 39).

17 KG to MZ, 1925, in *A Self-portrait*, p. 82; 'golden chains' in KG to MZ, 21 May 1921.

18 As well as 70 regular theatres, New York also boasted around 800 movie theatres.

19 MH Journal, 21 May 1924, and a number of letters between them, Sept. 1924 to May 1925.

20 St Sergius was a local saint, a martyr who became popular as a saint in the fifth and sixth centuries. The inhabitants of Bsharri gifted the land around his shrine to the Carmelites in the sixteenth century, and they built the existing monastery there.

21 So much so that there was a punning rhyme: *al-Rabita al-Qalamiyya*, the Pen Club, was known as *al-Rabitah al-Qadahiyya*, the Drinking Club, a *Qadahiyya* being a glass for arak.

22 *KGLW*, pp. 388–9, 395.

23 Witter Bynner to Lorraine M. George, 13 Feb. 1941 (in Kraft (ed.), pp. 166–7).

24 Witter Bynner to Idella Purnell Stone, 30 Dec. 1930 (in Kraft (ed.), p. 92).

25 See MH Journal, 26 June 1913, 31 Aug. 1913, 10 Nov. 1917.

26 *KGLW*, p. 394.

27 Sheban (reprinted in Sherfan (ed.), *A Third Treasury of Kahlil Gibran*, p. 77).
28 Gibran declared himself to be a 'wet', opposed to Prohibition, on the grounds that it didn't work and that a little wine was good for you: MH Journal, 3 Feb. 1917.
29 Douglas, p. 24.
30 Mikhail Naimy (1950), p. 171. The Gibrans too take this story as genuine: *KGLW*, p. 349. Typically, Barbara Young implies that it was her to whom Gibran made this remark (p. 12), just as elsewhere she makes herself Gibran's partner in conversations lifted from Mary Haskell's journals.
31 Reed, pp. 61–2, 102–5. Among the Delphics, Gibran was particularly close to Syud Hossain, the editor of *The New Orient* magazine, and Sarojini Naidu, poet, feminist and colleague of Mahatma Gandhi, who became the first female President of the Indian National Congress in 1925. Just as Gibran's studio was called 'the Hermitage', so Orozco's was called 'the Ashram'.
32 KG to MH, 19 March 1923; he complains about the book also in MH Journal, 12 July 1921, 14 July 1921, 22 July 1921, 5 May 1922 (unless this is another book which never materialized).
33 See p. 221. Gibran hoped the poem would be banned again, and so generate publicity and sales for the book: MH Journal, 5 Aug. 1921.
34 It can be found in English in *The Storm*, but it is also printed in *A Second Treasury of Kahlil Gibran* as 'The Master's Journey to Venice'.
35 MH Journal, 30 Dec. 1915.
36 We first hear about such sayings in MH Journal, 31 Aug. 1920, but then in a thick burst thereafter: 3 Sept. 1920, 7 Sept. 1920, 10 Sept. 1920, 3 Jan. 1921. However, Gibran continued to write them long after they dropped out of Mary's journals. Perhaps his confidence in his English was now such that he no longer felt the need to run such short pieces by her.
37 *The Prophet* sequel: MH Journal, 30 Aug. 1921; *The Way of the Seven Days*, MH Journal, 3 Sept. 1920. It is possible that the idea of the seven-day journey was taken over for an Arabic poem, since Kahlil told Mary in 1922 that he was up to the sixth day of such a poem, in which a pessimist changes gradually, day by day, into an optimist (MH Journal, 30 Sept. 1922); but I have not been able to identify this Arabic poem.
38 For instance, he told Mary that his 1922 three-month summer in Scituate, south of Boston, was a refreshing time, during which he wrote some of the best Arabic poems he had ever written (MH Journal, 12 Nov. 1922); and in 1924 he told her that he had been contracted to write ten pieces for *Al-Hilal* in Cairo (MH Journal, 26 May 1924). These pieces included 'Your Thought and Mine', which has been translated by Ferris in *Spiritual Sayings*. See also n. 83 for further Arabic writings from the 1920s.

39 Two of these new friends – Claude Bragdon and A.E. – would write glowing tributes to him: see bibliography. On p. vii of vol. 2, issue 4, Hossain himself praised Gibran as a 'genius', repeated the pseudo-Rodin quote from the Knopf publicity, and went on: 'There is no more sincere and authentic or more highly gifted representative of the East functioning today in the West.'
40 Editorial, pp. 95–6 of vol. 2, issue 1.
41 It is not surprising that it is one of Gibran's more ethereal pieces, since the legend on which it is based is also strange. Iram is said to be a mysterious city of gold and precious stones which was built by Shaddad ibn 'Ad, but then disappeared in the desert. However, once every forty years, Iram reappears, and happy is the man who sees it.
42 And ignoring the occasional short English piece that was published in unusual outlets, such as 'Snow', an inferior poem printed by the New York *Herald Tribune* as a Christmas offering on 22 Dec. 1929.
43 For instance, 'You know *The Prophet* means a great deal in my life. All these 37 years have been making it' (MH Journal, 8 Nov. 1919); 'That book means more to me than all my other work' (MH Journal, 31 March 1921); 'It's the only book I ever spent so long on' (MH Journal, 19 May 1922); '*The Prophet* is the first book in my career – my first real book, my ripened fruit' (MH Journal, 16 June 1923). See also MH Journal, 11 April 1915, 18 April 1920; KG to MZ, 9 Nov. 1919.
44 The most important references are: MH Journal, 12 June 1912, 7 Sept. 1912, 6 April 1913, 4 Sept. 1914, 14 Nov. 1914, 11 April 1915, 21 April 1916, 24 March 1918, 6 May 1918, 31 Aug.–1 Sept. 1918, 14 April 1919, 18 Aug. 1919, 20 April 1920, 20 May 1920, 20 Aug. 1920, 25 Aug. 1920, 27 Aug. 1920, 31 Aug. 1920, 7 Sept. 1920, 10 Sept. 1920, 14 Sept. 1920, 17 Sept. 1920, 5 Feb. 1921, 1 March 1921, 12 July 1921, 8 Aug. 1921, 30 Aug. 1921, 2 Sept. 1921, 6 Sept. 1921, 9 Sept. 1921, 19 Jan. 1922, 8 March 1922, 14 April 1922, 5 May 1922, 16 May 1922, 30 May 1922, 11 Sept. 1922, 7 Oct. 1922, 31 Dec. 1922, 2 Jan. 1923, 16 June 1923, 23 June 1923; MH to KG, 11 June 1918; KG to MH, 12 Dec. 1920.
45 Quoted in Daoudi, p. 99; it seems to be a paraphrase of what Gibran told Claude Bragdon (see Bragdon, p. 146). It reflects the words of the Prophet in the book (p. 105, Penguin edition): 'Was it I who spoke? Was I not also a listener?' Much the same sentiment appears in KG to MZ, 9 Nov. 1919 and 3 Dec. 1923, where more mystically Gibran speaks of being written through by God.
46 MH Journal, 17 Sept. 1920, 21 April 1922, 5 May 1922, 9 May 1922, 19 May 1922, 30 May 1922; KG to MH, 19 March 1923, 17 April 1923, 30 April 1923.
47 Perplexingly, however, she asked him in 1923 about the book called the 'Commonwealth', as if that were different from *The Prophet* and a future

book he was still mulling over (MH Journal, 16 June 1923). Perhaps he was holding that title in reserve for the book that was to become *The Garden of the Prophet*.

48 MH Journal, 4 Aug. 1919, 8 Nov. 1919, 10 Sept. 1920, 30 Sept. 1922; see also KG to MZ, 9 Nov. 1919: 'This is a book which I thought of writing a thousand years ago.'

49 Quoted in Daoudi, p. 100.

50 At one stage Gibran seems to have toyed with the idea of ending with a numerologically significant number of counsels (MH Journal, 31 Aug. 1920); but ultimately he let the themes themselves decide the number.

51 Naḍeem Naimy (1975); for Almustafa as Gibran's alter ego, see Chapter 10, note 23.

52 MH Journal, 2 Jan. 1923. On the second book, *The Garden of the Prophet*, see MH Journal, 10 Sept. 1920, 14 Sept. 1920, 8 March 1922, 30 May 1922, 2 Jan. 1923, 16 June 1923, 26 Nov. 1923, 8 June 1924; KG to MH, 16 May 1929. In *The Syrian World*, April 1929, he announced its publication later that year, but this was as much as anything an attempt to force himself to work on it, and it still remained disorganized two years later when he died. Young tells her version of the posthumous compilation of the book on pp. 119 ff. of her biography, but see the valid criticisms of Hawi, pp. 240–42, and Daoudi, pp. 54–5; she included pieces which Gibran probably did not intend to be part of this book.

53 MH Journal, 7 Oct. 1922.

54 Young, p. 119. The third part of the trilogy is mentioned, for instance, in MH Journal, 23 June 1923.

55 Knopf recalled (vol. 1, p. 48): 'Whenever I saw Gibran in the few years of life that remained to him after 1923 and gleefully reported how well *The Prophet* was doing, his reply was always the same – he shrugged his shoulders and said: "What did I tell you?"'

56 Already by 1920 people were beginning to pester him for copies of various counsels: MH Journal, 21 April 1920; see also MH Journal, 5 May 1922.

57 *Publishers Weekly*, 11 Dec. 1995, p. 23. The idea of a film was first floated in 1932 (*KGLW*, p. 409). *The Broken Wings* was made into a film in 1968.

58 MH Journal, 31 Dec. 1922. They saw in the New Year in New York by reading through the whole book together.

59 MH Journal, 4 Sept. 1914, 7 Sept. 1920.

60 MH Journal, 30 May 1922, which more or less repeats the same sentiment from 16 May 1922.

61 Gibran himself acknowledged this progression: MH Journal, 16 May 1922.

62 See especially MH Journal, 11 May 1918, 12 May 1922.

63 MH Journal, 20 Aug. 1920.

64 Penguin edition, p. 118.

65 Penguin edition, pp. 68, 40.
66 See p. 191.
67 Penguin edition, p. 123.
68 KG to MH, 26 Nov. 1923.
69 MH to KG, 2 Oct. 1923.
70 Several years later, George William Russell (A.E.) added his weight to those who read *The Prophet* as a piece of Eastern philosophy. With half an eye on the back-cover blurb, he wrote: 'I do not think the East has spoken with so beautiful a voice since the *Gitanjali* of Rabindranath Tagore as in *The Prophet* of Kahlil Gibran' (p. 168).
71 One of the less pleasant tasks facing the thorough researcher into Gibran is that he has to wade through two volumes of alleged commentary on *The Prophet* by the disgraced cult leader Bhagwan Shree Rajneesh (Cologne: Rebel Publishing House, 1987). The output is impressive – just short of 1,000 pages – but the content less so. Rajneesh starts from the premise that Gibran did truly glimpse reality, but only glimpsed it. Now he, Rajneesh, will give us the full story. His justification? 'Speaking on Kahlil Gibran is a very rare, almost impossible thing because I am not a poet – I am poetry. I am not a painter; I am the painting' (p. 18). Then the commentaries proceed, with plenty of digressions on subjects from his own Buddhahood, to travelling on a Bombay train, to the injustice of his treatment at the hands of the US government, and so on. His thoughts on the subjects covered by Gibran are very similar to Gibran's, in the sense that they occupy the same order of generality. As usual with Rajneesh, he displays impressive book-learning and oratory; but it takes a fanatic to describe Jesus as a 'fanatic, a bit insane' who needed a good dose of Eastern meditation to calm him down! The books are not so much commentaries as a vehicle for his own ideas.
72 Hanna (1973), p. 66.
73 Young, p. 99; MH Diary, 12 Dec. 1927.
74 MH Journal, 11 Jan. 1919.
75 Barbara Young says three times (p. 95).
76 Dreams of Christ: KG to MH, 25 March 1908; MH Journal, 19 April 1911 (with the implication that the dreams are fairly frequent – say, about two or three a year); KG to MH, 7 Feb. 1912; MH Journal, 10 Jan. 1914, 9 May 1917 (hasn't dreamt of Christ recently), 9 and 12 June 1919 (hasn't dreamt of Christ for about a year), 30 Dec. 1919, 14 July 1921 (he also dreams about Shakespeare, Blake, Keats and Shelley), 27 May 1923. Discussions about Christ: MH Journal, 7 Dec. 1910, 10 March 1911, 15 June 1912, 6 April 1913, 24 Aug. 1915, 25 Aug. 1915, 26 April 1916, 6 Jan. 1918, 14 April 1919, 9 and 12 June 1919, 6 Aug. 1919, 25 Aug. 1920, 7 Sept. 1920, 10 Sept. 1920, 3 Jan. 1921, 8 Jan. 1921, 5 Feb. 1921, 8 Feb. 1921, 18 April 1922, 16 May 1922, 16 June 1922.

77 p. 77.
78 Translated in full by Anthony Ferris in *Secrets of the Heart*. Gibran once asserted that the word translated 'meek' in the Bible means, rather, 'calm' and 'understanding' (MH Journal, 8 Jan. 1921). It is true that the Greek word *praos* can mean 'calm' or 'self-possessed', though 'understanding' is going a bit far; but he may be thinking of some Syriac word, since he occasionally used to claim affinity with Christ through their shared knowledge of Syriac.
79 Bragdon, p. 144.
80 KG to MH, 29 April 1909; MH Journal, 11 Oct. 1911.
81 Favourable reviews: *New York Times* (P. W. Wilson), New York *Herald Tribune* (John Holmes), New York *Evening Post* (Paul Eldridge: 'There are drawings in this book so extremely delicate and lovely that they seem to have been created from the very stuff of dreams'); Manchester *Guardian*. Less favourable: *The New Republic*. These are all the reviews I have seen, though there may be more.
82 See also 'The Last Guest', a prose-poem written some time towards the end of Gibran's life and preserved in Shehadi's collection of reproduced manuscripts.
83 *Assilban* is translated by Anthony Ferris in *Spiritual Sayings*. In their 1981 edition of *Lazarus* and *The Blind*, the Gibrans revealed the existence of three other short, unfinished plays written in English towards the end of Gibran's life – *The Banshee*, *The Last Unction* and *The Hunchback or the Man Unseen*. These have never been published, though a little of their content is summarized by the Gibrans. Since, as I have already had occasion to mention, the Gibrans refused me access to the material in their possession, I have no further idea about the contents of these fragmentary plays. Occasionally, in Mary's journals, we hear about other unwritten plays – for instance, one Gibran planned to write for Lionel Barrymore (MH Journal, 18 April 1920). There are also five otherwise unpublished Arabic plays, all short and all dating from the 1920s, collected by Antoine al-Qawwal in his *Uncollected Works of Gibran* (that is, works not included in the monumental edition of Gibran's Arabic writings by Mikhail Naimy), which was published in 1993 by Dar Amwaj in Beirut. The titles of these plays are: *The Unseen Man*, *Between Night and Morning*, *The Coloured Faces*, *The Beginning of the Revolution* and *The King and the Shepherd*.
84 MH Journal, 26 April 1914; Diary, 13 May 1926.
85 MH Journal, 3 June 1915, 20 June 1915, 30 June 1915, 23 April 1916.
86 MH Journal, 21–22 July 1916.
87 He reminded Mary of its existence in 1923, and read her as much of the poem as existed then, commenting that it was the best English he had ever

written (though to my mind it is often rather plodding), and that he intended to change every 'thou' in it to 'you' – for which we may be thankful: MH Journal, 16 June 1923.

88 KG to MH, 16 March 1931, 22 March 1931.

89 p. 237.

90 Under the rubric 'Round About Parnassus', *Saturday Review of Literature*, 28 March 1931, p. 696.

91 See especially Glen Mullin's review of *Twenty Drawings* in *The Nation*, April 1920, pp. 485–6. Chapin's remark on this aspect of Gibran's artwork is perhaps fairest: 'Blake he is not. Gibran – a much lesser but real star – he is.'

12 Death and After

1 *KGLW*, p. 394; Mikhail Naimy (1950), p. 218.

2 *A Self-portrait*, pp. 91, 94.

3 Barbara Young to Margaret Crofts, 23 April 1931.

4 See Douglas, pp. 475–8.

5 Victor Hugo, in an 1871 sonnet.

6 MH Journal, 12 Aug. 1921.

7 MH Journal, 12 Aug. 1921; KG to MH, 6 Jan. 1909.

8 *The Vision*, p. 80.

9 *The Procession*, trans. Kheirallah, p. 42.

10 MH Journal, 13 Nov. 1915.

11 *A Self-portrait*, pp. 84–6.

12 MH Journal, 30 July 1917, 30 July 1919. 'Perhaps a man may commit suicide in self-defense' (*Sand and Foam*, p. 40).

13 April 1931, p. 21.

14 The poems and speeches, and a great deal of other material relating to Gibran's death, are reprinted in the April 1931 issue of *The Syrian World*, which is almost entirely devoted to eulogy of Gibran. The issue contains several other poems as well (of which one, by Leonora Speyer, is half good), and reprints Gibran's famous 'Message to Young Americans of Syrian Origin', as well as a robust response, 'A Pledge', by Cecil J. Badway, 'a young American of Syrian origin'.

15 Nevertheless, Father al-Douaihy got into some trouble as a result of the funeral service. It emerged only in the 1980s (see the 'Afterword' to *KGLW*, p. 432) that a well-meaning trouble-maker from the Maronite congregation in New York wrote to the Archbishop of Boston accusing Gibran of being apostate. The Archbishop's office wrote a stiff letter or two to al-Douaihy, but he defended his right to bury Gibran, and argued that his friend was

actually more religious than most people, and therefore had more right to a religious ceremony.

16 Barbara Young in *The Syrian World*, op. cit., p. 24.

17 MH Diary, 13 April 1931.

18 In her diary for 15 April, Mary remarked that she found Gertrude Stern 'hysterical'. Since, as we now know, Gibran had asked her to marry him just the year before, her emotional state is less surprising.

19 The ceremony received an appallingly inaccurate write-up in the Boston *Evening Transcript* for 14 April 1931.

20 Letter dated 19 May 1931. Barbara's approach to *The Garden of the Prophet* was equally cavalier: see Chapter 11, note 52.

21 Mrs William Brown Meloney to KG, 1 Oct. 1930; KG's reply, 6 Oct. 1930.

22 See Pilpel and Zavin.

23 MH Journal, 6 June 1911, 16 June 1911; KG to MH, 14 Nov. 1913. For an outline of the 1911 will, see p. 137; the 1913 will sounds like a mere adjustment of the 1911 one.

24 His royalties for the six months ending 31 Dec. 1930 were $2,476.94 and £6.13.1d.

25 Pilpel and Zavin, p. 154.

26 'Profits from *The Prophet*', *Time*, 15 May 1972; see also Dempsey.

27 MH Journal, 30 Aug. 1913.

28 *New York Times*, 25 July 1931, p. 13.

29 See the report in the *New York Times*, 20 Sept. 1931, Section 1, p. 20. The story was picked up all over the States, e.g. by the *Kansas City Star* for 22 Sept. 1931.

30 Harte, p. 1212.

31 Turner, p. 54. For a description of the appearance of the tomb before its 1990s' refurbishment, see Kayrouz, pp. 99–104.

32 As for other signs of recognition, there are three non-Lebanese monuments to Gibran known to me: the one in Boston which I mentioned on p. 132, the one in Washington to which Jonathan Yardley took such exception (see pp. 222–3), and I am told that there is one in Mexico, but I have not been able to confirm this. In Lebanon, there are plaques and monuments all over the place, as one might expect: at the house in Bsharri purporting (undoubtedly falsely) to be his childhood home, in the entrance to the present building of his old school in Beirut, and so on. Gibran's lyrics have also inspired songs, both popular and serious. I cannot prove that when Ewan MacColl wrote 'The First Time Ever I Saw Your Face', the beautiful love song which was a massive hit for Roberta Flack, he was thinking of the movement in Gibran's poem 'The Beloved', from the first glimpse to the first kiss to physical consummation, but it would not be the first instance of unacknowledged borrowing from Gibran. In the excellent 'Julia', from the Beatles' *White*

Album, John Lennon and Paul McCartney twice echo *Sand and Foam*. 'Half of what I say is meaningless, but I say it just to reach you, Julia,' is their adaptation of 'Half of what I say is meaningless, but I say it so that the other half may reach you'; and a little later in the song we hear, 'When I cannot sing my heart, I can only speak my mind,' which is a close paraphrase of another aphorism from *Sand and Foam* (see pp. 285–6). Mr Mister drew on *The Broken Wings*. At a more serious level are the cappellas by American composers Howard L. Richards and Thomas Benjamin. The former's 'Song of the Flower' (1981) and the latter's 'Sing and Dance' (1980) are both indebted to Gibran. In his collection *Windsongs*, composer Jean-Pierre Dantricourt included a piece called 'The Garden of the Prophet'.

33 Reported in *Time*, 13 Aug. 1965.

34 The word-of-mouth experience was duplicated in the UK: see John St John, *William Heinemann: A Century of Publishing, 1890–1990* (London: Heinemann, 1990), p. 290.

35 p. 144.

36 Penguin edition, p. 71.

37 p. 15.

38 *Sand and Foam*, p. 24.

39 He told Mary that in response to the criticism he would try to make the connections of thought plainer (MH Journal, 29 March 1921). See also MH Journal, 31 Dec. 1917, the implication of which is that he had been charged with vagueness.

40 Penguin edition, p. 118.

41 *Sand and Foam*, p. 23.

42 p. 84.

43 *Painted Veils* (1920), p. 214 (Modern Library edition).

44 For sustained analyses of his thought see Ghougassian, Hawi, Ross, Sheban and Sherfan. Ghougassian even labels him an existentialist and, somewhat bizarrely, thinks that it is only academic prejudice that has kept him out of the histories of modern philosophy.

45 Lasch (1979), who used the word in the title of his best-selling book on the 1970s, *The Culture of Narcissism* (just as Tom Wolfe described it as the 'Me Decade'), has been justly criticized by, e.g., Clecak. It may be true that a proportion of American society conforms to Lasch's picture, but he makes it sound as though he is discussing the whole, not a part.

46 See especially the convenient list in Heelas, Appendix 1.

47 Roszac (1975), pp. 26–9.

48 KG to MZ, 6 April 1921.

49 He conceived a desire to own such a fragment in 1915, and used to pester Mary, until she bought one for him, which had been found near the great meteor crater in Arizona. On his interest in the stars, and on the meteorite:

KG to MH, 13 Dec. 1912, 9 Dec. 1915, 19 Dec. 1916, 3 Jan. 1917; MH to KG, 6 Dec. 1915, 12 Nov. 1916; MH Journal, 26 April 1914, 26 Dec. 1915, 28 Dec. 1915, 3 Jan. 1921, 8 Feb. 1921.

50 MH Journal, 17 Sept. 1920.

51 p. 25.

Bibliography

There have been very many books and articles on Gibran in English and Arabic, and in other languages too (chiefly French); this bibliography can make no claim to be exhaustive, though it does accurately reflect my reading, or at least as much of it as is worth revealing. While being thorough on English works about Gibran (apart from the numerous reviews I have read), where other, more general books are concerned, I have mentioned only the most important.

Books by Kahlil Gibran

Nubdah fi Fan al-Musiqa (*On Music*, a pamphlet) (New York: Al-Mohajer, 1905)

Ara'is al-Muruj (*Brides of the Meadows*, referred to by Gibran as *Nymphs of the Valley*) (New York: Al-Mohajer, 1906). Translated by H. M. Nahmad as *Nymphs of the Valley* (New York: Knopf, 1948), and by J. R. I. Cole as *Spirit Brides* (Santa Cruz: White Cloud Press, 1993)

Al-Arwah al-Mutamarridah (*Spirits Rebellious*) (New York: Al-Mohajer, 1908). Translated by H. M. Nahmad (New York: Knopf, 1948)

Al-Ajnihah al-Mutakassirah (*The Broken Wings*) (New York: Mir'at al-Gharb, 1912). Translated by A. R. Ferris (New York: Citadel Press, 1957) and by J. R. I. Cole (Ashland: White Cloud Press, 1998)

Dam'ah wa-Ibtisamah (*A Tear and A Smile*) (New York: Atlantic, 1914). Translated by H. M. Nahmad (New York: Knopf, 1950).

The Madman: His Parables and Poems (New York: Knopf, 1918)

Al-Mawakib (*The Procession*) (New York: Mir'at al-Gharb, 1919). Translated by M. F. Kheirallah (New York: Arab-American Press, 1947)

Twenty Drawings (New York: Knopf, 1919)

Al-'Awasif (*The Tempests*) (Cairo: Al-Hilal, 1920)

The Forerunner: His Parables and Poems (New York: Knopf, 1920)

Al-Bada'i' wa-'t-tara'if (*The Beautiful and the Rare* or, as Gibran preferred, *Best Things and Masterpieces*) (Cairo: Yusuf Bustani, 1923)
The Prophet (New York: Knopf, 1923)
Sand and Foam (New York: Knopf, 1926)
Kalimat Jibran (*Spiritual Sayings*) (Cairo: Yusuf Bustani, 1927). Translated by A. R. Ferris (New York: Citadel Press, 1962)
Jesus, the Son of Man (New York: Knopf, 1928)
Al-Sanabil (*The Spikes of Grain*) (New York: As-Sa'ih, 1929)
The Earth Gods (New York: Knopf, 1931)
The Wanderer: His Parables and Sayings (New York: Knopf, 1932)
The Garden of the Prophet (New York: Knopf, 1933)
Lazarus and His Beloved and The Blind (Philadelphia: Westminster Press, 1981)
Paintings and Drawings 1905–1930 (New York: Vrej Baghoomian, 1989)

Anthologies

A great many of Gibran's Arabic pieces have been collected in various anthologies. There is a good deal of overlap between these anthologies, but this is not always immediately obvious, since different translators and editors give different pieces different titles.

(a) Translated by Juan R. I. Cole: *The Vision* (Ashland: White Cloud Press, 1994)
(b) Translated by Margaret Crosland (from French editions):
The Eye of the Prophet (London: Souvenir Press, 1995)
Visions of the Prophet (London: Souvenir Press, 1996)
(c) Translated by Anthony R. Ferris:
Secrets of the Heart (New York: Philosophical Library, 1947)
Tears and Laughter (New York: Philosophical Library, 1947)
The Voice of the Master (New York: Citadel Press, 1958)
Thoughts and Meditations (New York: Citadel Press, 1961)
Between Night and Morn (New York: Philosophical Library, 1972)
Most of the pieces translated in these books by Anthony Ferris are also collected in either *A Treasury of Kahlil Gibran* (New York: Citadel Press, 1951) or *A Second Treasury of Kahlil Gibran* (New York: Citadel Press, 1962).
(d) Translated by Andrew Ghareeb: *Prose Poems* (New York: Knopf, 1934)
(e) Translated by Adnan Hydar and Michael Beard: a few pieces in Salma Jayyusi (ed.), *Modern Arabic Poetry: An Anthology* (New York: Columbia University Press, 1987)

(f) Translated by Joseph Sheban: *The Wisdom of Gibran: Aphorisms and Maxims* (New York: Philosophical Library, 1966)

(g) Translated by John Walbridge:

The Storm: Stories and Prose Poems (Santa Cruz: White Cloud Press, 1993)

The Beloved: Reflections on the Path of the Heart (Ashland: White Cloud Press, 1994)

(h) Translated by many of the above, various pieces in:

Suheil B. Bushrui (ed.), *An Introduction to Kahlil Gibran* (Beirut: Dar el-Mashreq, 1970)

Gregory Orfalea and Sharif Elmusa (eds), *Grape Leaves: A Century of Arab American Poetry* (Salt Lake City: University of Utah Press, 1988)

Robin Waterfield (ed.), *The Voice of Kahlil Gibran* (London: Penguin, 1995)

Reproductions of manuscript extracts of several of Gibran's English works can be found in William Shehadi, *Kahlil Gibran: A Prophet in the Making* (Beirut: The American University of Beirut, 1991)

Collections of letters

A Self-portrait, translated by Anthony R. Ferris (New York: Citadel Press, 1959)

The Letters of Kahlil Gibran and Mary Haskell, edited by Annie S. Otto (Houston: Southern Printing Co., 1970)

Beloved Prophet: The Love Letters of Kahlil Gibran and Mary Haskell, edited by Virginia Hilu (New York: Knopf, 1972)

Unpublished Gibran Letters to Ameen Rihani, translated by Suheil B. Bushrui (Beirut: World Lebanese Cultural Union, 1972)

Gibran: Love Letters, translated and edited by Suheil B. Bushrui and Salma H. al-Kuzbari (Oxford: Oneworld Publications, 1983) [This book was first published by Longman under the title *Blue Flame: The Love Letters of Kahlil Gibran to May Ziadah*]

Works exclusively about Gibran

Suheil B. Bushrui, *Kahlil Gibran of Lebanon* (Gerrards Cross: Colin Smythe, 1987)

Suheil B. Bushrui (ed.), *Kahlil Gibran: An Introductory Survey of His Life and His Work* (Ibadan: Ibadan University Press, 1966)

Suheil B. Bushrui and Paul Gotch (eds), *Gibran of Lebanon: New Papers* (Beirut: Librairie du Liban, 1975)

Suheil B. Bushrui and John Munro (eds), *Kahlil Gibran: Essays and Introductions* (Beirut: Rihani House, 1970)

Shiv Rai Chowdhry, *Gibran: An Introduction* (Delhi: Javee and Co., 1970)

M. S. Daoudi, *The Meaning of Kahlil Gibran* (Secaucus: Citadel Press, 1982)

Joshua L. Ditelberg, 'Kahlil Gibran's Early Intellectual Life, 1883–1908' (MA thesis, University of Pennsylvania, 1987)

Joseph P. Ghougassian, *Kahlil Gibran: Wings of Thought*, in *A Third Treasury of Kahlil Gibran* (New York: Citadel Press, 1975)

Jean and Kahlil Gibran, *Kahlil Gibran: His Life and World* (New York: Interlink Books, 1974)

Suhail S. Hanna, 'An Arab Expatriate in America: Kahlil Gibran in His American Setting' (PhD thesis, Indiana University, 1973)

Khalil S. Hawi, *Kahlil Gibran: His Background, Character and Works* (Beirut: American University of Beirut, 1972)

Yusuf Huwayyik, *Gibran in Paris* (New York: Popular Library, 1976)

Wahib Kayrouz, *Gibran in His Museum* (Bsharri: Bacharia, 1995)

Mikhail Naimy, *Kahlil Gibran: A Biography* (New York: Philosophical Library, 1950)

Annie S. Otto, *The Parables of Kahlil Gibran: An Interpretation of His Writings and His Art* (New York: Citadel Press, 1963)

Annie S. Otto, *The Art of Kahlil Gibran: Visions of Life as Expressed by the Author of 'The Prophet'* (Port Arthur: Hinds, 1965)

Martha J. Ross, 'The Writings of Kahlil Gibran' (MA thesis, University of Texas, 1948)

Joseph Sheban, *Mirrors of the Soul* (New York: Philosophical Library, 1965)

Andrew D. Sherfan, *Kahlil Gibran: The Nature of Love* (New York: Philosophical Library, 1971)

Andrew D. Sherfan (ed.), *A Third Treasury of Kahlil Gibran* (New York: Citadel Press, 1975)

Barbara Young, *This Man from Lebanon* (New York: Knopf, 1945)

Articles about Gibran

Anon., 'Kahlil Gibran Dead', 'Body of Kahlil Gibran Starts Back to Syria', 'Gibran is Honored in Native Lebanon', *New York Times*, 11 April 1931, p. 19; 25 July 1931, p. 13; 20 September 1931, p. 20

Anon., 'Funeral Services for Syrian Artist', Boston *Evening Transcript*, 14 April 1931, p. 14

Anon., 'Obituary Notes', *Publishers Weekly*, 25 April 1931, p. 2111

Anon., 'Fifteen Years of Mounting Sales', *Publishers Weekly*, 2 April 1939, pp. 1451–2

Anon., 'The Prophet's Profits', *Time*, 13 August 1965, p. 77

Anon., 'A Land, a Poet, a Festival', *Aramco World*, July/August 1970, pp. 5–7

Anon., 'Profits from *The Prophet*', *Time*, 15 May 1972, p. 50

Claude F. Bragdon, 'Modern Prophet from Lebanon', in *Merely Players* (New York: Knopf, 1929), pp. 139–47

Witter Bynner, 'Kahlil the Gibranite', in *The Borzoi: Being a Sort of Record of Ten Years' Publishing* (New York: Knopf, 1925), pp. 43–6

Louis Chapin, 'Another Side of Gibran', *Christian Science Monitor*, 7 February 1973, p. 16

Howard W. Cook, 'Johan Bojer and Kahlil Gibran', in Carl Gad, *Johan Bojer: The Man and His Works* (New York: Moffat, Yard, 1920), pp. 27–9

John K. Cooley, 'A Man with a Flair in His Soul', *Christian Science Monitor*, 4 June 1970, p. 19

David Dempsey, 'Improvement', *New York Times Book Review*, 23 November 1952, p. 8

Jean and Kahlil Gibran, 'The Symbolic Quest of Kahlil Gibran: The Arab as Artist in America', in Eric J. Hooglund (ed.), *Crossing the Waters: Arabic-speaking Immigrants to the United States before 1940* (Washington: Smithsonian Institute Press, 1987), pp. 161–71

Josh Greenfeld, 'The Marshmallow Literature and the Gang That Whipped It Up: Rod McKuen, Walter Benton, and Kahlil Gibran', *Mademoiselle*, March 1969, pp. 206–7

Suhail S. Hanna, 'Gibran and Whitman: Their Literary Dialogue', *Literature East and West*, 1968, pp. 174–98

A. C. Harte, 'Burial of a Poet', *Christian Century*, 30 September 1931, pp. 1212–13

Victor Howes, 'What is the Secret of Gibran's Success?', *Christian Science Monitor*, 4 June 1970, p. 19

Stefan Kanfer, 'But Is It Not Strange That Even Elephants Will Yield – and That *The Prophet* Is Still Popular?', *New York Times Magazine*, 25 June 1972, pp. 8–9, 24, 26, 28, 30

Mikhail Naimy, 'A Strange Little Book', *Aramco World*, November/December 1964, pp. 10–17

Nadeem Naimy, 'The Mind and Thought of Kahlil Gibran', *Journal of Arabic Literature*, 1975, pp. 55–71

Robin Ostle, 'The Literature of the *Mahjar*', in Albert H. Hourani and Nadim Shehadi (eds), *The Lebanese in the World: A Century of Emigration* (London: The Centre for Lebanese Studies, 1992), pp. 209–25

Robin Ostle, 'The Romantic Poets', in Muhammad M. Badawi (ed.), *Modern*

Arabic Literature (Cambridge: Cambridge University Press, 1992), pp. 82–131

A. J. Philpott, 'Memory of Kahlil Gibran Recalled by Exhibition', Boston *Daily Globe*, 10 December 1946

Harriet Pilpel and Theodora Zavin, 'The Curious Will of Mr Gibran', in *Rights and Writers: A Handbook of Literary and Entertainment Law* (New York: Dutton, 1960), pp. 153–5

Alice E. Raphael, 'The Art of Kahlil Gibran', *The Seven Arts*, March 1917, pp. 531–4

George W. Russell (A.E.), 'Kahlil Gibran', in *The Living Torch* (New York: Macmillan, 1938), pp. 168–9

Sheila Turner, 'Tales of a Levantine Guru', *Saturday Review*, 13 March 1971, pp. 54–5, 70

Various, in *The Syrian World*, 19 February 1929, pp. 29–33

Various, in *The Syrian World*, 5 April 1931, pp. 17–48

Jonathan Yardley, 'The Eternal Kahlil Gibran: Never Has One Prophet Done so Little to Deserve so Much', *Washington Post*, 8 October 1984, pp. D1, D9

American history and society

Henry Adams, *The Education of Henry Adams* (1907; Harmondsworth: Penguin, 1995)

Frederick L. Allen, *Only Yesterday: An Informal History of the 1920s* (New York: Harper and Row, 1931)

Cleveland Armory, *The Proper Bostonians* (New York: Dutton, 1947)

Ann Douglas, *Terrible Honesty: Mongrel Manhattan in the 1920s* (New York: Farrar, Straus and Giroux, 1995)

F. Scott Fitzgerald, *The Crack-up*, ed. Edmund Wilson (New York: New Directions, 1945)

Martin Green, *New York 1913: The Armory Show and the Paterson Strike Pageant* (New York: Charles Scribner's Sons, 1988)

Emily Hahn, *Romantic Rebels: An Informal History of Bohemianism in America* (Boston: Houghton Mifflin, 1967)

M. A. de Wolfe Howe, *Boston: The Place and the People* (New York: Macmillan, 1903)

Nathan I. Huggins, *Protestants Against Poverty: Boston's Charities, 1870–1900* (Westport: Greenwood, 1971)

Henry James, *The American Scene* (1907; Harmondsworth: Penguin, 1994)

J. Stillson Judah, *The History and Philosophy of the Metaphysical Movements in America* (Philadelphia: Westminster Press, 1967)

Christopher Lasch, *The New Radicalism in America (1889–1963)* (New York: Knopf, 1965)

Henry F. May, *The End of American Innocence* (New York: Knopf, 1959)

Keith N. Richwine, 'The Liberal Club: Bohemia and the Resurgence in Greenwich Village, 1912–1918' (PhD thesis, University of Pennsylvania, 1968)

Caroline F. Ware, *Greenwich Village 1920–1930* (Boston: Houghton Mifflin, 1935)

Walter M. Whitehill, *Boston: A Topographical History* (Cambridge, Mass.: Harvard University Press, 1959)

Peter W. Williams, *Popular Religion in America: Symbolic Change and the Modernization Process in Historical Process* (Englewood Cliffs, NJ: Prentice-Hall, 1980)

Edmund Wilson, *The Shores of Light: A Literary Chronicle of the Twenties and Thirties* (New York: Farrar, Straus and Young, 1952)

Edmund Wilson, *The American Earthquake: A Documentary of the Twenties and Thirties* (Garden City: Doubleday, 1958)

Edmund Wilson, *The Twenties: From Notebooks and Diaries of the Period* (New York: Farrar, Straus and Giroux, 1975)

Arabic literature

Roger Allen, *The Arabic Novel: An Historical and Critical Introduction*, 2nd edn (Syracuse: Syracuse University Press, 1995)

Muhammad M. Badawi (ed.), *Modern Arabic Literature* (Cambridge: Cambridge University Press, 1992)

John A. Haywood, *Modern Arabic Literature, 1800–1970* (New York: St Martin's Press, 1972)

Salma K. Jayyusi, *Trends and Movements in Modern Arabic Poetry*, 2 vols (Leiden: E. J. Brill, 1977)

Tahir Khemiri and G. Kampffmeyer, *Leaders in Contemporary Arabic Literature*, Part I (Berlin: Deutsche Gesellschaft für Islamkunde, 1930 = *Die Welt des Islams* 9.2)

Matti Moosa, *The Origins of Modern Arabic Fiction* (Washington: Three Continents Press, 1983)

Reynold A. Nicholson, *Translations of Eastern Poetry and Prose* (Cambridge: Cambridge University Press, 1922)

Charles G. Tueley, *Classical Arabic Poetry* (London: Kegan Paul International, 1985)

Lebanese/Syrian history and society

Engin D. Akarli, *The Long Peace: Ottoman Lebanon 1861–1920* (Berkeley: University of California Press, 1993)

George Antonius, *The Arab Awakening: The Story of the Arab National Movement* (Philadelphia: J. B. Lippincott, 1939)

Robert B. Betts, *The Druze* (New Haven: Yale University Press, 1988)

Frederick J. Bliss, *The Religions of Modern Syria and Palestine* (New York: Charles Scribner's Sons, 1912)

Charles H. Churchill, *The Druzes and Maronites under the Turkish Rule from 1840 to 1860* (London: Bernard Quaritch, 1862)

Leila T. Fawaz, *An Occasion for War: Civil Conflict in Lebanon and Damascus in 1860* (Berkeley: University of California Press, 1994)

Robin Fedden, *Syria: An Historical Appreciation* (London: Robert Hale, 1947; repr. 1965 as *The Phoenix Land*)

Charles Glass, *Tribes with Flags: A Dangerous Passage through the Chaos of the Middle East* (New York: Atlantic Monthly Press, 1990)

George Haddad, *Fifty Years of Modern Syria and Lebanon* (Beirut: Dar-al-Hayat, 1950)

Philip K. Hitti, *A Short History of Lebanon* (London: Macmillan, 1965)

Philip K. Hitti, *Lebanon in History from Earliest Times to the Present*, 3rd edn (London: Macmillan, 1967)

Albert Hourani, *Minorities in the Arab World* (London: Oxford University Press, 1947)

Albert Hourani, *Arabic Thought in the Liberal Age, 1798–1939* (London: Oxford University Press, 1962)

A. C. Inchbold, *Under the Syrian Sun*, 2 vols (London: Hutchinson, 1906)

Lewis G. Leary, *Syria: The Land of Lebanon* (New York: McBride, Nast, 1913)

Isaac Riley, *Syrian Home Life* (New York: Dodd, Mead, 1874)

Kamal S. Salibi, *The Modern History of Lebanon* (London: Weidenfeld and Nicolson, 1965)

Kamal S. Salibi, *A House of Many Mansions: The History of Lebanon Reconsidered* (London: I. B. Tauris, 1988)

Hisham Sharabi, *Arab Intellectuals and the West: The Formative Years, 1875–1914* (Baltimore: Johns Hopkins University Press, 1970)

Ethel S. Stevens, *Cedars, Saints and Sinners in Syria* (London: Hurst and Blackett, 1927)

Colin Thubron, *The Hills of Adonis* (London: Heinemann, 1968)

Lebanese/Syrian immigrants in the States

Anon., 'The Foreign Element in New York: The Syrian Colony', *Harper's Weekly*, 3 August 1895, p. 746

Anon., in *The Independent*, 30 April 1907, pp. 1007–13

Anon., 'Syrians in the United States', *Literary Digest*, 3 May 1919, p. 43

William I. Cole, *Immigrant Races in Massachusetts: The Syrians* (Boston: Massachusetts Department of Education, n.d. [1921])

Philip K. Hitti, *The Syrians in America* (New York: George H. Daran, 1924)

Eric J. Hooglund (ed.), *Crossing the Waters: Arabic-speaking Immigrants to the United States before 1940* (Washington: Smithsonian Institute Press, 1987)

Albert Hourani and Nadim Shehadi (eds), *The Lebanese in the World: A Century of Emigration* (London: Centre for Lebanese Studies, 1992)

Philip M. and Joseph M. Kayal, *The Syrian-Lebanese in America: A Study in Religion and Assimilation* (New York: Twayne, 1975)

Beverlee T. Mehdi, *The Arabs in America 1492–1977: A Chronology and Fact Book* (Dobbs Ferry: Oceana Publications, 1978)

Lucius H. Miller, *Our Syrian Population: A Study of the Syrian Communities* (Saratoga: R&E Research Associates, 1968)

Alixa Naff, *Becoming American: The Early Arab Immigrant Experience* (Carbondale: Southern Illinois Press, 1985)

Gregory Orfalea, *Before the Flames: A Quest for the History of Arab Americans* (Austin: University of Texas Press, 1988)

Psychology

Reuben Fine, *Narcissism, the Self and Society* (New York: Columbia University Press, 1986)

Gary Forrest, *The Diagnosis and Treatment of Alcoholism* (Springfield: Charles C. Thomas, 1975)

Gary Forrest, *Alcoholism, Narcissism and Psychopathology* (Springfield: Charles C. Thomas, 1983)

Mario Jacoby, *Individuation and Narcissism: The Psychology of Self in Jung and Kohut* (London: Routledge, 1990)

N. Schwartz-Salant, *Narcissism and Character Transformation* (Toronto: Inner City Books, 1982)

Relevant biographies and studies

Shelley Armitage, *Kewpies and Beyond: The World of Rose O'Neill* (Jackson: University Press of Mississippi, 1994)

Christina H. Baker (ed.), *Diary and Letters of Josephine Preston Peabody* (Boston: Houghton Mifflin, 1925)

Emily Balch *et al.*, *A Heart That Held the World: Helena Stuart Dudley* (Boston: privately published, 1939)

Tony Brown (ed.), *Edward Carpenter and Late Victorian Radicalism* (London: Frank Cass, 1990)

Ellen F. Clattenburg, *The Photographic Works of F. Holland Day* (Wellesley: Wellesley College Museum, 1975)

Bruce Clayton, *Forgotten Prophet: The Life of Randolph Bourne* (Baton Rouge: Louisiana State University Press, 1984)

Charles F. Cummings, 'Thomas Raymond Brought City Wealth of Expansion', Newark *Star-Ledger*, 24 April 1997, p. 4

Catherine Fehrer, *The Julian Academy, Paris 1868–1939* (New York: Shepherd Gallery, 1989)

Jean Gould, *Amy: The World of Amy Lowell and the Imagist Movement* (New York: Dodd, Mead, 1975)

Grace Guiney (ed.), *The Letters of Louise Imogen Guiney*, 2 vols (New York: Harper and Brothers, 1926)

Estelle Jussim, *Slave to Beauty: The Eccentric and Controversial Career of F. Holland Day* (Boston: David R. Godine, 1981)

Alfred A. Knopf, *Portrait of a Publisher 1915–1965*, 2 vols (New York: The Typophiles, 1965)

James Kraft (ed.), *The Works of Witter Bynner: Selected Letters* (New York: Farrar, Straus and Giroux, 1981)

James Kraft, *Who is Witter Bynner?* (Albuquerque: University of New Mexico Press, 1995)

Joe W. Kraus, *Messrs. Copeland & Day* (Philadelphia: George S. MacManus and Co., 1979)

Mabel Dodge Luhan, *Movers and Shakers* (New York: Harcourt, Brace, 1936)

Patrick Mahony, *Maurice Maeterlinck: Mystic and Dramatist* (Washington: The Institute for the Study of Man, 1979)

Weston J. Naeff, *The Painterly Photograph, 1890–1914* (New York: Metropolitan Museum of Art, 1973)

Nadeem Naimy, *The Lebanese Prophets of New York* (Beirut: American University of Beirut, 1985)

Gregory Orfalea, *US–Arab Relations: The Literary Dimension* (Washington: National Council on US–Arab Relations, 1984)

Stephen M. Parrish, *Currents of the Nineties in Boston and London: Fred Holland Day, Louise Imogen Guiney and Their Circle* (New York: Garland, 1987)

Alma Reed, *Orozco* (New York: Oxford University Press, 1956)

David Reynolds, *Walt Whitman's America: A Cultural Biography* (New York: Random House, 1995)

Hyder E. Rollins and Stephen M. Parrish, *Keats and the Bostonians* (Cambridge, Mass.: Harvard University Press, 1951)

Robert A. Rosenstone, *Romantic Revolutionary: A Biography of John Reed* (Cambridge, Mass.: Harvard University Press, 1990)

Douglas Shand-Tucci, *Boston Bohemia 1881–1900*, vol. 1 of *Ralph Adams Cram: Life and Architecture* (Amherst: University of Massachusetts Press, 1995)

Chushichi Tsuzuki, *Edward Carpenter 1844–1929: Prophet of Human Fellowship* (Cambridge, Mass.: Cambridge University Press, 1980)

Marguerite Wilkinson, *New Voices: An Introduction to Contemporary Poetry* (New York: Macmillan, 1919)

Romanticism, Symbolism, Decadence

Maurice Bowra, *The Heritage of Symbolism* (London: Macmillan, 1943)

Maurice Bowra, *The Romantic Imagination* (Cambridge, Mass.: Harvard University Press, 1950)

Edward Carpenter, various books, collections of essays, individual tracts and pamphlets

Joseph Chiari, *Symbolism from Poe to Mallarmé* (London: Rockcliff, 1956)

Henri Dorra (ed.), *Symbolist Art Theories* (Berkeley: University of California Press, 1994)

Ralph Waldo Emerson, various works

William Gaunt, *The Pre-Raphaelite Tragedy* (London: Jonathan Cape, 1941)

William Gaunt, *The Aesthetic Adventure* (London: Jonathan Cape, 1945)

Robert Goldwater, *Symbolism* (New York: Harper and Row, 1979)

Francis Grierson, various essays

Elizabeth G. Holt (ed.), *A Documentary History of Art*, vol. 3: *From the Classicists to the Impressionists* (Garden City: Doubleday, 1966)

Philippe Julian, *Dreamers of Decadence: Symbolist Painters of the 1890s* (London: Pall Mall Press, 1971)

Cecil B. Lang (ed.), *The Pre-Raphaelites and Their Circle*, 2nd edn (Chicago: University of Chicago Press, 1975)

Richard Le Gallienne, *The Romantic '90s* (1926; London: Robin Clark, 1993)

Maurice Maeterlinck, various collections of essays

Madeline Mason-Manheim, *Hill Fragments* (New York: Brentano's, 1925)
Perry Miller (ed.), *The American Transcendentalists: Their Prose and Poetry* (Garden City: Doubleday, 1957)
Friedrich Nietzsche, various works
Mario Praz, *The Romantic Agony*, 2nd edn (London: Oxford University Press, 1951)
George R. Ridge, *The Hero in French Romantic Literature* (Athens: University of Georgia Press, 1959)
George R. Ridge, *The Hero in French Decadent Literature* (Athens: University of Georgia Press, 1961)
Auguste Rodin, *On Art and Artists* (New York: Philosophical Library, 1957)
Arthur Symons, *The Symbolist Movement in Literature*, 2nd edn (New York: Dutton, 1919)
Edmund Wilson, *Axel's Castle: A Study in the Imaginative Literature of 1870–1930* (New York: Charles Scribner's Sons, 1931)
William Butler Yeats, 'A Symbolic Artist and the Coming of Symbolic Art', *The Dome*, December 1898, pp. 233–7
William Butler Yeats, 'The Symbolism of Poetry', *The Dome*, April 1900, pp. 249–57

The 1960s, 1970s, and the New Age

Philip D. Beidler, *Scriptures for a Generation: What We Were Reading in the '60s* (Athens: University of Georgia Press, 1994)
Peter Clecak, *America's Quest for the Ideal Self: Dissent and Fulfillment in the 60s and 70s* (New York: Oxford University Press, 1983)
Marilyn Ferguson, *The Aquarian Conspiracy: Personal and Social Transformation in the 1980s* (London: Routledge and Kegan Paul, 1981)
Wouter J. Hanegraaff, *New Age Religion and Western Culture: Esotericism in the Mirror of Secular Thought* (Leiden: E. J. Brill, 1996)
Paul Heelas, *The New Age Movement* (Oxford: Blackwell, 1996)
Christopher Lasch, *The Culture of Narcissism: American Life in an Age of Diminishing Expectations* (New York: Norton, 1979)
Timothy Miller, *The Hippies and American Values* (Knoxville: University of Tennessee Press, 1991)
Theodore Roszac, *The Making of a Counter Culture* (New York: Doubleday, 1969)
Theodore Roszac, *Unfinished Animal: The Aquarian Frontier and the Evolution of Consciousness* (New York: Harper and Row, 1975)
Steven M. Tipton, *Getting Saved from the Sixties: Moral Meaning in Conversion and Cultural Change* (Berkeley: University of California Press, 1982)

Index